The Complete Guide to Fencing

Authors:

Dr. Berndt Barth (introduction 2.1, 2.3, 2.4, 3.4)
Dr. Heinrich Baer (5)
Jochen Färber (10)
Dr. Michael Hauptmann (2.5)
Claus Janka (6, 9, Successes)
Manfred Kaspar (7)
Peter Proske (6)
Joachim Rieg (8)
Dr. Gabor Salomon (7)
Dr. Arno Schimpf (2.2)
Andreas Schirmer (1)

Overall editing: Dr. Berndt Barth

Berndt Barth & Emil Beck (Eds.)

The Complete Guide to Fencing

Meyer & Meyer Sport

Original title: Fechttraining
Meyer & Meyer Verlag, 2005 (2nd Ed.)
Translated by Susanne Evens, Petra Haynes
AAA Translation, St. Louis, Missouri, USA
www.AAATranslation.com

British Library Cataloguing in Publication Data
A catalogue record for this book is available from the British Library

Bernd Barth & Emil Beck (Eds.)
The Complete Guide to Fencing
Oxford: Meyer & Meyer Sport (UK) Ltd., 2007
ISBN 10: 1-84126-191-2
ISBN 13: 978-1-84126-191-1

796.86 BAR oclc 10/12/06

© 2007 by Meyer & Meyer Sport (UK) Ltd.
Aachen, Adelaide, Auckland, Budapest, Graz, Johannesburg,
New York, Olten (CH), Oxford, Singapore, Toronto
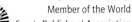 Member of the World
Sports Publishers' Association (WSPA)
www.w-s-p-a.org
Cover Design: Jens Vogelsang
Printed and bound by: B.O.S.S Druck und Medien GmbH, Kleve
ISBN 10: 1-84126-191-2
ISBN 13: 978-1-84126-191-1
E-Mail: verlag@m-m-sports.com
www.m-m-sports.com

Contents

Preface

This book is an extremely successful symbiosis of the practical and the theoretical. Emil Beck and Berndt Barth, two distinguished fencing instructors, have produced and published this book of basic principles on the subject of "fencing training" in collaboration with successful fencing trainers and scientists.

Emil Beck, the ingenious trainer, who in the 1970s intuitively developed a completely new training method for fencing, virtually embodies the athletic success of the German fencers. Since that time, his methodology and the modern fencing style significantly shaped by him, have received broad international recognition and emulation.

Berndt Barth, a long-time instructor of training science at the renowned German College for Fitness Training in Leipzig, Germany, laid the scientific foundation for the education of several generations of degreed physical education instructors and fencing experts.

The participating authors have contributed their knowledge and experience.

I am certain that this book serves the continuing development of modern fencing. For this reason it will also contribute to the modernization of our beloved sport of fencing, thus increasing its appeal. May the many suggestions in this book fall on fertile ground and assure that the sport of fencing can meet the demands of the modern world of sports.

Dr. Thomas Bach
President of the German Olympic
Sports Union (DOSB)

Preface

This book, "The Complete Guide to Fencing", represents in effect the final step toward the merging of the two German fencing associations that were newly founded 50 years ago, after World War II.

After annexation of the five new national associations founded in former East Germany in 1990, the integration and coalescence of the structures, the active fencers, the trainers and coaches, and the functionaries, the discovery and learning process in training methodology was also quickly addressed.

The German fencing sport's smooth consolidation of the two fencing associations founded after World War II, also became apparent in the fact that the German Fencing Confederation's national team was guided to the so far most successful World Championships in Essen in 1993, by the two publishers together as team leader and head coach. This same sense of community is also expressed in the publication of the book "The Complete Guide to Fencing", to which the most renowned German fencing trainers and scientists were able to contribute their vast technical knowledge. In our amateur sport the importance of quality of training continues to grow. Trainer qualifications and participation of the fencers themselves in the training process are key components of future development.

The last publications of the most important books on fencing training in Germany date far back. The "Tauberbischofsheim Fencing Lessons" by Emil Beck, were last published in 1978, the textbook "Fencing" under the direction of Berndt Barth, was last published in 1979. The publication of this very accessible textbook for fencing training is rather overdue. The success of the German fencers justifies – in fact, makes it obligatory – that we tell others how we train. Only international development will insure the future of fencing. Fencing as a martial art sport thrives on competition.

My special thanks to Emil Beck and Berndt Barth, whose initiative made it possible that this book can be published during our anniversary year. I would also like to thank all of the "co-authors", who participated in the book's production via their contributions.

Erika Dienstl
Honorary President
German Fencing Federation

Preface by the authors

With "Tauberbischofsheimer Fencing Lessons", Emil Beck, in 1978, published the foundation of his education and training system established since 1952.

One year later, under the direction of Berndt Barth, a group of authors consisting of trainers and training scientists from the German Fencing Confederation (DDR), published the second, much revised edition of their textbook "Fencing", with the experiment of fencing training based on scientific theories.

It is an open question whether or not the vision of Emil Beck, or the reference by the Federal Commission for the Advancement of Competitive Sports, to the yet to be created "training doctrine in the sport of fencing" listed in the preface to the "Tauberbischofsheimer Fencing Lessons", was the decisive factor.
At any rate, Emil Beck used his first personal meeting with Berndt Barth on the occasion of an international épée tournament in the spring of 1981, to suggest collaboration on the publication of a book. "You have a great theory, and we are more successful in the practical area. That lends itself perfectly to a collaboration."

Right after the Olympic boycott in1980, and with the particularly tense relationship between the two German nations, this was an almost utopian suggestion.

Eighteen years later the time has come. A team of twelve trainers, and scientists and journalists actively working in the sport of fencing implemented the plan – teaching training in the sport of fencing. In doing so, they succeeded in combining the different attempted training concepts of both former German fencing associations into one uniform and innovative training doctrine.

The authors chosen for this work represent the "current German training doctrine in the sport of fencing". It clearly was the authors' intention to retain the proven contents and the overall structure of the forerunners, to integrate newer findings, theories and methods from contributing exercise science-oriented fundamental sciences, to edit them for application in fencing training, and to supplement them with generalized teaching methods and experiences from successful trainers.

At the same time the manuscripts from those authors of the text book "Fencing" from 1979, who are not involved in "Fencing Training", were of some use. This applies in particular to Dr. R. Frester (psychology), Dr. K. Gottschalk (medicine), Dr. F.-J. Müller, (saber), P. Stanitzki (épée), and the illustrations of H. Hausmann.

"The Complete Guide to Fencing" is a reference book for training in competition-oriented fencing. Structure and content are geared toward the demands of coach and trainer instruction. It is a great source for suggestions to fencers who want to reflect on their training. Not everything in this book will be new to everyone. There also won't be a completely satisfactory answer to some questions. Sometimes they don't even exist yet. But readers should still have confidence in the book's statements. Much of it is theory driven, wherever possible backed by exercise science, and supported by the enduring success of German fencers[1] over the years.

The purpose was not to create a recipe book for fencing training, but rather to impart the knowledge needed to design one's own training.

We are always open to advice and suggestions.

The authors

---

[1] In view of the frequent use of the word "fencer" we would like to emphasize that these statements equally refer to female fencers. Special annotations are included in matters that are specific to women's fencing.

Introduction:
Essential information regarding terminology

Fencing terminology combines technical sports terms, i.e. language specific to the training process, competition language, which is primarily based on French regulations, as well as science terminology from disciplines of sports science.

The technical language used in German fencing was in turn shaped by the most varied developmental influences, but in particular by the international fencing masters and trainers who have been working in Germany for centuries. By development we refer to the influence of the nations leading the world-fencing scene at any one time, mostly Italy and France, later Hungary and the Soviet states. The fencing masters that coined terminology came primarily from Italy, France, Hungary, Poland and Russia.

Here is a select example to chracterize the situation:
"Rimessa" (also "Rimesse") is the Italian term for an attack that continues, is repeated, or prolonged on the same, or – via disengagement – focused on a different target area. However, in French terminology one differentiates between "Remise" (same target area) and "Reprise" (different target area). If, in addition, any extra footwork is required, what the Italians will call a "Reprisa d'Attacco" (also Raddoppiamento dell'Affondo") becomes a „Reprise d'Attaque (also "Redoublement") for the French, while in the English-speaking world it is called "Continuation of attack". The Russians differentiate the "Powtornie Ataki" according to the opponent's behavior, depending on whether he parries, performs an incorrect riposte, or delays the riposte.

For instance, the French will occasionally also refer to a "redoublement" as only the footwork – lunge-dragging the supporting leg forward – as a lunge. In striving towards adequate German translations of these variations one struggled with continued attack, continuation of attack, and repeat attack, etc., without being able to vary the semantic content of these terms. Add to that translation errors and occasional misspellings in adopted terms, that were taken for granted and have become standard terms in some terminologies. "Cercle" is an example of this.

And then there are always the "fundamentalists" from a particular "school", who will only accept one view (sometimes the only one they know), or those whose views belong in historic essays and who cannot accept that the terminology evolves along with the fencing methods.

The following considerations serve as a **basis for communication** that is the foundation of this book:
Competitive fencing is a modern dueling sport characterized by the contest between two fencers. This occurs by means of planned performances and action sequences

based on conscious decisions, which are called strategies. This is the case in military theory, psychology, mathematical game theory, politics, and, aside from some other areas, also in competitive sports. This is explained in Chapter 2.4. When fencers analyze a fencing competition with regard to strategy, the fencers' reciprocal actions can be identified as strategic elements according to their place and character. Thus strategic elements are actions that can, from a strategic aspect, be defined as attack or defense elements respectively. Their main and sub groups (basic strategic elements) are characterized by the same or similar strategic characteristics. That is why such a classification does not only contribute to communication between advocates of different schools, but also conveys overall conceptual clarity. In addition grouping, such as the system of basic strategic elements is based on, offer convenient starting points for the methodical design of training. This will become particularly apparent in chapters 6, 7 and eight.

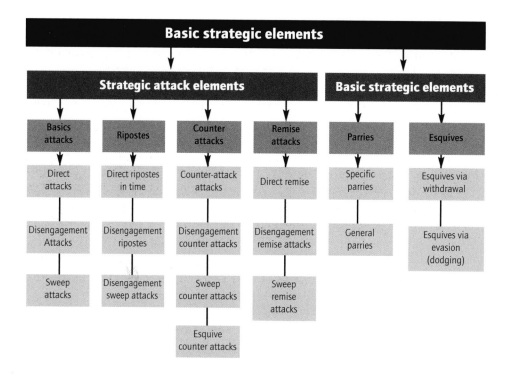

Fig. O.-1: Classification of basic strategic elements

Strategic attack elements are attack actions that have the goal of making a hit.
- *Basic attacks* are attack actions that are executed against a non-attacking opponent without a direct link to previous attack or defensive actions.

Specific strategic elements, that are identified in the technical language according to the appropriate touch, disengagement or sweep actions and the position of the weapon, as direct thrust, direct cut, angulated thrust, disengagement thrust, cutover-cut, sixte-bind-thrust, quarte-beat-cut, sixte-glide, flick, can be found under the group or class name for basic attacks.

- *Ripostes* are attack actions that immediately follow a successful defensive action. They respond to an opposing attack action. One differentiates between direct riposte, disengagement-riposte, cutover-riposte, glide-riposte, etc.

- *Counter attacks* are attack actions that take direct advantage of the opponent's preparatory actions or direct attack actions for one's own attack. They are identified as disengagement in time, cutover in time, counter thrust, stop hit, block thrust, prise de fer, etc.

- *Remise attacks* are attack actions that follow directly after a failed attack. Like the other attacks, they are identified by the type of weapon movement in relation to the opposing blade, i.e. as direct, disengagement, and sweep-remise attacks.

Strategic defense elements are actions that have the goal of fending off the opponent's attack actions.

- *Parries* are defensive actions that prevent an opposing hit through movements with one's own weapon. They are referred to as septime pressure parry, octave beat parry, quart glide, sixte counter pressure parry, etc. One differentiates between general parries (defends multiple target areas and planes) and specific parries (most often in response to provoked or anticipated, therefore known attacks).

- *Esquives* (displacement parries) are defensive actions that prevent an opposing hit through body movements. They are referred to as retreating, dodging to the right, ducking, volte, etc.

For the sake of clarity, a conscious decision was made to forego listing each individual and possible strategic element. Every fencer can define his fencing actions if he refers to the main groups and the description of the fencing technique elements. Using the French and Italian terms shows that the terms of historic origin and those used in the FIE-Reglement can easily be incorporated. It is not a coining of "new terminology", but the creation of a systematic framework.

In practical fencing, established names were used for some sequences of basic strategic elements and for certain strategies. This applies in particular to "feint attacks, parry ripostes, and attacks with second intention."

- From a strategic-tactical point of view, feint attacks are combinations of two or more attack elements. The first attack (with double feint attacks the first and the second attack) serves to provoke mostly anticipated parries, to uncover unprotected openings, and to make a hit with a disengagement attack.

  All strategic attack elements serve as feints. The feints are identified by the strategic attack element that is used as a feint, by the number and type of parries, and by the attack element that finishes the feint attack.

  Example: battuta–thrust feint–disengagement thrust, feint-riposte with cutover, feint-counter attack (feint in time).

- *Parry-ripostes* are combinations of parries and ripostes. The favorable measure created by the opposing attack is used to make a hit. They are identified by the parry that was used and the riposte that was used.

  Example: Septime press parry–disengagement riposte, quart glide-(direct) riposte, sixte parry-glide riposte, etc. A parry riposte that follows a parry-riposte is called a counter parry-riposte.

- *Attacks with second intention* are combinations of two attack elements and one defensive element, or of two attack elements. With a feigned attack the opponent's attention is diverted from the true (second) intention and he is challenged to a parry-riposte or a counter-attack. The hit is made with a second parry-riposte (counter parry-riposte) or a counter attack (counter time).

The classification of technical elements that are the basic components of every movement action in fencing is done in a similar way. The structure of movements and their function are the classification characteristics. This makes it possible to describe the special characteristics of each individual group, as well as the positions and movements, in a generally binding and non-weapon specific way, to point out possible variations, and to strive for conceptual clarity.

We will forgo the classification and description of technical elements (basic technical elements). Basic references are provided in Chapter 2.3. The combinations are described in connection with the weapon-specific solution to the strategic-tactical tasks in Chapters 6, 7 and 8.

1 Divided like the country – the sport of fencing in post-1945 Germany

Like the country itself, the history of German fencing after 1945 was divided until the fall of the Berlin Wall. As Europe lay in ruins after World War II, there could be no immediate thought of fighting with épée, foil and saber. The Allied Forces had made sure of that on Dec. 17, 1945, with the Allied Control Council Directive 23. They viewed fencing, as well as any other martial arts sport, as a paramilitary exercise and a threat to peace. It took four years until the Allied forces revoked the ban and realized that the fencers with their blunted weapons were no bloodthirsty warriors.

Meanwhile, the Iron Curtain had been closed, East and West were no longer just cardinal directions, and the Federal Republic of Germany and the German Democratic Republic were a political reality. At first, enthusiasts in the West made efforts toward the **renewed founding of the German Fencing Federation (DFB), which was launched on Dec. 17, 1911, in Frankfurt,** on the initiative of Jacob Erckrath de Bary. Arbitrarily, meaning without the authority of the Allied forces, they tackled the reconstruction of the DFB. A foundation assembly was held on November 27, 1949, on the floor of the upper house of the German parliament in Bonn, which was attended by representatives from 157 fencing clubs and departments. Only six months later, did the Allied High Commission indirectly approve this surge ahead, by officially abrogating the ban.

In the DDR (German Democratic Republic), it took a few more years for the reconstruction of the sport of fencing, which was viewed as elitist, to begin. **On June 15, 1952, the "Fencing Section" was founded at the sports commission in Berlin,** where Karl Fischer, Herbert Schmiedel and Albert Gipp successively took charge. In addition fencing departments were formed in Leipzig, Erfurt, Magdeburg, Halle, Berlin, Zella-Mehlis, Gera, Rostock, Chemnitz and Dresden. At the end of 1951, 47 sections had already begun their training operation.

The first fencing tournaments within the DDR were already being held in Leipzig in July and October of 1951. The first DDR championships were held a year later, where Georg Neuber of Motor Dresden became champion in both foil and saber. But there was a shortage in fencing attire, and especially in blades, which led to limited training and competition activity.

Nevertheless, it became possible to expand the activities to an international level. At the end of 1952, Czech and East German fencers competed in Prague and Gottwaldov. This was the prelude to numerous competitions with other socialist countries, of which the USSR and Hungary, with their know-how, provided a significant impetus for increased performance.

In spite of intensive work in the youth area, fencing initially remained a sport that inspired little interest. By 1961, the number of organized members of clubs and departments had barely risen to 4200; only after 1971 did that number go up to about 7500. Not enough to produce top fencers that could bring international glory and success.

The kidnapping of the FIE president and its consequences

But before German fencers were once more permitted to compete on the world scene, feelings of resentment within the international fencing organization FIE had to be aired out. Although the FIE president at the time, Jacques Coutrot, whose godfathers included the German Erckrath de Bary, on Nov. 29th, 1913, pleaded for the reentry of the DFB, it was still rejected by the FIE Congress in 1951.

It had not been forgotten that the FIE president Paus Anspach, who was in office from 1933 to 1948, had been kidnapped in the summer of 1940, by Reinhard Heydrich, the head of the Gestapo. The reason: fencing enthusiast Heydrich himself wanted to become FIE president. To this purpose he kidnapped Anspach and had the entire FIE archive confiscated and brought to Berlin, where it burned in 1945. The Belgian was also carried off to the capital, where he was aggressively, but unsuccessfully, asked to resign.

This knavery bestowed upon the DFB another year of international ostracism. Only at the FIE Congress on March 28, 1952, did a majority vote for the reentry of the (West-) Germans. This meant that the DFB fencers' participation at the Helsinki Olympics, which marked the beginning of a slow but glorious climb to the world's fencing elite, was secured.

The fencers in East Germany had to wait longer to become members in the world association. After two applications for membership, in 1952 and 1954, were declined, the 37th FIE Congress decided on May 12, 1956, in Milan, to admit the Fencing Section of East Germany. Thus the road to the international title competitions was now open to the Germans from the East as well.

An organizational prerequisite to this was the founding of the German Fencing Confederation (DFV) on July 20, 1958, at the central delegates' conference of the Fencing Section in Leipzig. Alfred Röll became the first president, followed by Rudolf Hansen and finally Rolf Borrmann. The latter led the organization for 20 years, until 1990.

The first big showdown between the now internationally acceptable fencers from East and West came before the Olympic Games in Rome in 1960, and in Tokyo in 1964, where united German teams participated for the last time. During the elimination rounds the East German fencers suffered great disappointments, as none of them could prevail against the rivals from the West. This was particularly bitter before the Japan Games, because the good results at the World Championships in Danzig in 1963 had inspired much hope. The defeat of the repeated team-world champions Italy by the East German épée fencers, and the consequent fifth place finish, was the first major international success for the DFV.

But East Germany's fencing revival was limited. The small base of talented junior fencers was one reason, the lack of broad promotion of this cost-intensive individual sport, was the other one. Fencing, where international contacts and the global competition advance success within its community, did not fit into East Germany's competitive sports system. Anyone who could not guarantee medals found little support.

For the active fencers in the DFB however, the whole world was wide open, yet successes did not come automatically and in huge numbers. During the 50s and 60s, big celebrations were only sporadic. Ilse Keydel, who got third place in Brussels in 1953, won the first World Championship medal after World War II. But one name stood out above the rest: Heidi Schmid. She took second place at the World Championships in Paris in 1957, at the tender age of 17, exactly 20 years after the final World Championship victory of the legendary Helene Mayer, thus steeling the female German foil fencers.

The fencer from Augsburg created a sensation at the Rome Olympics, where she won a gold medal on September 1, 1960. In the following year, she also won the World Championships in Torino, Italy, as well as the students' World Championships, and was the first female fencer to be voted "Athlete of the Year". The thread of success broke in Tokyo, host of the 1964 Olympics: Heidi Schmid was eliminated in the intermediate round. But Helga Mees of Saarbrücken made the breakthrough and won the silver.

During that time, which was shaped by the formative influence of fencing geniuses such as Christian d'Oriola (France) and Eduardo Mangiarotti (Italy), the male German foil fencers did not get a stab in. However, as a team they made up an accurate group, which won World Championship-silver behind the upcoming fencing power, USSR, in Budapest 1959. One year later, at the Olympics, they also landed the bronze medal.

But it took nearly another decade before the foil of an exceptional German fencer could keep the world elite in-check: Friedrich Wessel. The Bonn fencer immediately landed a double coup by securing the World Championship title both in Cuba in 1969, and in Ankara in 1970. The Olympic crowning of his career was denied this pure amateur, who passed up participating in the 1971 World Championships in favor of pursuing his law degree, which likely cost him a medal one year later in Munich.

At that time, gold, silver, and bronze medals in épée and saber were only the stuff dreams were made of. Only in the era of Emil Beck, the originator of the (West-) German fencing miracle, would the entire armory get a new polish, whereby the Germans only broke through the phalanx of the Eastern Europeans in saber after its electrification in the mid-80's, combined with new training methods and rule changes.

Fencing did not fit into the East German system

East Germany lacked the resources, the freedom of movement, and the support for someone like Beck to create a similar revival of the fencing sport, such as was possible in the other Germany. In view of the sparse sponsorship by the state, for which medals and world records were symbols of the socialist system's superiority, it is in fact surprising that East Germany was able to claim any successes at all. Initially the saber was the hardest-hitting weapon there. At the Olympic games in Mexico City in 1968, the East German team took a remarkable fifth place, and was fourth three years later, at the World Championships in Vienna. But the East German fencers could only come close to medaling, such as Torsten Kühnemund of Potsdam, whose fifth place finish at the 1988 Olympics represented the best result in international individual épée fencing.

The big scores in foil fencing started to happen after Claus Janka took charge of that weapon within the East German organization. At the World Championships in Hamburg in 1978, and at the Boycott Games in Moscow in 1980, the East German male and female national foil fencing teams moved into focus with a fourth place finish respectively. Incidentally, in the year between, a female quartet that included Mandy Niklaus, had won gold at the student World Championships. In 1982 in Rome, the athlete from Dresden United won the first (bronze) medal for East Germany at fencing World Championships. Of all things, a West German fencer, Sabine Bischoff, nearly bungled that historic success. She sent Mandy Niklaus into the semi-finals, but in the final round she got revenge in the fight for bronze.

Peter Proske was one of her trainers, whose subsequent protégé, Udo Wagner of Dresden, won Olympic silver in foil fencing in 1988, thus presenting East Germany with its greatest fencing triumph to date. Like many of his colleagues, Peter Proske, who was the athletic director of the Tauberbischofsheim fencing club until 2004, after the turning point, switched over to training centers throughout Germany.

The world's most successful fencing club in Tauberbischofsheim also became a magnet for a number of top athletes from East Germany. After the fall of the Berlin wall, Uwe Römer, Ingo Weissenborn, and Udo Wagner moved to the Baden region and with their skills were able to prevail even in the "new Germany".

The last East German champion, Weissenborn, became the first foil fencing world champion of the reunited Germany in Budapest in 1991, namely in the duel for gold against Thorsten Weidner (TBB). "After this victory I feel liberated", Thorsten said at that time. He had received his first lessons from Lok Bernburg, and had drawn attention with his spartakiad victories in foil fencing and saber. Together with his companion Wagner, he was part of the East German foil fencing team that won World Championship silver in 1983, and bronze in 1986, as well as the German team that won the Olympic title in 1992.

Synonymous with fencing: Emil Beck

In the old Federal Republic one man, whose name would become synonymous with fencing, set new standards: Emil Beck. Born on July 20, 1935, in Tauberbischofsheim as the youngest of a family of 13, and first becoming aware of the sport in 1951 at a movie theater, he became the epitome of the medal smith. He created a new fencing school, built an efficient training center around the "FC TBB", cleared many obstacles out of the way, and by the early 70s had made the small town in the Baden region world famous.

The statistics of Beck's success are phenomenal. During the three decades from 1968 until 1998, his Tauberbischofsheim fencers won tons of titles and medals: 18 Olympic medals, 74 world and 28 European championships are a proud record. Add to that 34 European and 129 World Cup victories, as well as 399 German national titles. This achievement is unparalleled in the world and is essentially credited to Emil Beck, who gave up direction of the Tauberbischofsheim Olympic base on July 31, 2001, ending his career.

Of all things two triumphs in épée fencing, the most fickle of all weapons, marked the starting point of a new fencing era. In 1973, the German team won a sensational gold medal at the World Championships, providing the "Goeteborg Miracle". At the same time Beck experienced the first low point of his career at the Olympics in Munich in 1972, when the German fencers, against all expectations, did not win any medals.

That was definitely not the case in Montreal in 1976. Alexander Pusch, the épée genius, refined his 1975 World Championship success with an Olympic victory, which he snatched away from his teammate Jürgen Hehn. In the end the club also won silver. The big Olympic coup was landed by the men's foil fencing team, of which Thomas Bach was a member. He later continued the parry-riposte game in the sports-political arena on the International Olympic Committee (IOC), where he moved all the way up to vice president.

Since the Montreal Olympics, Germany ranks amongst the fencing elite such as Italy, France, or Russia. Since then there have been many highlights and a few lows, as well as a number of excellent athletes whose talent and character have given a face to this fringe sport.

Alex Pusch, who actually won his third title at the 1978 World Championships in Hamburg, was a kind of "Franz Beckenbauer" of fencing. Amongst the community of épée "players" in the 20th century, this was only accomplished by Italy's miracle weapon, Edoardo Mangiarotti, and Alexander Nikantschikow from the former USSR, as well as the Frenchman Eric Srecki. When Pusch, spoiled by his early successes, did no longer produce, the star of Elmar Borrmann, who in 1983 became the second German épée world champion, appeared on the horizon. Seven years later, Thomas Gerull surprisingly managed to do the same. Four years later Volker Fischer did it.

But after that the stage belonged to Arnd Schmitt of Heidenheim, who, like Pusch, was gifted and headstrong. Like his famous predecessor, he also became Olympic Champion in Seoul in 1988, but unsuccessfully struggled to become individual world champion at ten differernt World Championships (1985-1998). Only in 1999, was he able to break the spell and, – once again in Seoul – won the world champion's crown he was missing. Oliver Lücke, who only won his first (bronze) medal at the World Championships in 2001 at age 37, had to wait a long time for a big individual success.

South Korea was not only a highlight in Schmitt's career, but also a general milestone in the history of the DFB. This was largely due to the female foil fencers, Anja Fichtel, Sabine Bau and Zita Funkenhauser, who, in that order, won gold, silver and bronze, and together won another gold medal. This women's trio was the most effective team German fencing has ever produced. In the forefront was Anja Fichtel, whose successes and charisma overshadowed Helene Mayer, Heidi Schmid and Cornelia Hanisch. But "Conny" Hanisch of Offenbach, who produced a World Championship title-trilogy with her wins in 1979, 1981 and 1985, also reached enormous popularity, which even allowed her to win the title of "female athlete of the year" (1986).

Fig. 1-1:
Anja Fichtel and Alexander Pusch, two of Germany's most successful and popular fencers.

Anja Fichtel in fact never received this honorary title, but with her Olympic triumph, her two individual World Championship gold medals (1986/1990), and a total of ten World Championship medals, as well as ten national individual titles, she outstripped all of her predecessors.

Moreover, this Tauberbischofsheim fencer became the darling of the media like no other fencer before her. Much to Emil Beck's displeasure, she was quite outspoken, going on the attack off the strip, posed in the nude for magazines, and did not let pregnancy and the birth of a child interfere with her career. Sabine Bau, who landed a big surprise of her own after her superior rival retired, did not manage herself as spectacularly. In 1998 she finally got lucky and triumphed at the World Championships in La Chaux-de-Fonds. Twice more, in 1999 and 2001, she managed to land World Championship silver before she ended her career in 2003. At the Sidney Olympics in 2000, Bau had to leave the limelight to her Tauberbischofsheim teammate, Rita König, who got second place.

Many say that becoming the best in the world in men's foil fencing is fencing's crowning glory. Five German athletes have accomplished this: Friedrich Wessel was the first in 1969 and 1970, then Matthias Gey in 1987, Alexander Koch in 1989 and 1993, Ingo Weissenborn in 1991, and Peter Joppich in 2003. Only one touch kept Ralf Bissdorf from becoming the first German Olympic champion in foil fencing at the Olympic finals in Sydney in 2000. Duplicity of events: at the Olympic games in Los Angeles in 1984, Matthias Behr also missed the gold medal by one touch.

Only one German could become number one in saber fencing at World Championships in the 20th century, namely Felix Becker, who was world champion in Athens in 1994. One of the precursors preparing the laborious ascent into the international elite was Jürgen Nolte, who won eight national championships between 1980 and 1990, and was a noteworthy sixth at the 1986 World Championships; better results had been achieved before him by Gustav Casmir with a medal win at the (unofficial) Olympic in-between games in 1906, and his nephew Erwin Casmir, who achieved even better results with a fourth place fnish at the 1936 Olympic Games Berlin. In the late 90's, a new generation of German saber fencers prepared to set out. At the forefront was Wiradech Kothny, who had become European champion in 1999, and had won two bronze medals (individual and team) at the Olympics in Sidney in 2000.

Women's saber fencing only gained admittance to the World Championships one year before the turn of the millennium and has been part of the Olympic program since 2004. Of the German lady fencers Sandra Benad became a successful pioneer in this new discipline. The Eislingen native was able to take third place in the 2000 World Championships. One year later, at the European Championships in Koblenz, Germany, she won individual silver and led the saber team to win the title.

The women have been competing in épée fencing at the World Championships since 1989, whereby the Germans have been amongst the world elite since the beginning, as the team victories from 1988 (at the yet unofficial World Championships) and 1990, or the second place finish at the 2003 World Championships demonstrate. The DFB had to be patient until 2001, when Claudia Bokel was able to pocket the fist individual World Championship title. But other experts, such as Ute Schaeper, Eva-Maria Ittner, Katja Nass, Denis Holzkamp, and Imke Duplitzer, were also getting close to reaching this giant goal. They were runners-up at the World Championships in 1989, 1991, 1994, 1998 and 2002, and won the silver medal at the Olympic games in 2004.

But the success of an athletic association does not only consist of athletic merits. One of the greatest challenges for German fencing was the German reunification and the coalescence of the two associations. The fact that the sports-political threads were spun with the lighter foil, abandoning the rattling of sabers, was proven at the German Fencing Congress on December 8, 1990, in Bonn. By the sportsmanlike professional interaction between the fencers and the preparedness of the majority of representatives of both German fencing associations even in times of political confrontation, the regional associations Mecklenburg-Vorpommern, Brandenburg, Sachsen, Sachsen-Anhalt, and Thuringia were admitted to the DFB in the spirit of chivalry, and the seal was set to the union of fencers.

"This is our contribution to fair play. For us that term is not just lip service", said DFB president, Erika Dienstl. In 1986, the native of Stolberg near Aachen in the Rhineland, was the first woman after Erwin Casmir (1949-1957), Otto Adam (1957-1972, Elmar Waterloh (1972-1978), and Klaus Dieter Güse (1978-1986), to be elected to the top of the DFB.

Fig. 1-2:
The "unification presidents":
Erika Dienstl for the DFB
(West) and Dr. Berndt Barth
for the DFV (East) with the
1990 unification motto

The final act of the DFV of the former East Germany was its disbandment on Dec. 31, 1990. In May of that year, Dr. Berndt Barth was elected president of the DFV. The last chairman of the East German organization became vice president, and later secretary general of the DFB. The fact that another man from the German East, Claus Janka, also became sports director proves, that the fencers wanted unification also for the sake of fair play.

It was not expected that fencing, like some other sports, would see a long-term performance increase due to reunification. A number of excellent athletes from the new German states were able to make the leap to the national teams, but the continuous, systematic, and successful schooling of talent for world-class competitions developed only slowly. However, there is a lively fencing culture in cities like Berlin, Potsdam, Leipzig, Dresden, Halle, or Jena that may become the basis for a new revival in the East.

Chronology of the history of Geman fencing post-1945
(Compiled by Andreas Schirmer)

12.17.11	**Founding of the DFB in Frankfurt**
1939-45	World War II
12.17.45	Allied Control Council Directive 23 for the ban on fencing in Germany.

West Germany	East Germany
11.27.49 Re-founding of the German Fencing Federation (DFB) in Bonn	
1951 First post-war German championships.	
6.15.51	**Fencing Section is founded by the German Sports Committee in Berlin.**
3.28.52 Readmission of the DFB into the World Federation F.I.E.	
1953 Ilse Keydel wins the first World Championship medal.	
5.12.56	**East Germany's Fencing Section is admitted to the F.I.E.**
7.20.58	Founding of the East German Fencing Association in Leipzig.
9.1.60 Heidi Schmid becomes Olympic champion	
1963	East Germany's épée team gets fifth place at the World Championships in Danzig.
1968	East Germany's épée team gets fith place at the Mexico City
1969 Friedrich Wessel becomes first German foil champion.	Olympics.
1973 First World Championship victory by German épée team.	
1975 Alexander Pusch becomes first German épée world champion.	
1976 Pusch and DFB men's foil team become Olympic champions.	
1978 First World Championships in Germany (Hamburg) – Pusch world champion.	Women's and men's foil teams get fourth place at World Championships.
1979 Cornelia Hanisch wins first of three World Championship titles.	Women's foil wins Students' World Championships.
1980 Boycott of Moscow Olympics.	Women's and men's foil teams get fourth place at Olympics.
1982	Mandy Niklaus is first female East German fencer to win
1984 German épée and women's foil team Olympic champions.	World Championship medal (3)
1986 Anja Fichtel becomes youngest world champion in history.	
1988 Seoul Olympics. DFB wins seven medals and nationas ranking, Fichtel, Schmitt, and women's foil team win gold.	Udo Wagner is second to win first Olympic medal in individual foil.
1989 First time German World Championship medals in saber team (silver) and Felix Becker (bronze).	

1989 German reunification

12.8.90	**Admission of regional associations "East" into the DFB.**
1991	Ingo Weißenborn becomes first (foil) world champion after merging of fencing associations.
1992	German men's foil and women's épée teams become world champions for the second time.
1993	World Championships in Essen; hosts win 11 medals and nation ranking; Alexander Koch, men's foil and women's foil team world champions.
1994	Felix Becker becomes fist German world champion in saber.
1995	Atlanta Olympics; Arnd Schmitt flag bearer for entire German team; only women's foil team takes bronze.
1998	Exhibition competition in women's saber at World Championships; Sandra Benath takes seventh place.
1999	World Championships in Seoul; 6 medals; gold for Arnd Schmitt and women's foil team; Wiradech Kothny becomes European champion.
2000	Kothny wins first Olympian saber medal since 1906; five medals total in Sydney.
2001	First European Championships in Germany; Men's foil and women's saber teams win titles in Koblenz; Claudia Bokel becomes world champion in women's épée.
2002	At World Championships Andre Wessels takes second in individual and wins gold with men's foil team; Imke Duplitzer and Britta Heidemann take silver and bronze in épée.
2003	Peter Joppich becomes world champion; Simon Senft becomes European champion in men's foil.
2004	Women's épée teams won silver at the Athens Olympics; the men's épée team won bronze. Richard breutner becomes European CHampion in men's foil.
2005	For the third time after Hamburg in 1978, and Essen in 1993, World Championships take place in Germany, this time in Leipzig.

2 Performance structure, performance capacity, and performance development

2.1 Demand and performance structure

2.1.1 Demand profile and performance structure

Many fencing trainers picture the "ideal" fencer as "fast as a sprinter, a technical virtuoso like a violinist, and savvy as a chess player". Further attributes are elegant and fierce, goal oriented and persistent, strong willed and disciplined, and tall and slender respectively.

On the one hand this is correct because there are many individual factors involved in fencing performance. Fencing is certainly not comparable to sports in which the result or performance capacity is primarily defined by the pre-eminent significance of one criterion, like a marathon runner's endurance, a weight lifter's strength, or a gymnast's technical acrobatic skills. Even the most brilliant technician won't be successful in fencing if his action is not executed quickly and at the right moment, and the most persistent fencer will lose if he does not hit the opponent, but rather misses him.

On the other hand, fencers with good competition results have a rather varying appearance. There are world champions who are over six feet tall, and there are others who are around five feet tall. There are very elegant fencers, but also successfully fencing athletes with an unorthodox fencing style. There are the savvy strategists and clever tacticians, as well as the relatively one-sided, very fast reacting and strong fencers. Most often, particular talents or developed strengths are the basis for the fencers' various, individually preferred ways of fighting (performance style). There is a strongly generalized differentiation between the so-called "fighters" and the "tacticians".

Fencers who are labeled *fighters* are those who can, due to good special-temporal orientation, act and react quickly, consequently and strongly – regulated by impulse – in quickly evolving fight situations.

Tacticians are fencers who anticipate emerging situations or actively prepare for them with tactical maneuvers respectively, and successfully handle the contest with the opponent based on predominately reflexive decisions after strategic-tactical considerations, aided by complicated motion sequences.

With this two-sided examination it can be concluded, that fencing is a very complex sport that requires a multitude of special performance abilities and qualities for successful execution. But it can also be concluded that these performance requisites are related and in part alternately complement or compensate (balance) each other respectively.

Previous opinions on the performance structure of fencing – the inner structure of the concrete fencing performance or the factors involved in achieving performance and their interdependence respectively – are based on requirements analysis and the idea that the individual abilities and physical characteristics involved in the complex performance, as well as other components, can be combined into "complex performance factors". These complex factors are shown in schematically simplified form as a performance structure model.

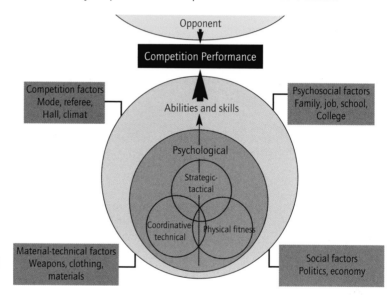

Fig. 2.1.-1: Schematic performance structure model in fencing

At the core of the illustration are the *abilities and skills* that are tied to the *character system*. In the above illustration these are shown as circles:

- **Physical fitness abilities and skills** combined with the physical-organic prerequisites (build, support and musculoskeletal system, cardiovascular system, muscles, nerves, sensory organs, etc., and the respective developmental status of strength, speed and endurance).

- **Coordinative-technical (movement regulating)** abilities (muscular coordination, movement perception, movement visualization, ability to control movements) and developed **sports-technical skills.**

- **Strategic-tactical abilities, action-regulating skills and processes** (feeling, perceiving, visualizing, thinking), developed or acquired, respectively, strategic-tactical knowledge and ability, as well as the ability to act.

- Around this core the **psychological abilities and skills** form a relatively independent complex, because the psychological influence factors of cognition (planning, evaluating, decision making), incentive (interests, goals, desires, expectations) and emotion (joy, anger, confidence, insecurity) influence the three other areas.

External factors (schematically shown as rectangles) influence the fencer's specific ability to act (the performance and the result) insofar as the
- **psychosocial factors** (family, school, college, job, friends, etc.),

- **social factors** (environment, evaluation and endorsing of performance through social classification, public effects, allocating of resources, sports scientific findings, etc)

- **material-technical factors** (competition material, weapons, clothing, to the point of special sports equipment for training) and

- **competition factors** (competition mode, location of competition, performance evaluation by referees, etc)

can become performance benefiting or performance inhibiting. By controlling this entire complex Emil Beck organized and secured the successes of his Tauberbischofsheim fencers for many years.

The intertwining of the factors in the schematic illustration of figure 2.1.-1, suggests the reciprocal linkage. The comprehensive classification of the psychological abilities and skills symbolizes their general significance.
Modern future-oriented approaches in the examination of the performance structure try to illustrate the correlation between the factors, their "internal functioning", with an integral concept. It is that mutual conditionality or structural and functional linkage of biological processes of the energy regulation (fitness level), the sensorimotor processes of the movement regulation (technique/coordination), and the mental-cognitive processes of the action and behavior regulation (strategy/technique), combined with the situation-outlasting, character-specific (cognitive, emotional and motivational) dispositions, that characterize the substance of a fencer's performance and performance capacity structure.
For a better understanding of the suggestions for modern fencing training in the following chapters, they are preceded by a summary and brief explanation of the most important starting positions.

1. The athletic performance of a fencer is the complex result of the actions of a personality. Based on the performance capacity of the apparatuses and functions, the multifaceted linkages between abilities, characteristics and skills have an effect on the level of competitive performance, the attitude towards coping with the demand, and the individual ability to act.

2. The individual performance requisites (abilities, skills, characteristics, etc.) are, with regard to their completeness and their participation in achieving the athletic performance, not definable at present. Therefore fitness reports and exact performance predictions are only possible by approximation. The "bio-psychosocial entitiy fencer" manages the type of sport as well as the discipline-specific bias of the performance capacity (structurally and functionally), in terms of a "self-organization" through the frequent accomplishing – on training methodical grounds – of the specific demands in training and competition of the sport and the discipline. This process takes place irrespective of what we already know about it in detail.

3. There is no special ability "as such", but just the abilities of the fencer for concrete activities, actions or movements. That is why no claim of validity for other spheres is being sought with those statements regarding "personality" and its structure. Intended are references to the entire personality, with regard to the activity (actions, movements), but only to the specific areas of demand affected by the sport of fencing. A fencer's performance capacity is purposive. Fencers are highly specialized and therefore most often only successful in one discipline.

4. Since fencers accomplish equal athletic performances (procure victories) with very different physiques, different action repertoires, and different fighting manners, it is beneficial and essential to address the fencers' individual characteristics and to assess or to create respectively, compensation alternatives.

Typical compensation alternatives for fencers are compiled in table 2.1.-1, as per research results by Rodionov, 1979

Table 2.1.-1: Typical compensation alternatives in fencing (as per Rodionov, 1979)

Deficiencies	Compensation
In strategic thinking	Through speed of motor reaction and execution.
In the spreading of attention.	Through speed of perception and thought operations. Accuracy of muscular movement differentiation.
In the shifting of attention.	Through fast motor reaction, situation anticipation and feel for tempo.
In the speed of motor reaction.	Through feel for measure and tempo, situation anticipation, spreading of steady attention, strategic-tactical thinking.
In the accuracy of muscular movement differentiation.	Through constant attention, speed of motor reaction, good feel for tempo.

5. The fencers' individual performance requisites are structured "hierarchically" on different regulation levels, according to the concrete demands. That means, that the complex performance factors identified in fig. 2.1.–1, do not act side by side as a "performance structure" but are, as function- (also regulation) levels, inferior or superior in a hierarchical sense, are in a "double hierarchical relationship" to each other. With this type of "holistic concept" following synergistic conclusions (Pickenhain, 1996; Janssen et. Al, 1996) an attempt is made – admittedly with a much-simplified model – to explain the interrelationship between the sub-systems and their "internal functioning".

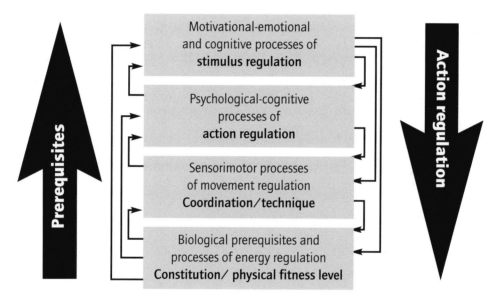

Fig. 2.1.-2:
Relationships of function levels of the action system (schematic)

This "double hierarchy" becomes apparent in that, on the one hand, the organism's existence and the biological processes of the energy regulation in the, for the trainer comprehensible, form of strength, speed and endurance are prerequisite to the fencer's ability to execute the fencing technique quickly, accurately and reliably, to perceive the opponent's behavior, make accurate decisions and set goals, feel anger or joy (left arrow to the top).

On the other hand, the action control occurs when the fencer sets goals, becomes motivated to achieve them, devises action programs, and chooses certain goals, ways, and means. Only then does the execution or conversion respectively, of the goal and situation appropriate movement programs (motor implementation) and the activation of the energy providing processes (right arrow to the bottom) occur.

The entirety of the performance and performance action is determined at the stimulus regulation level. The action, motion, and energy regulation is involved to a certain degree. In this context, what is important to the trainer is the knowledge that the stimulus level is superior to the action regulation level, in contrast the motion and energy level is inferior.

Competition failure or just one error can be caused by a decision that is not situation appropriate for an incorrect action (i.e. counter attack instead of parry-riposte), as well as a tardy (missed time) or inaccurate movement in the sequence (too big; too small) or the target (missed target). Or the fencer just didn't really feeL like it.

2.1.2 Demand structure and training tasks

These performance structure issues become important to the trainer, when practicing and training by goal formulation, determination of the necessary training content to reach the goal, training means and training methods are to be directed to where the fencer trains according to the demands, and that the targeted physical-organic movement-regulating, psychological-cognitive and emotional-volitional prerequisites and processes are developed and linked in a structurally ideal (according to the requirements) way. Regulation that meets the demands must be learned and continuously perfected and stabilized.

In a much-simplified version one can imagine that the human organism is a self-regulating system, in which strain that is caused by athletic training acts as a "disturbance of equilibrium". The organism attempts to balance these and tries to adapt. It is the trainers' job to optimize these adjustments to the strain. Development (improvement) always occurs when an athlete's existent performance requisites are not sufficient, and he can only complete the task or demand under personal exertion.

The trainer finds his basis for orientation in the demand structure.
Demand analyses are established during individual analytical steps that are executed with precision, applying methods of training science specific to high-performance sports.

1. The task analysis asks about the characteristics and the structure the fencer has to cope with during competition, and the conditions under which this occurs (first column of the structure plan in table 2.1-2). For instance, during the fencing fight the desire to win is most essential at the hierarchical upper level; at the lowest level the strain capacity is the constant alternating of forward and backwards movements, during which the fencer cannot fatigue.

2. Derived from this are
   - the behavior patterns, actions and movements essential to task execution, and
   - the performance requisites inventory essential to behavior, actions and movements (second column of the structure diagram).

(Self-assurance and organic-muscular load tolerance are prerequisites to the examples mentioned above.)

3. When tasks executed during training (third column) correspond to tasks performed during competition (first column), then performance rerequisites (second column) of the character and structure essential to task execution, are developed.

This applies to the "construction" of requirement profiles for long-term training plans, which focus more on a versatile foundation, as well as the optimum preparation of fencers for international championships. This provides the trainer with a kind of "time table" for his responsible job.

Table 2.1.-2, on page 34, shows the relationship between the demands of fencing and the necessary performance requisites, the training exercises and the monitoring. The intent is to simplify the complexity and the complex correlations with the aid of such a "structure plan", so that a trainer can follow them anytime, and continue to advance and adapt them creatively to concrete prerequisites and conditions, and make them applicable.

Demands, performance requisites and training implementation have an inner connection that was linked, in the overview, to the assertions regarding complexity, the hierarchy of the regulation levels, and self-organization.

Significant to training are observations in the horizontal rows on the respective regulation level, as well as in the vertical columns in terms of the mutual interdependencies.

For the trainer, the proportionate weighting of the sub-systems involved in the complex fencing performance is only reasonable within these limits.

In Chapters 2.2 to 2.5 the analytical steps for the individual regulation levels and performance factors are addressed, based on this performance structure model. Performance factors are "lifted" as sections from the schematic performance structure model (fig. 2.1.-1) and broken down further.

Table 2.1.-2: Structural plan of fencing training

Regulation level	Demands made by competition	Prerequisites to fulfill demands	Training tasks for learning	Monitoring for review
Motivation Emotions	Success motivation Performance enjoyment Exertion readiness Desire to win	Social wellbeing Confidence in success Self-confidence Desire to win	Conveying positive goals and performance-oriented values Assuring sense of achievement Avoiding compulsion	Observation of self and others Asking questions and having conversations Sociopsychological methods Competition analysis
Strategy Tactics	Concentration Fight determination Clever thinking Quick decision-making	Certainty on rules Perception Strategic-tactical thinking	Imparting knowledge Perception training Situational training Many competitions	Perception-, reaction-, and decision-making tests Training and competition analysis
Technique Coordination	Quick, accurate, reliable movements and skills adapted to the opponent	Motor experiences Sense of movement Variably adaptable motor control ability	Motor learning training Stabilizing training Application training under varying conditions	Evaluation of technique Biomechanical evaluation Competition analysis
Physical fitness Energy regulation	Explosive and quick movements without fatiguing; ability to handle strain and recover	Ability to handle organic-muscular strain Specific power Ability to recover quickly	Versatile fitness training Rhythmic conditioning exercises Rhythmic conditioning exercises	Fitness-oriented performance tests Biological and biomechanical performance analyses

2.2 Basic pedagogic and psychological principals of fencing

2.2.1 Functional conditions in fencing and their psychological dimensions

The amount as well as the variability of the motor performance requirements, of the technical-tactical abilities and skills, and the general external conditions, require specific performance, action, and behavioral qualities on part of the fencer, to achieve top efficiency during the concrete competitive situation.

The pedagogic-psychological work process should allow for two dimensions: one is the dimension "fencer", with analysis of the fencer's individual basic physical structure and the training programs to be developed based on that; the other is the dimension "fencing", with analysis of the specific requirement characteristics of this particular sport, and the psychological preconditions for successful task execution on part of the fencer, resulting from that.

In the heavily tactical-technical dueling sport of fencing, the basic motor characteristics that clearly come to the fore are speed-, movement-, and coordination-based factors in the fencer's training, whereas, by comparison, in the endurance-based sports the cardiopulmonary system and metabolic kinetics decisively support or limit the performance processes. These different physical requirement criteria of the particular sport also inevitably determine the content of the psychological interventions for the improvement of the fencer's cognitive, volitional and emotional characteristics.

The activity related particularities of fencing are elaborated on below according to subordinated characteristics, and descriptions of the possible psychological concomitants are provided.

(1) The time level
Criterion
Fencing is a multi-task activity over an extended period of time, with intentional and unintentional temporal interruptions, against different opponents, with an increase in qualitative demand during the course of a competition. Beyond that, the exact fixation of the fight times is often not possible. Therefore the fencer has to stay "in shape" for an extended time period – often for several days during competitions –, and must even be able to increase his performance towards the end.

Psychological aspects
The quality level of the ability to adapt and reorganize is the central regulating variable for the competitive performance.

The fencer must be able to "produce" his optimal psycho-physiological excitation level according to the particular tournament situation, and use it to increase his concentration capacity. In doing so, he has to build up an ideally functioning activation status directly before the fight, regulate the same according to the fight progression, and afterwards immediately initiate the relaxation process. If this conscious tension exchange does not succeed during the course of the day as well as during the fight, there is a danger of continuous tension with the effect of an often considerably limited ability to concentrate, thus limiting performance capacity.

(2) The confrontation level
Criterion
The focus here is not on faster, higher and further, overcoming obstacles, or battling physical barriers. The object of the contest in fencing is always the opponent with all of his physical and psychological strengths or weaknesses respectively.

Thus a fencer's performance always develops as a result of exerting one's action- and skill-related abilities under the impact of the respective opponent. Similar to the sports of wrestling, boxing and judo, in fencing the opponent of course actively joins in the happenings:

He tries to act himself (to make hits), but also tries to react (ward off attacks). Consequently the opponent's psychological qualities must also be incorporated in one's own strategic-tactical action plan (see Chapter 2.4).

Psychological aspects
Subjective perception and information processing processes play an important role in the execution of actions. The degree of development in characteristics such as anticipation ability, confident decision-making, focused concentration, the ability to react quickly and accurately, decisively determines the correct choice and the effectiveness of attack and defense alternatives, and thus the success or failure of a fight.

Since the international fencing elite of all arms possesses a nearly equally strong technical-tactical action potential today, the principal objective is to optimally apply one's own action capabilities and skills in decisive fights (stress situations) under the existing situation-dependent conditions, and thereby implementing or asserting respectively, one's competition strategy and tactics. Here the fight finally turns into a contest with the opponent's psychological capacity, with his strengths and weaknesses.

(3) The valuation/evaluation level
Criterion
During a fight the fencer is constantly confronted with successes (self-initiated hits) and failures (hits received). Performance-based action and behavior can hereby be decisively facilitated or inhibited, depending on how the fencer experiences and processes success or failure in this particular situation.

Next to this internal, subjective evaluation there is an additional behavior influencing, external valuation dimension: the decision of the referee (particularly in foil and saber fencing). If this objective decision is inconsistent with the subjective evaluation of the fencer, another stress condition has occurred and needs to be regulated.

Psychological aspects
Dealing with successes and failures on the side of the fencer, in particular the issue of psychological success and failure related stability is an important success factor. In addition, "evaluation stress" must be reduced, on the one hand, by practicing making definite, distinct hits, but on the other hand, by also actively training stress management during the instruction process.

(4) The external level
Criterion
With regard to the performance-influencing basic external conditions, particular attention is directed at the spectators (i.e. background noise, manifestations), the facilities where the competitions are held (i.e. associations with previous competitions at the same location; general conditions such as lighting, size, position, retreat options), and the opponent's reputation (attitudes, i.e. "He can hardly be beaten!", "Others have already lost against him!")

Psychological aspects
A fencer's inability to cope with these conditions leads to highly increased excitation, initiated by the activation of the endocrine axis (hypothalamus-pituitary gland-adrenal cortex), with the adjustment reaction of nervousness, tenseness, uncertainty and feat. False estimation of one's abilities and skills, and disruption of the ideal functioning of the psycho-physiological excitation level, often characterizes the fencer's performance related actions. Here the athlete must learn to regulate his aspiration level according to the demands of the situation to consciously initiate relaxation, and to specifically apply concentration-promoting methods.

The listed demand and functional conditions for the sport of fencing necessitate a complex, integrated education of the fencer. Training the psychological abilities and skills is an indispensable prerequisite to the implementation of technical, coordinative, strategic-tactical, and fitness-related qualities. The quality of the development of psychological performance characteristics determines the quality of athletic activity during training and competitions, and vice versa.

Kunath (1978), phrases this "bidirectional communication" as follows: "The psychological is always tied to activities. Whereby the biotic aspects of a human being prevail over the psychological in people's activities and actions." But person and environment are not firmly coupled from the outset; rather their relationship is only established and specified by actions. In this sense, athletic actions are not just a peripheral motor process, but activities that are largely psychologically regulated as well as regulating the physiological.

According to this, action regulation means "the enabling of the personality" to, specifically and appropriately, independently control and regulate its actions based on mental images, operations and conditions, in a concrete situation, allowing for comprehensive action-related goals, and under consideration of the concrete external and personal action-related conditions." (Konzag & Konzag, 1980). These characteristics and abilities are developed during the process of the fencer actively dealing with his environment, particularly during athletic "pressure situation".

2.2.2 Fundamentals and prerequisites for the development of psychological abilities and skills

2.2.2.1 The person-environment interrelation in fencing

The external and internal (personal) action requirements and their interdependencies are described in fig. 2.2.-1.

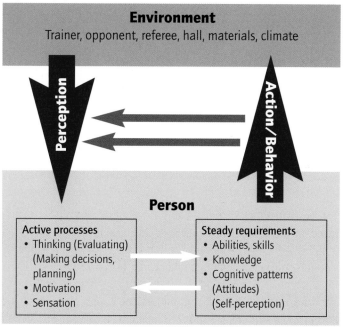

Figure 2.2.-1: Main requirements for the interaction of a fencer with his environment from a psychological point of view: perception – information processing (thinking) – behavior/ action (as per Eberspächer, 1993)

The specific functional conditions of the sport (multi-tasking, different opponens, variable fight times) point to the significance of the perception process. Perception volume and -intensity impact the ability to convert and anticipate and thus the reaction speed and the functioning of the fencer's tactile-kinesthetic apparatus.

2.2.2.2 Psychological abilities and skills (psychophysiological model)

Cognitive, motivational and emotional abilities influence physiological processes (hormonal, nervous, immunological) and in turn are influenced by them. The resulting functional disturbances or enhancements determine the fencer's action-regulating behavior. Figure 2.2.-2 illustrates these connections. At the same time the neuromuscular information necessary for successfully completing tasks and the sensorimotor information communicated through the feel for the blade or measure is primarily influenced by the current emotional state of the fencer.

Here the development of the mental systems that influendce performance capacity, as well as the perception ability and the accepting of body-specific feedback signals are a significant concern.

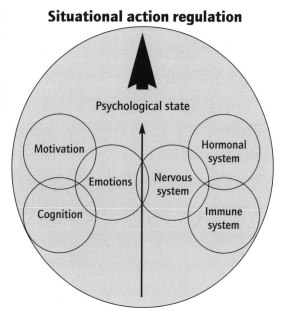

Fig. 2.2.-2:
Factors of the mental system and the neurophysiologic level.

The hormonal system and the endocrine gland act as the controls. The interplay between these factors decisively determines the quality of the situation-dependent coordinative abilities. A highly specialized eye-hand-leg-coordination fulfills its purpose only if it can be simultaneously applied in a highly variable manner.

This only works under optimum system conditions, which are particularly vulnerable during stress situations. Fig. 2.2.-3 explains these complex "head-body" connections.

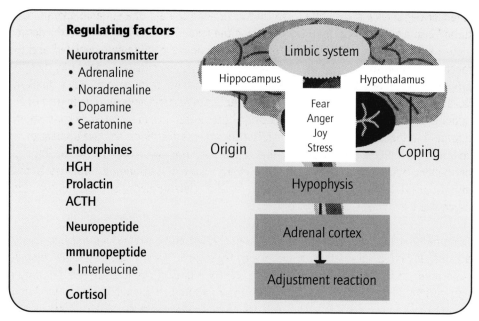

Fig. 2.2.-3: The psycho-physiological network and its impact factors

2.2.2.3 Psychological impact factors

(1) Cognitions

The fencer must contemplate courses of action for handling demands in complicated situations. But the process is always the same: An initial state must be turned into a target state. In between is a barrier that complicates the turnover or momentarily makes it appear impossible. Thus thinking becomes problem solving, whereby alternatives are tested for their suitability through test actions (mental operating and testing processes).

The TOTE-model (Test-Operation-Test-Exit) very clearly illustrates this process, as it combines the cognitive and motor dimensions of action (cp. Fig. 2.2.-4).

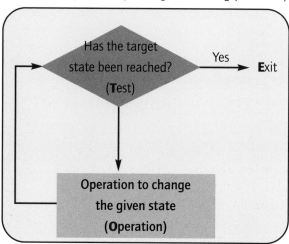

Fig. 2.2.-4:
The TOTE-model: Actions/
problem solving in sports
(Miller, Galanter & Pribram,
1973)

A fencer perceives a given state (test) that must, with the aid of a suitable operation, be turned into a target state. After the operation the fencer checks (test) to see if the desired state has been achieved. If this is the case, the action is considered completed and the fencer moves on to the next action (exit). Thus athletic actions are constantly merging progressions of test-operation-test exit. Problem solving requires productive thinking, novelty and creativity. At the same time varying training conditions and the impact of the opponent play a central role in fencing. The fencer obtains the tactile-kinesthetic information that provides the vital impulses for the specification and development of his coordinative abilities specifically during the interaction with the opponent. Through permanent actions and test actions the overall level of sensorimotor abilities is thus improved. These are important steps in the development of competition-proof psychological abilities.

Cognitive patterns play an important role in the planning, evaluating and deciding of actions or action alternatives respectively. These are "classification systems" learned over time, that can promote or inhibit situation-dependent actions. The situation-appropriate and effective processing of information can be highly irritated during situations of psychological strain. Athletes and trainers sometimes lose track during these situations.

This is when cognitive patterns as subjective coordination systems are helpful in sorting things out. But their effects can become problematic in the area of preconceptions and stereotypes: "I won't be able to win against him/her anyway"; "At this tournament I have been knocked out for years during the 32nd, at the latest." Such thinking definitely shapes the perception, experience and actions of the fencer in a negative way

The fencer's self-image is a frame of reference that determines how the fencer acts specific to a situation. This image is updated according to the situation, and strongly influences the fencer's motivational and volitional qualities. Since the self-image is established in the course of personality development, changes – particularly of negative self-images – are not realizable in the short-term. Here the goal must be to "unlearn" old, negative ways of thinking and to train and "anchor" new, positive action and behavior patterns. This is where the trainer is being challenged: A variable training design with the integration of elements containing strategic-tactical, coordinative-technical and psychological requirements, serves the development of a solid self-image with regard to abilities and skills.

Motives are another frame of reference. This is a matter of "perpetual preconceptions regarding cognitive processes", with which the individual fencers perceive identical situations differently and evaluate the outcome and the consequences of their actions differently (Heckhausen, 1980). Fig. 2.2.-5 shows the thought processes of planning, evaluating, deciding and linking to the steady "classification systems" within the scope of the fencer's information processing processes.

(2) Motivation

The ability to effectively motivate oneself is considered a sign of competence of a good trainer.

Motivated actions/behavior is critically influenced by three factors:

- The fencer's expectations regarding the results and consequences of his athletic actions, which have been evaluated as being important to him.
- The activity-related stimuli of a task that has been posed, or the currently given situation respectively.
- Experiences from similar situations in the past and the results achieved at that time, or the evaluation and consequences of these results respectively.

Regulation of cognitive actions

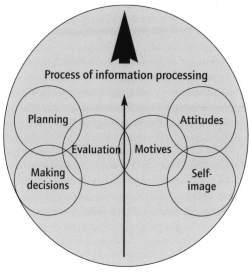

Figure 2.2.-5:
Cognitive processes and their subjective coordinating systems

The trainer should be able to integrate motivation-aiding measures into his methodical training repertoire. An important factor is the creation of suitable inspirational conditions in daily training situations, i.e. giving tasks that are characterized by elements of curiosity, adventure and challenge. A second important aspect is the promoting of experienced probabilities of potential outcomes to actions, i.e. giving tasks in the sense of "moderately new", meaning the fencer should have the sense that he possesses the necessary action-related qualifications (knowledge, skills), and that, with optimum effort, he will easily be able to complete the task to his own satisfaction. In doing so, fencers usually prefer tasks that lead to positive, desirable consequences, or to the least negative, undesirable consequences possible. Additional influencing factors at work here are also the personal constraints (self-image, motives, attitudes). It is ultimately a matter of developing the factors that influence achievement potential and promote motivation, and their subjective classification systems with regard to the planning, execution and control of actions (q.v. Chapter 4.2).

What happens in a fencer's head when a specific task if given? He considers whether or not he can do it. Past experiences in similar situations help him to do so. Eventually, there are interferences by certain cognitive patterns ("I have never been able to do that!"; "That is much too difficult!"). Ultimately the fencer sets his own abilities with regard to the difficulty of the task and the potential consequences to his acting or not acting. He asks himself: Is it worth it or not?

But actions don't always have rational explanations. Rheinberg (1991) emphasizes the significance of the activity's appeal during the inducement to act. There are action incentives that lie in the execution of the activity itself. Csikszentmihalyi (1985) speaks of being "completely absorbed in the activity", the flower life. The fencer feels optimally challenged, the action sequences are clearly defined and merge smoothly, concentration seems to happen on its own; one forgets about the time and occasionally about oneself. One does not perceive oneself as apart from the activity but is one with it.

Fig. 2.2.-6 illustrates the situational, motivation-based action influencing factors and their superordinated, relatively steady personal determinants.

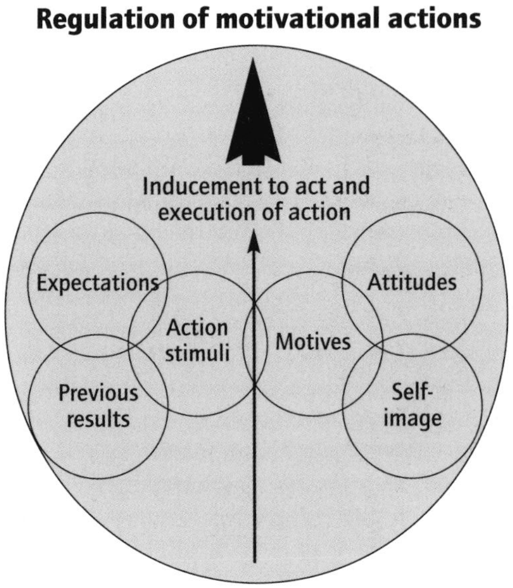

Regulation of motivational actions

Inducement to act and execution of action

Expectations · Action stimuli · Motives · Attitudes

Previous results · Self-image

Fig. 2.2.-6;
Situational and personal factors of performance-motivated actions and behavior

(3) Emotions

More or less intensely experienced emotions go hand in hand with every action. Ongoing or anticipated emotions together with cognitions and acts of volition initiate behaviors, maintain them, or cause interferences and transitions to differently motivated behaviors. Based on their more or less positive or negative quality, emotional states induce basic basal behavioral directions – toward something or away from something. As a result emotions have a behavior adjusting, organizing and energizing funtion. In doing so they exhibit three determinants:

- *A cognitive component:*
  Emotions always have a connection to the fencer's individual assessment of a situation, meaning they are the results of the representation and processing of knowledge.
- *A physiological component:*
  Activation- or deactivation-states respectively, go hand in hand with emotional processes that can promote or interfere with athletic actions (excitation level).
- *A behavioral component:*
  Emotions are reflected in the fencer's expressed behavior and performance during concrete situations.

Emotions always imply a positive or negative assessment on the part of the fencer. Criteria may be personal desires and goals, personal characteristics and abilities, and the norms and standards considered to be binding. Fig. 2.2.-7 clarifies these evaluating criteria and their bearing on the fundamental influencing factors of emotional states or processes.

Particularly strong emotions lead to a decline in quality during the execution of an action, to the interruption or avoidance of actions. Fear of failure promotes behavior based on failure-avoidance. Fear triggers safety-seeking behavior. Thus emotions also have a highly motivating function. From an athletic point of view a high degree of emotional stability is therefore very important, because the ongoing emotional state can functionally impact other psychological or physiological processes. With regard to the fencer, one has to particularly consider a disruption of the entire sensory activity: altered cognitive behavior, decreased speed of reaction, inadequate ability to adapt, absence of tactile-kinesthetic information, unclear sensorimotor information (coordination, orientation).

These are critical qualities with regard to the feel for blade and measure.

External and internal developmental conditions, influencing mechanisms and evaluating criteria of emotions therefore require continuous monitoring during the training process.

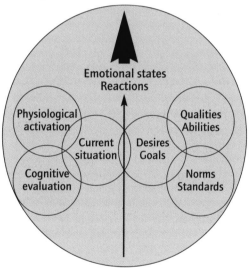

Fig. 2.2.-7:
Regulation factors and evaluation conditions of emotional processes

2.2.3 Methods for learning and stabilizing mental training programs

The situational and personal conditional factors of cognitive, motivational, emotional processes and states require continuous monitoring and adaptation during training and competition events. What works during training is far from having competitive validity. Precisely that motivational-emotional competitive stability is a critical success factor in fencing. It impacts the strategic-tactical, coordinative-technical and concentrative

qualities, particularly in crucial situations. Psychological training should therefore always go hand in hand with certain training-methodological elements that promote these methods, and that ultimately really make the competitive transfer possible. The fencer must possess specific behavioral- and performance-related qualities, based on an extensive, variably applicable repertoire of motor skills, which enable him to implement his technical-tactical abilities and skills in the respective competitive situation.

In detail, the following psychological training methods are applicable, whereby the effectiveness of these methods presupposes the fencer's unlimited willingness to cooperate:

- Learning relaxation techniques (progressive muscle relaxation, autogenic training) for activation training in varying situations.

- Practicing soliloquizing (positive affirmation) for coping with psychologically stressful situations.

- Alertness regulation in decisive situations through recognition of switching points in the action and focusing attention on them.

- Imagination regulation to improve quality of movement, emotional stability and confidence by establishing mental training programs (i.e. for motion sequences, fights, tournaments, feared opponents).

These methods must find their expedient complement in training. Accepting and trusting the trainer are imperative preconditions thereto. The following are desirable methodical combinations:

- Short breaks after very intensive, concentrative strain with optimized regeneration via relaxation techniques.

- Constant changing of offered stimuli, combined with a frequent change in the psychological demands made on the fencer. Only with this interplay will a concentrative adaptation process be initiated, promoted and stabilized.

- Setting goals and presenting tasks that continuously enhance the fencer's motivational structures (constantly creating new challenges).

Finally, within the scope of the psychosocial environment, coordinating training schedules with school, college and job (study and work schedule) must be addressed in particular. Here precise time management is essential. In doing so the fencer should never have the feeling that he is not spending enough time on any one thing.

2.3 Fundamentals of fencing technique

2.3.1 Fencing technique characteristics

*Fencing **technique** refers to the distinguishing techniques that have been tested in practice, and are practicable with regard to the fencer's qualifications and the resolution of the specific movements.*
Technique in fencing is not self-serving and is not subject to direct performance evaluation (like, for instance, gymnastics or ice skating), but it is a component of the combative operations. Through technique, the decision made regarding the direction of the engagement is motor appropriate and reliably implemented.

Technique serves as an external model for the action of movement and manifests itself on the basis of the individual movement visualization (as an internal model) or appropriate action programs within a special system of simultaneous successive partial movements respectively, which adapt to the constant changes in the combative situations. It utilizes the fencer's existing psycho-physiological powers (nervous system, muscular system) and the material-technical conditions (weapon, strip) to resolve the action-related task. It is immediately apparent, that technique cannot be regarded as something separate but must only be viewed in connection with the other components that impact the complex performance in fencing.

Technique is the method for resolving a combative task and, together with the psychological particularities of cognition and analysis of the combative situation and the strategic-tactical component – the mental resolution to a combative task –, is of considerable importance to the fencing performance.

High athletic performances in modern fencing are achieved anywhere where traditional dogmas and views of an abstract technique that was only formalized according to external characteristics, have been overcome.

The Russian fencing school in particular (i.e. Arkadjew, 1968, or Tischler, 1996), and the system Beck implemented in Tauberbischofsheim in 1978, have contributed considerably to that end. This made fencing an exceedingly dynamic martial arts sport.

Observations made at competitions, film analysis and biomechanical research have shown that the top-fencers in the world break out of the "classic forms" of external fencing criteria.

A criterion of good technique is its effectiveness in resolving combative tasks, ultimately hitting the opponent and preventing opposing hits. And since every combative situation is subject to a certain 'non-repeatability", every situation-adapted

resolution method has generally binding, as well as individually and situation-dependent (thus not generally binding) characteristics.

Generally binding is a model of the form of movement execution as basic technique abstracted by the world-class fencers.

Basic fencing technique

The technical elements, the basic components of every combative action in fencing, are classified under structural and functional aspects. This makes it possible to present the particularities of the individual groups of positions and movements in a generally binding and non-weapon specific way, to point out possible variations and strive for conceptual clarity.

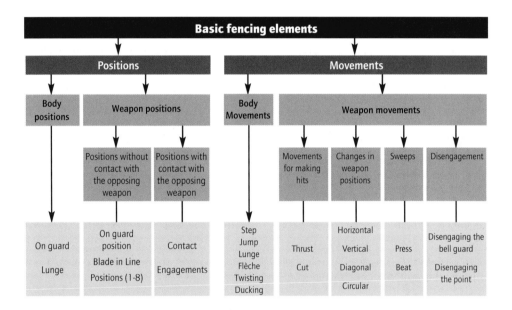

Fig. 2.3.-1: Technical elements of fencing

We will forgo descriptions of the individual techniques. The illustrations of the technical elements are accompanied by basic directions. The combinations are explained in Chapters 6, 7 and 8, in connection with the weapon-specific resolution of the tactical task.

Positions

Positions are typical momenta of the fencing movements that frequently repeat themselves in the course of a fight. They are starting and ending, as well as reversing momenta, and they conduce to a more specific description of the combative action. We differentiate between *body positions* and *weapon positions* (arm, hand, and weapon positions).

Body positions

The fencing position is the most expedient starting and ending position of all leg and body movements on the strip. It ensures favorable conditions for all movements and is characterized by the following criteria (fig. 2.3.-2):

- Position of the feet relative to the line of fencing.
- Location of the body's center of gravity and,
- Rotation of the shoulder and pelvis relative to the fencing line.

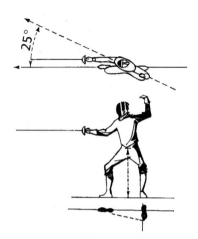

Fig. 2.3.-2: Fencing position

The foot of the lunging leg is positioned at a right angle, approx. 1.5-2 feet in front of the supporting leg. The body's center of gravity lies vertically above the support surface. The main support points are the pads of the feet. The rotation of shoulders and pelvis relative to the fencing line is approx. 25°. Deviations from this fencing position (aspired to by beginning fencers) by successful fencers are usually tactically or biomechanically motivated, but frequently are anatomically or physiologically contingent, and are not necessarily judged as being incorrect.

For example, the position of the lunging leg at a right angle to the center of the supporting leg is the most favorable option with regard to balance. The location of the body's center of gravity depends on the distance between the feet in fencing position, the amount of leg flexion in the ankles, hips and knees, and the tilt of the torso. Typical variations, aside from the characterized position, are the high/narrow and the deep/wide fencing positions. It is possible to shift the body's center of gravity forward (attack position). Lifting the heel of the supporting leg off the strip (starting position if the heel is rotated out additionally) is particularly biomechanically advantageous before a lunge or a running attack (flèche).

The fencing position is not a static element, but is essential for loose and quick movements and therefore should be as natural as possible.
The lunge is characterized in the description of the lunge.

Weapon positions

We distinguish between the arm and weapon positions (without contact, with contact) according to their position relative to the opposing weapon.

- Positions without contact with the opposing weapon

Fencing position. With regard to the fencing position, the arm and weapon position is weapon-specific and individually different. From the basic position (cp. fig. 2.3.-2) the arm and weapon position can vary on any plane.

The hand of the fencer and the blade of the weapon are points of reference for the more specific determination of the "lines" and the differentiation of target areas (fig. 2.3.-3).

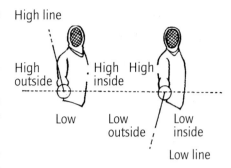

Figure 2.3.-3: Lines and target areas

The imaginary horizontal line through the center of the guard divides top and bottom; the blade divides outside and inside. "Blade in line" describes the outstretched, weapon-bearing arm threatening the opposing target area. The position of the weaponless arm, in the basic position (except saber – see fig. 8.5, pg. 302) it is bent, sideways and up, is subject to individual changes and is not an essential fencing element.

Positions are defined positions of the weapon-bearing arm and the weapon in relation to the fencer's own body. We differentiate between eight fundamental positions, which are depicted here non-weapon specific and sequential with their numeric definition (fig. 2.3.-4).

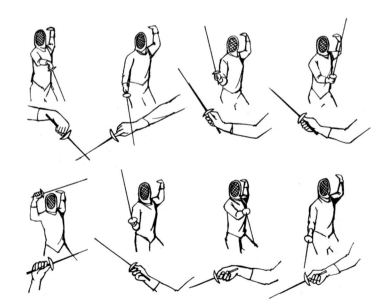

Fig. 2.3.-4:
Positions
1. Prime
2. Second
3. Tierce or Third
4. Quart
5. Quint or Fifth
6. Sixte
7. Septime
8. Octave

Table 2.3.-1: Names of basic positions

Name of position	Relation to the body[1]	Arm position	Hand level[*]	Fist rotation	Point position	Additional tips
First position **(1) Prime**	Left	Bent halfway, horizontal in front of body	Level of left shoulder	Pronated	Front-low, knee level	
Second position **(2) Second**	Right	Bent at an obtuse angle	Level of pelvis	Pronated	Front-low, thigh level	Similar to eighth position
Third position **(3) Tierce**	Right	Bent at an obtuse angle	Level of waist	Pronated	Right-front-high	Similar to sixth position
Fourth position **(4) Quarte**	Left	Bent at an obtuse angle	Between chest and waist	Slightly supinated/ pronation possible	Left-front-high	
Fifth position **(5) Quint**	Top	Bent halfway	Right front above the head	Pronated	Left-front-high, above head	
Sixth position **(6) Sixth**	Right	Bent at an obtuse angle	Between chest and waist	Slightly supinated	Right-front-high	Similar to third position
Seventh position **(7) Septime**	Left	Bent at an obtuse angle	Chest level.	Slightly supinated	Left-front-low, thigh level	
Eighth position **(8) Octave**	Right	Bent at an obtuse angle	Level of pelvis	Slightly supinated	Right-front-low, thigh level	Similar to second position

[1] for a right-hander

50

A more detailed description of the positions (in relation to the body, arm position, hand level, fist rotation, location of point of the blade) is given in table 2.3.-1, pg. 50.

Depending on the combative situation, variation of these numerically identified positions on any plane (up and down, outside and inside, steeper or shallower, away from the body and towards the body) is possible and necessary,

- *Positions with contact with the opposing weapon*

All positions in which the weapons (blades) of both fencers come in contact are called *engagements* or *touches*.

Engagements are positions in which the fencer uses his blade to dominate the opponent's weapon by using the leverage of middle against foible, forte against middle or forte against foible respectively. Engagements are preceded by changes in position and thrusting sweeps.

In the line of an engagement the fencer is protected from a direct thrust (closed engagement). The fencer, whose blade is being engaged, is unprotected against a direct thrust (open engagement).

Contacts are touching positions during which the characteristic of an engagement (against direct thrusts) is not present with either fencer. The relationship is neutral, even if one fencer has more or less of an advantage. Engagements are contacts that are carried out in the upper as well as the lower line. Engagements are identified by the positions of the fencer performing the engagement (compare to fig. 2.3.-5a).

Contacts are neutral; they are usually named after the position the fencer, who provokes the touch, wants to assume (compare to fig. 2.3.-5b – it is a septime touch if the rear fencer provoked the relationship.

Fig. 2.3.-5: a – Sixte bind: b – Septime touch   a   b

Movements

Body movements

During a fight the fencer uses different forms of locomotion. These are basically steps, leaps, lunges, and flèches; less often lateral, vertical or twisting movements.

The step forward from the fencing position is executed by simultaneously pushing off with the supporting leg and setting the lunging leg forward. For the fencing position the supporting leg is dragged behind. The movement of the lunging leg begins by lifting the toe (back position) or the heel (on guard) respectively, depending on the body's center of gravity.

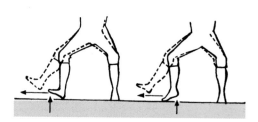

Fig. 2.3.-6:
Forward step (different beginning)

The backward step begins simultaneously with the pushing off of the lunging leg and the setting back of the supporting leg, and ends with the dragging behind of the lunging leg. From a tactical aspect, other variations are also possible; for instance, the step forward can begin with the dragging behind of the supporting leg and end with the setting forward of the lunging leg.

With the forward and backward step, while learning the basic technique, there is approx. one foot of ground gained; in a combative situation the range, speed and rhythm constantly vary. Some variations are cross steps, side steps, leaps, cross leaps and double quick, which can be performed forward and backward.

The lunge is the movement most frequently used by a fencer while approaching for an attack. The push-off is done with the back leg (supporting leg). The resulting force from the horizontally and vertically working strength of the supporting leg remains in effect for the duration of the lunge, as compared to the force progression of the front leg (lunging leg), which consists of a push-off phase from the floor and a momentum phase (fig. 2.3.-7).

The amount of strength applied during push-off determines the speed and range of the lunge. The curve of movement of the body's center of gravity varies in height, depending on the direction and volume of force; the position of the torso varies from leaning forward to standing vertically, even slightly leaning back. Lunges vary in length.

The maximum length of a lunge is contingent on anatomical-physiological qualifications (flexibility).

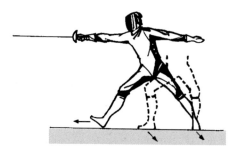

Fig. 2.3.-7: Force action during a lunge

The primary purpose of the non-weapon bearing arm's movement is to maintain balance, and it is performed from the top to the bottom/back.

In its final phase the lunge is fixed by firmly standing on the sole of the supporting leg, or is lengthened by standing on the pad of the foot, or by sliding the leg forward, respectively. The lunging leg breaks the forward movement or lengthens the lunge by swinging back.

The recovery to the fencing position is done by actively bending the supporting leg and at the same time pushing off with the lunging leg, by dragging the supporting leg behind, or by simultaneously bending both legs with a jumping motion.

The flèche is a start-like forward movement from the fencing position, or from a short lunge with a brief loss of balance and a strong push-off with both legs. Flèches are differentiated by the way the body's center of gravity is shifted forward. This occurs by either pushing off with both legs (see fig. 2.3.-8a), by powerfully jerking the torso forward (see fig. 2.3.-8b), or (less frequently) by setting back the lunging leg (see fig. 2.3.-8c).

After pushing off, the supporting leg is placed in front of the lunging leg. Breaking steps restore balance.

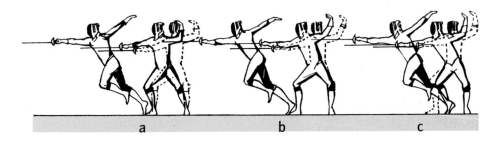

Fig. 2.3.-8: Variations of the flèche

Movements with the weapon

• *Hitting movements*

Hitting movements are performed by extending the arm and guiding the weapon with the hand in such a way, that the point of the weapon (in a thrust) or the edge (with a cut) respectively, touches the opposing target area.

The arm extension occurs either before the body's forward movement, simultaneously with it (main form), or at various times during this movement.

• *Changing the weapon position (position change)*

Changes from one position to another as a result of arm-, hand-, and finger movements are done with arched or circular motions. With the change of positions the lines are changed, the sectors of the target area are covered or uncovered respectively.

The position changes are identified by the direction and form of the weapon-bearing arm's line of movement. Changes in a horizontal or vertical direction are identified as direct (see fig. 2.3.-9a), in a diagonal direction as semi-circular (see fig. 2.2.-9b), and in an elliptical or circular direction as circular changes (see fig. 2.3.-9c).

Fig. 2.3.-9: Changing positions

a – Direct position changes: 6-4, 4-6, 8-7, 7-8, 6-8, 8-6, 7-4; but also 4-3, 3-4 or 7-2.2-7 and 2-1, 1-2, etc.
b – Semi-circular position changes: 6-7, 7-6, 8-4, 4-8; but also 3-7, 7-3, 3-1, 1-3, 6-1, 1-6, 4-2, 2-4, etc.
c – Circular position changes: 6-6, 4-4, 8-8, 7-7; but also 6-3, 7-1, 2-8, etc., if the changes are circular and not done by turning the arm, the hand or the weapon.

- *Sweep movements*

Sweep movements with arm and weapon are used to remove the opposing weapon (most often in a threatening position) from the open line. These movements are performed beat- and thrust-like. Thrusting sweeps end in engagements; thrusting ones most often end in a blade position without contact. They are executed from the line or from a position with prior or simultaneous position change respectively, and are identified by the final position and the type of action against the opposing weapon.

The relationship of the weapons during thrusting sweeps corresponds to that of the engagements. In a beat-like sweep (battuta) the most advantageous effect is achieved by middle against middle. In a beat-like sweep the movement of the weapon happens very quickly. By flexing the muscles of the wrist and fingers the weapon is suddenly fixed in the desired final position. Thus the beat effect (whip-like) is heightened by the blade's residual momentum, and vibration of the blade is prevented.

• *Disengagement movements*

These movements with a weapon are used to evade an engagement, contact, or a sweep movement. Disengagement movements are done by evading the bell guard (disengagement – see fig. 2.3.-10a) or point (cutover – see fig. 2.3.-10b) of the opposing weapon. Depending on the line, the disengagement of the opposing weapon will be high, to the side, or low, and in the final phase always away from the opposing weapon into an open sector.

During disengagements the weapon is moved with wrist movements around the opposing weapon in an arch. Cutovers evade the opposing point of the blade over high, over low, or to the side. They are performed by finger movements and by bending the weapon-bearing arm in the wrist and elbow.

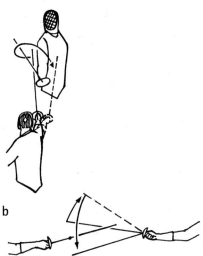

Fig. 2.3.-10:
Disengagements, a – Disengagement of the opposing bell guard (disengagement), b – disengagement of the opposing point of blade (cutover)

2.3.2 Technical requirements of a fencer

The technical demands on a fencer result from the demands of the fight and its particularities.

There are two basic types:

1. Movements (techniques), which are used to score hits and prevent opposing hits. They are elements of select combative actions, (i.e. movements that are necessary for attacks, counter attacks, parries, etc).
   A fencer is successful if he can perform the following movements:

- Very quickly. He will beat the opponent to the punch.
- Very accurately. He hits the opponent, evades the opponent's movements, and is moving efficiently.
- Very reliably, so that the quick and accurate movements will also succeed during interfering actions by the opponent and in case of psychological fatigue and strain.
- Variably, to adapt the movements deviating from the basic form and in speed and rhythm "situation appropriate", to that of the opponent.

2. Movements a fencer has to perform to press the opponent, to investigate him, deke him, distract and outmaneuver him.
   A fencer will do this well when

- He possesses a versatile repertoire of movement elements, which he can combine differently (consciously and unconsciously).
- He can vary the "design" of his movements, i.e. is able to consciously demonstrate (covering lots of ground, challenging, improvising).

Without carrying out a detailed technique analysis, the trainer should always remember with regard to self-monitoring, that technique in fencing never has an independent function and can only be judged by "external" (spatial) movement parameters, but rather is determined by the purpose and the type of combative task. The particularity of the task, including the resulting motivation, impacts the characteristics of the motion sequence to the point of choosing the neurological mechanisms used. A movement that is performed slowly is regulated differently than one that is fast. There are substantial differences between a movement performed according to a movement outline that is also result-oriented ("targeted"), and a sensorimotor movement that is regulated ("guided").

This, for the process of technique acquirement in fencing, extremely important difference between executions that outwardly appear alike, is intended to clarify an example from the industrial psychology (Hacker, 1973, pg. 68) of varying proficiency in "typewriting." To accomplish the "blind 10-finger system" of the perfect secretary is not only a more frequently practiced process of a similar activity compared to a beginner, but also a fundamentally different process. The beginner searches for the letters and gets practice in searching. The practiced secretary doesn't search, she "strikes".

For her the "technique" of striking the keys has become a totally dependent moment in the overall event of writing –like the technique is in relation to fencing for a good fencer. And just like it isn't possible to make the qualitative leap from perfected searching to the "blind 10-finger system" (one has to learn the other technique from the start), it is not possible in fencing to acquire a technique from a more frequently practiced technique based on the principle of "accuracy before speed", that can be applied as a component of the combative action in competition. Specific techniques

must be taught as specific techniques right from the start. Based on the principle of this statement, this example can of course also be applied to fast typing on the computer or playing piano.

That was actually the revolutionizing element of the "Tauberbischofsheim fencing lessons" (cp. Chapter 3.3).

2.3.3 Technical-coordinative performance requisites

Basic prerequisites for acquiring technique are the elements that are hierarchically subordinated to technique in the training "structure diagram" (table 2.1.-2): the organic-muscular/fitness-related stress and performance requisites. These are addressed separately in Chapter 2.5.

The specifically technical-coordinative performance requisites are differentiated as follows:

1. Prerequisites for sensorimotor regulations
The fencers regulate the motion sequences during the phases of technical instruction and perfection on the basis of motion-sensing signals that are extensively reflected as a "sense of movement" and decisively determine the current regulation ability and −readiness.

The effectiveness of the motor learning process most definitively depends on how sophisticated and precisely the information from one's own body and the environment, that is needed for the motion sequence can be apprehended (perceived), and is recognized as a "sense of movement".

2. Prerequisites for intellectual regulation
This means that the fencers also possess enough knowledge, skills, and perceptions about the aspired to target technique, and are able to convert these cognitive (awareness) prerequisites during the execution of movements. This is the sequence of the trainer giving verbal descriptions and instructions for corrections: "Knee out!"; "Elbows to the inside!"; "Extend the arm sooner!"; "Don't swing!", etc. The fencer must comprehend this, interpret it, and convert it into corrected movements.

Regulative functions, meaning tasks that impact the motor learning-, perfecting-, and stabilization process, share both processes: verbally or optically communicated information combined with real movement perception.
Helpful for this are:

3. Movement experience
The more general movement experiences (also motor skills, movement patterns or motor behavior patterns) a fencer has, the faster he will learn and perfect the specific fencing techniques.

Most people have acquired general movement experiences – i.e. walking, running, skipping, jumping, gripping, rolling – during their normal developmental process, at recreation activities, or during PE class at school. All of these movement experiences must be constantly activated and broadened. Exercise and supplemental sports broaden movement experiences, ensure the all-around or many-sided "bio-psychosocial" perfection, and create necessary balance and diversion.

Particular movement experiences in connection with coordinative performance requisites in fencing significantly improve learning aptitude. The confident handling of the overall fencing technique repertoire and the associated movement requirements are thereby connected: confidence to move in the fencing position, or skill in handling a fencing weapon as an "arm extension".

In fig, 2.3.-11 the performance requisites essential to functional-reliable movements, are "lifted" as an extract from the performance structure model as it is shown in fig 2.1.-1.

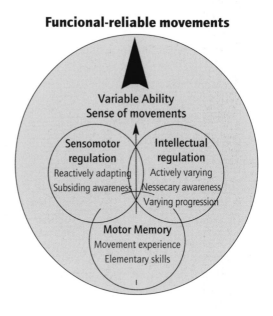

Fig. 2.3.-11: Schematic model of technical-coordinative performance requisites

2.3.4 Fundamentals and teaching methods for technical training

Technical descriptions of standardized basic techniques with suggestions regarding their instruction are dominant in most fencing textbooks. Suggestions for technical instruction are offered from countless concepts and variation possibilities, which were passed down more or less traditionally or derived from comprehensive sports technical concepts.

There is no sensible alternative to the notion that technical instruction must be carried out diligently and continuously. But a tedious mechanical execution under the same condition is not necessary, rather a variable execution dependent on the situations and conditions under which the combative actions take place. The ability to adapt the execution of the basic technical elements to the respective combative situation, and to successfully finish them, even upon extension of the conditions during the execution, is essential to the individual and situation-dependent execution of the movements.

Table 2.3.-2: Overview of the learning process for fencing technique (according to Schnabel)

Aspects of the learning process / Learning phases	First learning phase — Acquirement of "basic technique"	Second learning phase — Acquiring of technique "variability"	Third learning phase — Acquirement of technique "plasticity"
Completing specified motor tasks	Successful execution of movement elements and simple connections on a relatively passive partner.	The technical elements and their connections are variably executed according to the concrete fight situation.	Successful completion of movement task, even under changing conditions during execution.
Execution of movement	Execution is consistent with the most important movement characteristics of basic technical elements. Flow of movement, rhythm of movement, and looseness are not yet sufficient.	The execution corresponds to the conditions of the fight situations. Deficiencies in coordinative progression and effectiveness surface with opposing action during execution, psychological strain, amongst others.	Execution is uniformly good, even under more difficult conditions.
Muscular coordination	Increased tensing of all muscles; clenching of leg and arm muscles.	Clenching of muscles only occurs during more difficult and particularly unexpected situations.	Efficient use of muscles, even under more difficult conditions.
Movement perception	Basic technique is acquired kinesthetically. Details of execution and demonstration remain unclear.	Movement perception is more differentiated. Different pressure ratios and positions are explored.	Movement perception is very precise. Good feel for blade and measure.
Methodological control	Focus and motivation create and maintain learning readiness. Creating of coordinative qualifications, demonstrating, explaining, Acquired practicing (deductive).	Deepening and reinforcing of goal and motives. Differentiated demonstrating and explaining. Controlled practicing in varying situations against different opponents. Differentiated correcting.	Differentiated deepening and reinforcing of goals and motives (continued development of learning readiness). Complex and combat-like training. Further constant monitoring and correcting.

Many recommended teaching paths are geared to the linear ascension method:
- Practice under simplified conditions and with support.
- Practice under standardized, not disordered conditions.
- Practice under varying conditions, whereby the occurring changes are familiar or predictable (anticipatable).
- Practice under varying (situational) conditions, whereby the conditions are unfamiliar or not predictable to the fencer. In table 2.3.-2 on page 59, the learning process is summarized on the basis of several selected aspects.

In another learning model developed for fencing, Müller subdivides into learning phases and learning steps, and in doing so includes newer research results on the motor learning process.

Table 2.3.-3 Learning phases and learning steps of the learning and perfecting process of the fencing technique (Müller, 1995).

1. Learning phase	Acquirement of basic skills (Basic structure)
1. Learning step	Acquirement of motion sequence
2. Learning step	Development of movement skill with overriding attention to movement speed.
3. Learning step	Stabilizing of movement skill with special consideration to progression accuracy and target precision under retention of movement speed.
2. Learning phase	**Acquirement of variability of movment skill**
1. Learning step	Linking of different movement skills to movement chains.
2. Learning step	Stabilizing of movement skill with situation change before movement execution.
3. Learning step	**Expansion of variability.**
3. Learning phase	Acquirement of plasticity of movement skill Ability to "reactively" correct motion sequences during suddenly occurring interferences by the opponent. "Skill adaptation".

Learning phase: Acquirement of basic technical skills

1. Learning step: Comprehending the motion sequence

The fencer learns to execute the motion sequence described and demonstrated by the trainer at a moderate speed and to describe the movement characteristics. Fig. 2.3.-12 shows the graphical and verbal description of the movement characteristics of a lunge as an example.

Movement characteristics

1. *Momentum comes from the forward leg (lunging leg).*
2. *The lower lunging leg is jerked forward and at the same time the supporting leg is forcefully extended.*
3. *The body's center of gravity first moves forward in a horizontal direction, before it moves downward in a curve due to the no longer existing momentum of the lunging leg and the effects of the law of gravitation.*
4. *The torso is always held upright.*
5. *The weapon arm is forcefully extended with the momentum from the lunging leg.*

Fig. 2.3.-12: Movement characteristics of a lunge

2. Learning step: Reinforcing (automating) of the movement for the overriding proficiency of speed and rhythm.

By repeating the movement under standardized conditions, with the goal being a speed-oriented execution, the fencers acquire a movement automatism with a chronologically graduated impulse pattern (time structure or impulse-timing pattern). It is generally thought that the time structure is stabilized after 200-300 repetitions. This applies to qualitatively correct repetitions as well as incorrect ones. The latter is then considered "error training".

3. Learning step: Perfecting progression accuracy and target precision.

By maintaining the speed of movement, a predetermined "technical model" is aimed for. The fencers have a clear goal and monitor or correct respectively, the accuracy of the

progression accuracy and target precision via this predetermined "norm". But since this norm is not determined on an exclusively biomechanical basis, the trainer's corrections must also apply to cognitive and sensorimotor functions. Only then emerges the "muscle sense awareness" necessary for the continued development, that provides the precondition to self-monitoring and self-correction (additional information thereto in Chapter 4, "Youth training").

2. Learning phase: Acquirement of variability

1. Learning step: Combining (linking) various technical elements into movement sequences
There rarely are complications when the individual technical elements "only" have to be connected to each other, i.e. be executed consecutively. In doing so the respective time structures remain largely unaffected (for instance, step forward and a subsequent step backward). When elements whose time structures also merge are linked, new impulse-timing structures must be established. This applies, for instance, when linking a forward step-lunge, because here the individual muscle impulses overlap.

2. Learning step: Conscious variation of movement execution
On the one hand, this is about temporal and rhythmic variations of movements and combinations of movements, to actively adapt them to the opponent's movements. The time structures are "stretched" or "compressed".

On the other hand, the fencer must be enabled to execute technical elements and combinations temporally-spatially according to the requirements (adapted), if the situational change occurs prior to movement execution.

3. Learning step: Learning variations on the basic technique
During this stage of technical perfection, variations of the technical models in the sense of "independent techniques" are developed into skills. Here "good technique" becomes the "situation-appropriate and singly best execution". It is understood that this happens only after the basic techniques have been mastered, or the fencers would prematurely receive one-sided training.

3. Learning phase: Acquirement of the ability to "vividly" modify technical elements and combinations
The goal is the fencers' ability to reactively (as orientation-based reactions) adapt or correct respectively, their motion sequences during unfamiliar and suddenly occurring interfering actions by the opponent.

This "implementation quality" also referred to as "vividness of technique" or "skill adaptation", is essential during, for instance, parry reflexes or "feints on sight". This is accomplished during the training process when automated movement patterns the fencer cannot anticipate, are suddenly required.

Surely there are various other models and variations for successfully teaching fencing technique. But it is just as likely that, particularly in fencing training, methodical errors will "creep in".

In view of this, several **universally valid details** must be noted:

1. All coordinative-technical exercises are "norm controlled" and have a definite specification with regard to movement execution and objective. They enable cognitively regulated actions (How and why do I want to accomplish what?), a sense of right and wrong with regard to the effort (What do I need to do for the right execution?), and the development of muscle sense awareness (Does my sense of movement coincide with the actual execution?)

    Mental images of the target technique have an overriding goal oriented function. Mental images as a basis for execution orientation that form through constant feedback regarding one's own motion sequences possess an overriding regulative function.

2. Movement visualization or sense of movement (movement sensation) respectively, and imagining the movement significantly contribute to the qualitative improvement of technical training and must be developed systematically. Suitable methods and impact procedures are: psycho-muscular and ideo-motor training and their substantiation, descriptions of the sense of movement and sense of execution, observation of actual technical sequences, finding the causes of failed executions, execution with verbal monitoring, exchange of experiences amongst the fencers, and more (also see Chapter 2.2 thereto).

3. Every trainer certainly has his way, his methods and his experiences. Nonetheless, there isn't just that one preferred option at any one time. Often the "linearly ascending learning path" is supplemented by the parallel instruction of learning, reinforcing and stabilizing, with constant implementation under varying conditions (no fencing trainer would consider waiting to let a fencer compete until after he has perfect command of the techniques).

    There is also the opposite way: from diversity and variation always back to specification and detail.
    A conscious changing of methods is advantageous in preventing a "methodical monoculture", which would diminish the learning effect. Wherever possible, the fencers should also train with different trainers.

4. Specific preparation, familiarization and review are necessary before starting technical training (this really applies to any kind of training): preload, in particular activation and motivation (more information hereto in Chapter 5).

The repetitions for an exercise variation and the amount of break time in between the exercises and sequences cannot be generally specified. Every trainer has know-how in this area based on experience.

An exercise, a particular sequence, etc, should be repeated until it is successful, and as long as the fencer still has the desire to improve it or to repeat the exercise equally well. For this the trainer has to inspire attentiveness and motivation in the fencer. Getting joy out of practicing and improving is a pledge to success.

5. In technical training the didactic principle "from the familiar to the unfamiliar" should be adhered to. General as well as specific (already acquired) movement experiences can be used for the "familiar". This speaks in favor of starting out with tasks that are similar, and to begin with the instructions and corrections only after the initial trial attempts. Structure-determining technical elements that were developed correctly from the start and are available as basic technical patterns, allow the fencer to utilize available motor and sensor resources while learning new movements, and effectuate the learning process.

At the same time, the elements and combinations that have been trained the most should be "finished", instead of working predominantly on weaknesses. This creates clear action components for combative qualification and enables the fencer to recognize his own weaknesses and correct them.

2.3.5 Criteria and methods for technique analysis

Every trainer's most important control procedure for technique analysis is movement observation. Primarily qualitative criteria are drawn on by means of fixed characteristics of the intended manner of execution (target technique), to evaluate the level of training.

Monitored and evaluated are:

• *Precision of movement*
Precision of movement expresses accuracy and is measured by the degree of consistency between the executed and the given movement. Regardless of whether the analysis deals with a result oriented (movement task fulfilled or not, meaning hit the target, parried or accomplished) or a process-oriented movement (specified flow parameters and characteristics adhered to or not, meaning no swinging, limited space, shortest way) respectively, target value and actual value are compared, variations are determined, the problem resolution is evaluated against the anticipated results, causes for errors are determined, and corrections are made.

Technique model – head cut

Movement characteristics

1. Point is guided directly to target area via arm extension at elbow joint.
2. At the same time the hand is raised to shoulder level (avoid movement to inside).
3. Final beat with fingers and wrist, followed by the blade slightly bouncing off the target area.
4. Hit is made with the forward part of the edge (4-6 inches).

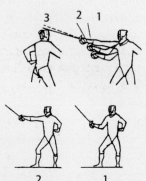

Error	**Suggestions for corrections**

F1 Cut begins with swinging motion (point is guided back).

K1 Improved movement coordinationa and perception are needed.

Execute initially slow, then gradually faster arm movement without swinging motions.

F2 Final beat is not initiated by fingers and wrist. Blade does not bounce off mask.

K2 Grip is held too tightly and too rigid in the wrist.

Several final beats with extended arm with emphasis on loose grip.

F3 Arm and hand are raised too much during arm extension; the forearm as a target area is uncovered too much.

K3 Causes are incorrect movement percep-tion or insufficient coordination.

Repeat explanation and demonstration. As a practice aid only the hand is guided at first; for monitoring a saber, which cannot be touched, is then held above the arm at eye level.

F4 Hit does not land with the edge but rather with the blade.

F4 incorrect   F4 correct

K4 Initially execute movement slowly and pay attention to rotation of edge in direction of opposing target area. Gradually increase speed.

F5 During the arm extension the hand is guided to the inside; the outside cover of the arm is suspended.

F5 correct   F5 incorrect

K5 Saber is held too lineally, causing the fencer to guide his fist to the inside to be able to make a hit.

Explanation and execution of counter attack to the arm outside for monitoring purposes ("safety reflex").

Figure 2.3.-13:
Objectives, possible executions and errors and suggestions for corrections of a head cut in saber fencing

Accuracy in specifying the goal significantly impacts the quality of the analysis. The more accurate and sophisticated the fencer's skill level is, the more precise and sophisticated the specification and analysis must be. At the more advanced training levels this can scarcely be accomplished with just observation. Here the trainer must resort to video recordings and their detailed evaluation and, if necessary, biomechanical measuring methods. The latter are indispensable to the objective monitoring of the speed of movement. Fig. 2.3.-13 on page 65, exemplifies goal specification, execution or error possibilities respectively, and suggestions for corrections, with a cut to the head in saber fencing.

- *Constancy of movement*

Here the training level with regard to technique and its steadiness is monitored by the degree of consistency of repeatedly executed motion sequences.

The goal of technique training is to ensure that with each repetition the learned technique is of equal quality. Movements that are executed with lots of consistency and are largely automated (done unconsciously) as motor elements of the combative action are called motor skills.

- *Rhythm of movement*

The rhythm of movement reflects primarily the temporal-dynamic parameters of the technique: time structure, dynamic structure of acceleration and deceleration or the duration and intensity of the force impulses.

External monitoring criteria for the rhythm of movement is the timing. That is why externally the rhythm of an extraneous movement is more likely to be heard than seen.

Systematic observation of competitions and detailed technical evaluation ultimately provide the critical clues as to the fencers' actual technical training level. In the long run the success criteria of the competition itself – scoring hits or missing the target, or parrying or not parrying long enough respectively –, reveal whether a fencer is technically good or not.

Occasionally trainers say that during training their fencers are in perfect command of the technique, but during competition they miss the target or forget everything they learned. Then it should be determined if in fact the technique required in competitions – fast and accurate, steady and variable – has been practiced, or if the technique was perfected like that of a gymnast's or a diver's. And that just does not work in fencing (hereto also Chapter 2.2). In addition every trainer should prepare selective competition analyses and also take into consideration the technique-based errors.

On the one hand, since monitoring possibilities available to trainers during the training process are mostly for the external movement characteristics (precision of movement) and,

on the other hand, the decisive learning impulses are imparted on the fencer by the complete internal given value of the target technique (internal images), important new ground could be broken in technical training with the fencers' ability to self monitor and self evaluate. More on that in Chapter 4, "Youth training".

2.4   Fundamentals of fencing strategy and tactics

2.4.1 Characteristics of strategy and tactics

The entirety of behavior, actions and operations of fencers and teams, that are aimed at the total use of personal performance qualifications in the sense of the best possible competition results, under consideration of the rules of competition, partner and opponent conduct, as well as the external conditions, are referred to as tactics, or differentiated as strategy and tactics.

Strategy is the fencer's plan for his actions and his behavior, with which he preplans and determines actions with regard to his conduct while competing, and individual combative actions, under consideration of the rules of competition, personal strengths and weaknesses, the strengths, weaknesses, and possible behavior patterns of the opponent or opponents, and the conditions anticipated at the competition. In connection with a strategy, the individual combative action is referred to as a strategic element (compare to "introduction", fig. 0.-1).

A competitor uses strategies by anticipating future events during competition, meaning he mentally goes through his behavior alternatives and chooses the option most advantageous to him. Strategies are also basis for short- and medium-term preparation concepts and long-term training plans.
The opposite of a behavior pattern that uses strategies would be behavior where a fencer makes decisions regarding the continuation of the competition as the case arises. In doing so he has to let himself be guided by accumulated memories from many different situations, or he has to choose, under the pressure of time, from an abundance of possible variants.

While the strategy takes into account – but does not influence – the opponent(s)'s possible decisions during behavior planning, the tactic applies to the implementation of prepared actions for the execution of the strategy. **Tactic** involves everything that in practical language is often referred to as "preparation". It orientates to the judgment process during situations as prerequisite to the determining and implementing of expedient methods that may deke or influence the opponent, and it contains the necessary knowledge and skill to do so. The goal of a tactic is to initially forgo the actual result yielding action, in order to, with additional actions,

- obtain information needed for an accurate evaluation of the combative situation (observation, exploration, investigation).

- give the opponent little or false information respectively, (dekeing, concealing) and

- create favorable conditions for the execution of the result-yielding action (maneuvering, feinting, provoking).

Tactics are necessary when it is difficult to reach the goal, and one has to decide to take one or more intermediate step(s) to first provide the means for reaching the overall goal.

2.4.2 Strategic tactical demands on a fencer

Specific to fencing is that in each case two fencers with opposite interests interact. Each wants to hit the other with his fencing weapon more often than he himself is getting hit.

Within the scope of the stipulations specified in the rules (conventions), both fencers can freely choose between different possibilities in terms of actions and behavior. The fencer who can, with approximately equal athletic and technical qualifications, more accurately and faster recognize the opponent's intended actions and behaviors, makes the right decisions and tries to outsmart the opponent, will be victorious.

With regard to a fight action (an attack or a parry), the fencer has to
- recognize the emerging combative situation and comprehend its significance with regard to his own actions, meaning, to analyze and interpret the action-related conditions and the opponent's actions.

- think about what possibilities there are for opposing actions, meaning, mentally creating ways and action programs, and anticipatorily deliberating the likelihood of their success.

- choose the most advantageous action alternative to act situation-appropriately.

Next to a general fight readiness and the confidence to win, fencing makes the following strategic-tactical demands on the fencer:
- Constant attention to the changing between concentration and spreading, and conscious perception of all details in the opponent's behavior via passive observation or active exploration.

- Accurate anticipation and situation comprehension.

- Active maneuvering to create an advantageous contest situation.

- Mental comparison to previous situations.

- Quick, situation appropriate decisions under consideration of existing competition experiences, and

- Veiling of one's own intentions to have the mental advantage over the opponent.

The fencers' strengths and weaknesses in managing these demands shape each fencer's respective fighting style. The compensation possibilities (compare table 2.1.-1) have led to three principal decision making possibilities in fencing.

Decision-making type 1	Decision-making type 2	Decision-making types 3
Acts/decides with "firm" intent	Acts/decides according to "thought pattern"	Acts/decides according to the "situation"
Waits for opportunity: "if-then"	Mental concept: "either-or"	Without previous thought "let's see what happens"
Advantage: anticipates situation	Advantage: acts variably	Advantage: situation appropriate
Disadvantage: hardly variable	Disadvantage: delayed action	Disadvantage: can be caught by surprise

Fig. 2.4.-1: Decision making types in fencing (according to diagrams by Rodionov, 1979)

With **decision-making type 1**, the fencers act according to a previously determined strategy and wait for an opportune situation.

The advantage to such a course of action is that the situation can be anticipated and the decision is made very quickly. For instance, the fencers execute their hits with a predetermined attack, do not react to feigned actions or feints, or tend towards a particular type of parry-riposte or a counter-attack respectively.

The disadvantage is without a doubt the limited variability and susceptibility with regard to feints and second intention.

With **decision-making type 2** the decisions are heavily prepared through imagined operations. The fencers mostly have two or three different action alternatives "in their heads" and choose according to the current situation.

The advantage is that the fencers are more variable and are harder to "figure out". During the contest they solve their tasks with an "either-or" approach. They apply alternatives from various action groups (basic strategic elements), for instance attack or defense. But one can also choose alternatives from within a group, for instance a direct or a feint attack, quarte or sixte parry.

The disadvantage with this decision-making type is the time delay in decision-making.

With **decision-making type 3** the fencers forgo preliminary strategic consideration and make decisions intuitively "from the gut" depending on the current situation, based on the motto "let's see what happens".

The advantage is that the fencers are able to act situation-appropriate at any time, providing they are capable, and possess a large action repertoire and many experiences.

The disadvantage is that decisions have to be made on a case-by-case basis and the contest progresses without a theoretical concept. And when it isn't going well, they are helpless. They are lacking a strategy (back-up strategy) for such cases.

The characteristic behavior during athletic contests typical in fencing (duel behavior) is explained with the following requirement dimensions:

Situation-appropriateness: Based on specific cognitive-, thought-, and decision-making processes, the fencer implements an extreme degree of consistency between the demands of the contest situation and his subjective performance options.

Being goal oriented: Based on high motivation, achievement-oriented attitude regarding the contest, a highly developed level of sport-specific, volitional contest-related qualities, and an outstanding psycho-physiological state, the fencer can implicitly implement a high-quality victory oriented strategy, even under extremely difficult fight conditions.

Originality: Based on the fencer's personal character, his individuality and personal style respectively, are expressed.

Steadiness: Even in difficult situations or situations of extreme strain can the fencer maintain the consciously controlled actions necessary for reaching the goal (also compare to Kirchgässner & Barth, 1982).

2.4.3 Prerequisites for strategic-tactical performance

The fencer's handling of the strategic-tactical demands requires a series of primarily psychological processes, which can be clearly classified as data processing steps.

Fig. 2.4.-2 offers a simplified diagram of the in reality always interactively proceeding processes.

With the cognition-linked processes (information intake) the fencer creates a subjective "map" of the concrete situational requirements and gives the absorbed information a personal meaning for his actions.

A distance to the opponent (measure) that is not objectively definable in centimeters, subject to the extent of one's own movement options, e.g. step or step forward lunge, is subjectively referred to as middle or wide measure.

If the distance becomes "dangerous" to one's own defensive safety, it receives the subjective meaning: "critical measure – open quickly!"

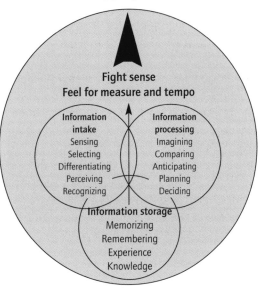

Situation appropriate behavior

Fight sense
Feel for measure and tempo

Information intake
Sensing
Selecting
Differentiating
Perceiving
Recognizing

Information processing
Imagining
Comparing
Anticipating
Planning
Deciding

Information storage
Memorizing
Remembering
Experience
Knowledge

Figure 2.4.-2:
Schematic model of strategic-tactical performance requisites

It is similar with the perception of the positions of the blade and movements.

The *intellectual processes* (mentally processing and saving the information) have the function of analyzing the respective situation, to relate it to one's own action possibilities, to consider the opponent's intentions, to find solutions or make decisions respectively (primarily linked to short-term memory), and to acquire the knowledge required for that purpose and to memorize the results of one's own actions as well as the opponent's (long-term memory).

All these processes possess a different degree of consciousness and range from "fully conscious" (watching an opponent, establishing an action plan) to "unconscious" (feel for measure and tempo, readiness to act).

The quality of the strategic-tactical actions depends on the speed, the accuracy, purposefulness, variability and steadiness of these processes. Since these processes dominantly define the competitive fencing style, scientific research is being done to determine the specific aptitude for individual fight behavior via details about individual strengths and weaknesses (compare table 2.4.-1 and fig. 2.4.-1). Such research results are compiled in table 2.4.-1.

Table 2.4.-1: Relationships between preferred action motive, fighting style, and personality traits (according to research by Bitechtina, Tischler & Daskevitch, 1976, with top Russian saber fencers (r = correlation coefficient)

Action motiv	Absolute success	Sure success	Avoiding failure
Personality traits	Self-controlle (r = 0,875)	Psychological stability (r = 0,870)	Fear of failure (r = 0,826)
	Emotional stability (r = 0,913)	Initiative (r = 0,860)	Willingness to take risks (r = 0,923)
	Independence (r = 0,976)	Good mood (r = 0,870)	Aspiration level (r = 0,815)
	Aspiration level (r = 0,905)	Dependability (r = 0,715)	Justification (r = 0,892)
	Originality (r = 0,854)	Self-confidence (r = 0,868)	Spontaneity (r = 0,826)
Preferred behavior	Initiative Short fights	Controlled Complicated	Temporizing Passive
	Attack	**Defense Riposte**	**Counter-attacke**

2.4.4 Strategic-tactical training

Strategic-tactical training is geared towards the development of abilities and skills for situation-appropriate, goal-oriented, and purposeful action and behavior.

The contest-related requirements are made comprehensible, the psychological qualifications for the intake, processing and saving of information are developed (Chapter 2.2), and the fencers are prepared for actively, psycho-cognitively coping with varying demand situations.

During the strategic-tactical training the fencers are enabled to,

• comprehend action and information intake demands more quickly and accurately.

• find optimal solution strategies.

• make situation-appropriate action-related decisions.

The essential training tasks are:

1. The acquiring, systematization, and strengthening of strategic-tactical proficiency with regard to possible and situation-appropriate action and behavior alternatives, including knowing the contest regulations.
2. The ability to quickly and accurately comprehend demand situations.
3. The ability to mentally examine various solution variants, and the refinement of the strategic-tactical nimbleness of mind with regard to action-based decision-making and tactical action preparation.
4. The development of the specific forms of strategic-tactical action and behavior like, for instance, probability-related behavior, measure-related behavior, and situation-related anticipation.
5. The development of the operative or situation-related memory respectively.

During training one must always bear in mind the indivisibility of knowledge transfer and practical application, or thinking and experiencing respectively (hereto also Chapter 3). Regulative function also derives the knowledge for the fencer via the link with feedback from one's activity. The knowledge transfer and acquisition should be linked to the applied sports activity.

From a strategic aspect the training mainly focuses on
- the comprehension of situations that are relevant to the action,
- mentally dealing with solution variants,
- developing a specific nimbleness of mind (fencers think in terms of fencing actions),
- expanding the volume of the "situational memory" and
- developing the ability to anticipate situations and probability-related behavior.

A few suggestions for the planning of strategies are primarily intended to help those trainers and fencers who so far have not worked much with strategies. In each case the starting point is, that one must be able to realistically evaluate one's abilities, skills, and the current level of preparation, and that one possesses a minimum of information regarding the opponent's possible strategies. For this one must analyze one's recordings from past competitions, observations of the opponent against other fencers, as well as information from teammates or the trainer respectively.

Every strategy must be victory-oriented. *At the same time inexperienced fencer in particular should take note of the following recommendations:*
- In a contest with a more powerful opponent one should not engage in his repertoire, but rather use a rarely used strategy that is unfamiliar to him. The risk can be equally big.
- A less powerful opponent can be defeated at a low risk and under little strain via concentrated fighting. Incautiousness can balance the chances for victory.

- Fencers with powerful attacks must be defeated with well-prepared attacks. Good defenders must be provoked into attacking.
- Fencers who attack in a frenzy or with feints can be successfully dealt with through counter attacks. Fencers who prefer counter attacks are fought with direct attacks and surprise sweeps.
- Fencers who defend themselves with multiple parries should be countered with feints or attacks with second intention.
- Physically small fencers competing against bigger athletes should favor sweeps or sweep counter attacks.

The baseline for the contest should be determined, and the application of strategic elements and their consequences should be preplanned under consideration of such recommendations.

The question of repeating successful elements is answered differently. On the one hand the opponent has been warned by the hit he received, but on the other hand, an advantage can become apparent with a successful execution, particularly with that element.

Strategic planning is important for the preparation of competition fights and contests. On the one hand it facilitates active participation in the training process, but on the other hand it can also impede successful fighting if there is too much strategic thinking during the fights. Because the cause for slow or missing reactions in specific, even unambiguous and favorable, situations can not only be a "snoozing" issue but often is a "thinking" issue. That is why the trainer's acclamations and interjections during fights are not always useful.

Tactical training is oriented to the ability
- to explore (identifying the opponent's intentions and options).
- to defilade (veiling one's intentions).
- to implement specific maneuvers (blade and measure maneuvers to create favorable conditions for one's actions).

Tactical aids are any consciously executed actions and assumed positions that serve the exploration, dekeing and maneuvering of the opponent, regardless of which part of the body they are performed with and whether or not the weapon is moved in doing so. Their scope ranges from the simplest technical element to basic strategic elements to combinations.

Investigating, dekeing and maneuvering the opponent – in essence attempting to identify his intentions – , bluffing with regard to one's intentions, and to maneuver in such a way that will bring about favorable conditions for one's actions, is essential to the tactical contest. The fencer's ability to explore, deke and maneuver demonstrates his tactical maturity.

We differentiate between the following groups of tactical actions (preparatory actions):

- *Feigned actions:* Attack and defensive actions whose purpose it is to explore (investigate) the opponent's intentions and to divert from one's own intentions (disguise).
- *Maneuvers:* Actions that create favorable situations for the successful implementation of strategic elements.
- *Feints:* Attack actions that are intended to create openings and confuse the defense.

There is general agreement that there are no fixed norms for the execution of this or that bluffing or investigating action.

The tactical actions work very differently and change depending on the element's repetition during the fight. Thus the same element can solve various tactical tasks, and can produce totally different reactions from the same fencer in a different situation, or from another fencer in a similar situation. That is why tactical tasks instead of tactical actions "as such", are described and practiced.

Exploring the opponent

The goal of the exploration is to recognize the opponent's fight behavior, technical potentialities, and psychological-ethical and fitness-related condition. Among other things, the following questions must be answered for this purpose:

- How does the opponent react to sudden and unexpected attacks?
- How does the opponent react to individual elements of the attack (feint, beat, et.al)?
- Which attack methods does the opponent prefer and how does he implement them?
- How do the symptoms of an opponent's unfocused and careless condition become apparent?
- How quick is the opponent?

Feigned attacks (beginning of the attack only, individual elements or the complete attacks with minimal forward movement) that are executed suddenly and with a varying rhythm, serve the investigation of the opponent's defense.

The feigned defense serves to explore possible attack by the opponent. In doing so this or that defensive action is suggested in a seemingly jumpy manner, to discover how the opponent will behave.

The overall condition can be identified by all of the opponent's reactions, his gestures and movements. Specific subtasks during the fight also require the appropriate investigative methods. In doing so, the tasks continue to become more difficult, because the opponent is consciously working against the exploration. If the opponent reacts (flinches) to a feigned attack, the following questions arise:

- Was that intentional or not?
- Does the opponent know what he did?
- What was that the start of, a parry or a counter-attack?

To recognize this requires considerable competitive experience as well as strategic-tactical and psychological knowledge.

Camouflaging
The purpose of camouflaging is to give the opponent false perceptions regarding one's strategic-tactical intentions, technical options, and psychological-physiological requirements. An attack one wants to execute suddenly and as a surprise to the opponent is camouflaged via, among other things, slow, seemingly carefree movements and through suggested defensive actions, which decrease the opponent's alertness and prudence.
A counter-attack can be camouflaged by reacting to opposing attacks with retreating and parries, thus disguising the true intent.
Gestures that suggest resignation and fatigue camouflage fight readiness.
Deliberately slow and lethargically executed feigned actions disguise fitness-related readiness.
The principal task of camouflaging is to consciously work against the opponent's exploration. Camouflaging is "pretend lying on the strip".

Preparing the attack
A well-prepared attack is the surest way to making a hit because the attacker has the initiative and can start the attack at the moment he is most ready. However, that does not mean that one should continuously attack, but that it should happen at the right moment with a situation-appropriate attack. The attacker creates the most favorable situation for an attack for himself through his own tactical actions (maneuvers). Here one differentiates between general and concrete preparation for an attack.

The general attack preparation creates favorable conditions for various attacks. The opponent's initiative is repressed, his defensive readiness is restricted, and the start of an attack is camouflaged. Measure maneuvers make it more difficult for the opponent to correctly estimate the measure. By repeatedly playing the distance game (lengthening and shortening the measure), one maneuvers the opponent into a favorable measure for one's attack and camouflages the start of the attack.

Unlike the classic break down of near-, middle-, and wide measure, the descriptions of which are subject to footwork, one refers of "critical measure" with regard to strategy and tactics. This means "dangerous measure" when one is being attacked, and "favorable measure" when one intends to attack. The critical measure varies depending on the individual and the situation, and is subject to the speed, reactions, and physical size of the fencers, as well as the type of weapon.

Cornering the opponent at the end of the strip is one particular form of the measure maneuver. By actively maneuvering with steps forward, sliding the lunging leg forward, bending the torso forward, short lunges, etc., the opponents who fight their fights with overly wide measures are passive or save themselves during an attack by retreating, are cornered at the line at the rear limit of the strip. Some fencers also allow themselves to be pushed back and use that to break the opponent's concentration and tempt him into becoming careless. But doing so with good opponents is very risky.

Maneuvers with the weapon (fencing phrase) disrupt the opponent's systematic fight composition, restrict his initiatives and unnerve him. Particular rhythmic and non-rhythmic blade movements (contact, engagements, beats, changes, feints, etc.) keep the opponent occupied and force specific movements on him. The direction and the moment of one's attack are thus camouflaged. In a fight measure maneuvers are usually linked with weapon maneuvers. Many fencers adopt their own distinctive phrases and measure play.

The attack preparation is specific when the attack is intended to begin at a previously planned moment or a very specific attack is being prepared. This highest level of attack preparation cannot be described in detail here. But it must be pointed out that for this investigating, disguising and maneuvering must be mastered so perfectly, that the opposing activity and non-activity can be accurately judged and affected.

Preparing the defense

Actions for the preparation of defense have already been touched on in connection with exploring and camouflaging. Therefore we will limit ourselves to preparing the defense against specific attacks we have provoked the opponent into making.

Provocation is meant to control the opponent's initiatives and direct his actions, without giving the impression that his initiative is being inhibited. He must seemingly be able to outsmart us. For this purpose certain maneuvers are executed to tempt him into specific attacks. The intended behavior, whether parry-riposte or counter attack, is camouflaged. Basic forms of provocations are those positions referred to in old fencing books as "invites". A sixte-invite is intended to provoke the opponent into an attack high/inside or low.

The provocation or challenge is direct if the opponent is provoked into an attack as a direct result of the immediate fight situation that is created by the challenger.

Example: Fencer A moves as though he intends to execute a quarte engagement attack; fencer B takes the bait and launches a displacement-counter attack. A is prepared for the counter attack and defends himself with a sixte parry-riposte or a circular quarte parry-riposte.

A provocation or challenge is indirect if the opponent was challenged to an attack that logically results from recognizing the challenge.

Example: Fencer A maneuvers as though he intends to execute a quarte engagement attack, but does it in a way that B recognizes his intention. He is thereby directly provoked into a disengagement thrust-feint-disengagement thrust attack. A is prepared and responds with a quarte parry-riposte or a stop hit.

The advantages of a prepared attack where the fencer knows ahead of time exactly which defensive actions to choose, compared to the unprepared one where the opponent can catch him of guard, hereby become apparent. But not every defense can be prepared, and therefore every fencer needs to have a defense system with which he can defend himself, based on his reflexes, during surprise attacks.

Particularly beginners should keep the following tactical suggestions in mind:

- During every training or competition fight, after receiving or making a hit, the actions should be analyzed to determine how and why the hit occurred.

- An intention that was revealed through an unintentional gesture should be replaced with another or, via a renewal, should be consciously used as a disguise.

- Versatility in a fight makes it possible to catch any opponent off guard. It does not show primarily in a multitude of different fighting actions, but rather in the breadth of their variations. Later on both become significant.

- In a fight with an unknown opponent it must quickly be determined through exploration how the opponent attacks and how he defends himself. Always be at the ready for defense!

- When fighting near the line at the rear limit of the strip one should never allow the opponent to come near, and with respect to the direction, must attack him with unexpected actions to the weapon. Advanced fencers also use the second intention.

- Against fencers who successfully use sweep attacks, one's weapon must be in constant motion or held very low.

- Fencers who unsettle the fight with a fast tempo must be fought with calm simple actions. Do not respond to the opponent's actions.

- Opponents who don't perform well in a near measure should be tempted into close quarters with measure maneuvers.

- Counter attacks should only be carried out after several deliberate retreats. Retreats tempt the opponent into starting his attacks unfocused and stereotypical, during the first phase.

- The attack preparations of aggressively attacking fencers should be disrupted. This is done with, among other things, feigned attacks, feigned counter attacks, and active playing with the measure that is confusing with regard to direction and rhythm.

Every fencer should memorize the following guideline and try to put into practice the suggestions contained therein:

To be active, abrupt, decisive, and to act quickly, to disable the opponent's initiative, create false perceptions for the opponent regarding one's options and intentions, to force unfavorable situations on him and force him to do that which he is least good at, and to utilize for oneself that which works best.

A specific training component of strategic-tactical training is **situational training**.
Modern illustration models refer to the two basic phenomenon, perception function and recognition. A precondition with regard to perceiving every situation composed of partial signals is the synchrony of the individual signals belonging together, which become linked if they regularly occur simultaneously. In doing so, a "signal perception complex" picked up in a particular moment spans all of the sensory organs involved.
The segregated training of the senses is of little practical use.

The possibility of perceiving situational changes within a fraction of a second – a very important skill for a fencer – rests on the assumption that an information selection takes place inside the brain, and that changes to only some components of these complexes are always sufficient for identification. With many similar renewals these reduced signal combinations in their characteristic structure are fixed in such a way, that the fencer quickly and accurately recognizes them when they recur. But since every situation in its entirety is subject to a certain nonrepeatability, a kind of "frequency distribution with compression at mean values" occurs in terms of situation categories. That is why the fighting actions are also grouped into strategic (action-) elements and categories.

Now this should not scare the fencing instructor, because the human brain independently "organizes" and "saves" the different observation objects with regard to the respective goal according to common and separate characteristics, provided that the patterns (situations) are repeated often enough.

Since nearly every trainer has learned to drive, a general comparison between fencing and driving for the purpose of describing the methodic steps, presents itself.
- First skills are acquired. The driver familiarizes himself with the rules of the road, learns the road signs, their meaning and the respective appropriate behavior. The fencer does the same things, but he does them in fencing.
- Next a goal is set. Whether he needs to turn left, go straight or to the right respectively, in the situation of an intersection with signals, is perception determining for the driver. It is similar for the fencer. The situation for an attack is different than that of a defensive situation or a counter attack. So the fencer has to know what he wants to do or what he should do. And it is always better when he wants to! Attitudes, interests, motives, and needs are important regulators that can influence perception positively as well as negatively.

- Now the driver finds out which situation characteristics (traffic lanes, directional signs, traffic signals, motorists and cyclists) are significant in what way. And the fencers learn the important relationship between information (measure, position, direction of movement, blade position, etc.) and situation.

- And then it's practice, practice, practice, and that as much as possible in real situations. The driver has to drive the car and the fencer has to fence, preferably like or in a real fight. Putting your fencing book under your pillow at night will not help you become a world champion.

If in the beginning the situation characteristics are still consciously perceived and monitored, associations (connections) between the characteristics belonging together for the respective situations increasingly develop. Perceiving many situations and their evaluation "at a glance" becomes a matter of course.

These perceptions are also the basis for the so-called "feelings"; for the fencer they are the "measure feel", the "blade feel", the "tempo feel", and particularly the complex "fighting sense". Situations are perceived or recognized more quickly. Deviations from the saved pattern are signaled immediately.

In summary it can be said:
The speed of correct decisions is approximately equally influenced by perception and thinking. Both processes have a complex nature, are reciprocally linked, and with proper practice can already be improved in early childhood.
Important factors are:
- Strategic-tactical skills regarding possible and situation-appropriate actions and behavior alternatives.

- The ability to quickly and accurately perceive a situation.

- Mentally dealing with different solution alternatives and nimbleness of mind with regard to action- and behavior-based decisions.

- Specific forms of strategic-tactical behavior, particularly measure-related behavior, probability related behavior, and functional memory.

- Experiences from fights with many different fencers.

- A positive attitude regarding strategic-tactical training tasks, and "mental freshness".

Possible excessive intellectual demand from the strategic-tactical training sometimes feared in young fencers, only occurs if the fencers are not motivated for the task or the

demands are placed in such a way that they cannot be solved yet. That is why, with all the necessity of methodical steps for the development and training of strategy and tactics, it is important to see to it that conduct and behavior that is to be set, including the emotional-volitional particularities characteristic to fencing, must occur under competition-appropriate conditions.

The specific methods thereto are compiled in table 2.4.-2.

Table 2.4.-2: Methods for strategic-tactical training

Basic methodic form	Didactic-methodological tips for strategic-tactical training
First communication	Explain significance of action/behavior. List and explain situational conditions. Demonstrate as fight-like as possible.
Perfecting	Repeat, monitor, and evaluate/motivate under standardized and varied conditions. Complicate conditions (e.g. information reduction).
Implementing	Repeat against different opponents. Step-by-step expansion of repertoire. Constant evaluation of training results.
Instructing	Tasks for all possible decision-making types. Implementation of given strategic schemes. Investigation/maneuvering of opponents; Camouflaging.
Improvising	Finding situation-appropriate actions by oneself. Defined, differentiated evaluation of solutions.
Imitating	"Role play" regarding typical/anticipated behavior of main or "feared opponents" respectively.
Handicap	Increased demand through restricted room for maneuver, interference, and additional strain.
Competition	Performance monitoring, tests, reviews, Fights focusing on training, development, and review.
Behavior programs	Specification of verbal orientation focal points. Formulaic forming of intent and self-control.
Extreme training	Extreme demands under consideration of individual performance requisites.

But ultimately only participating in many competitions with opponents at the same or higher level leads to promising fight behavior.

Fencing makes fencers, competitions makes competitors.

The results from strategic-tactical actions and behavior are processed as experiences, and gain individual significance.

2.4.5 Criteria and methods for the monitoring of strategic-tactical performance requirements and performances

The monitoring of psychological performance requisites essential to strategy and tactics is primarily done through tests.

Tasks are given which require the regulation prerequisites that are to be measured for their solution. The activating stimulus or the signal, as well as the answer, can be general or closely approaching fencing technique.

The following are used in fencing:

(1) **Reaction tests**, during which the fencers have to react as quickly as possible to optical, acoustic or kinesthetic-tactile signals.

- An object – gymnast's baton, fencing glove, coin – is dropped. It must be stopped by hand or with the weapon before it touches the floor (fig. 2.4.-3).

Fig. 2.4.-3:
Testing reaction with a gymnast's baton

- A timer is activated (a contact or photo sensor with the hand) with a signal-light, sound, touch, or by withdrawing touch. The fencer stops the timer with a motion (finger pressure, thrust with the weapon. The time and failed attempts are measured.

(2) **Decision-making tests**, that are similar to reaction tests, only the fencers have to decide between two, three, or more alternatives. Fig. 2.4.-4 shows a measuring station that has been used successfully for many years at the Deutsche Hochschule für Körperkultur (German Academy for Fitness Training) in Leipzig, Germany.

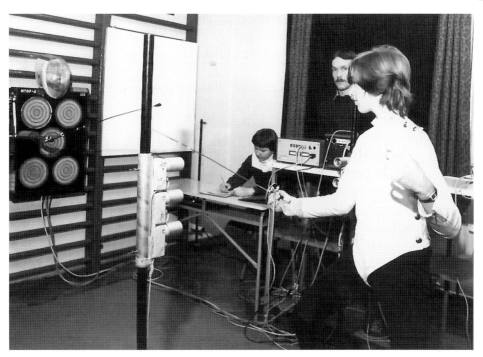

Fig. 2.4.-4: Measuring station (DhfK Leipzig)

- The tester holds a coin in each of his hands. The fencer has to catch the respective coin being dropped – right, left, or both. The successful attempts are counted.

- The fencer is given the task to react to colored lights, different sounds or numbers, etc., and must choose various, though specified, solutions.

(3) Perception tests, to determine how accurately and quickly the fencers can perceive signals or complex patterns.
- By briefly looking at slides, the fencers have to identify, for instance, the number of symbols (or the number of different symbols) on each slide.

(4) Very different **anticipation tests, probability tests, or concentration tests** are conducted in a similar way. Every trainer has his own tasks, apparatuses and compilation methods. Attention should be paid to,
- exact test instructions and adherence thereto.

- exact indexing of the results.

- motivation of the fencers' for the best possible test performance, and

- careful (not overrated) interpretation of the results.

But the most important monitoring method is the competition analysis.
The simplest form is the result analysis in which all available competition results (placement, victories and defeats, hits scored and received) are collected and analyzed.

With respect to training control measures, it is of interest to know which fencers (right or left fencing, big or small fencers) victories had been won against and which fencers had been lost against.
Which actions a hit was scored and prevented with, and what the reasons were, is recorded during specific fight observation. Errors have a strategic-tactical cause if the situation is not recognized, or recognized too late or evaluated incorrectly, as the case may be, and if the fencer's decision is inexpedient or too late.

When such observations are carried out over an extended period of time and analyzed with the fencers, they result in important leads for the improvement of training.

A very simple method is to keep tally sheets of the executed fight actions and their results. If prepared forms are used it can even be done without much effort by the fencers who are not participating in the fight. The models list all of the results the trainer needs. Even basic frequency scales allow for interesting conclusions.

Progression logs and fight analyses based on scientific methods, video footage and complex computer-video systems, are suitable for more detailed deductions. Experienced fencers and their trainers also have access to observation data from important opponents, and can therefore develop specific strategic-tactical concepts and are better able to prepare for future fights.

2.5   Physical fitness requirements of a fencer

2.5.1 Characteristics of physical fitness

Traditionally the term "fitness" is associated with strength-, endurance-, and speed related abilities. Physical fitness performance requisites characterize the physical abilities that are primarily determined by energetic processes.

Corresponding to the training and competition demands on the intensity and duration of movement as well as the strain-break regiment, the fitness related abilities enter into typical interrelations (fig. 2.5.-1).

The goal in fitness training is the morphologic-functional perfection of the essential functional systems (e.g. cardio-vascular-, respiratory- and nervous-muscle system), as well

as the energy providing and resynthesizing processes, including the associated regulations. During the schooling process, the execution of movements and actions required for training or competition must become more economical, stable and efficient.

The schooling of fitness related abilities can only be put into practice during the execution of movement. In this respect every fencer requires a specific fitness level that corresponds to the demands of his discipline. At the same time fitness training results in very close connections to the coordinative abilities (e.g. in speed training), the psychological abilities, and the technical-tactical performances.

Ensuring economical and efficient movements and actions in training and competition

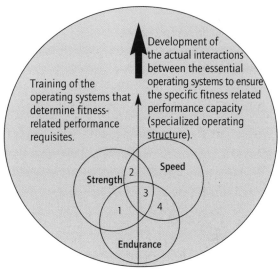

Fig. 2.5.-1:
Interaction between the abilities strength, endurance and speed, shown as an operating model based on the adaptation of biological measurement categories.
1 = strength endurance   3 = power endurance
2 = power   4 = speed endurance

Well-developed fitness related abilities are an important precondition to handling the necessary workload requirements during training, and for steady, high performances at fencing tournaments.

Dynamic performance development and the great power density call for a fencer who is quick, explosive, and persistent. Such requirements are substantiated by the fact that dynamic footwork, powerfully explosive lunges, situation-appropriate and quick reaction and movement times must be carried out during the entire tournament.

The entire body of training methods for the development of fitness related abilities can be categorized by different factors. This facilitates the training methodological orientation and thus the implementation of fitness training.

From a workload method point of view, it is necessary to differentiate between fitness training with general and fitness training with specific physical exercises (general and specific fitness training).

General fitness training is training with movement patterns that are not identical to the typical movement or respective components of fencing movements: among others, reaction and relay games, running exercises, working out with dumbbells, throwing and thrusting exercises, as well as bicycling. Such forms of exercise do not provide an immediate improvement in the fencer's competitive performance, but they do optimize the operating systems that are essential to the respective basic ability, and create the prerequisites for fencing-specific training.

Fitness oriented footwork and lessons, footwork with a weight jacket, lunges against a rubber band, among others, are examples of specific fitness training. In specific fitness training the movement patterns and required workloads are similar or identical to those of a competition. They serve the immediate improvement of fencing performance.

In doing so, the fitness related performance requisites by means of fencing specific workload requirements are addressed in such a way, that interrelations such as are required for a successful fencing competition (specialized functional structure), are established. At the same time, interrelations with the other fencing performance determining performance factors are optimized and stabilized.

Furthermore, the individual fitness related abilities can be distinguished by additional criteria, which will be addressed briefly in the following paragraphs.

2.5.2 Endurance and endurance training

Endurance is the performance requisite that gives the fencer the ability to handle long lasting workload demands without major performance decrement due to fatigue.

While endurance is crucial to the performance result with long lasting workload demands, it impacts the performance result with short-term workload demands. The latter applies to fencing. Overall the endurance-training portion in fencing is quite small.

Improved endurance in fencing

- ensures the energetic requirements for a dynamic fighting style for the duration of the competition, as well as fewer errors.
- promotes better concentration and mobilization.
- is a requirement for increased workload tolerance and compatibility.
- ensures faster recovery (regeneration) during lulls in fights and training breaks.

The most important classification possibilities for endurance are compiled in table 2.5.-1.

Table 2.5.-1: Schematic classification of endurance methods according to lactate-speed-graph and heart rate

Classification according to **dominant load factor**	Workload duration:	Short-term endurance 25 sec. to 2 min. medium-term endurance > 2 min. long-term endurance > 10 min.
	and movement intensity, respect.:	Intensive Extensive
Classification according to **type of energy allocation**	Aerobic endurance (= basic endurance I)	
	Anaerobic endurance (= basic endurance II)	Anaerobic/alactic acid Anaerobic/lactic acid
Classification according to mass/ size of the **utilized musculature**	Local endurance Regional endurance Global endurance	(also: local strength endurance)
Classification according to **type of physical exercise used**	Overall endurance Specific endurance	
Classification (of methods) according to **basic work-load demand structure** (break-workload arrangement)	Duration method (DM) (no breaks)	Continuous method Alternating method
	Interval methods (IvM) (short rewarding breaks)	Short-term IvM or intensive IvM Medium-term IvM Long-term-IvM or extensive IvM
	Competition/moni-toring methods (CM) (restoring breaks)	Duration of competition Below duration of competition

2.5.2.1 Basic endurance

Basic endurance is the critical achievement-related foundation for substantial training and competitive demands. It is certain that with an increase in aerobic capacity, regardless of whether training is done with general or specific exercises, the tolerance with respect to intensive workloads increases. An improved basic endurance level ensures increased mobilization ability, improved energy balance, and is a requirement for fencing-specific endurance training. Basic endurance training occurs primarily at the start of the training year and during longer intervals between important competitions.

Basic endurance I (also called stabilization or economization interval) characterizes the endurance development under a dominant oxidative-aerobic metabolic state; in the lactate

area more than 1 to 4 mmol/l. Under these conditions the organism's oxygen demand can be secured. The goal is increased movement intensity in a completely aerobic metabolic state and an increased workload capacity and workload tolerance, as well as the ability to regenerate after dealing with general and specific workload demands.

The typical methods for basic endurance training I in fencing training are the continuous method as well as the extensive interval method (see fig. 2.5.-2).

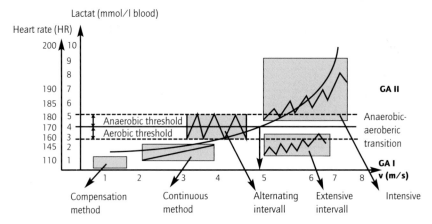

Fig. 2.5.-2:
Schematic classification of endurance methods based on the lactate-speed graph and the heart rate

Continuous method

Workload volume:	12 min. (youth fencer – Cooper Test")
	30 min. (competitive fencer continuous running)
	(first without, later with specified distance)
Intensity:	Pulse rate 140-160 (= medium speed)
Training exercise:	General
Training effects:	Economization of cardio-vascular work.
	Improved oxygen absorption.

The training in the basic endurance training II interval (also developmental interval) promotes endurance development in a dominantly glycolic-anaerobic metabolic state; in the lactate area 4 to approx. 10 mmol/l. At the same time the fencer consciously creates an "oxygen debt". The objectives are increased realizable intensities under anaerobic conditions, as well as an improved lactate tolerance. During the first two stages of long-term performance build-up the BE-II training should be irrelevant. During the subsequent training stages the BE-II training can, with the aid of the intensive or short-term interval method, be used selectively. Of much greater significance for fencing is the training of the aerobic-anaerobic transition, for which the alternating method is particularly suitable.

Alternating method

Workload volume:	5 x 1200 m-runs
Intensity:	Alternate between maximum and slow speeds
	(e.g. lap 1 – alternate 75 m jog, 25 m sprint
	lap 2 – alternate 25 m jog, 50 m sprint
	lap 3 – alternate like lap 1)
Break:	5-6 min.
Training exercise:	General
Training effect:	Ability to transition between aerobic and anaerobic metabolic demand:

- for changes in speed and rhythm during a fight.
- "feel" for the differentiation between powerful and medium strength effort.
- Regeneration in spite of light workload.

The 12-min. run ("Cooper Test") has proven beneficial in the evaluation of basic endurance level in fencing. That is the purpose of the following evaluation chart 2.5.-2, which has been tried and tested for many years:

Table 2.5.-2: Standard values for the evaluation of the basic endurance level – 12 min. run according to: Pahlke & Peters, 1079, pg. 359 (Note: for girls apply 200 m less respectively.)

Evaluation	Age									
Excellent	2600	2650	2700	2750	2800	2850	2900	2950	3000	3050
Very good	2400	2450	2500	2550	2600	2650	2700	2750	2800	2850
Good	2000	2050	2100	2150	2200	2250	2300	2350	2400	2450
Satisfactory	1600	1650	1700	1750	1800	1850	1900	1950	2000	2050
Insufficient	1000	1050	1100	1150	1200	1250	1300	1350	1400	1450

The following figure 2.5.-3 shows the performance development of a successful épée fencer after several weeks of endurance training.

The fencer trained 2 x week, whereby the duration method was used first, followed by the alternating method. During the remaining training time, training was alternately fencing specific or strength training. The test design consisted of a 6 x 1200 m-run at a specified speed and a break of approx. 30 sec. (see fig.) between the individual runs.

Workload profile: 6 x 1.200 m				Test 1	Test 2	
				10.04.97	28.06.97	
	(1.000 m)	Planned time	Actual time	HR direct	HR direct	Difference
	05:40	06:48	06:48	130	121	9
	05:20	06:24	06:24	150	135	15
	05:00	06:00	06:00	180	151	29
	04:40	05:36	05:36	187	176	11
	04:20	05:12	05:12	195	185	10
	04:00	04:48	Aborted		191	
Heart rate after			2 min	145	128	17
Heart rate after			5 min	136	110	16

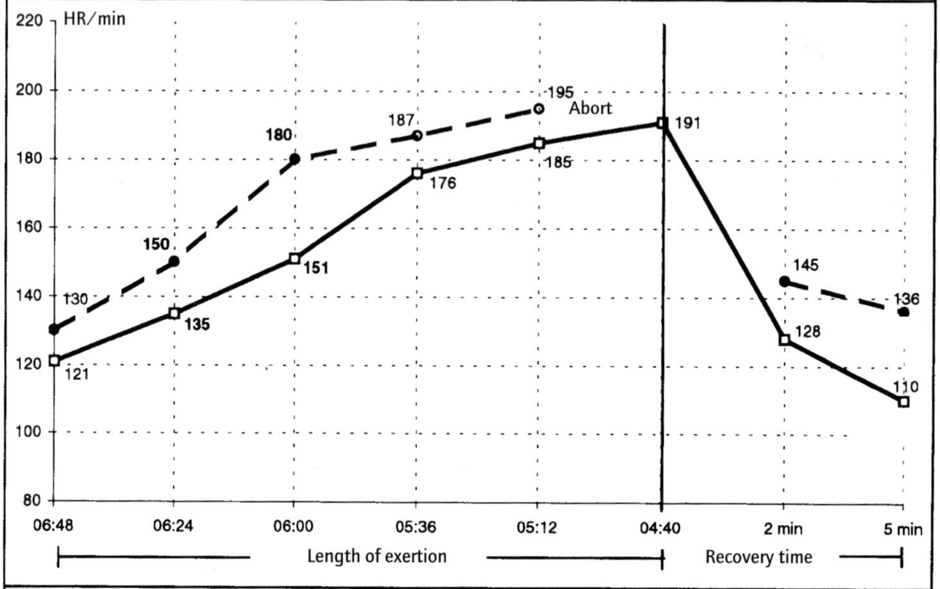

Results	Test 1	Test 2
Aerobic threshold (Lipometabolism 1.8 mmol)	5:20 min/1.000 m HR 150 bpm	5:00 min/1.000 m HR 151 bpm
Aerobic/anaerobic threshold (4.0 mmol/l lactate threshold)	5:00 min/1.000 m HR 180 bpm	4:40 min/1.000 m HR 176 bpm

Fig. 2.5.-3: Developmental progression of the endurance level after a training phase with emphasis on endurance development of a successful épée fencer.

After the training phase, the aerobic threshold had been improved from 5:20 min to 5:00 min (1000 m). At the same time the heart rate went down from 150 bpm to 135 bpm. In the aerobic/anaerobic transition area the fencer increased his speed from 5:00 min to 4:40 min.; the heart rate went down from 180 bpm to 151 bpm. The resting pulse rate also improved, indicating recovering capability.

Overall the training effect consists of an economization of the cardio-vascular performance and an improved mobilization capability and stamina, which infers an increase of concentrative qualities that is essential during a long tournament.

2.5.2.2 Competition-specific endurance

Competition-specific endurance training along with its training means and workload requirements is orientated to the fencing competition. These are, for instance, fitness lessons, endurance oriented footwork, or fencing fights, which may be of aerobic-, anaerobic-lactic acid or anaerobic-alactic acid design. Command of at least the basic technical fencing elements and their combinations are necessary for this.

Extensive interval method	
Workload volume:	5-8 fights up to 10 hits; if possible with time target.
Break:	Until pulse has gone down to approx. HR 12bpm
Training exercise:	Specific
Training effect:	Improved fight speed with more situational peaks in exertion. Fewer blunders due to fatigue.

2.5.3 Strength and strength training

Strength as a performance requisite characterizes the fencer's ability to overcome resistance and hold resistance respectively. Strength is developed relative to the required and realized demands respectively. The design of the workload factors (workload intensity and workload volume, as well as their determining subfactors, the type of physical exercises, the quality of movement execution) and the workload procedures which can be referred to, in the broadest sense, as methods and organizational-methodic forms, are particularly crucial to the direction and speed of strength increase.

The object of strength training is:
- Increased muscular load capacity to be able to realize current and future movement and performance requisites.

- Stabilizing the passive locomotor system through harmonic muscle development.

- Developing the muscular capability to perform longer, more powerful, explosive strength efforts during fencing movements and actions.

The significance of strength training and the design of its content are very different during the various phases. During the initial training stages, strength training has a strictly general character directed towards the sport type, and should conform to the principle of versatility. With an increase in training age and during the course of training years respectively, the exercise selection and workload structure are more and more orientated to the specificity of fencing.

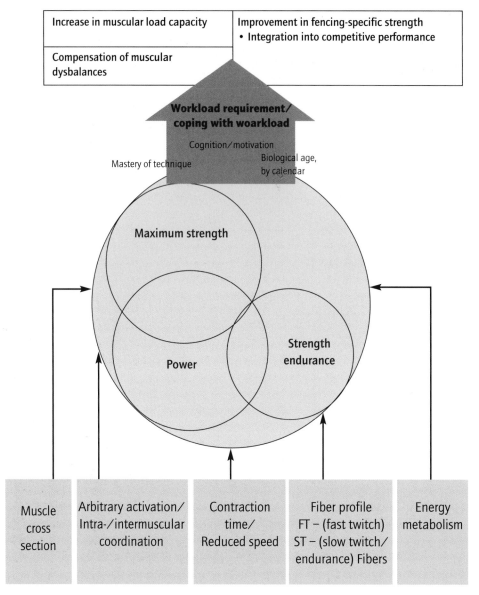

Fig. 2.5.-4: Illustration of the essential biological and performance factorial prerequisites for strength development, as well as the objectives of strength training in fencing.

The most important classifications in strength training are compiled in table 2.5.-3.

Table 2.5.-3: Classifications of strength training

Classification according to the main effects of strength training	Maximum strength-, power-, strength endurance training		
Classification according to the manner of muscle contraction	Dynamic	resist (concentric) release (eccentric) reactive (eccentric-concentric, plyometric)	
	and static strength training		
Classification according to the type of physical exercise used	General specific strength		
classification according to the organizational-methodic form	Circuit-, Set-, Station training		
Classification (of methods) according to the basic structure of resistance requirements	Basic form alternating resistance	Variation increase	*Example* *80% to 100% MR* *e.g. pyramid method*
		$\dfrac{80\,\%}{5\,x}+\dfrac{85\,\%}{4\,x}+\dfrac{90\,\%}{2\,x}+\dfrac{95\,\%}{3\,x}+\dfrac{100\,\%}{1\,x}$	
		decrease	*variant as per Watkins*
		$\dfrac{100\,\%\,WM}{10\,x}+\dfrac{75\,\%\,WM}{10\,x}+\dfrac{50\,\%\,WM}{10\,x}$	
		(MR = Maximum repetitions)	
		increasing-decreasing	*from 30% to 60% and back to 30% MR* *Dbl. pyramid method*
		$\dfrac{30\,\%}{15\,x}+\dfrac{40\,\%}{14\,x}+\dfrac{50\,\%}{13\,x}+\dfrac{60\,\%}{12\,x}+\dfrac{50\,\%}{13\,x}+$ $\dfrac{40\,\%}{14\,x}+\dfrac{30\,\%}{15\,x}$	
		Contrast method	
		1.-2. Serie: $\dfrac{(80\,\%\,MK}{4\,x}+\dfrac{40\,\%\,MK)}{3\,x}$ 3.-5. Serie: $\dfrac{(90\,\%\,MK}{3\,x}+\dfrac{50\,\%\,MK)}{2\,x}$ 6.-7. Serie: $\dfrac{(80\,\%\,MK}{4\,x}+\dfrac{40\,\%\,MK)}{3\,x}$	
		(3 min. break after each series)	
	Constant resistance	*Method of submaximum strength effort*	
		$5\,x\;\dfrac{(\,90\,\%\,MK\,)}{2\text{-}4\,x}$	

2.5.3.1 Maximum strength and training for maximum strength

Maximum strength capacity gives the fencer the capacity for maximum random muscle contractions. We differentiate between dynamic and static maximum strength capacity. Maximum strength is the basis for great power or strength endurance based performances. This means that the fencer's maximum strength level should be so high that it can become fully effective during brief fencing movements.

Maximum strength can be increased through muscle hypertrophy (profile enlargement), as well as by improving intramuscular coordination (higher rate of activated motor units). Forced maximum strength training with an effective workload structure is only recommended during and after puberty. During the preceding stages of life the focus should be on increasing the relative (maximum-) strength.

This is essentially done by means of brief workload duration and explosive strength efforts with minor additional loads. For 9-10 year olds the resistance should be a maximum of 30% and for 11-13 year olds a maximum of 50% of their body weight.

> ***Statistic strength training is also effective:***
> Length of exertion: 4-8 sec.
>
> Intensity of exertion: minimum of 75% of the possible maximum exertion
>
> Repetition break: approx. 1 min.
>
> Repetitions/exercise: 5-10 x (if possible at 2-3 different angles)
>
> Exercises per muscle: 2-3

It can also be used in combination with dynamic strength training for the specific strengthening of weakened muscles, for targeted posture training, for strength-preserving training of injured fencers, or to prepare for static strength requirements (fencing position).

Dynamic maximum strength training to improve intramuscular fitness includes forms of exertion, which use so much movement resistance that they only allow eight movement repetitions at a minimal rate of movement. As a rule these are exercises with a high weight resistance of 80% and 100% of the maximum strength (% MS).

Additional conditions are a preferably rapid strength development, a low number of repetitions and sets, as well as relatively long recovery times. The goal is to increase maximum strength through improved intramuscular coordination.

Workload intensity:	80%-100% MS
Speed of movement:	preferably fast
Workload volume:	low
Per training unit:	4-5 exercises (stations)
Sets/exercise:	2-3
Breaks:	4-5 min.
Organizational-methodic procedures:	station training
Method:	pyramid method (see above)
Preparation and evaluation:	at least 15 min. and 10 min. respectively (for trained fencers)

this form of maximum strength improvement is dominant among competition oriented fencers.

2.5.3.2 Power and power training

Power ability is a fencer's ability to resist loads at a highly reduced speed. The goal of power training is to increase acceleration as well as the residual speed of the body (e.g while lunging) or the weapon (while thrusting).

Power training is associated with forms of physical strain that are largely similar to the typical competitive performance and movement structure in terms of acceleration and speed requirements. With general power training the bandwidth of resistivity can be 30% to 70% of the maximum strength. Higher external resistance should improve the strength component and lower external resistance the speed component of power. Additional workload preconditions are relatively low workload volumes that should fall within a range of up to six sets and 1-8 repetitions per set. The breaks between sets serve an extensive recovery to prevent a decline in the speed of movement due to fatigue; based on experience these should be approx. 4-6 min. With specific power training the possibilities of variations with regard to external resistance are limited. Wrist or ankle weights on the weapon-bearing arm or around the ankles should not exceed 1/4 lb, weight jackets not more than 11 lbs.

Reactive forms of exertion (also: plyometric training or training by the "shock method") are a very effective form of training the explosive strength effort. It is a "release-resist" combination with extremely brief linking of both work phases, referred to as the stretch-shortening cycle. A larger increase in muscle tension is achieved during the short-term movement reversal phase than during the purely resisting or releasing forms of exertion.

Typical are, for instance, low jumps with immediate vertical or horizontal take-off from the deceleration phase (low-high jumps), whereby floor contact must be extremely brief.

2.5.3.3 Strength endurance and strength endurance training

Strength endurance ability is the fencer's ability to resist fatigue during repeated strength efforts. That is why it is increasingly viewed as a form of endurance training (local muscle strength endurance) (among others Harre & Leopold, 1986). In fencing strength endurance is significant to the improvement of muscular workload tolerance and is supposed to enable the fencer to repeat the powerful strength efforts required during training and competitions, with equally high efficiency.

Typical for strength endurance training is doing as many repetitions as possible in individual exercise sets, and rather short breaks. In general strength endurance training one chooses additional loads of between 40% and 70% MS. Lower movement resistance (< 40% MS) combined with substantial workload volume boost strength endurance for very long lasting competition loads timewise, with emphasis on the endurance component. Higher movement resistance (50%-70% MS) promotes strength endurance for medium and short competitions with emphasis on the strength component. The most important control factor in strength endurance training is the rate of movement as it essentially determines the manner of energy production.

Circuit training with the direct goal of improving muscular workload tolerance and the longer-term preparation for forced strength training, is particularly well suited for large groups of young athletes.

Workload volume:	10-12 stations		3-5 complete circuits
Workload duration:	30-45 sec.	Later	10-20 sec.
Resistance:	Low		Medium
(Subject to exercise execution, body position, or similar)			
Workload intensity:	Medium		Maximum rate of movement
Breaks:			
Change stations:	30-60 sec.		20-30 sec.
Between circuits:		3-4 min.	
Method:	Extensive		Intensive interval method

In specific strength endurance training the workload requirements should act as "power endurance". For instance, footwork aided by the short-term interval method.

Fig. 2.5.-5 shows the strength training of a successful foil fencer. The system of a multi-week strength build-up becomes apparent through exact specification of the content design for the individual phases.

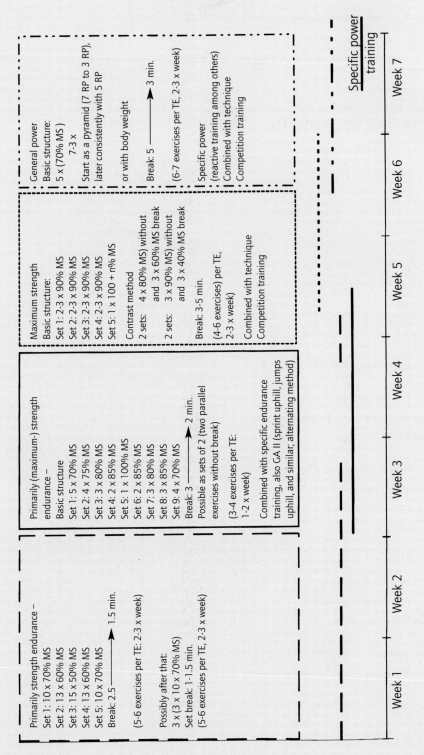

Week 1 — Week 2 — Week 3 — Week 4 — Week 5 — Week 6 — Week 7

Specific power training

Primarily strength endurance –
Set 1: 10 x 70% MS
Set 2: 13 x 60% MS
Set 3: 15 x 50% MS
Set 4: 13 x 60% MS
Set 5: 10 x 70% MS
Break: 2.5 → 1.5 min.
(5-6 exercises per TE: 2-3 x week)
Possibly after that:
3 x (3 x 10 x 70% MS)
Set break: 1-1.5 min.
(5-6 exercises per TE, 2-3 x week)

Primarily (maximum-) strength endurance –
Basic structure
Set 1: 5 x 70% MS
Set 2: 4 x 75% MS
Set 3: 3 x 80% MS
Set 4: 2 x 85% MS
Set 5: 1 x 100% MS
Set 6: 2 x 85% MS
Set 7: 3 x 80% MS
Set 8: 3 x 85% MS
Set 9: 4 x 70% MS
Break: 3 → 2 min.
Possible as sets of 2 (two parallel exercises without break)
(3-4 exercises per TE: 1-2 x week)
Combined with specific endurance training, also GA II (sprint uphill, jumps uphill, and similar; alternating method)

Maximum strength
Basic structure:
Set 1: 2-3 x 90% MS
Set 2: 2-3 x 90% MS
Set 3: 2-3 x 90% MS
Set 4: 2-3 x 90% MS
Set 5: 1 x 100 + n% MS
Contrast method
2 sets: 4 x 80% MS) without
          and 3 x 60% MS break
2 sets: 3 x 90% MS) without
          and 3 x 40% MS break
Break: 3-5 min.
(4-6 exercises) per TE,
2-3 x week)
Combined with technique
Competition training

General power
Basic structure:
5 x (70% MS)
7-3 x
Start as a pyramid (7 RP to 3 RP),
later consistently with 5 RP
or with body weight
Break: 5 → 3 min.
(6-7 exercises per TE, 2-3 x week)
Specific power
(reactive training among others)
Combined with technique
Competition training

Fig. 2.5.-5: Phase of a successful (active) foil fencer's forced strength build-up (May-June)

2.5.4 Speed and speed training

Speed as a determinate coordinative-fitness related performance requisites enables the fencer to quickly react to stimuli and to process information respectively, as well as to execute movements or motor actions under easier and/or sport-specific conditions with maximum movement intensity, whereby a short workload duration eliminates limiting of the performance due to fatigue. Speed is the most significant fitness related ability in fencing.

The development of the various types of speed should begin very early on. Thereby the speed training portion of the young fencer's overall training time is quite large, and even at the top constitutes a considerable performance reserve as action speed combined with technical-tactical training.

The following goals are associated with speed training:

- shorter reaction time and/ or processing of stimuli and information ("mental" agility).
- improved "motor" speed.

The following model (fig. 2.5.-6) is derived from the various speed systemizations.

Muscular-energetic (fitness related) requirements

Elasticity/ flexibility Length of muscle fibers
Creatine phosphate/ Muscle temperature
length of ATP reproduction
Contraction time/shortening speed Portion of FT fiber

Action speed	Speed of an individual movement	Locomotor speed
	Acceleration ability	
	Noncyclical————————→ Cyclical	
	Speed of movement	

Complex speed (= speed performance)

Choice reaction	Elementary reaction	Speed during lengthening-shortening cycle	Frequency speed Tapping
Reaction speed		Contraction speed Coordinative speed	

Basic speed

Prereflex/innervation reflex, sensorimotor regulation, neuromuscular control
Regulation of intra and intermuscular coordination
(Fiber type recruiting, synchronization, stimulation and repression)
Nerve conducting speed
Nerval-informational (Coordinative requirement)

Volitional, cognitive, motivational and emotional qualities

Fig. 2.5.-6:
Classification model of speed related abilities

2.5.4.1 Basic speed

Basic speed (also elementary speed) comprises the highly constitutional psycho-physiological requirements of speed-related abilities (e.g nerve conducting speed, length of prereflex and reflex innervations respectively, and the ratio of slow contracting ST and fast contracting muscle fibers FT). The limits of basic speed development are primarily determined by the central nervous and neuromuscular control and regulation mechanisms, which are "fixed" early on and must therefore be trained at an early stage.

Reaction speed

Although, under narrow consideration, reaction speed can be assigned to psychological as well as motor abilities, it is occasionally counted among speed related abilities (Harre & Leopold, 1986). It characterizes the fencer's fastest possible motor reaction (choice reaction) to a recognized signal.

In fencing reaction speed in its manifestation as a choice reaction is significant in determining performance. Therefore it should be developed at a very early stage, initially starting with simple reaction exercises involving acoustic, tactile, kinesthetic, and optical stimuli – whereby the latter should dominate –, to the point of situational training.

The following preconditions should be warranted for reaction speed training:
- Requiring short reaction times.
- Versatility in terms of information type, intensity, and duration of the included physical exercises and their execution.

This includes such forms of exercise as take-offs, fixed reactions to familiar signals that can also be given in random order (e.g., sit down to the "hot" signal, lie on your back to the "cold" signal, etc.).

The repeating of fast elementary or choice reactions to information of varying design (optical/acoustic, loud/quiet, irregular time intervals between individual commands, varying technical-tactical fight situations with alternative solution options, and such), have proven to very effective:

- Training under pressure of time.

- Low volume per training unit as well as the number of repetitions per exercise. The length of breaks in between the individual exercise complexes should be approx. 2-5 minutes long and actively designed.

- If reaction times increase due to decreased concentration and symptoms of fatigue, the form of exercise should be changed or training should be discontinued.

2.5.4.2 Complex speed

Complex speed always manifests itself in close connection with the other performance requisites, and characterizes movement and/or action related performances that can be carried out in a very short period of time. In subsequent stages of training it is methodically barely distinguishable from power training, which is why basic conclusions with respect to workload methods also apply to the development of speed of movement.

Action speed

Of the complex speed subcategories action speed is most significant to the successful structuring of a fencing competition. Since it is closely linked to technical-tactical training it is included in Chapter 2.4.

Speed of movement

Speed of movement refers exclusively to the motor components of an action and manifests itself in short-time executions of movement. On the one hand these are based on well-developed elementary speed abilities, and on the other hand they also depend on the level of the other personal performance factors.

Fundamental workload method requirements are:
- Sub- to super-maximum intensities (achieved by, for instance, running downhill on a gradient of up to 3º).
- A workload duration of approx. 7 seconds, consequently very short distances (approx. 20-30 m), but with short-time explosive movement execution.
- Long, restoring breaks.

In doing so, the chosen exercise must be mastered with respect to sport technique. The following training means are available to the fencer:

Coordination-, frequency-, and progressive runs, "flying starts", relay competitions, playing catch, little games, skipping in place, while moving, over small obstacles or markers, uphill/downhill/horizontal sprints: approx. 20-25 m (basic athletic training) up to 60-70 m (advanced training) with variations (uphill/downhill, on varying surfaces).

3 Basic methods of fencing training

The nature of fencing training is to strive for higher performance capacity and better performances and results through active exertion. The more methodical and goal oriented the fencer's performance readiness (pedagogic-psychological process) and performance capacity (training method process) is affected, the better it all works. Fencing training can be performed in various implementation areas: beginners' training and junior performance sports, competition oriented popular sports, and senior sports, professional sports and disabled sports. The different goals of the implementation areas are significant with regard to the volume and intensity of training, whether the training is intended to develop and stabilize performance capacity, or if the aim is – and this applies to popular sports and senior sports in particular – to improve the quality of life and to delay an age-related decline in performance capacity.

The complexity of a fencer's performance capacity was referred to in Chapter 2 in connection with performance structure. This chapter will cover the basic methodic principles in fencing training.

3.1 Training goals, content, means, and forms of training organization

Training goals, training content, training means, training methods and forms of training organization do not function segregated from each other, but rather through their interactions with each other. That is why one also refers to goal-content-aid-method-relation.

The main goal in fencing training is focused on the complex fencing performance. Its result can be measured by the complex performance capacity, but ultimately really only by the success at a competition while competing against others. This requires complex, specific training.

The subgoals correspond to the preconditions that have to be accomplished in training to reach the main goal. Subgoals can be in-between goals that correspond to the periodic performance build-up. But they can also correspond to individual performance elements of the performance structure. For instance, it can become necessary to periodically increase development of the specific fitness related abilities of power and endurance as preconditions to the effective use of technical-tactical actions. Or a higher level of the psychological preconditions of concentrated

attention and anticipation ability may be necessary to ensure the effective use of technical-tactical abilities and skills. On the other hand, the fencer has to learn to implement the improved fitness related abilities and the higher level of psychological preconditions during the respective fighting actions. This means that individual factors in specific stages of training can also develop successively or more strongly (accentuated) (c.p. fig. 3.6.-1).

But one should never become too far removed from the ideal structure essential to the respective competitive performance.

It is just as wrong to develop strategic-tactical abilities before the basic technical skills have been acquired. It would also be inexpedient to develop and stabilize technical elements without tactical reference and without the necessary speed (see fig. 3.6.-1).

The development and perfection of technical-tactical abilities and skills, the teaching and refinement of psychological behavior and performance characteristics, as well as the optimal development of fitness related abilities appropriate to the specificity of fencing represent firmly linked and interactive sides of an integrative process.

The realization of a training goal occurs primarily via the training content which itself determines the use of training means and methods, and the best forms of organization for that purpose.

- The **training content** determines what needs to be done to achieve the goal.

- The **training means** that are to be used for that purpose show what the aspired to goal can be realized with.

- The **training methods** characterize the "we" in these processes.

A select example demonstrates how important it is to always view these relations within their context.

"Footwork" as a training exercise is a specific training aid that can be used for the goals "learning technique" or "rhythm training" or "specific endurance development". It is understood that for learning technique one does not apply the duration method or the situational training method. Thus the goal (e.g., rhythm training) always determines the content (step forward – lunge and drag the foot), the aid (footwork) and the method (acquired practice and repetition method).

Readers interested in theory should consult a reference book on training theory. We recommend Schnabel, G. Harre, D. Krug, J. & Borde, A. (Hrsg.) (2003).

That is why this segment does not include all assertions of the general methodology, but mostly brings out methodic highlights and important fencing-specific details. The wealth of information from successful German trainers and foreign trainers working in Germany, and particularly the textbooks and publications on fencing methodology, could be utilized for this purpose.

3.1.1 Exercises without a partner

These exercises allow the fencer to execute all fencing technique elements and their combinations with or without a weapon. In doing so, the positions and movements are learned and monitored in their proper execution and coordination. All actions are performed without another fencer's counteraction. This has the advantage of calm, standardized conditions with minimal emotional influence, for the execution of movements.

The fencers can concentrate on the individual tasks and vary technical details, tempo and rhythm without the opponent's influence, and learn new or, in terms of coordination, complicated combinations. For the purpose of self-monitoring, it is to the fencer's advantage to occasionally perform these exercises in front of a mirror. Practicing with the eyes closed particularly develops the kinesthetic sense (sense of movement). The following is a preferred method for practicing without a partner:

Independent practice
Practicing independently is the basic method for learning or training the elements and combinations of fencing technique. The trainer issues and explains the tasks and demonstrates the process; then the fencers train independently. But in doing so the trainer's control is in no way suspended. He continually observes the group and corrects individual fencers. If there are commonly occurring mistakes, independent work is discontinued and the necessary corrections are gone over with the entire group.

It is recommended to introduce a few organizational standards within each group. Restlessness can thereby be avoided and favorable organizational conditions can be created for demonstrations and corrections.

By way of independent practice the fencer can concentrate on the essentials of execution according to his training level. He is not distracted by signals that are not characteristic to fencing, like commands, whistling and such, that define the beginning or progression of the individual actions. Furthermore, independent practice under the trainer's control instills conscious and positive behavior with regard to the training process, independent initiative, and develops the fencer's determination.

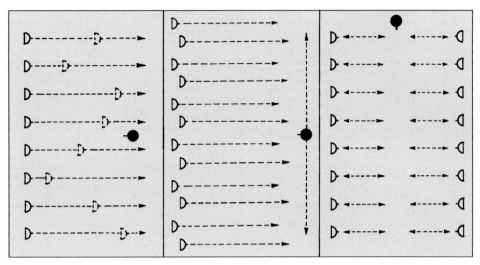

Fig. 3.1.-1:
Forms of organization for independent practice without a partner

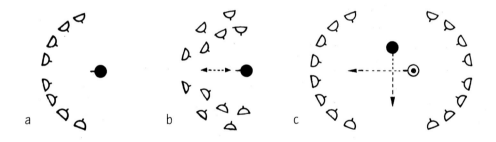

Fig. 3.1.-2:
Forms of positioning for demonstrations, tips, and corrections (to be assumed
independently by fencers after command is given)

Execution of action upon command or signal
Execution of individual elements
This methodical process becomes necessary when the dissection into individual elements
is essential to a consistent, correct execution of a combination.

If, for instance, the object is to learn the basic technical structure of a counter parry-
riposte, a complete dissection is possible in such a way, that each time after a signal one
of the subsequently listed elements is executed individually:

1 – Arm extension
2 – Lunge
3 – Return to lunge
4 – Parry
5 – Arm extension
6 – Lunge

or

1 – Attack (arm extension and lunge)
2 – Return with parry
3 – Riposte with lunge

Counting can be supplemented with knocking or optical signals. This method is fencing-specific and is seldom used, and then only very briefly.

Execution of actions or combinations

Another form is one where the trainer each time just indicates the start of the overall action with a signal, thereby achieving major compactness. The trainer can control the workload and with a large number of repetitions with little break-time, the fencer can also develop fitness-related abilities.

These exercises are performed in rows or line-outs. "Conditional signals" that are still used occasionally (e.g., 1 knock = forward step, 2 knocks = backward step, lifted left arm = forward leap, lifted right arm = lunge) are not well suited for this as they communicate combinations of signals that are not required in fencing. A special form of signaling or signal planning is achieved when the end of one fencer's exercise or combination is the signal for the next fencer to begin. Suitable forms of organization are rows, wide line-outs, squares, or circles (fig. 3.1.-3).

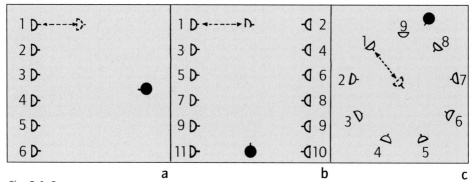

Fig. 3.1.-3:
Positioning for special signaling during on-command exercises

In addition this form has considerable emotional impact. It promotes attentiveness and livens up instruction. At the same time the fencers can observe correct and incorrect executions by the others.

Simulated actions as signals

Here the suggested action by a trainer or fencer serves as a signal to the other or others to execute the actions. The fencer has to mentally process the optical information and, in accordance with the simulated situation, has to choose and execute his own action.

The trainer gives the group the task of maintaining a certain measure between himself and the group, or to react with defensive elements to a simulated attack. Thus the opening of a particular target area, for example, necessitates an attack.

Practice example

Trainer executes	Fencer answers with
Step forward	Step backward
Two steps backward	Two steps forward
Lunge and return to fencing position forward	Two steps backward – one step
Thrust with lunge	Step backward – parry
Step backward with quarte position	Thrust with step forward – lunge

This practice game can be supplemented as needed. But a few basic tactical skills are required. Important is that the trainer is clearly visible to all fencers. Left-handed fencers stand on the right side. The distance between trainer and group is such that there is no weapon contact (fig. 3.1.-4).

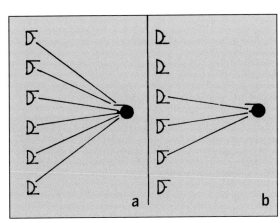

Fig. 3.1.-4:
Forms of positioning:
a – correct, b – incorrect

Shadow fencing and mirror fencing

The main purpose of this form of practice, which is also analogously used in other martial arts and game sports, is the "contest" with an imaginary fencer. The fencer has to visualize the opponent's actions in order to evade or anticipate them, or to repel them.

He can tactically substantiate his own actions and successfully execute them without the "mock opponent". Previously learned and practiced elements and actions are executed as preparatory actions to explore the mock opponent and to maneuver or to mask one's intended actions. In mirror fencing one's mirror image represents the imaginary opponent. In doing so the trainer can also ascertain how much imagination his fencers have and how well they comprehend fencing as a martial art sport.

Forms of competition

The learned and trained elements and actions are reviewed at regular intervals in the form of a small competition. The executed and applied elements and actions are judged based on the basic stipulations specified by the trainer or the training program.

The fencers receive information regarding their performance level, which has a stimulating effect on the further training process. The emotional interest, particularly in young fencers, can be increased by, for instance, presenting the best from each group with a symbol (pennant, cup) signed by a popular fencer, and by maintaining a public performance and evaluation survey (similar to a position table).

These reviews can be centered on:
- the best execution of a movement structure.

- the error free execution of a combination.

- the furthest lunge relative to body height, or the quickest lunge.

- the error free and quick execution of actions following the trainer's action, et al.

3.1.2 Exercises on training devices

Auxiliary training devices are typically "conditional opponents". They are primarily used for perfecting scoring movements and attack elements. The choice of accurate footwork relative to the distance from the target, accuracy and the exact handling of the weapon are immediately visible by the result. An armed thrusting arm serves the monitoring of the correct execution of actions while observing the opposing weapon (sweeps and parries, engagements and contact). Combinations with time measuring devices serve the monitoring of speed and movement execution.

"Fencing robots" that generate considerable construction and acquisition costs, are only expedient for training and performance reviews if their actions and reactions can surpass the maximum performance capacity of a partner.

Otherwise partner exercises and trainer lessons make more sense.

Fig. 3.1.-5: Fencing dummy with target.

The following illustrations show common training devices.

Fig. 3.1.-6:
Thrusting silhouette with multiple target points.

Fig. 3.1.-7:
Thrusting silhouette with armed thrusting arm.

The practical value of the thrusting silhouette with an armed thrusting arm increases considerably if the arm can be attached alternately on the right or left, top or bottom, and can be variably adjusted at the shoulder, elbow and hand, or has spring flexibility.

Fig. 3.1.-8:
Transportable fencing dummy

All auxiliary devices are constructed or mounted in such a way that their target area is level with the target area of the fencer standing in fencing position. The auxiliary devices are used to perform thrusts from near, middle, and wide measure with an extended arm, with a step forward, with a lunge or a step forward or leap-lunge respectively. The correct footwork relative to the distance was chosen, if in a thrust the blade has a slight bend.

The thrusts are executed form different positions, after position changes, and with varying target points. They can be executed from contact or engagements, and can be combined with a push or beat to the weapon. One of the special auxiliary devices may be preferred depending on the type of weapon and the goal of the exercise.

The portable thrusting dummy is used for cuts in saber fencing, the thrusting silhouette or the thrusting dummy are used for foot thrusts in épée fencing. Sweep attacks with any weapon type, and hand or arm hits in épée or saber fencing require an armed thrusting arm.

The exercise requirements are increased via prepared fencing phrases and measure play. Various forms of competition increase the incentive.

To avoid injuries, any exercises performed on a device with an armed thrusting arm absolutely require approved fencing attire and a mask.

3.1.3 Partner exercises

During partner exercises the elements and actions to be practiced are performed with a partner whose actions are conditionally active. The partners take turns in giving each other requirements for executing particularly those actions that are dependent on the opponent's behavior. This includes all disengagement movements, defensive actions, ripostes, counter attacks and combinations, among others.

The movements to be executed will only be successful if the partners are responsive to each other's actions. This requires mutual support, empathy, and attentiveness. Through clearly defined tasks, partner exercises provide both fencers with a learning and training objective. Personal "adoptions" between weaker active fencers and good fencers teach camaraderie and positive social behavior within the training group, the club, or the national team (also see Chapter 4.2).

Frequent changing of partners prevents acclimatization to one partner and is emotionally effective.

Alternate execution of exercises

One of the two fencers issues the necessary requirements (measure, blade position or movement, tempo) so the other can execute the agreed upon action. For example, to be able to execute an attack quarte battuta-disengagement thrust the partner has to resort to the quarte parry after the quarte-battuta. Only then is a disengagement thrust by the opponent possible.

To start the same fencer executes several actions before the two partners switch roles. Later the actions are executed alternately. It is recommended to assign trainer tasks to the conditional partner. This will augment his attentiveness and heightens his interest. In the above exercise the attacking fencer practices the specified attack, the fencer issuing the requirement practices tactical provoking or feinting actions.

The personal acquirement process can be shortened through alternating active analysis of the respective partner's mistakes. Here three fencers can also work together at one time. One fencer issues the requirements, the second one practices, and the third acts as "trainer".

Cyclical execution of exercises

This form of practice is also known as parry-riposte game or riposte cycle. The object is for the partners to execute mutually conditional attacks in cyclical progression that are each repelled with a specific parry. The elements that need to be learned are thereby repeated many times. The riposte corresponds to the attack action by the beginning partner.

With this form of practice the technique of each element or action can be practiced to the highest degree of complexity, by designing the exercise so it can be repeated cyclically.

Varying the measure with different footwork, varying the speed and the rhythm during execution as well as the chance to score hits, creates additional requirements.

The quarte parry-riposte will exemplify typical variations of this form of training:

- Partner A stands in near measure and tries to hit the opponent high/inside by extending the arm and slightly bending the torso forward.

- Partner B assumes quarte parry and directly ripostes high/inside.

- A parries on his part with a quarte parry and ripostes, etc. (fig. 3.1.-9).

If the advance is made with a forward step the partner defends himself with a parry and step backward.
If partner A attacks from a middle measure with a lunge, the parry is executed standing or with a small step backward respectively, but the riposte is executed with a lunge.

There is constant alternating between lunge and return to the fencing position. Depending on the task, the measure can also be negotiated with short lunges, forward leap – lunge, forward step – half lunge, etc..

This basic exercise with the suggested measure variations can be further expanded with tempo and rhythm variations. One or both partners get the chance to score a real hit on their partner with an accelerated, quick riposte. In any case, the riposte play is continued in calm progression (regardless of whether a hit was scored or the partner parried). Critical is the sudden transition from a relatively sedate parry-riposte play to a serious action.

If the parry is executed with a forward step in these variations, different options for the coordination of leg and arm movements arise.

- The complete backward step with a parry and the riposte with a forward step.

- Setting the supporting leg back with the parry and dragging the lunging leg behind with the riposte.

- Setting the lunging leg forward with the parry and following behind with the supporting leg with the riposte (this creates a close quarters situation).

During advanced stages of training various parries (direct, circular, quarte, sixte, septime, etc.), various ripostes (direct, disengagement, cutover), remise attacks, and other basic elements are incorporated into the riposte play.

Practice example

Partner A performs	Partner B performs
Straight thrust high/inside	
	Parries with quarte parry and ripostes inside/low with a lunge
Parries with octave parry and ripostes high	
	Parries with quarte parry and ripostes high/inside as a feint
Wants to parry with a direct quarte parry	
	Disengages this parry
Parries the disengagement thrust with a circular quarte parry and ripostes high/inside.	

Thus the original situation has been restored and the second or additional cycle respectively, can begin.

With this exercise form it is important to make sure that the structure of the movement is preserved. An unnecessary speed increase during the execution of the cycles must be avoided. Speed increases result from changes in rhythm. The parry should occasionally be skipped to test the sincerity of the partner's attack.

3.1.4 Combative exercises

This form of training (also called "Contres") occupies an intermediate position in the transition from training to competition. In terms of fight actions the technical-tactical elements learned and stabilized thus far continue to be perfected in a "combat-like" way. By the same token one could also say that technical-tactical elements of the competition are taken out and trained separately under stipulated conditions.

The goal is for a fencer to meet his partner, who is acting with maximum resistance, in a predetermined situation. In doing so one partner is primarily the attacker, the other the defender. Both can place the decisive hit; depending on the task, the attacking fencer can do so with basic attacks, remise attacks, and feint attacks, the primarily defending fencer with return or counter attacks. The basic situation is as follows:

The defending fencer assumes the fencing position in such a way that moving back further becomes impossible or can be closely directed. A wall, a bench, a chair, or something similar serves as an obstacle. Markings on the strip (lines, symbols) afford control while retreating (fig. 3.1.-10).

Fig. 3.1.-10:
Starting position for "combat-like" exercises"

The attacker assumes the fencing position at the specified distance and tries to hit the opponent with an action known to the defender (predetermined), or with one of two or more options (elective). The attacker determines the timing of the start of the attack.

This requires that the attacker:
- Conceal the start of the attack and the attack option.
- Execute the attack consistently and quickly.
- Execute the actions with accurate technique.

This requires that the *defender*:
- Recognize the beginning and the type of attack.
- Execute the parry and riposte correctly and at the right time.

In doing so, the attacker increases his power and perfects his technique as well as the consistent use of the attacks. The defender essentially improves his concentration, perception ability and reaction speed.

Practice examples
The defender stands in fencing position. The attacker has the task of attacking with a straight thrust from the middle measure. The defender does a quarte parry and ripostes high/inside.

Possible variations:
- The distance (near, middle, wide measure).
- The relationship of the starting positions of the blades (free, touched, engaged).
- The type of attack (high, low, straight, with disengagement, with cutover, with sweep).
- The parry (from prime to octave).
- The riposte (high, low).

- *Exercises with attack preparation.* The attacker gets the opportunity to conceal his attack by playing with the measure, fencing phrase, or measure play and fencing phrase. Attention must be paid to strictly sticking to the task and maintaining the starting distances at the beginning of the attack.

- *Exercises in time.* The defender changes positions arbitrarily (between all options, only direct, only semi-circular or circular or both, rhythmic or non-rhythmic). The attacker seeks the tempo for an attack on the opening being uncovered (with a direct or disengagement attack). The exercise becomes more fight-like if the attacker is in a wide measure and the defender executes steps forward and backward with the position change. The attack then follows on one of the defender's steps forward. The attacker anticipates the step, and in doing so the expected blade movement from the defender.

- *Optional execution of different attacks.* The basic alternative here is the choice between a basic attack and a feint attack. In doing so the choice should be such that the feint is directed against the target area that can also be hit with a basic attack (e.g., either straight thrust or thrust feint-disengagement thrust, or quarte engagement thrust or quarte engagement-thrust feint-disengagement-thrust respectively).

Appels and short, hard beats may be permitted as an additional maneuver to conceal the attack.

One can see from the few basic exercises listed and their possible variations, which can be used individually or in different combinations, how varied the application of these "combat-like exercises" can be.

There are no limits to the creative initiative of trainers and fencers. All exercises are also suitable as forms of competition.

Methodological tips

- Due to the great emotional effect, increased monitoring and good organization is necessary. Forming a line-out under the trainer's supervision as well as changing partners in a circle or groups of three with independent monitoring by the respective non-practicing fencer, have proven successful. The attackers and defenders should switch or partners should be changed after about 4-10 attacks.

- The situation and the task must be clearly specified. With optional execution of attacks the number of alternatives for beginners should not be more than two, for intermediates four to five.

- Characteristic mistakes in the execution of "combati-like exercises", which the trainer or the fencer who has been named "assistant" must pay particular attention to, are:

For the attacker:

- Nonstop attacks (they lead to technical errors and slow down the attacks).

- Rhythmic time slices between attacks (they make the defender's job easier).

- Slow or recognizable start of the attack due to indecisiveness or lack of power.

- Inconsistent execution of the attack to avoid getting hit by a possible riposte.

For the defender:

- Early (before start of the attack) execution of parry.

- Indecisive or late parry due to lack of concentration or lack of reaction capability.

- Technically inadequate (too wide or too short) parries.

- Attempted evasive movements to the back or side.

- Parrying without riposte.

The defenders are at a disadvantage because the amount of time needed to execute an attack from the middle measure is shorter than that of the defensive action. The defender must anticipate the moment and the direction of the attack.

3.1.5 Schooling and training fights

Schooling and training combat (also called schooling and training assaults) is a direct preparation for applying learned fighting actions in a competition. The so far closely restricted situations during "combative exercises" are expanded and made more competition-appropriate. The object of such fights is to create and recognize the strategically-tactically based situations, to choose and correctly execute the technique, and to seize the right moment.

Categorically dispensing hits is not the focus here, but rather solving specific, precisely specified, combat-like training tasks. This requires constant supervision and correction by the trainer. Experience shows that without constant monitoring by the trainer the so-called schooling and training fights quickly turn into so-called "open fencing fights" in which the desire to score hits impedes the solving of defined, specific training tasks.

The fencers then tend to almost exclusively execute their favorite actions and neglect their broad development. Without monitoring or self-monitoring technical and tactical mistakes can become set and consequently are difficult to correct. The fencers must be trained to strictly adhere to the tasks. As soon as the fencers internalize the tasks, options, and execution forms of the schooling-and training fights, this form of training becomes very popular. Progress in learning occurs very quickly.

The two fencers who face each other in schooling and training fcombat are opponents who, within the limits of the task definition, keep each other from realizing their intentions. The schooling and training fights are complex but depending on the task to be solved, can have technical, tactical, and fight-related sub-goals.

As diverse as a fight can be, all of the special goals and forms of engagement in the schooling and training fights vary just as much. The following are descriptions of a few examples.

3.1.5.1 Fights with technical goals

These serve to perfect and stabilize the fighting technique.

Technical accuracy in fighting actions
It is not the dispensed hits that are assessed, but rather the partner's technical inaccuracies (swinging movements during the thrust, undefined parry, incorrect coordination) are counted as hits.

If an error occurs the schooling fight is suspended, the error is analyzed, and the fight is continued until one of the fencers has "dispensed" a predetermined number of hits.

Technically accurate execution of attack elements
To win the fencer must fence with technical accuracy. The jury or the referee makes a decision according to the rules of the competition. A trainer or an authorized fencer can also make judgments on technically correct execution. The hit is only valid if both issue a "yes".

Repeating actions that were unsuccessful due to technically inaccurate execution
In the case that an action was unsuccessful due to a technical error, the original fight situation is reconstructed, and the unsuccessful action is repeated until a technically positive result is achieved.

Technically accurate and quick execution of a riposte
In doing so, the attacker is required to immediately continue his first attack. A scoring machine set on the shortest time or the referee respectively, decides if the riposte was really fast.

Staying balanced and observing the line
For this the width of the strip is reduced with chalk to 8-16 inches. Technically faulty posture and crossing the side boundary line (with one or both feet) result in a hit.

3.1.5.2 Fights with technical and tactical goals

These fights are more similar to the real combative action, as technique and tactics are linked.

Hitting a specific target area
With the incentive of a higher score the fencer is supposed to focus his attention on strong or weak areas in his attack or his defense.

Target area preferred in attacks by beginners:

- Foil – high/inside, but not high or low/outside.

- Epée – the arm, but not the head.

- Saber – head and side, but not the arm inside.

Tasks can be to only hit high/outside, head or arm inside, or in a fight hits to these areas are awarded two or three points. The fight then continues until a predetermined number of points has been reached.

This approach promotes accuracy, training of not yet solid actions, and eliminates weaknesses.

Specified elements of attack and defense

Here the process is similar to hitting a specific target area. To apply learned elements, stabilize "special actions", or eliminate weaknesses particular elements that can be used to hit or defend are specified or are awarded an appropriately higher score. The tactical emphasis is on deceiving and maneuvering the opponent who knows approximately hich fighting actions will be used. A combination of both options, hitting the specific target area with a specific element, increases the difficulty and requires the fencer to act deliberately.

Repeated elements do not count

This form serves to expand the competition repertoire. One can either bar every basic element or just not permit the same combination during the course of the fight.

A similar form with the opposite goal is that one or two elements are specified and must be executed in different tactical situations.

Without counter-attack

This serves primarily to develop decisiveness and consistency in an attack and to stabilize and perfect the defender's most important parry reflexes.

3.1.5.3 Fights with tactical goals

Fights for the exploration of the opponent

The trainer gives one or both fencers one or more tasks with specific elements or actions for hitting the opponent. These elements or actions should be recognized by the opponent or observing teammates. Whoever was explored most vaguely due to skillful camouflage or recognized the opponent's intentions respectively, is the winner. Not too much attention should be paid to technique. That would detract too much from the actual task.

Fights for mastering the strip

For this purpose the strip is divided with chalk into smaller sections (3.5-5.5 feet). Aside from the regularly scored hits every lost section of the strip is assessed with a penalty hit without interrupting the fight.

Fights for training specific engagement situations

+ With one hit (with an imaginary score of 4-4 or 14-4)
  This requires a maximum of concentration and a healthy risk based on tactical fencing moments.

+ At the end of the strip and the last three feet
  In these situations critical strategic-tactical mistakes are often made in a state of excitement.

Finally a few methodological suggestions regarding the application of schooling and training fights:

- Both fencers always receive clearly formulated training tasks for all schooling and training fights.
- The trainer handles the selection of partners for the fights. In case of performance differences a limit can be placed on the number of hits allowed. Partners should be switched often.
- Every type of schooling and training fight has advantages and disadvantages. Focusing on just one area can have an adverse effect on other factors. The key is a balanced relationship and skillful composition.
- In all cases schooling and training fights should conclude with a free fencing fight. Here every fencer should be given plenty of leeway for his actions. Any errors that crop up should be addressed no sooner than the next training session.

3.2   Lesson with the trainer

The lesson (also individual lessons) is the trainer's individualized instruction with the fencer. In doing so, the trainer is partner as well as opponent and teacher depending on the different content of the tasks. This offers advantages to the process of training individualization that cannot even be equaled by good partner training and competitions. But it must be noted that the trainer can only work with one fencer at a time, in contrast the others must train relatively independently.

That is why careful consideration must be given to when lessons are necessary, which training contents can only be addressed with lessons, where they are advantageous, and when the same goals can just as well be realized with group instruction in form of exercises without a partner, with auxiliary devices, with the various forms of partner training and the schooling and training fights. A private lesson is always something special for the fencer taking the lesson. A lesson with the trainer should never be considered a matter of course or even as a "service on demand".

3.2.1 Lesson goals and purposes

Nearly all goals in specific fencing training can be tracked through lessons.
The primary focal points are:
(1) Emphasizing and training of technical and tactical details of elements of fighting actions, as well as assessing and developing fight situations.
　　　Specific criteria are:
- Nearly imperceptible measure changes.
- Minor changes in the position and pressure ratio of the weapons or the various movement amplitudes of the weapon arm.

- Particular postures or movements as points of reference for possible follow-up actions.
- Subtleties in the progression of movement during specific or evolving situations, among others.

The fencer should have a mental and motor understanding of these fight-determining intricacies. If he can manage this with the trainer's help it will be the foundation for his continued development and his effectiveness as a partner during partner exercises. He will thus be able to direct his own training and recognize his mistakes in a competition.

(2) Finding mistakes and suggesting their elimination
Often the trainer is able to notice specific mistakes and particularly their causes more quickly during the hands-on activity with the fencer rather than by pure observation. Here the trainer can refer to his own wealth of experience as a fencer. As a result means and methods are identified as ways to eliminate these mistakes in continued training.

(3) Communication between fencer and trainer
For advanced fencers the lesson is a means of tactical communication between fencer and trainer. In joint training alternative solutions are developed and acted out. In addition the lesson serves to consistently call the fencer's attention to the breadth of his own action repertoire.

(4) Implementing training focal points
It is not possible to resolve a training focal point during a half hour lesson, it is however important to be instructionally effective at, for instance, nodal points:

- It is relatively easy for a good trainer to restore a fencer's self-confidence and confidence while teaching a lesson after failures in training or competition, by choosing specific elements and exercises, as well as offering praise and encouragement.

- If there are any tendencies towards "arrogance" and carelessness during training the trainer can call attention to mistakes and imperfections during the lesson, thus sending a reminder for objectivity.

- For some fencers lessons before the competition help lessen a certain amount of overexcitement or turn inactivity into activity.

Overall the educational and emotional value of a trainer lesson with the fencer is in no way inferior to the value of any form of training. The lesson should never be viewed as a form of punishment but rather as a distinction. Its educational value is not that of "if you don't train diligently I'll work you over in a lesson", but rather "because you have trained so hard and have progresses so well you will get a lesson!"

Only those fencers, who show focus in their training in the other training forms, receive private lessons.

Depending on the task, the lessons are differentiated by technical, tactical, and fight oriented preparation.

Lessons for technical preparation aim to develop the ability to execute the fighting actions and their combinations within their motion sequence during evolving situations.

Lessons for tactical preparation are intended to enable the fencer to successfully realize strategic goals by exploring, camouflaging, and maneuvering.

Lessons for fight oriented preparation serve to train perception and quick resolution (reaction, reflex) of fight moments.

Beyond that the lessons can also be used to resolve various other tasks (e.g., warm-up lesson, competition preparation lesson, fitness lesson, exam lesson, schooling lesson, etc.). However, these forms will not be elaborated on as they are only special forms of the already mentioned basic variations, and are not much use in the overall training process.

Besides, the effort-usefulness ratio is disadvantageous.

3.2.2 Lesson organization and design

Lessons usually last 20-50 minutes. The following orientations for the individual variants are the result of workload testing:

- For technical preparation: 20-30 min. with 3-5 short breaks for recovery and comments.

- For tactical preparation: 20-30 min. with 3-5 short breaks.

- For fight oriented preparation: 2-3 work phases of about 5-10 min. with 3-5 minute breaks in between.

In its basic structure the design of a lesson corresponds to that of a training unit. A brief, specific warm-up of about 2-3 minutes with routine exercises focuses particularly on loosening up and improves concentration. The warm-up is done before the lesson, independently or with a partner.

Then follows introduction of the task for the main part. The trainer explains the lesson goal, the exercises to be practiced, elements or combinations and the stipulations for their execution. This is done via brief and precise verbalization. This includes defining the trainer's actions, his starting and finishing positions, the different movements of the weapon arm, among other things, as well as the basic action.

The fencer should know from the start if he needs to prepare for agreed actions, for two or three alternatives, or various unknown actions. During the interruptions or breaks respectively, new tasks are assigned, suggestions offered, and corrections made. The work phase should not be interrupted by explanations. It suffices to use agreed gestures, signals or brief verbal comments for information purposes.

The lesson should end with a brief slow-down phase along with routine, successful exercises. At the end of the lesson the fencer should thank the trainer.

3.2.3 Trainer's technique during lesson

The tasks listed require good, specific preparation on behalf of the trainer. It is presupposed that the trainer giving the lesson is familiar with modern fencing technique and regularly works on perfecting his skills. He has the ability to create and diversify various tactical situations.

He creates fight moments through sudden, quick actions and transitions from defense to attack and vice versa, and demands the fencer's constant attention. Anyone who does not possess these abilities and skills should not give lessons until he has perfected his own skills.

The damage a bad lesson can cause is worse than any possible benefit. To be able to persistently execute attack and defensive actions, maintain an overview of the respective situation and recognize the mistakes the fencer is making, and not to fatigue too quickly, the trainer avails himself of a special trainer technique during the lesson.

In the trainer's main position his legs are slightly bent and in stride position with approximately one foot of space in between. The center of gravity is located over both legs and slightly forward, respectively. The weapon arm is slightly bent, the weapon is at the same level as that of the fencer. The weaponless arm hangs down, bent halfway (fig. 3.2.-11).

Fig. 3.2.-1: Trainer position during lesson

This position is comfortable, relaxed, and allows free forward and backward movements "traveling steps", cross steps, and running.

For the attack the trainer uses short lunges or a kind of drop start (fig. 3.2.-2).

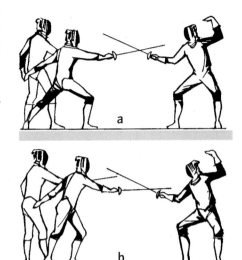

Fig. 3.2.-2: Trainer attack during the lesson

But to carry out of certain tasks it is also necessary to briefly work in fencing position as well as execute real attacks with a lunge or flèche. Every one of the trainer's movements must have a specific purpose. Routine beats that are mostly executed habitually without an actual purpose, are of little use to the fencer. He becomes inured to them. This can have an adverse effect in a competition. Such a beat only has meaning if it is intended to, for instance, emphasize the final moment of a thrust in order to demand a faster execution and suggest a late parry.

Aside from the systemized fencing knowledge the trainer also imparts personal knowledge, skills and experiences during the lesson. As a rule he can only really create such fight moments as those he has observed, analyzed, and personally tested in a real contest. In fencing clubs, where several trainers are employed, it should be a matter of course to confer with each other, help each other and possibly alternate lessons. A trainer who doesn't practice regularly falls behind.

Every trainer personifies a particular type of fencer. It is important to take note of that, because it can have a positive as well as a negative effect on the mutually good understanding between trainer and fencer. Not every fencer can or should personify the trainer's fencing type. It is just as difficult, if not downright impossible, to copy specific peculiarities of another trainer's lessoning style. While it may be outwardly successful, the subtleties, the essence of the situations and moments, will be missing. Exchange of experiences and constant work on oneself are preconditions to being a trainer who gives individual lessons to his fencers. Propriety, mutual understanding and trust between trainer and fencer, as well as optimism lay the foundation for a successful lesson.

3.3 "Tauberbischofsheim fencing lessons" as per the "Emil Beck System"

Irrespective of the preceding generalized positions for the lesson, the "Tauberbischofsheim fencing lessons as per the "Emil Beck System" deserve to be presented separately,

There probably isn't another fencing school in the world that has perfected and successfully implemented a system of lessons that build on each other, for the perfection of competitive technique in fencing as it was done in Tauberbischofsheim, by, and later under the direction of, Emil Beck.

Fig. 3.3.-1:
Emil Beck demonstrates "his" lessons with world champion and Olympic champion
Alexander Pusch in front of a distinguished audience.

The "Tauberbischofsheim fencing lessons" distinguish themselves by the following characteristics:

1. The lessons focus on schooling those motion sequences that are most commonly used for each respective weapon. They are systematically classified and condensed into activity units. This modular system proves to be particularly economical and effective. It is based on the perception that the totality of motion sequences in fencing is composed of individual actions, which, on their part, can be used in any combination.

Accordingly, activity units and action complexes can be constructed via combinations of specific motion sequences, which will remain logical and thus manageable.

The starting basis for each lesson is a single on guard position out of which the combinations of movements are combined. If, for instance, the fencer is given the on guard position sixte, he knows that the lesson will be structured as follows: the first activity is composed of a sixte battuta thrust as preparation, followed by a change to sixte parry-riposte. The second activity unit consists of the same preparation followed by a change to sixte parry-riposte with disengagement. The variations are then run through in that order.

The lessons are designed for épée and foil. They are each comprised of four steps with 2-4 lessons, each consisting of 12-17 activities. The athlete practices each activity with seven different forms of footwork. A complete lesson lasts 20-40 minutes. The trainer determines the number of repetitions in a motion sequence based on the fencer's technical skill level. The movement elements of the defensive activities should be trained in approximately the same volume as the offensive ones (see: Beck, 1978).

2. As can be seen in the two examples from the overall repertoire selected for better comprehension, an explanation of the first activity with all forms of footwork is always given at the beginning of a lesson or at a change in the motion sequence respectively. The following activities within the structure are only described for execution in a standing position. The corresponding footwork can be taken from the first activity.

The description is based on the assumption that the trainer and the fencer are right-handed. If two left-handers face each other, the execution of the lesson should be mirrored. If there is a difference in hand preference between the partners, an analogous application is recommended.

Example 1: Foil fencing lesson, step 1, lesson 1

The trainer is in low on guard position; the athlete engages with octave. The trainer breaks out of the engagement and threatens the athlete with a low line.

1.1   Standing:
Circular octave beat – chest thrust.

1.2   With step forward:
Circular octave beat – step forward, chest thrust.

1.3   With lunge:
Circular octave beat – with lunge, chest thrust.

1.4   With step forward, lunge:
Circular octave bind – with step forward, hold bind – with lunge, chest thrust.

1.5   With jump forward, lunge:
Circular octave bind – with jump forward, hold bind – with lunge, chest thrust.

1.6   With step backward:
With step backward, circular octave parry – chest thrust.

1.7   With jump backward, lunge:
With jump backward, circular octave parry – with lunge, chest thrust.

1.8   With flèche:
Circular octave beat – with flèche, chest thrust.

2.1-8 New activity:
Circular octave bind – side glide.

3.1-8 New activity:
Circular octave beat – chest feint – semi circular quarte parry – half disengagement thrust at side.

4.1-8 New activity:
Circular octave beat – chest feint – semi circular sixte parry – thrust to side.

5.1-8 New activity:
Circular octave beat – circular chest thrust (against) change to octave parry.

6.1-8 New activity:
Circular octave engagement – carry-over to quarte – chest glide.

7.1-8 New activity:
Circular octave engagement – carry-over to quarte – side glide.

8.1-8 New activity:
Circular octave beat – back thrust.

9.1-8 New activity:
Circular octave cutover – back thrust.

Example 2: Epée fencing lesson, step 3, lesson 2

The trainer is in low on guard position; athlete engages with octave. Trainer breaks out of the engagement and threatens the athlete with a high line.

1.1 Standing:
Semi-circular quarte cutover – wrist thrust high – sixte parry – chest thrust – change to quarte cutover – wrist thrust high – safeguard: low line – octave parry – side glide.

1.2 With two steps forward:
Semi-circular quarte cutover – with step forward, wrist thrust high – change to quarte cutover with step forward, wrist thrust high – safeguard: octave parry – side glide.

1.3 With step forward, lunge:
Semi-circular quarte cutover – with step forward, wrist thrust high – change to quarte cutover – with lunge, wrist thrust high – safeguard: octave parry – side glide.

1.4 With two steps forward, lunge:
Semi-circular quarte cutover – with step forward, wrist thrust high – change to quarte engagement with step forward, hold engagement– cutover – with lunge, wrist thrust high – safeguard: octave parry – side glide.

1.5 With step forward / jump forward, lunge:
Semi-circular quarte cutover – with step forward, wrist thrust high – change to quarte engagement – with jump forward, hold engagement – cutover – with lunge, wrist thrust high – safeguard: octave parry – side glide.

1.6 With two steps backward:
With step backward, semi-circular quarte cutover, wrist thrust high – with step backward, change to quarte cutover – wrist thrust high – safeguard: octave parry – side glide.

1.7 With step forward, flèche:
Semi-circular quarte cutover with step forward – wrist thrust high – change to quarte cutover – with flèche, wrist thrust high.

2.1-7 New activity:
Semi-circular quarte cutover – wrist thrust high – sixte parry – chest thrust – change to quarte cutover – wrist thrust low – safeguard: high line – semi-circular sixte parry – carry over to quint – chest glide.

3.1-7 New activity:
Semi-circular quarte cutover – wrist thrust high – sixte parry – chest thrust – change to quarte cutover – thigh thrust – safeguard: high line – semi-circular sixte parry carry over to prime – chest glide.

4.1-7 New activity:
Semi-circular quarte cutover – wrist thrust high – sixte parry – chest thurst – change to quarte cutover – foot thrust – safeguard: high line – semi-circular sixte parry – foot glide.

5.1 Standing:
Semi-circular quarte cutover – wrist thrust high – sixte parry – remise pronated wrist – safeguard: high line – semi-circular quarte parry – foot glide.

5.2 With two steps forward:
Semi-circular quarte cutover – with step forward, thrust supinated wrist – with step forward, remise pronated wrist – safeguard: semi-circular quarte parry – foot glide.

5.3 With lunge:
Semi-circular quarte cutover – with lunge, thrust supinated wrist – remise pronated wrist – safeguard: semi-circular quarte parry – foot glide.

5.4 With step forward, lunge:
Semi-circular quarte bind – with step forward, hold bind – cutover – with lunge, thrust supinated wrist – remise pronated wrist – safeguard: semi-circular quarte parry – foot glide.

5.5 With jump forward, lunge:
Semi-circular quarte cutover – with jump forward, thrust supinated wrist – with lunge, remise pronated wrist – safeguard: semi-circular quarte parry – foot glide.

5.6 With two stepds backward:
With step backward, semi-circular quarte cutover – thrust supinated wrist – with step backward, remise pronated wrist – safeguard: semi-circular quart parry – foot glide.

5.7 With step forward, flèche:
Semi-circular quarte cutover – with step forward, thrust supinated wrist with flèche, remise pronated wrist.

6.1-7 New activity:
Semi-circular quarte cutover thrust supinated wrist – sixte parry – remise thigh – safeguard: high line – semi-circular sixte parry – circular thrust chest (against) change to quarte parry – high line (opposite sixte).

7.1-7 New activity:
Semi-circular quarte cutover – thrust supinated wrist – sixte parry – remise foot – safeguard: high line – semi-circular quarte parry – glide side.

8.1 Standing:
Semi-circular quarte cutover – thrust pronated wrist – octave parry – remise supinated wrist – safeguard: thrust chest – high line (opposite sixte).

8.2 With two steps forward:
Semi-circular quarte cutover – with step forward, thrust pronated wrist – with step forward, remise supinated wrist high safeguard: thrust chest (opposite sixte).

8.3 With lunge:
Semi-circular quarte cutover – with lunge, thrust pronated wrist – remise supinated wrist – safeguard: thrust chest (opposite sixte).

8.4 With step forward, lunge:
Semi-circular quarte bind – with step forward, hold engagement – cutover – with lunge, thrust pronated wrist – remise supinated wrist – safeguard: thrust chest (opposite sixte).

8.5 With jump forward, lunge:
Semi-circular quarte cutover – with advance jump, thrust pronated wrist with l unge, remise supinated wrist – safeguard: thrust chest (opposite sixte).

8.6 With two steps backward:
With retreat step, semi-circular quarte cutover – thrust pronated wrist – with retreat step, remise supinated wrist – safeguard: chest thrust (opposite sixte).

8.7 With step forward, flèche:
Semi-circular quarte cutover with step forward, thrust pronated wrist – with flèche, remise supinated wrist.

9.1-7 New activity:
Semi-circular quarte cutover – thrust pronated wrist – remise chest – high line (opposite sixte).

10.1-7 New activity:
Semi-circular quarte cutover – thrust pronated wrist – remise thigh – safeguard: high line – semi-circular quarte parry – circular thrust chest (against) change to sixte parry – high line (opposite quarte).

11.1-7 New activity:
Semi-circular quarte cutover – thrust pronated wrist – remise foot – safeguard: high line – semi-circular quarte parry – glide chest.

12.1 Standing:
Semi-circular quarte cutover – thrust chest – high line (opposite sixte).

12.2 With step forward:
Semi-circular quarte cutover – with step forward, thrust chest (opposite sixte).

12.3 With lunge:
Semi-circular quarte cutover – with lunge, thrust chest (opposite sixte).

12.4 With step forward, lunge:
Semi-circular quarte engagement – with step forward, hold engagement– cutover – with lunge, thrust chest (opposite sixte).

12.5 With jump forward, lunge:
Semi-circular quarte engagement – with jump forward, hold engagement – cutover – with lunge, thrust chest (opposite sixte).

12.6 With step backward:
With step backward, semi-circular quarte cutover – thrust chest (opposite sixte).

12.7 With flèche:
Semi-circular quarte cutover – with flèche, thrust chest (opposite sixte).

13.1-7 New activity:
Semi-circular quarte engagement – glide chest.

14.1-7 New activity:
Semi-circular quarte beat – thrust chest – high line (opposite quarte).

15.1-7 New activity:
Semi-circular quarte beat – feint chest – quarte parry – thrust chest – high line (opposite sixte).

16.1-7 New activity:
Semi-circular quarte beat – double feint chest (against) quarte sixte parry – thrust chest – high line (opposite quarte).

17.1-7 New activity:
Semi-circular quarte beat – circular thrust chest (against) change to sixte parry – high line (opposite quarte).

If the lesson is a tournament lesson, then one or the other action will suddenly be parried or riposted unannounced, or a counter action or one of the many other possible surprise alternatives respectively, is carried out.

3. Preparation for the lesson with the trainer is based on the ideomotor principle. It is precisely this distinctive feature of the "Tauberbischofsheim fencing lessons" that utilizes sports psychological findings regarding ideo-motor training in an outstanding way.

The insight that regularly repeated, conscious speaking, thinking, and imagining (imagining oneself) of the motion or action sequences practiced (post processing) or to be practiced (preparation) during the lesson, facilitates the learning and training process, was utilized here. This applies to fencers who are learning techniques and action sequences, as well as to fencers who have mastered techniques and actions for some time, On the one hand, with the latter imagination and execution errors may creep in over time, which have to be recognized early on. On the other hand, imagination is subject to fluctuations, as is generally known. Images can, for instance, fade during phases of increased athletic training. The fencer can comprehend the movement or action progression respectively, via a simple verbal description. Specific, and particularly spatiotemporal characteristics of the images (especially the measure and the tempos) can and should be reviewed through sport specific methods.
When a fencer applies one of the "Tauberbischofsheim fencing lessons" for the first time he should have at least some rough images of their progression. The fencer needs an image of what the exercises he wants to execute should look like. The images are based on knowledge from the lessons he can refer to (see example) and on programs that have been stored in memory. The only way the fencer can imagine a movement or action he has to learn or perfect is by referring to the images he has stored of them.

The mental reproduction of a movement perception or motion sequence stored in memory is dominant within the movement concept, which is at the center of the technically accentuated lesson. It contains kinesthetic, optic, tactile, staticodynamic, and possibly acoustic portions, which in their complexity reflect the dynamic, temporal, and spatial relationships between the elements of movement.

- The **spatial component** of a movement concept includes the external characteristics (positions, stance, nodal points, measure, etc.).

- The **temporal component** includes timing, duration, and speed of the sequential or simultaneous movements.

- The **dynamic component** includes strength effort, muscle tension, and rhythm of the movements.

Personal movement experiences especially influence the dynamic parameters of the movement concept.

Movement visualisation also changes in the course of the learning process with regard to its complexity. For the beginner it contains primarily the nodal points of the motion sequence. In the course of learning it becomes more precise and detailed. Once the fencer has acquired the movement skills, an image with a reduced content and fewer nodal points will be sufficient for him (see fig. 2.3.4).

The advantages of a targeted utilization of movement and action visualization during the TBB fencing lessons result from their significance to the development of the fencer's action-related ability:

- They interact with the movement and action program and contribute substantially to its development, and

- they are prerequisite to the processing of information the fencer receives from the trainer, as well as directly from his own movement or action execution.

Ideomotor training in connection with the TBB lessons can be used primarily to resolve the following tasks:

- Speeding up the learning phase for relearning, stabilizing, or newly acquiring movements or parts of movements respectively.

- Preserving motor skills during training breaks due to illness or injury.

- Improving sensorimotor regulation ability, for instance the sense of movement and rhythm.

- Heightened awareness of coping in training because the fencer must verbally describe and mentally pervade the motion sequence.

- Improved concentration and sensorimotor preparation for the motion sequence prior to the lesson.

It is advisable to insert a relaxation phase between the ideomotor preparation of the lesson and the lesson with the trainer.

4. The lessons are executed as "block training" (for instance a weekly cycle). The fencer knows prior to each week which lessons await him that week. The first week's lesson also marks the beginning of his mental training for the rest of the week. This lesson scheme can of course only be used for the technical lessons. But it has the advantage of having fixed written lessons that all trainers are familiar with, so that each one of them can instruct every fencer.

To elevate a technical lesson to the level of a tactical or competitive lesson, it is adapted to the individual fencer.

Due to the largely predefined scheme, which the trainer is also bound by, he has to constantly mentally deal with the activity units as well. Thereby the trainer also trains mentally and, in fact, due to the large number of daily lessons he does so far more than the individual athlete. This type of mental "trainer training" has the effect of improving the trainers' manual skills, which gives them the capacity for fight-like instruction and expands the palette of their technical skills.

5. Finally it must be considered that the success of the "Tauberbischofsheim fencing lessons" are essentially based on the fact that Emil Beck exuded great suggestiveness and emotionality while giving lessons, which incited the fencer to the highest degree of concentration and exertion readiness. Only thereby was it possible to execute activity sequences with optimal speed and to stabilize them by repeating them often.

3.4   Basic orientation for fencing training

Fencing training is a very complex process. Important characteristics are workload-, demand-, and adaptation processes, mental and sport motor training and learning processes, as well as pedagogic, pedagogic-didactic, and training-methodological approaches. At the same time, placing demands on the fencer and the fencer coping with demands is the most significant emotional aspect of the training process (also see Chapter 2).

Below is an analysis of several important **basic orientations for fencing training** with varying significance to the individual areas of implementation.

Fencing training is goal-oriented
This purposefulness manifests itself in the fact that the entire training, as well as the individual demands, every task, every procedure, every method used in training, is directed towards a goal. In doing so a distinction should be made between

performance goals over longer time periods and in-between goals set for medium or even short time periods. To be effective, each individual training unit must be executed with purpose. Goals should not only be established to increase athletic performance or complex performance capacity, but also for sub-tasks, such as, for instance, technique development or development of action-related ability. The development of psychological performance requisites or components and the resolution of educational tasks should also be approached with determination. Goal-oriented training is a precondition to methodicalness and systematics. Focusing on a goal promotes purposefulness, which substantially orientates, motivates, and regulates athletic activity. That is why we also refer to the goal-content-means-method relationship.

Fencing training is methodical and systematic

The training methodology in fencing utilizes accredited orientations for training from other sports combined with the generalized experiences of successful fencing instructors and fencing schools. This manifests itself in ideas and plans for performance development overall, as well as the development of individual performance requisites or components respectively. In doing so there is a conscious progression from a specific initial state to a designated, relative final state. At the same time the education process is optimized and incorrect workloads for the fencers are prevented (hereto Chapter 5). Methodicalness and systematics also help to link important components of the training process (e.g., training and competition, local training and course training, training workload and workload outside of training).

The methodicalness begins by clearly displaying all of the important dates for the training and competition year. That applies to all competitions with designated levels of importance, important job-related, school-related, or private appointments, performance monitoring and tests, sports medical check-ups, and the time breakdown of the training and competition year into goal and task-related periods and phases or sections. In the end the structure of the main competitions determines the training structure (interdependence of goals, content, means and methods).

Multi-year concepts (also conceptual outlines) are jointly worked up and deliberated on by teams of trainers, and are the basis for the yearly training plans for that respective time period. In high performance training these plans are supplemented by individual training plans. Strategic plans represent a certain in-between step between a yearly plan and the preparation of a training unit. They incorporate the results of the previous training segment (also school-, job-, or illness-related absences) and provide specifics on the essential tasks and content of each training unit.

Strategic plans for 1-3 week time periods have proven of value in fencing. They are also basis for the training between competitions during the competition period. Since the various basic forms (group and individual training plans) and types of training plans (multi-year plans, yearly training plans, strategic plans) essentially have identical basic components in all sports, please refer to general literature on training science (Schnabel, G. Harre, D. Krug, J. & Borde, A. (Hrsg.) (2003).

Fencing training is a formative and educational process

Athletic training can only be realized through the fencer's actions on the basis of demands. At first it is not dependent on whether the demands made on the fencers come from outside, for instance from the trainer, or if they are self-imposed by the fencers according to their goals and based on self-discipline related thereto. Both are possible. In each case they develop an emotional and intellectual relationship with the requirements and their accomplishment. In training they process or handle observations, impressions, resistances. This happens by way of high workloads, complicated exercises, and difficult or uncomfortable training partners, or through occurrences like victory and defeat. They are also confronted with other insights from practical sports (e.g., strategy and tactics) and sports science (e.g., tolerance of the connective and supportive tissue system).

At the same time the fencers' age, educational background, training and competition experiences play a significant role. The overall social environment also has an effect on them. They are confronted with standards that regulate the athletic activity and with which a personal relationship must be developed. This includes fencing sport-compatible behavior according to the rules of competition and behavior that is in line with the group standards of the respective training group, the club, or the select team. Performance standards, if necessary for the nomination to an important competition, are also effective in terms of formation and education.

All of these influences add to the development of the fencers' individual relationship with the sport of fencing, fencing training and competition. The field of activity of training and competition does not insubstantially shape the fencer's personality. This shaping can occur spontaneously or be pedagogically controlled.

The specific and methodical formative influence is particularly effective in the training of young athletes.

Fencing training is primarily an individual process

On principle the training is geared toward individually developed and individually operating fencers. Training cannot be effective without consideration of the individual peculiarities. For instance, a training group of young athletes can have accelerated and delayed fencers who require particular attention and a special approach. Other individual training requirements result from characteristics of physical build, state of performance, athletic ability, experience, psychological peculiarities, or individual strategic fighting concepts.

On the other hand, performance capacity in fencing initially cannot be developed without partner training. One cannot fence without other fencers. This is consistent with the character of fencing as a dueling sport. It becomes really obvious in team competitions. The respective performance depends heavily on partners during the competition and partner performance in training. Any types of assistance and positive psychological motor influences, as well as a cheerful training atmosphere depend considerably on the group climate.

Fencing training is theory driven

As a result of scientific work, modern fencing training can be based on a well-drawn up training theory. The training expert has access to a system of insights and skills that allow for a relatively specific and methodical approach. These insights and skills were derived from the laws of performance development. This refers to the structure diagram for fencing training shown in Chapter 2, and orientational basis for training and performance control.

From that arise requirements regarding the relationship of training load, demand, and performance development, the ratio of training load and recovery, and the indivisibility of formation and education in the training process, as well as the methodical steps in technical or strategic-tactical training, the contradictory effect of endurance and power training on the muscle, among other things. Particularly in professional sports, methodologists, biomechanical engineers, physicians, psychologists, and educators increasingly contribute to the training process, gain new insights, and put them directly into practice. Even qualified trainers benefit from the processing of scientific findings.

A responsible fencing trainer must be required to base his own work on the respective current level of scientific knowledge and continue to educate himself. Most of the problems in fencing require a multidisciplinary approach. In doing so the collaboration of fencers and trainers is essential.

3.5 Competitions

As previously mentioned, the performance capacity sought in fencing is based on a psycho-physiological potential that is complex in structure, as well as specific sports-technical and strategic-tactical skills. During the training process there is, aside from the need for intermittent concentration on individual performance factors, the requisite to also develop the performance capacity in its complexity or according to the structure respectively. In fencing this can only happen through the indivisibility and with the interaction of training and competition. Competitions therefore are not just target goals in training but also means to performance development. They are training means, as well as training goals. Competing against high-ranking opponents or training partners enrich the competition experience and, with proper training-methodological application, lead to heavy loading of the fencers, and the stabilization of sports-technical and strategic-tactical skills. On principal, psychological competitive qualities can only be developed through competitions with varying degrees of difficulty.

Competitions as training means

Unlike the schooling and training fights, competition fights do not place restrictions on the fencers' technical, tactical, and fight-related options. In competition fights the fencer reassesses the effectiveness of his technical skills, and his action-related ability and its stability during the various fight situations and against different opponents. He gains confidence in his actions and monitors his physical fitness level and his mental state. He checks the efficiency of his competition preparation and his break arrangement between the individual competition fights, and he learns how to prepare himself for each fight during the course of the tournament.

Most important is to gain fight experience from the most diverse fight situations and with the most diverse opponents. This task can only be accomplished almost exclusively in competition fights.

In training only approximately realistic competition-specific situations can be created. Additionally it must be noted that, aside from the large fencing centers, the number of relatively equally strong opponents in a club is not very large. Each of these opponents has strengths and weaknesses and certain peculiarities in the way they fight which, after many fights, everyone is familiar with.

After frequent fights against each other, this can lead to stereotypical behavior and to a greater vulnerability against other unfamiliar opponents. In addition there is a lack of inner excitement and occasionally of the complete mobilization of available options. Such fights, which are executed without inner interest, are often more damaging than beneficial.

Precondition to the participation in competitions is that the fencer possesses the physical, psychological, technical and strategic-tactical prerequisites needed to resolve the competitive tasks that are given. The minimum requirement for fighting a competition fight is that the fencer has mastered a basic attack and several defensive elements in their basic technical form, and knows how to tactically apply them. Also required are a proper weapon, competition attire that is in accordance with safety regulations, basic knowledge of competition rules, and a cheerful, optimistic attitude. The joy of competing against the opponent should not be clouded by any unpleasant occurrences. The competition organizers, the group leader, and every trainer hereby carry a major responsibility.

The degree of difficulty of the competitions goes up with an increase in performance capacity. Fights against opponents of equal strength are preferable. But individual stronger opponents should not be avoided.

Number and character of the competitions are based on the period of the yearly training cycle, and the training level and performance class of the fencers.

When evaluating the competition results it is important that the achieved victory or placement is not rated higher than the training level that is evident in the competition result. How the result was achieved must always be taken into consideration.

Every good trainer tries to objectify the state of his fencers' performance through focused observation of the competitions. In doing so, he must primarily register the effectiveness of the fighting actions and any occurring mistakes. Ranking points and positions are definitely not enough.

In accordance with the training level and performance class, the following orientations are issued to competitions that are intended for performance build-up:

Fundamentals training (age 11/12)
- The competitions are highly motivating as a form of training and workload.
- The competition content is geared specifically to the adaptive line of the sport and discipline.
- The competition mode is simplified, the rules are adapted to the respective ages.
- Official competitions are to be combined with the monitoring of training goals.
- The competitions are spread out evenly throughout the year.
- There is no specific preparation for competitions during fundamentals training.
- The competitions provide conditional information regarding specific aptitude at the rate of training complexity to result.

Buildup training (age 13/14)
- The competitions have a dual function: form of training and official performance record.
- The temporal orientation occurs in varying periods.
- No modification of the rules of competition, but goal-dependent mode changes.
- The competitions are very important to the development of specific adaptability.

Continuing-, performance, and high performance training (age > 16, > 18, > 19)
- The competitions play a major role and possess central regulatory function:
  + in the increasing of complex performance.
  + for performance realization to peak level.

+ The competitions are the form of training with the highest specific degree of integration and self-controlling effect.
+ The competitions are modified in the course of the year; their importance depends on the timing of the maximum specific function level (main competition of the year).

Competition highpoint

The highpoint of the competition (main competition) is the crowning point and final goal of a training year or a multi-year training cycle. All training-related events and the majority of competitions are secondary. As a rule, the training year is oriented to the competition highpoint. Two highpoints in one year are an exception and only possible if they are far enough apart so the fencer can physically recover and get prepared again.

In past years, the interest of the FIE, the tournament organizers, the sponsors, and of course also the fencers, has led to an enormous increase in important tournaments. The competitive season spans 8 to 10 months. Many competitions require a certain short-term preparation and interrupt the long-term preparation. This is contrary to the principles of effective and methodical training for the main competitions of the season (World Championships, Olympics), and inevitably leads to a slower general development and a decreased absolute performance capacity. Every trainer and fencer must be well aware of this.

Objectively it is not possible to be well prepared for every competition and at the same time want to strive for optimal performance development.

Immediate competition preparation

Competition highpoints require special preparation. In its overall structure this immediate competition preparation is a yearly training cycle reduced to a few weeks. After a brief recovery break (usually after the last qualifying competition for the highpoint) follows a preparation phase with an increased volume of the initially versatile, later specific training. After that the performance is built up and stabilized. The immediate competition preparation cannot make up for what was missed during the training year.

The immediate competition preparation serves to stabilize the existing performance level in accordance with the state of the performance, and to mobilize possible additional performance reserves. Competitions during the phase of immediate competition preparation serve the buildup, stabilization, and control of performance capacity.

But qualification for the highpoint should have already happened before the start of this training phase, because the psychological preparation and attitude is very important to the upcoming competition.

Top fencers must have access to adaptively sufficient periods of training and competition workload, as well as recovery time. This can be achieved by:

- Differentiating important and unimportant competitions.

- Courage to set limits if systematics suffer due to competitions.

- Competition series during phases of increased intensity (cycles).

- Periodic complete abstinence from competition to preserve mobilization options and for reactivation.

- Paying attention to physical recovery after important competitions.

- Frequent monitoring of progression and state of adaption via control competitions with performance diagnostics (performance control).

3.6 Methodical steps for the development of a fencer's competitive skills

The complex and complicated structure of performance in fencing, how it works in every fight (compare Chapter 2.1), requires the complex development and parallel perfecting of all the abilities, skills, and qualities involved in achieving performance. This pertains to the indivisibility of technique and tactics. Executing a movement with accurate motor movement is not enough to successfully resolve a fight situation.

In training attention should be paid right from the start to the most appropriate adaptation of fencing-specific skills to strategic-tactical requirements. The connection between fitness-related and movement regulating abilities and technical-tactical skills should also be taken into account, because fitness-related and movement regulating abilities make up the basic requirements for optimal development and application of technique and tactics in fencing. This applies to the beginner as well as the top fencer, the latter on a higher level.

Of equal significance are the relationships that exist between technique, tactics, as well as fitness and the fencer's personal characteristics.

None of these factors are developed automatically. Their development is as elementary as possible and as complex as necessary. This principle should be taken into account with regard to the teaching method, the choice of training means and forms, and with training design. In order to provide a reasonably clear description of this extremely long and complex process, it will be broken down into four steps and summarized in the following specifications.

Step 1: Development of versatile fitness-related and movement regulating fundamentals and learning of basic technical-tactical skills

While developing fitness fundamentals, which at this level is done primarily with a variety of training means (supplementary sports), aside from the all around training, the development of power stands in the foreground.

The skills of the sports used for fitness training (particularly game sports) are learned step by step. This is of advantage to the fencer's continued development and at the same time creates a broader pool of versatile movement experiences.

The development of basic fencing movement skills happens through the repetition of motion sequences under standardized conditions, after an accurate demonstration by the trainer. After some initial habituation exercises with the weapon in the unnatural fencing position without strict error monitoring, the technical elements are first executed while standing, later with movement. A broad repertoire of technical elements that are schooled relatively simultaneously helps in gathering specific movement experiences, and supports the development of movement-regulating (fitness-related) requirements.

The regimented training under standardized conditions, good monitoring, and accurate error correction are necessary, but should not be prolonged. Exercise combinations and fight-like tasks ensure a versatile training session. Training means are exercises without a partner, exercises on training devices, and partner exercises with a passive partner.

With increasing confidence, movement accuracy and fluent execution, the technical elements, with regard to tactical requirements, are differentiated and diversified. This applies primarily to the coordination of legs and weapon arm depending on the distance from the fencing dummy or partner. Leading off with reactive requirements for the execution of techniques increases the difficulty and provides new requirements.

As the skill level goes up the continued perfecting of technique can be combined with the development of fitness-related abilities. Performance comparisons and contests can promote the readiness for competitive fencing and the fun of competing against others.

During this phase, a positive attitude about training, familiarization with hygiene procedures, pursuit of excellence, development of fight readiness and other psychological traits are the focal points of personality development. This requires joyful training without monotony and with a constantly increasing demand. Sports and combative games provide the necessary balance to what initially seems not very emotionally affective development of basic technique.

Step 2: Perfecting fitness-related abilities that are characteristic of fencing, as well as strengthening and application of basic technique according to the specific fight situation

In this step the abilities characteristic of fencing, such as power and specific endurance, are developed during the continued diverse perfecting of all fitness-related abilities.

The technical elements are executed systematically while determining the number of repetitions, the tempo of the execution, and by means of additional tasks, alongside the stabilization of the motion sequence for the development of fitness-related abilities. Attention should be paid to the consistant quality of the motion sequence. The training workloads must always include elements of the target performance and must "anticipatorily" lay foundations for coping with future requirements.

Strengthening the basic technique while applying it in fight situations (basic technical-tactical skills) still occurs under relatively consistent conditions. A typical,new moment in this step is the contest with an opponent.

The execution of elements is temporally and spatially dependent on the opponent. The perfecting and differentiating of movement skills with regard to the fight situation occurs under these conditions. Training means are exercises on training devices and partner exercises that are executed alternately and cyclically. "Fight-like exercises" and fights, particularly with technical goals, are essential.

*Step 3:   Continued perfecting of fitness-related abilities and development of basic
strategic-tactical elements in their situation-specific application.*

Physical fitness is perfected primarily through special exercises. Every adaptive reaction is aimed at the distinctive and idiosyncratic impulse combination for the subsequent fencing performance (special exercises), and to assure good workload capacity (supplementary exercises).

At the same time, the continued development and stabilization of individual fitness-related abilities should be elementary and should be done together with the technical-tactical skills.

With increased strengthening of the technical-tactical skills, the opponent's activity level is gradually heightened. The exercise conditions become more situation contingent, meaning more dependent on the opponent's behavior. The technique becomes variably accessible in accordance with the opposing conditions. A change in conditions occurs via the opponent's changing of the measure, and through a change of position, rhythm, and the pressure ratio of the weapon. The fast action tempo required for this creates additional problems.

The strategic-tactical abilities and skills are developed in such a way, that a specified strategic goal may be realized through targeted creating and utilizing of fight situations (exploring, camouflaging, maneuvering). Depending on the fencer's prerequisites, education level, and fighting disposition, one or several situations with specific or varying maneuvers are prepared.

Equally important is the training of reaction ability in present, anticipated, or not anticipated fight moments. Developed are primarily defensive reflexes, reaction and differentiation capacity and anticipation ability.

This requires the interaction and the competing actions of both opponents. Only then do realistic fight situations develop that require the kind of reactions and well-coordinated movements and movement combinations that are recognized as being expedient and purposeful fighting actions. This complex schooling of technical-tactical abilities and skills corresponds to the character and desire of the fencer who seeks out the opponent and the fight-like combative situation.

Training means consist primarily of "fight-like exercises", schooling and training fights, as well as individual lessons. If the fencers perpetually make the same technical-tactical mistakes (bad habits, heavy one-sidedness, coordination errors, among others), it becomes necessary to fall back on the sub-method. Here the specific individual characteristics of the technical-tactical mistakes must be differentiated. Individual phases, difficult movement combinations, and particularly the incorrect elements are pulled out of the complex and practiced separately. Such mistakes are quickly overcome by intensive practice of the individual elements through good monitoring and conscious self-monitoring. Effective are monitored partner exercises and lessons on technical preparation.

Step 4: Perfecting and stabilizing the fencer's competitive ability

A fencer's competitive ability is the complex ability that directly determines the performance during a competition based on the individual performance factors. It is the connection between psychological and motor processes that are needed to resolve combative tasks.

Perfecting and stabilizing fighting ability happens primarily through fight-like forms of training, practice competitions, and competitions. The fencers apply their perfected skills and abilities in various fight situations, and against different opponents, review their options and gather fight experience. They continue to gain confidence in their actions. It is just this kind of enrichment of the fight experience through fight-like forms and competitions that is most important to the development of competitive ability. In terms of method, the focus here is not on success (the emotional effects), but rather on applying and reviewing under realistic conditions that which has already been learned.

This requires a conscious approach to the training fight as a methodical training step. Only a seriously fought fight – and that includes trying out new resolution options – creates nearly realistic situations. The more realistic the situation, and the more accurately it is perceived, the more valuable are the images that are stored as experiences. For instance, during less serious fights the partners mostly face off in a near measure, because it is also less strenuous during an attack. They get used to the near measure, then unconsciously behave the same way in competition, and wonder why they don't have a chance against the opponent's attacks.

All of these fights should have specific methodological tasks, and if necessary be interrupted briefly to describe and correct mistakes (specific tasks like exploring, camouflaging, maneuvering, specific elements, attack spurts, standard situations, final meter, starting command of the president of the jury, tie, etc.). If these fights are primarily for reviewing purposes, then the competition results and the training level determined on the basis of observation are of equal importance.

Training means and-forms are schooling and training fights, various forms of competition, and also fights with the trainer.

In fig. 3.6.-1 on page 144, the goals and tasks for the parallel performed strategic-tactical and technical-coordinative training are summarized and compared in sequential steps.

Between the two specific fencing training columns one can view the most expedient primary forms of training. The bottom four steps, shown in ascending order approaching the competition, can also be implemented in the form of individual lessons.

BASIC METHODS

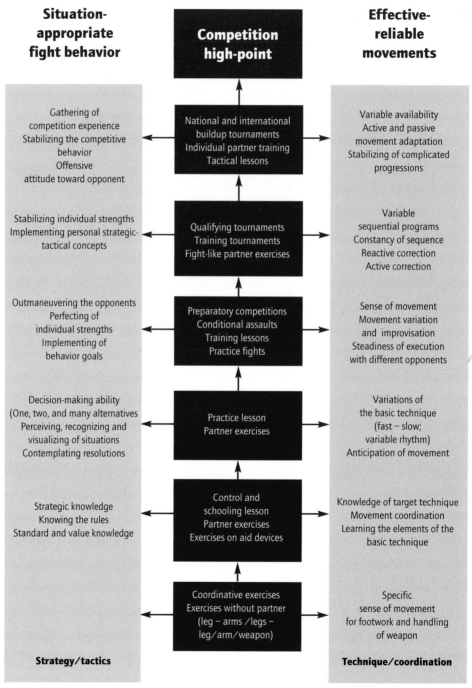

Situation-appropriate fight behavior

Competition high-point

Effective-reliable movements

| Gathering of competition experience Stabilizing the competitive behavior Offensive attitude toward opponent | National and international buildup tournaments Individual partner training Tactical lessons | Variable availability Active and passive movement adaptation Stabilizing of complicated progressions |

| Stabilizing individual strengths Implementing personal strategic-tactical concepts | Qualifying tournaments Training tournaments Fight-like partner exercises | Variable sequential programs Constancy of sequence Reactive correction Active correction |

| Outmaneuvering the opponents Perfecting of individual strengths Implementing of behavior goals | Preparatory competitions Conditional assaults Training lessons Practice fights | Sense of movement Movement variation and improvisation Steadiness of execution with different opponents |

| Decision-making ability (One, two, and many alternatives Perceiving, recognizing and visualizing of situations Contemplating resolutions | Practice lesson Partner exercises | Variations of the basic technique (fast – slow; variable rhythm) Anticipation of movement |

| Strategic knowledge Knowing the rules Standard and value knowledge | Control and schooling lesson Partner exercises Exercises on aid devices | Knowledge of target technique Movement coordination Learning the elements of the basic technique |

| | Coordinative exercises Exercises without partner (leg – arms /legs – leg/arm/weapon) | Specific sense of movement for footwork and handling of weapon |

Strategy/tactics

Technique/coordination

Fig. 3.6.-1:
Methodological training steps of strategic-tactical and technical-coordinative training

144

3.7 Training control

The main purpose of training control is the purposive, regulative effect on the training process via planning, monitoring, evaluation and control methods. Training control should help to systematically develop athletic performance capacity and athletic form.

Figure 3.7.-1 is a schematically simplified illustration of the training process and the function of training control.

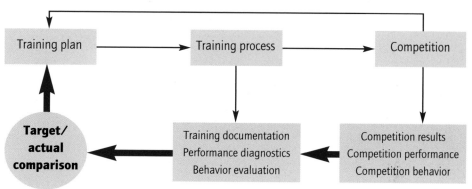

Fig. 3.7.-1: Schematic illustration of training and performance control

The training plan is designed by a training team or by the trainer himself (for the group or an individual fencer, short-, medium-, or long-term).

For an interdisciplinary approach, the training team also includes specialists in the concerned fields of knowledge and activity, doctors of sports medicine, psychologists, biomechanical engineers, and physical therapists. The fencers should be included in this process.

The tasks designated in the training concept or plan, are carried out during the training process. The planned increase in performance capacity through training should bring about better results at competitions.

The competition results are stated more precisely by means of exact competition analyses. The training process is documented and controlled through performance analyses.

It is clear that training control only makes sense if all of the important elements necessary for control are available: training plan – training documentation – performance monitoring – competition analysis – and, of course, the instruments for regulation of the processes.

Training control in a sport as complex as fencing cannot reasonably be carried out with results from isolated status investigations, whether it is a lactate determination or a specific power-time-progression. Most often the process begins with comparisons between planned and completed training and the competition performance. This provides the trainer with insights into the interrelation of training and performance and statements regarding efficacy of training-methodological procedures. The last column of the training structure diagram (table 2.1.-2) shows the stages of goals, means and methods of performance control. It makes apparent how varied and complicated the designing of optimal fencing training is.

The starting point is always the specific developmental status of the fencer's performance capacity. The general target for the fencer who is to be trained is derived by comparison from the specificity of the performance structure of top fencers, and a training plan is then worked out. The plan can be for one training year, for a multi-year training segment, as well as for the overall development. This goal, which focuses on the developmental level of the individual factors as well as the complex fencing performance, defines the training process. The developmental growth with respect to the starting performance is determined through performance diagnostics (objectifying of sub-performances and performance requisites) and through competitions and the competition analyses that are performed at the same time. This performance increase, in turn is the starting point for determining the new goal.

3.8 Warming up before training and competition

The intended effectiveness of the training increases the importance and the value of the warm-up. The warm-up serves the fencer's optimal preparation for the imminent workload demands, as well as the psychological, functional-organic, strategic-tactical, and particularly the coordinative-motor aspects. The physiological functioning state that is essential to the training process is improved in terms of the "warm-up". Aside from improving the functional readiness of the organ systems, the goal of a general warm-up is, among other things, to increase flexibility and muscular activity, to loosen up tense muscles, and to elevate the "working temperature".

The *general warm-up* brings the overall functional readiness of the organ systems to a higher level. In contrast, a *specific warm-up* should achieve an improved adjustment of the correlation between sport-specific requirements and the activity of the central nervous system essential thereto, combined with the neuromuscular transmission behavior.

Thus an increase in the organism's performance capacity at the start of athletic activity is not only indicative of the change in the functional activity of the locomotor system, but also of an increase in the functional readiness of the central and peripheral nervous system. The concentration and reaction readiness essential to a superior training effect and the capacity for differentiated movement perception and control facilitates appropriate exercise repetitions from the beginning of specific fencing training, and prevents incorrect attempts. Here the ideo-motor training must also be classified as described in the "Tauberbischofsheim fencing lessons" (Chapter 3.3). That is why the exercises included in the specific warm-up must correspond to the fencing-specific requirements, such as concentration, reaction, coordination and speed. It is important that the fencer execute all requirements consciously and accurately.

The psycho-physiological function sequences that are essential to the "main part" of the training and competition are optimized through an appropriate warm-up program. The implementation of the warm-up process, and particularly its specific portion, should be greatly personalized. This also stimulates personal preparation ("collecting oneself") and any thoughts that might interfere with the training "stay outside". For the trainer the type and intensity of the warm-up is an "external indicator" of his fencer's training readiness.

The currently practiced tournament mode (unseeded fencers, no repechage, long breaks between fights) makes appropriate, individually designed and tested warm-up programs even more important. Many a top fencer has lost to seemingly weaker opponents in the first fight.

Figure 3.8.-1 illustrates the process of a fencer's personalized warm-up for competition-specific training or for a competition.

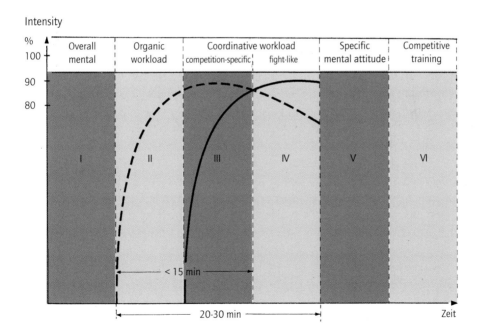

Fig. 3.8.-1: Warm-up before training and competition.

Phase 1: It includes the fencer's overall mental attitude in regard to the training requirements. It actually begins on the way to training and reaches its specific intensity upon entering the gym.

Phase 2: The task is a varied organic workload with the objective of activating the cardiopulmonary systems and the metabolism by gradually increasing the intensity through nonspecific and specific physical exercises. The intensity can reach up to 100% of the assumed physical performance capacity.

Phase 3: The warm-up program is supplemented by requirements that place high demands on the movement-regulating system (coordination), while retaining an intensive physical workload,

Phase 4: is necessary when competition-specific tasks must be resolved consecutively (fight-like training, training competitions, competition). For this the fencers pick their "favorite partner" and playfully perform small open fights. However, "serious" fights should also be incorporated prior to competitions.

Phase 5: After the physically active phase follows the fencers' specific mental tuning for the imminent training or competitive task. Movement and action visualizing (psychological) methods can also be applied during this phase.

In a sensible, specific warm-up that goes beyond the simple stretches and limbering exercises often seen, lie great reserves for a more effective use of available training time. Before the fencer is asked to train longer or more often, he should first train better. That begins with a proper warm-up. A trainer who begins a lesson with a fencer who is "not independently warmed up" relegates himself to a fencing dummy.

3.9 About the role of the trainer in the training process

The trainer occupies the leading role in the training and competition process. To the fencer he is the most essential and permanent important person. He has a strong influence on the fencer. Next to the trainer, particularly in professional sports, the doctor, the physical therapist, the psychologist, and the educator (i.e., the career advisor) also do extremely important work. It is primarily they who help shape the scientific character of fencing training. The doctor and the masseur largely ensure the fencers' welfare, set up prophylactic physical therapy procedures, take care of the fencers at competitions and in case of injuries and illnesses. Next to the trainer, of course, they are often considered as the fencers' confidantes.

Since other people, like team leaders, manager, teammates, officials, parents, relatives, teachers, and more, influence the fencers, these influences must be bundled and matched to the standardized goal and task. This can only be done through the trainer. That is why his capability and his leadership, which is based on trust, deserve a key role. By means of the options for individual lessons, fencing training offers excellent possibilities.

The young fencers are of course much more oriented to the trainer as the important person than is true of the experienced fencers, who are overall more independent and may have a more critical outlook on training and trainer. In this case a purely authoritarian leadership would almost certainly lead to failures. That is why the involvement of the fencers in determining training and competition goals, planning and evaluating training and competitions, determining strategy and tactics for competitions, training organization, and more, is in fact indispensable.

Positive training results are not achieved by affecting the training athlete, but on the contrary, through the athlete's active, close examination of the sport and himself.

To be able to do so, the athlete must already learn this in youth training. The children's fencing books "Learning Fencing" and "Training Fencing" were created for this purpose.

4   Youth training

Perceptions, experience, and knowledge regarding the design of systematic youth training in fencing are extensive, but also problematic. On the one hand, youth training employs means, methods, and forms of organization like those also used in other phases of long-term training and performance development. On the other hand, youth training has its own goals, content, and structure. The initial value and reference parameter for goals in youth training is the generalized requirement specification for fencing and its disciplines, and the performance structure of top fencers (compare Chapter 2.2). It is also important to know which skills or characteristics should be developed to what degree during which training stage and how to evaluate them, so subsequent training tasks can be derived therefrom.

Aside from the two comprehensive training goals in youth training

- development of fencing-specific action-related ability and
- development of physical workload tolerance, as well as the fencer's psycho-physiological stabilization, the ideal training path for the long-term, systematic and age-appropriate training for children in basic training as well as fundamental principals and advanced training, shown in figure 4.-1, is recommended.

Training phase	Age	Goals, main tasks and training forms
Basic athletic training	up to age 10	**Versatile base of motor prerequisites** and movement experiences Learning fencing up to the **beginner's exam** Dealing with success and failure in contests and first competitions, **happy communal experiences,** Predominance of **group training** General / specific training ratio 60% / 40%.
Basic training	age 11/12	**Speed and movement oriented** diverse motor development **Versatile technical training** (emphasis on speed and rhythm) and starting basictactical qualifications Developing **independence and long-term motivation** in fencing; learning **partner training** General / specific training ratio **50% / 50%**
Advanced training	age 13/14	Stabilizing of **diverse technical and tactical repertoire** combined with increased speed and reaction requirements Recognizing **particular strengths** and beginning development of particular strengthsthrough **individual lessons** **Competitions** have a dual function: complex training form and performance proficiency Beginning of winning and behavior-oriented training General/specific training ratio **30% / 70%**

Fig. 4.-1: Concept: Youth training in the DFB (from Barth & Wargalla, 1995)

4.1 Basic information on youth training

(1) A solid and versatile athletic preparation is a precondition to children's the long-term commitment to the sport of fencing and for a basic training that can be expanded on. This can be achieved primarily by improving the quality and effectiveness (the degree of efficiency) of the long-term structure of children's and youth training. While doing so, it would be unreasonable to aspire to specific performance development within increasingly younger athletes, thus overemphasizing competition results at the beginning of the developmental path.

(2) The often-required age-appropriate or age-dependent exercise-, training-, and workload organization for children and adolescents most often follows general biological, psychological, and pedagogic developmental models. These offer general guidelines for the training process, based on highly generalized mean data, to guide the evaluation of the children's individual level of development. It should be noted that the developmental steps for specific youth training should always be utilized in a positive way in terms of time segments of particular trainability, and not in the sense of particular protection.

Children are largely protected from excessive muscular demands by biological mechanisms (low content of glycolic enzymes in the muscle tissue, low catecholamine level) and are considerably more able-bodied and performance-motivated, and thus more workload tolerant and trainable than generally thought. However, extending the training time clearly causes a decrease in the effectiveness of the exercise and training effect. Not yet stabilized coordination patterns (technique patterns), particularly the rhythm-speed-characteristics essential to speed and accuracy-oriented techniques, can be negatively impacted (also called "error training").

(3) Important information regarding workload for children is as follows:
- Decreased workload tolerance of the support system, particularly the skeleton, thus avoidance of one-sided workloads.

- No strength training with weights that place lots of stress on the skeleton, particularly the spine.

- No training with injured (even slightly injured) children, even if they only have a cold.

- Differentiated requirements that are appropriate to the level of biological developmental and the training age even with group training (early bloomers, average, and late bloomers, beginner or more experienced).

The calendar age does not offer adequate orientation. In this age category the biological developmental age can differ by 2 to 3 years in either direction.

Thus a 12-year old child can biologically be like a 10-year old child (late bloomer) or like a 14-year old child (early bloomer). The biologically younger child will need time to mature and the biologically older child should not be overrated. The difficulty lies in making choices for each child, so the majority of attempts are successful and end with a positive result.

The concept of "training activity" is also geared towards personal goals, self-motivation, self-monitoring, and self-evaluation. An important educational goal in children's training is that the children learn to determine and thereby gently raise their own aspiration level and the difficulty level of the tasks.

As a rule, the children should always get plenty of sleep, should have a good diet, and sufficient relaxation and diversion.

(4) Children's training can be made more effective through better utilization of developmentally conditional time segments of good trainability. Without sacrificing variety, special attention must be paid to the skills and characteristics necessary for the subsequent fencing performance.

- Even at the preschool age, exercise forms of a technical nature that can be combined with reaction exercises are a good idea.

- Next to learning how to properly practice and train, the training of fundamental fencing-specific technical elements with respect to correct spatiotemporal structure (movement rhythm) and the perfecting of movement-regulatory (also coordinative) abilities, begins at early school age (age 7 to 10).

The children start out with the foil or saber. Competitive activities can begin around age nine.

(5) Children's training has extensive effects; it is educational (geared towards the children's overall personality development), instructive and adaptive (geared towards regulation and self-regulation processes/practice and training as a learning activity), socializing (acquirement of standards, rules, behavior patterns, dealing with expectations, cooperation in partner training – confrontation in competition), and is affectively effective (considerate of moods, sentiments and feelings, ensures positive experiences, processes wants and needs, takes place in a cordial, affectionate and open-minded atmosphere).

In the sport of fencing, which is primarily geared towards individual performances, group and partner training is particularly important and child-appropriate. In training, children mostly need other children. This develops a mutual sense of responsibility.
Figure 4.1-1 shows what children really want in fencing.

Fig. 4.1.-1:
What children look for
in fencing training

Most of all to fence

Interesting
training

Compete against
others

Lots of activity
and diversion

Performance comparison
with their peer

This development should not be hampered by too much focus on lessons with the trainer.

Encouragement
and solace

Approval
and praise

Children's training is not a reduced form of adult training. Competitive sports for children make sense from a pedagogical standpoint and are beneficial

Performance acknowledgement and progress

Experience success

Children's trainers who understand
their desires and concerns

when they are designed for an extended time period and are geared towards achieving top performances in the future (long-term performance buildup).

In fencing the best time to begin with systematic exercises and training is around age of eight. At this age the responsibility for the children's overall development takes precedence to training and competition standards.

(6) A concept that focuses on long-term youth training can only be successfully implemented if an adequate competition system is effectively embedded and has a motivating, valuing, and regulating function.
Competition content is determined by the fundamental goals and tasks of youth training.

Aside from fencing-specific competitions that primarily ensure sufficient motivation for the accelerated ("early bloomers") and those with more training experience, development-oriented competitions or forms of competition should focus more on regulating and evaluating fitness-related and coordinative versatility, quality of technical execution, and components of the "fighting and confrontation ability".

Competitions and contests contribute to the development of psychological stability, particularly success and failure stability, and therefore are important training means.

In contrast, "title competitions" often lead to undue performance pressure with children, due to an over-evaluation of results. The rewarding of youth trainers against the competition results of the children inevitably promotes this trend and induces premature specialization and one-sided training.

The structuring of competitions should therefore be age-related and have total workload limits.

(7) Good, meaning primarily versatile and educational, beginner and youth training that offers the children sufficient freedom of action, has positive repercussions with respect to the children's overall development process. It improves the specific and general learning conditions, and also produces positive, specific and general muscular and motor adjustment reactions. It creates and satisfies needs, adaptation-readiness and -ability, and the childlike impulse for independence and self-awareness.

During this process of practice, training, and competition while actively examining the associated diverse requirements, the children increasingly identify emotionally and individually with their sport, the training and competition, and the attained results.

Children with a dominant competition-oriented attitude (competition- and fight-oriented, success-motivated) will tend toward competitive sport-oriented training, while the others will orient towards the practicing, the social interaction or personal ability respectively, and will pursue fencing as an enjoyable leisure activity. Motivating training must increasingly take these individual differentiations into account.

In smaller clubs this is made feasible through differentiated tasks and goals. Larger clubs differentiate between competitive sport groups with result-oriented basic methodology and aptitude groups with primarily process-oriented methods. In children's training this differentiation should never be used as a measure of value for fencing training. Both areas are open to constant changeover.

(8) Currently there is no scientifically verified system for talent determination. Besides, in the area of children there are no compelling reasons for making early selections.

Since talent for future top performance in fencing is less characterized by the competitive performance that has been exhibited or the current development of so called "performance determining abilities" during childhood, but rather by the anticipated performance development potential in consideration of the present performance relative to the respective developmental age, a motivating and "aptitude-forming" training in fencing is most important.

This process should be accompanied by comprehensive and personalized training and development documentation. Youth training is training that develops aptitude and conserves and nurtures talent.

(9) Children's training presents a monumental pedagogic-psychological and methodological task. What and how a fencer will be in the future depends significantly on the quality of his first practice days, weeks, months, and years. "Investing" in the primarily pedagogic-psychological training, further training, and advanced training of children's trainers in particular, in the formulation and dissemination of pedagogic-methodological aids for the creative work of youth trainers, and the search for new training-methodological solutions are the most important matters for the continuity of fencing in its breadth and for the sustainment of performance capacity.

4.2 Pedagogic-methodological recommendations for youth training

The significance, specifically of those initial contacts with fencing and the first years of the learning process are pivotal to young fencers' future development. Anyone who wants to still enjoy fencing as an adolescent or adult or wants to successfully engage in a competitive sport as an adolescent or adult must already acquire the joy of fencing and the successful development essential to the pursuit of excellence during childhood.

What becomes of beginning fencers is most often determined at the beginning of their career. When beginning fencers enjoy practicing, curiosity can turn into enthusiasm.

But it can also happen that they don't return after the initial practice sessions because they think the whole thing is too boring, because the trainer constantly corrected them or did not pay any attention to them at all. Proper training for beginners has positive repercussions on the children's future development process.

It can be assumed that all coaches and trainers prefer a specific training method based on their own training and experience – may be even their successes –, are convinced by its effectiveness, and are not readily willing to deviate from it. On principal that would be correct. One can only expect success to come along if one is convinced of the effectiveness of a teaching path, a method, or a training means. But every teaching path, every method, every "fencing school", even the currently most successful one, perishes if it is not constantly monitored, corrected, improved, or expanded.

In practice there are more than a few examples where, after very positive training results, suddenly all "talent is absent", and one is certain that the training proceeded just like usual. And that is exactly why success was absent. There was a lack of necessary change. The biological predispositions of children are generally the same. But since the general performance development progresses, the training has to adapt as well. Lasting success is only achieved by regularly changing the instruction and the training (also see Chapter 3).

4.2.1 Practicing must be learned along with fencing

Meanwhile there are so many fencing books out that it is almost impossible for the poor trainer to know them all and choose the "right" book. Most of the time techniques and teaching paths are described and specified. The specifications are often heavily standardized, declared to be "time-tested", and "verified" by success. Unfortunately most of these tutorials do not sufficiently take into consideration the fencers themselves, although they are the most important aspect of the teaching and learning process.

The fencers, – regardless if they are really young and complete beginners–, are always subject to their own development, never just objects of our influence. Frequently they are not given enough space for their personal development, or better yet, the independence of our fencers is not sufficiently encouraged and utilized to improve the intensity and especially the quality of practice and training processes. A good youth trainer always thinks about how he does not only teach techniques or develop physical fitness in his fencing training, but how he can actively include the children in the practice and training process, so that next to improving the quality of the practice sessions he will also be better able to consciously facilitate the personal development of his fencers.

By practicing the fencers acquire movement skills, improve their fitness level, acquire tactical abilities, and psychological attributes. But not all practice is equally effective. There is always an important complex of influencing variables involved. Particularly critical are the quality of execution and the accuracy of error correction in technical-tactical training, and the volume and intensity-related workload in the development of speed, strength, and endurance.

One has to imagine, in a highly simplified way, that the human organism is a "self-regulating whole", and that the demands created by athletic practices affect that whole as "disturbances of equilibrium". The organism attempts to balance these "disturbances" and to adapt (compare Chapter 2.1). It is the trainer's job to optimize these adjustments to the demands, and to adapt them in such a way that the young fencer is neither under-challenged nor over-extended. And that takes place most effectively through the interplay of pedagogic control and independence.

4.2.2 Pedagogic guidance and independence

To the extent that the young fencers acquire certain movements, abilities, or behaviors, they become more independent with regard to the respective requirements, effectively increasing their operating range. Coping with difficult or different requirements becomes feasible. As a general rule this again requires close cooperation with the trainer, detailed pedagogic guidance as a prerequisite to the development of greater independence.

In a way each concrete training and development level has two areas of development, namely the area of present performance and the area of subsequent development (fig. 4.2.-1).

The area of present performance includes everything the fencers have already acquired during their previous development and training and can therefore handle more or less independently as a requirement. This level also offers options for increased performance, which the fencers are not yet able to achieve independently, but for which they have the qualifications based on their pervious development. Such performances are therefore initially executed under tutorial, after explanation, instruction and demonstration, by copying, with monitoring, encouragement and evaluation, etc. The possibilities that open up in an area of present performance characterize the area of subsequent development.

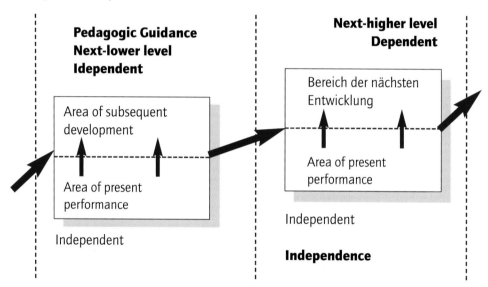

Figure 4.2.-1: Interplay of pedagogic guidance and independence

"Learning to practice", means gradually enabling the fencers to handle the requirements that extend beyond the area of present performance with increasingly more independence.

By practicing independently the fencers turn the area of subsequent development into the area of present performance. The opportunities for handling higher demands become the reality of individual behavior and capability. And with that an area of subsequent development is again opened, meaning prerequisites for handling higher demands – initially under tutorial and in cooperation – are created. Thus the proportion of pedagogic guidance by the trainer (primarily during lessons) to the independence of the fencers

(primarily in the forms of partner training (Chapter 3.1.3) and competitions) constantly changes. From working with the trainer (later it can be a teammate) the fencers move on to handling a requirement independently, but return to collaboration for higher demands. But this "return" is really advancement: the athletes continue to become more independent in training. The character of the pedagogic guidance must adapt to that and change. Of course none of these are simple and spontaneous processes. The fencers must be stimulated and their attention must be focused on the correct goals and focal points. Development-aiding conditions for practicing need to be created. But the success of the pedagogic influence depends primarily on how successfully the fencers can be prompted to actively participate in the practice process and enable them to do so. This also enhances the gathering of experiences at competition. The fencers then learn from success and failure.

4.2.3 Monitoring and evaluating as important learning actions

Learning actions, combined with learning goals and learning motives, represent an important action point for the guidance of young fencers during the training process, and for their ability to practice independently and self-dependently.

Learning actions are, for example:
- Observing motion sequences and creating sensorimotor (the motor sensation) and basic ideo-motor-based (motor perception-related) orientations (see Chapter 3.3 "Tauberbischofsheimer fencing lessons").
- Executing movements or fighting actions to drill them with respect to specified quality and effectiveness parameters (training practice) or
- Monitoring, evaluating, and judging one's own movements, actions, or behavior patterns, or those of others, with respect to stipulated quality and value standards.

As long as a fencer has not mastered a motion sequence or fighting action with the objectively required quality, the condition, sequences, sub-steps, ect. required for the achievement of objectives must be monitored and, if necessary, corrected and judged by the trainer. Next to determining the respective training goals (judging and action parameters), creating concrete and preferably complete orientational basis (progression and goal), and establishing learning readiness, monitoring and rating actions are very significant to the acquirement process.

Although monitoring and rating actions are closely related, both learning action categories have their specific functions.

Monitoring helps to determine if an executed movement or action satisfied the requirements of the learning task.

The following *evaluation* provides information regarding the degree (extent) of acquirement of action procedures relative to the goal. This is particularly important when new actions must be acquired, since any errors that develop at this juncture are very difficult to correct later, requiring additional effort.

Constant and detailed feedback is also extremely important to the acquiring and perfecting process, but beyond that it also has a motivating effect. That is why the trainer lesson is so important in fencing. In addition, in fencing it is very difficult to ensure this essential monitoring. That is because on the one hand the movement repertoire is extremely varied, opponent-dependent, and individualized, and there are inadequate objective monitoring and evaluating methods and criteria.

On the other hand the parallel, non-standardized partner training process in fencing enables the trainer to always just monitor one pair of practicing fencers closely and with lots of concentration. If a trainer gives lessons during group training, the other fencers' practice goes unmonitored even more frequently.

Here is a simple calculation: 12 athletes in the training group – one pair is specifically monitored, evaluated, and corrected – 10 athletes practice parallel without being monitored and corrected by the trainer. Result: more than 80% of specific technical-tactical training occurs without direct feedback from the trainer. Thus, if the best-possible learning progress is to be achieved, the athletes' ability to self-monitor and self-evaluate is indispensable.

Another result is directly linked to this: to the extent that the young fencers acquire certain knowledge, abilities, and skills with respect to self-monitoring and self-evaluation, they become more independent and confident, and become the subject of the practice and training process. As soon as the learning athletes are able to receive sufficient feedback from their own practicing that is not analyzed and evaluated for them by the trainer, a faster learning progress also becomes possible without added outside feedback.

Partner exercises and reciprocal lessoning during partner lessons (Chapter 3) as typical training forms in youth training are directly tied to reciprocal and personal implementation monitoring.

Through the ability to monitor and evaluate the actions of other fencers (the respective partner) the stage is set so that the athlete himself gradually thinks about his practicing and training, his movements, actions, and finally monitors and evaluates his behavior.

He becomes a partner to the trainer. In beginning and youth training that is the most prospective goal possible.

4.2.4 Monitoring and self-monitoring in training

Self-monitoring during practice is an important criteria for the level of independence and awareness with which the fencers participate in the practice and training process. As long as a fencer has not yet mastered a motion sequence (technique) or a fighting action, his compliance with the conditions, manner of implementation, etc., essential to the achievement of objectives, must be monitored and if necessary corrected. Up to now this was mostly done through external monitoring in the form of lessons with the trainer.

We will go on the assumption, that in the course of their training the fencers will increasingly be able to take this on themselves. The utilization of training time, particularly in technical and tactical youth training, could thereby be noticeably enhanced. But the ability to do so must be developed systematically. An important intermediate step in the learning athlete's taking over of the monitoring function is the mutual monitoring of the fencers. Initially it is much easier to observe "externally" on one's partner than on oneself to what extent an action result meets specific criteria, if the action execution proceeds according to requirements and regulations, and where variations and errors can be found and what their causes might be.

But partner monitoring is also a way to more accurately detect one's own variations and errors and to acquire the correct sequences. Self-monitoring techniques are acquired particularly because they are applied in monitoring others and are gradually carried over to one's own practicing and training. Mutual monitoring is a technique that can already be practiced with young beginning fencers (ages 8-10). We can remember from our own schooldays that the best learning progress always happened when we had to explain it to someone else.

The following suggestions for youth trainers yield the experience and suggestions of particularly Norbert and Gisela Meller (Barth & Meller, 1988) based on their use of this action-oriented training concept.

1. An important requirement is the readiness of the learning athlete to monitor himself and others (monitoring need) and allow himself to be monitored and corrected (monitoring trust). Most often this is achieved when the tasks that are given are difficult to resolve, or can only be resolved with particular effort, with the previous prerequisites. The "master" and "student" role-play in reciprocal practicing and training has paid off. It is easy to make the "master" aware of his special role, to clarify his responsibility to "the "student". The fencers take this task very seriously and really try hard. They often imitate their coach, so it can also turn into a self-monitoring opportunity for the trainer. The "master's" authority should not be undermined through direct intervention by the trainer.
- Assistance and suggestions for corrections are given via the "master".
- The quality of the "master" is measured by the learning progress of the "student".

2. The quality and effectiveness of practice is essentially determined by the orientational basis of the actions. With learning athletes the orientational basis develops through their processing and mentally reproducing instructions for the practice tasks, – the What?, How?, and What for?. For instance, Emil Beck creates such a basic orientation through mental training before lessons (Chapter 3.3). Aside from the mental preprogramming for optimum movement-readiness, the fencer is prompted to mentally penetrate the practice material. Depending on the fencers' goals and level of training, complete or more or less incomplete orientational basis are created. For tactical exercises they should be more incomplete in order to provoke tentative practicing. Guidelines for the athletes are precise and unambiguous descriptions of sequences, demonstrations with explanations of important nodal points in movements or actions, and also illustrations like those used in Chapters 6, 7 and 8 respectively, of the "children's fencing books "Learning Fencing" and "Training Fencing" (see literature).

3. The practice approach and the suggestions for corrections should be "pictorial" and take place in child and age-appropriate language.
Suitable for this is the "personalizing" aid, by pretending, for instance, that the weapon, a piece of sports or play equipment, or individual parts of the body have motives, emotions, or a will of their own:
- "Your weapon wants to make contact!"
- "Your blade doesn't want to be caught!" or
- "The ball is happy when it can travel really far!"

Language that is full of imagery like similes or metaphors is also suitable.
- The hand with the palm facing up is the "tray".
- The fixed way of holding a weapon with a French grip is called "birdie", because the hand is closed in such a way that a small, delicate bird could be held without being injured. The trainer's cue is: "Remember the birdie!"
- Everyone can imagine what it means when someone is "walking on egg shells".
Children readily accept such language and have fun with it. At the same time one does not have to forgo precise terminology.

At this point we will again point out that success depends on,
- how ready the fencers are to be monitored and evaluated by their practice partner.
- their desire to help the practice partner learn movements and actions faster through monitoring and evaluating, and
- what knowledge and skills the fencers have at their disposal to recognize their partner's
and their own errors, and make accurate suggestions for their correction.
In addition the fencers acquire monitoring techniques (monitoring actions) with which they can monitor and self-monitor.

A general prerequisite to success, of course, is the trainer's ability to identify with this kind of pedagogic concept and his command of the same.

In the following example several monitoring techniques are assigned to the learning and training tasks.

Learning and training task	Monitoring technique
(1) Comprehending the motion sequence.	• Description of the motion sequence. • Demonstration of the movement vertices ("nodal points") and the motion sequence in front of a mirror.
(2) Practicing the motion sequence	• Explanation of movement characteristics. • Showing the motion sequence in illustrated form. • Demonstration of the motion sequence with eyes closed.
(3) Stabilizing the motion sequence	• Reducing the various monitoring actions from (1) and (2) to nodal points and results monitoring. • Verbal emphasizing and illustratition of rhythm of movement. • Repeated execution with eyes closed and monitoring of results in front of a mirror.

For the youth trainer, of course there is the question of how to recognize which level of independent monitoring the fencer has already acquired. It is recommended to do so via various methods.

(1) Anticipatory monitoring and self-monitoring
This facilitates the analysis of movement and action series prior to execution. Incorrect exercises can thereby be avoided because the progression, the nodal points or possible errors are anticipatorily preconceived and corrected.

Anticipatory self-monitoring is complete when the motion or action sequence and the execution conditions (partner performance) can be described accurately.

The trainer will know which suggestions and aids, or demonstrations are still needed, if the description is incomplete or inaccurate.

"Homework" for which the fencers must read about, describe, or draw the movements and actions to be learned, is also suitable for acquiring this form of self-monitoring.

The young fencers may be given the following tasks:
The illustrations (figures 4.2.-2a and 4.2.-b) show six fencers standing in quarte position and six fencers standing on guard.

Fig. 4.2.-2: a – Quarte positions and b – on guard positions

Which of these positions are technically accurate? Color them green!
Which errors do you recognize in the other positions? Mark the major errors with red and the minor errors with yellow!
Which quick cue would you give to make sure your practice partner assumes the position correctly?

This procedure can be used for all positions, foot and blade work or combinations. The "instructor material for the training of sports assistants in fencing" (literature) contains 44 cards showing models and errors for foil and saber.

(2) Concomitant monitoring and self-monitoring
This occurs during the execution of movement and action, and facilitates immediate control and correction in the learning process.

Instruction by the trainer is done through verbal monitoring and rhythmic emphasis. To aid the execution the fencers, on their part, issue commands to themselves through concomitant speaking.

While the execution of movements should only be accompanied verbally during conveyance, initial attempts, and error monitoring, placing emphasis on time structures (rhythm) is extremely helpful and important for learning as well as perfecting.

Verbal accompaniment for an increase in speed during a step forward-lunge is such that the words are spoken increasingly louder:

STEP FORWARD – LUNGE!

The monitor immediately recognizes whether delayed or inaccurate perception, inaccurate mental processing, or a lack of coordination caused the fencer's practicing mistakes. Anticipatory and concomitant self-monitoring may be dispensed with after several error-free executions or the successful solving of tasks.

(3) Resultative monitoring and self-monitoring
Here the fencers check via the result after execution and the consciously "recalled" motion and action sequence, whether or not the execution was accurate or which errors need to be corrected.

A simple form of resultative self-monitoring is when the fencers execute movements several times with their eyes closed and self-monitor their final positions (also with a mirror) or have them monitored.

A few suggestions for the youth trainer outline the executions:
1. Demonstrate accurately. That saves a lot of correcting in the long run. Verbal accompaniment and emphasis promotes comprehension.

2. Wanting to practice means knowing how to practice. Wanting to correct errors means recognizing and knowing. But both must be learned first.

3. Keep your explanations brief and concise. Don't overdo the fencing talk.

4. Back off when the fencers correct each other. Don't make blanket judgments, but ask questions first.

5. Set high standards, but remember that fencing should be fun. Even a little progress is worth some praise.
   If you would like feedback on your work as a trainer, let an experienced trainer monitor you and occasionally ask your fencers.

4.2 The "Tauberbischofsheim model" for youth training in fencing

Germany's longtime successful youth training according to the "Tauberbischofsheim model" is based on the perception that with the increased specialization and thus increased performance-readiness and -capacity of the fencers, continued performance development in fencing is only possible through a substantial number of approximately equally strong training partners and the corresponding infrastructure for the development of athletic peak performances. A gradual "concentration" of the best fencers in a region at performance bases becomes inevitable.

The determining organizational, social, and psychological/pedagogical factors required for this should already be implemented during the initial phases of youth training and should be continually upgraded. Table 4.3.-1 shows the organizational structure required for the individual age groups and training levels.

Class	Training level	Age/School	Organizational structure
1	Basic athletic	To age 10	Talent sighting groups with training Elementary school collaboration of "school and club"
2	Basic training	Ages 11/12	Talent fostering groups in Elementary/Middle collaboration with school, club, and School association
3	Advanced training	Ages 13/14	Base training (state base), club, association (central events in state)

Table 4.3.-1: Training steps, ages, and organizational structure in youth training

The most important auxiliary support and training institutions during long-term youth training are shown in figure 4.3.-1 on page 167.

The fact that this can be implemented very successfully at the special Olympic fencing base Tauberbischofsheim, Germany, with the part-time boarding school "Modell Tauberbischofsheim", and the full-time boarding schools "Berghof" and "Haus der Athleten", can be seen by the top world performances achieved over many years by this center. Over the years a fencing center came into existence here whose infrastructure facilitated previously successful training from beginning to top international fencer.

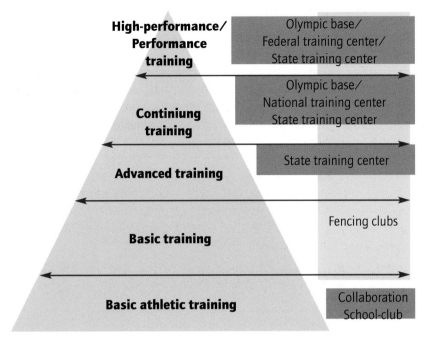

Fig. 4.2.-1:
Illustration of institutional support options during the phases of long-term performance development in fencing based on the "Tauberbischofsheim model"

As can be seen in figure 4.3.-1, the fencing center in Tauberbischofsheim, which is closely affiliated with its founder and sponsor, Emil Beck, also includes the national training center, as well as a training center for the state of Baden-Württemberg, where the young fencers can train together.

In addition there is a concept-based system of talent sighting and fostering through the association "Fechten Badisch-Franken" (Fencing Badisch-Franken) within a 25-mile radius of this fencing center. An instruction, training, and competition system that is supposed to facilitate age-appropriate, systematic, and long-term training, as well as financial assistance for fencing talents, was developed with the involvement of all the Tauberbischofsheim center's institutions and their resources, under consideration of the regional distinctions.

An important element of this concept is the seamless support transition – without switching clubs – of talented and competitive sport-motivated children and adolescents to the performance center in Tauberbischofsheim, and thus into the support system of German fencing. With regard to content and organization, this model adheres to the basic common structure of the German Fencing Federation.

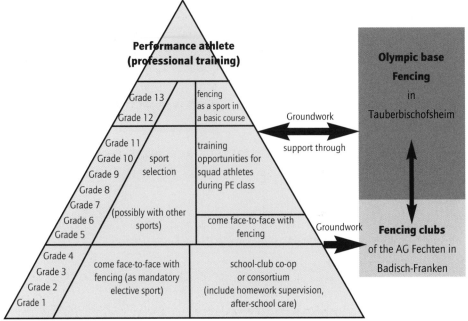

Fig. 4.3.-2: Talent sighting system –and fostering at the AG 'Fechten Badisch-Franken"

Basic athletic training and basic training

The purpose of the first step of basic athletic training is to discover whether the children are ready and able to participate in (competitive) sports training and whether they show a particular interest in fencing. The basic training as the second step of the training process serves additional talent sighting and development, the conveyance of fundamental and varied movement experiences, as well as sport-specific movement actions.

Basic tasks for athletic training within these two steps stem from the basic training guidelines for children and adolescents in the competitive sport of fencing, by the German Fencing Federation (literature).
Youth training is designed by fencing associations, fencing clubs, or fencing departments.

Important tasks are:
• Making training opportunities available to all children and adolescents interested in fencing and getting them involved in the association's volunteer work (area of popular sports).

• Advancement of talented children and adolescents, as well as long-term training with (individual) peak athletic performance (area of competitive sports) as a goal.

The association trainers and coaches are responsible for handling training and competitions; the associations' elected chairpersons are directly responsible for the organizational work within an association. Within the scope of their means, the associations take care of the respective basic conditions. Evaluation of the associations' work, and thus their financial funding, is done from the aspect of performance development. Criteria are, among others, the number of talent being advanced and their criteria-oriented training.

Important is that the instruction, particularly at the beginning of training and advancement, is directed by well-trained youth trainers. Several associations can share the financing of this.

Cooperation agreements between schools and associations offer excellent possibilities for implementing the following important functions:

1. Solid basic athletic training: The emphasis is on the development of movement-regulating (coordinative) abilities through varied training exercises. Numerous movement experiences should be conveyed, based on training that emphasizes having fun. This will provide a solid and vital coordinative and fitness-related foundation for future specific learning and technical training.
2. Forms of training that are "fun", should deepen the interest in the sport, and prepare for the joining of a fencing association and thus for regular training. Important in this context is a visible learning progress in the training of basic fencing techniques (basic elements of footwork, etc.).
3. Introduction of fencing as an (elective) mandatory sport as part of physical education; fencing is taught as a mandatory elective sport at interested schools as part of physical education. Emphasis is on grades 1 to 3. In doing so, the children get a better insight into the sport of fencing and are encouraged to take up regular training at a fencing association.

Fencing as a mandatory sport is currently limited to a specific period (approx. 10 hours of instruction). Together with the responsible PE-teachers the trainer works out a timetable that is implemented during the respective PE-classes.

The current experience in Tauberbischofsheim proves that subsequently 3 to 5 children sign up for fencing lessons.

The local associations are responsible for the organization and content design of these forms of training. The immediate training-related work is done by so called "talent trainers" who during this step already coordinate content with the "future" trainers.
Figure 4.3.-3 uses a training group of the AG "Fechten Badisch-Franken" as an example to illustrate the content-based methodological weighting in the course of a school-year.

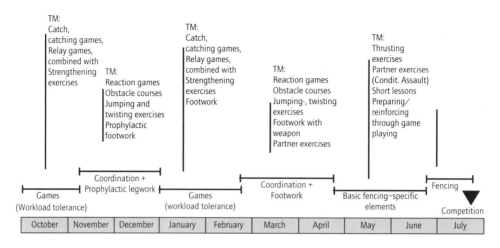

Fig. 4.3.-3:
Content-based methodological weighting of a training group from AG "Fechten Badisch-Franken

4. "Association crossover" talent groups.

   Association "crossover" talent groups are formed (based on locality or region) for the purpose of training effectiveness (larger groups, several training sessions per week, better performance comparison, social integration). They are formed and looked after by mentors at the completion of basic training. Continuous pedagogic, psychological, and social counseling, and supervision in form of homework or after-school care is carried out with the parents' approval, to safeguard the unity of scholastic development and athletic training.

Advanced and continuing training

The portion of fencing-specific training is gradually increased during *advanced training.*

Continued training characterizes the transition from youth training to performance-oriented training for young adults. In both phases the most capable fencers aspire to a spot on the national and international ranking list and prepare for participation in the Junior and Cadet World Championships. Joint training of performance-oriented fencers in large clubs with many equally strong fencers is an important prerequisite for this.

As a prerequisite to the increasing individualization of training, general and specific motor and psychological development monitoring accompany the overall talent fostering process. A prudent and responsible trainer identifies the performance capacity, the performance readiness, and the performance requisites of the fencers entrusted to him through tests, observations and evaluations.

To answer the question of what is meant by the "aptitude for competitive sport-oriented fencing" and how talent can be recognized, one has to refer to the structure of the performance-determining features that characterize a world-class fencing athlete.

If a child has regularly participated in training, additional factors are included in the fencing-specific aptitude diagnostics. This increases the validity of talent determination because one of the basic principles of aptitude diagnostics is that the aptitude for a specific activity can only be determined through the activity itself.

Additional aptitude criteria are:
- The level and the pace of progress in the acquirement of specific fitness-related, coordinative, and psychological abilities, skills and qualities, particularly the technical-tactical performance capacity; based on the relationship between biological development, training effort, and performance capacity, the biologically younger child with the same performance capacity and a previously lower training effort, is the more developable child.

- The status and development of the quality of competition performance; at the same time competition performance should not be viewed strictly by the number of victories achieved. Just as important as winning fights is that the fights are shaped by the abilities and skills that, in terms of a primarily perspective-oriented fencing performance capacity, have been purposefully developed by the trainer. Winning at any cost and without cosideration of the pedagogical and training requisites of certain training steps would be damaging to the purposive development of young fencers.

4.4 The children's trainer

It is understood that a youth trainer must first of all have command of "his trade" with the "weapon" to be able to demonstrate and utilize personal experience while conveying and correcting technique and fighting actions. He must understand the sport of fencing. He does not need to be a former world champion to do so. And he learned the basics of workload organization during his instruction as a trainer. But the trainer also has significant pedagogic and social functions that may be critical to the future development of the young fencers (compare Chapter 2.2).

First of all he is a role model the children try to emulate. Whatever the trainer says and does, how he conducts himself, and what he likes, sometimes carries more weight than the opinions of parents or teachers. A children's trainer should always be aware of that. He helps the children acquire rules and standards of social interaction within the social scope of action and to respect them, and in his capacity as role model, supports the education process at school as well as at home.

In daily fencing training many trainers emphatically prove that a homogeneous fusion of education and training can be implemented. That in doing so an unjustifiably high expenditure of time is not necessary is obvious to anyone who pays attention to the relationships and mechanisms of pedagogic guidance and care of young athletes.

We would like the children to enjoy coming to fencing training and go home with a sense of achievement. But what do we really mean when we say "children"? There are the diligent ones, the talented ones and the less talented ones, the precocious ones or the late-bloomers. Each is its own little personality with distinctly different prerequisites and its own developmental history, with desires and hopes, with existential orientations and needs. There are no "lazy" children and no "untalented" or even "bad" children. Each child is different from another! All of them are equally worthy of our attention, our care and love. Figure 4.4.-1 provides a graphic description of the job specifications of a children's trainer.

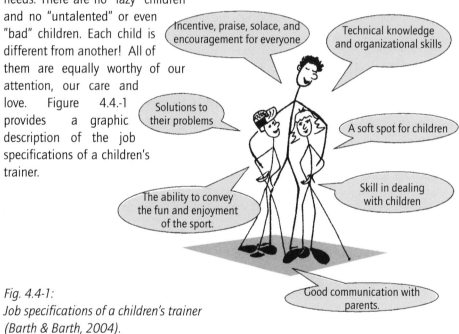

Fig. 4.4-1:
*Job specifications of a children's trainer
(Barth & Barth, 2004).*

The fencing trainer must be able to communicate and encourage, should be able to listen and identify with each child. He must give praise and solace. Sometimes he has to be critical, put the brakes on a hot head or issue a reprimand. But he always does so with respect for the little personality, – in short – he has "a soft spot for children".

At the beginning of training it is important to create a positive attitude and value system with regard to the trainer and training buddies. So-called rituals have proven very effective with this. They are stipulated procedures for the implementation of training, for corrections, or for the start or end of training, for the order in the fencing hall, and in the locker room and showers, for the storing of clothing and weapon, and much more. It saves

a lot of time and trouble in the long run, if these things are attended to from the very beginning. Sound behavioral qualities are developed through repeated practicing and applying of specified sequences during training or competition.
These include:

- Schooling of social behavior patterns for interaction with other children.
- Developing self-confidence and independence.
- Schooling to promote self-discipline and the ability for active cooperation.
- Increasing ambition and enthusiasm for fencing.
- Organizing time due to increased demands from school and sport, and much more.

Overall permanent performance motivation must be developed for the successful handling of long-term education and training processes, that will enable the future top fencer to achieve high-ranking international competition performances, and motivates the many others for a long lasting commitment to the sport and the association.

Positive reinforcement, the praising of even minor progress, strengthens the motives behavior is based on and at the same time pushes back the negative motivations.
The following forms of positive reinforcement have proven effective in children's training:

- Verbal praise or open approval.
- The trainer's delight or surprise over a result.
- Friendly eye contact with a child.
- An encouraging smile.
- Addressing the child before or after training, and much more.

The following things should be considered for the stimulation of positive behavior patterns:

- The chosen type of positive reinforcement should be one the child would really be happy about it. If the effect lessens, the type of positive reinforcement should be changed.
- Positive reinforcement is not a substitute for action-oriented methods; it builds on them and makes them effective.
- Frequent, relatively low-key positive reinforcement for even minor attempts are, as a rule, more effective with children than more infrequent, but stronger positive reinforcement.

The trainer's not so simple job is to select the practice material, the goal formulation, or the forms of competition for training in such a way as to ensure that each child receives positive reinforcement several times in the course of every training session.

5　Aspects of sports medicine in fencing

From a sports medicine point of view, fencing has a lot in common with other sports. It begins with the proper nutrition of an athlete, then goes on to a healthy lifestyle, endurance training, injury prevention and treatment of injuries, anti-doping regulations, vaccinations, protective clothing, and all the way to the highly specialized training of fighting actions. Some particulars that need to be considered in fencing training have already been addressed in the previous chapters. This was done primarily from the point of view of the training scientist and the psychologist. In this chapter the sports medicine specialist gets a chance to have his say. The topics to be represented are chosen from the perspective of **the sports medicine specialist's responsibility for the health and performance capacity of the fencers, as a partner to the trainer and the fencers**.

The job of the sports medicine doctor in the area of competition and performance-oriented fencing training is to help keep healthy athletes healthy and improve their performance capacity through systematic training.

The increase in performance demands and tournaments along with regeneration phases that are often too short heightens the significance of complex training and performance control. The persons involved have the difficult task of caring for fencers who, aside from their jobs and everyday life, pursue competitive sports like "pros", to be able to win against pros.

The tasks and responsibilities of sports medicine specialists are described in the following sections.

5.1　Healthy living

The first prerequisite for fencing competitively is certainly good health. That is why the primary goal in medical care is to maintain good health together with the high workload necessary for performance development.

The fencer himself can actually contribute significantly to this **by not consuming stimulants as much as possible**.

Smoking, for instance, causes narrowing of the blood vessels. This leads to poor circulation of the muscles, which of course will result in decreased performance due to the poor oxygen supply. In addition it causes an accumulation of carbon monoxide in the lungs. It adheres more easily to the hemoglobin and thus prevents the transport of oxygen

from the lungs to the muscles. In addition, even one cigarette a day blocks the bronchial system with phlegm due to a temporary paralysis of the bronchial cleaning mechanisms, which again diminishes the body's oxygen supply.

Everyone surely knows that **alcohol** interferes with coordination and concentration. Thus it is almost unfathomable to consume alcohol in training or at competition. The anti-doping regulations also prohibit alcohol consumption and punish it as an offense. Less well know is that alcohol interferes with the metabolism. In training we create a stimulus, which, among other things, should lead to an increase in muscle thickness and strength (compare Chapter 2.5). For this we need protein components, which are formed in the liver. But that is exactly where alcohol interferes with and prevents the generation of protein. Thus the after-training beer has undone many a training result.

Caffeine is an ingredient found in coffee, tea, energy-drinks, and in small amounts even in cocoa. It is intended to have a stimulating effect, but can easily lead to nervousness and tremulousness. This is certainly disadvantageous in fencing since fine motor skills are very important. Due to frequent incidences of abuse, caffeine of a certain concentration has been on the anti-doping list since 2003.

Drugs like marijuana (THC) have also been on the World Anti-Doping Agency's list of banned substances since 2004.

5.2 Toughening-up and increasing defense mechanisms

Next to avoiding an unhealthy lifestyle and damaging influences like the examples listed in Chapter 5.1, there are also ways to actively protect the body from infections, thereby safeguarding the training effort. Even a minor infection immediately leads to a decrease in physical fitness and similar to an injury, can mean a loss of several weeks of training time.

Building up antibodies means to improve the functioning and reproduction of white blood cells. Taking showers with long periods of cold water, and saunas has proven very effective for this purpose. A regimen of various extracts (Echinacea) also can help to improve defenses. However, a sports doctor should be consulted for this. Autologous blood treatments frequently used in the past can stimulate the body's defenses because the body has to develop antibodies to be able to catabolize the blood that is injected under the skin. Thereby every bruise, although painful, also increases the body's defenses. In life threatening situations due to infections injections of antibody concentrates are usually given to immediately help the body's defenses fight the pathogens. For example, an injection of the antiserum Tetagam is given for an injury just in case the "tetanus booster"

is overdue. Also, in case of a sudden trip that doesn't allow time for a vaccination, it is possible to receive the gift of immunoglobulin for the prevention of hepatitis.

In recent times it has been proven that the trace element zinc does not only activate white blood cells, but also causes them to multiply. Further details are included in the chapter "Nutrition" (5.3).

How the "psyche" can demonstrably control the immune system was addressed in detail in Chapter 2.2. This is indisputable: Emotional wellbeing is a protection from infection. In caring for his fencers the trainer can help significantly in the prevention of infection-related absences through empathy and intuition.

The ten rules for better health according to Russel Jaffa, can of course be modified or supplemented according to the specific situation at the club or the fencer's individual needs.

1.   Inhale deeply and avoid the pollutants in the air.

2.   If possible, eat only appropriate amounts of organic, natural foods
.
3.   Get to know yourself and live in harmony with yourself.

4.   Engage in a regular form of exercise that matches your physical ability.

5.   Take antioxidants (see Chapter 5.3, vitamins, minerals and trace elements).

6.   Laugh out loud at least once a day.

7.   Do relaxation exercises and meditate.

8.   Acknowledge your own successes and those of your training buddies, and forgive yourself and others for making mistakes.

9.   Stay cool – in your head and your spirit.

10. Feel better day-by-day.

5.3 Nutrition

Training and competition draws on the body's energy reserves and occasionally uses them up. The adenosine triphosphate (ATP) necessary for muscle function and release of energy must be extracted from carbohydrates, fat and if necessary protein. At first glycogen, blood sugar and fat are drawn on for energy supply. During extreme endurance requirements the body is able to burn up to 10% of its muscle protein.

The regulation of energy release consumes several enzyme systems, vitamins, and minerals, which are partially regenerated by the body, but must also be re-supplied through nourishment. Every activity leads to increased loss of fluids, particularly through perspiration. Fluids must be administered early on to avoid the premature onset of a drop in performance.

The demand for sensible nourishment before and after training, but also during competitions that last for many hours, particularly in fencing, is a result of these correlations.

To prepare for major and extended muscle activities the carbohydrate reservoirs in the muscles and the liver must be filled. This is best achieved when the basic nutrition consists of 60% carbohydrates, 10-15% protein, and the rest fat.

To consume such large quantities of carbohydrates is often a volume problem. Energy bars, including those made with milk, and similar foods are very popular but their fat content is always too high. Unfortunately the flavor of low-fat foods is often not acceptable to the palate and is therefore rarely consumed regularly because the flavoring used to improve the taste is primarily bound to fat. The disadvantage of an exclusively low-fat diet is the decreased vitamin intake, because many vitamins are again bound to fat. This vitamin deficiency must be supplemented if necessary.

A diet high in carbohydrates is particularly important during the final days before a tournament. The last meal should be consumed 2-3 hours before the competition. Sweetened beverages can still be dispensed shortly before competition. Aside from replenishing fluids, already spent energy can also be re-supplied through appropriate foods during competition breaks.

Adhering to dietary measures that promote regeneration, like eating after sports, is especially important since the body is in an anabolic metabolic state for hours after exhausting physical demands. At the same time an intense building up of tissue, particularly muscle tissue, takes place. At the end of a training day, depending on the workload, almost all glycogen reservoirs that should be refilled overnight are empty. They can be refilled by consuming carbohydrates soon after the physical strain.

The glycogen synthesis requires approximately .04 ounces of carbohydrates per 1 pound of body weight every two hours, or about 12.5 ounces in 24 hours. Suitable and of acceptable taste are noodles, bread, rice dishes, potatoes, and sugar. Vitamin B must be supplemented. Fluids should be rapidly replenished with water and juice mixes or sweetened tea, beverages containing honey, or other beverages that contain carbohydrates. A serving of meat, fish, or poultry, and low-fat milk products, plus fruits, vegetables, and salad follows the first meal containing lots of carbohydrates.

The proper intake of carbohydrates and the associated improved concentration and fitness level can even lower the risk of injuries.

But the most important requirement for a sensible diet is that of a low-fat diet. It is particularly important to look for hidden fats in order to avoid them. Only milk fat and oils are permitted. Since protein requirements do not exceed 12% of total calories even during major physical demands, but regular food already contains 15% protein, using a protein supplement or increasing meat intake is nonsensical and will more likely lead to problems such as excess weight and gout. These considerations show that especially today's trend of fast food that contains huge quantities of fat, and drinking beer after sports is totally wrong.

The right sports drink
Dehydration due to water loss from perspiring during intensive exertion and as a result of the warm insulating fencing attire is a problem for the athlete that should not be underestimated. Although the loss of fluids does not lead to a life-threatening crisis here as opposed to illnesses with diarrhea, even a relatively minor loss of fluids (loss of approx. 2% of body weight) leads to a noticeable loss of concentration and diminished muscular performance capacity. The loss of fluids also means a loss of minerals and trace elements.

These losses must be compensated for as quickly as possible. However, the intestine can only accommodate a limited water intake per time unit. Therefore it is often necessary to hydrate before competitions and certainly continue to do so during competition breaks, so a deficiency and consequential fatigue, cramps and loss of concentration can be avoided entirely.

The intestine's water absorption depends on stomach evacuation and osmotic pressure. Carbohydrates in particular influence stomach evacuation. According to research results the carbohydrate concentration should be 5%, because a carbohydrate concentration of 10% or more verifiably slows down stomach evacuation significantly. In this case his "water belly" would hinder the fencer more than he would improve his performance. That explains why soft drinks and juices that contain more than 1% carbohydrates are not suitable for fluid replacement. Additionally there is information suggesting that fruit acids contained in fruit juices also impair stomach evacuation. Also the addition of salts can hardly have a positive influence on evacuation.

Water absorption in the intestine is a completely passive process that is only dependent on osmotic pressure and suction from the particles dissolved in the water that are actively transported through the intestine. Glucose and table salt in particular can intervene here and improve water absorption.

The wall of the small intestine can absorb water at a rate of 1 ml of water per 0.155 sq. inch per hour. Through what is considered an optimal mix of approx. 7% carbohydrates and 25 mmol/l of sodium an increase to 4 ml can be achieved. But this means a fairly low carbohydrate intake. Next to the above-mentioned disadvantages, soft drinks and juices have an osmotic pressure that is too high. This has the effect of actually increasing water deficiency in the muscle tissue shortly after drinking, because the body first releases tissue water into the intestine to balance out the higher osmotic pressure of the beverage.

Consequently special sports drinks with the correct carbohydrate concentration and osmotic pressure are indispensable during major exertion and loss of fluids.
Climate control in airplanes causes a substantial loss of fluids through the skin, which goes mostly unnoticed and should already be balanced during the flight, but not with tea and coffee.

Vitamins, minerals, and trace elements
Next to losing water when perspiring the body also loses salt. Training and competition also lead to a loss of calcium and iron.

The metabolic processes leave behind free radicals. Toxins like nicotine and exhaust emissions also pollute the body with oxygen radicals. To neutralize these the body needs sufficient amounts of trace elements, minerals, vitamins, as well as other catchers of free radicals (antioxidants). This can be achieved through a diet of whole grain products, legumes, fruits, salad, and vegetables. With regard to eating meat it should be mentioned here that it serves mostly as a distributor of trace elements and minerals. Meat is less suited for protein delivery. Additional calcium supplements help prevent bone fractures, specifically fatigue-related fractures. Taking additional multivitamin supplements can be wise.

5.4   Heat stress and adapting to heat

Fencing equipment must conform to international safety regulations. Stricter regulations with respect to the overall equipment and their strict enforcement, particularly at competitions, have led to a significant decline in severe injuries.

Since the same dangers are present in training as are during competitions, fencing without a complete set of protective clothing cannot be tolerated. If trainers today still give lessons to their fencers without complete safety attire, they are being doubly irresponsible. They endanger their fencers and prevent their adapting to the realistic conditions of a competition. In cases of improper attire the trainer is definitely liable.

Fencing with blades that don't meet the FIE's safety standards is equally irresponsible.

In warm temperatures fencing attire often leads to considerable hyperthermia. That is why it makes sense to open the fencing jacket immediately after exertion from a lesson or a fight, and to change the t-shirt if it is wet.

Aside from the heat that is generated by the athletic exertion in the fencing uniform, high external temperatures can also create situations that have a negative impact on performance capacity and can cause fatigue.

Of the energy created by the muscle work, 75% is released in form of heat. The body tolerates heat accumulation above 104° only very briefly. Heat dissipation is determined by the skin's circulation and by perspiration. Only the perspiration that evaporates on the skin, and not the perspiration that drips off, cools. One liter of perspiration can extract approximately 700 thermal calories from the body in one hour.

The body temperature is regulated in one part of the brain. The skin's circulation and perspiration is controlled from there. The regulating processes of the brain can be improved through intensive training. Perspiration begins to form sooner during heat stress and larger quantities of sweat can be produced. But the necessary increase of circulation in the skin deprives the working muscles of blood.

The loss of salt from sweating can also be improved through heat training and can be reduced by 50%. Women, children, and older people are less able to perform in heat because they have fewer sweat glands in their skin. In addition, the core temperature of women increases slightly during the second half of their monthly cycle, so that a further decrease in heat tolerance can be expected during that time period.

The best method for avoiding heat-related loss in performance is to drink. Since feeling thirsty is not a good measure, the athlete should consume 1 to 1 1/2 quarts of a mineral beverage per 1 hour of exertion. The composition of the beverages should correspond to the recommendations in the previous chapter.

Training and competitions in extreme heat should start out with low workload intensity so the core temperature does not rise too quickly and the regulating mechanisms have time to engage. It is useful to spend some time in a cool place first, and the physically accentuated warm-up program should be limited in favor of coordinative and concentrative elements.

Heat acclimation takes 5-12 days. It can be done somewhat faster in humid heat than in dry heat. A workload of approximately 1.5 hours a day until a core temperature of 104° F is reached, or at least an endurance-oriented training, is necessary.

5.5 Doping and doping control

Even in ancient times athletes tried to improve their performance with various herbs and potions so they could honor the gods with their victories. The Incas gave their soldiers coca leaves to chew so they would be able to accomplish long all-day marches. In Europe the first reports of doping date back to 1850.

Over time it became more prevalent, and according to credible sources, in the 1960's 27% of all Italian soccer pros were doped. Only the deaths of doped top athletes have lead to the doping ban.

Doping control seeks to accomplish two important goals:
• First and foremost the same preconditions for those fighting against each other, and thus fair play,
• Preventing damage to the athletes' health.

Contrary to the optimization of diet, training process, or regeneration, doping is an attempt to increase the performance capacity in a non-physiological way by using a doping substance before or during competition and training.

Depending on their effect, doping substances are divided into different categories. One category includes stimulants like ephedrine and amphetamine; the other includes anabolics, beta-blockers, diuretics, and peptid hormones like Epo.
Since it has also been attempted to non-physiologically increase performance through blood transfusion, it is also considered a doping offense.

There are various reasons why doping is prohibited. First of all because of the fraudulent performance increase, in order to increase one's chances against the non-doped opponent. And that is extremely un-sportsmanlike, even if those performance increases are barely measurable with scientific tests. But more important are the health risks from toxicity, delayed damage, and finally the endangerment of others and one-self through uncontrolled actions cannot be ruled out.

A fundamental problem with doping control is that only those substances that are detectable are put on the banned substance list. Therefore many "performance enhancing" substances can currently not be controlled or fined at all.

Since top performances have not gotten worse since the introduction of tight controls it can be assumed that, with regard to increased performance, most of the doping panaceas were rather ineffective, and that there are far more reserves for performance development in the training qualification itself than none could ever achieve through doping.

That makes it all the more surprising that doping still goes on, even though many devastating long-term effects have clearly been proven and are well known.

Anabolics for instance, cause microsomia in children. Women adopt male characteristics and undergo voice changes, experience disruption of the menstrual cycle, loss of libido, and possible infertility. In addition anabolics cause liver damage, high blood pressure, mental health problems, paranoia, acne, weight gain, and liver cancer, as well as a weakened immune system with in increase of infections.

Beta-blockers are supposed to lower the stress level, but in reality they diminish performance capacity by approximately 10%.
Blood doping is supposed to have the same effects as high-altitude training, but it bears extreme health risks like hepatitis, etc.

Doping controls
The respective current version of the appropriate national and international bodies' anti-doping regulations are material to doping controls. After the final round of a fencing competition most of the time three fencers are chosen by drawing lots and then have to report to the doping control station within one hour. The fresh urine sample is taken under surveillance and filled into two containers, sample A and sample B, sealed and given a code. The analyses are subsequently performed in the authorized laboratories. If the fencer does not report for doping control he is considered a doping offender.

The medical treatment of fencers must be administered very cautiously. Of course they can be treated with medications as long as those are not on the list of banned substances. Taking banned substances is prohibited on principle, even if it is reported before the tournament or with a medical certificate on hand.
Doping controls during training are announced by the controller 24 hours before the test. These tests are only for anabolics.

According to the current regulations of the regulatory authority of the DSB, the absence of a fencer must be reported. Doping controls during training are also carried out in other countries and during training camps.

5.6 Training, preconditions, and goals

Every athletic activity is an adaptation stimulus to the human body. Training refers to the athletic activity that, as described in Chapters 2 and 3, leads to an increase in the performance capacity by systematically affecting the performance ability through effective procedures, methods and processes. The sports medicine specialist is involved in this process by supporting the trainer with training control. Aside from athletic failure,

incorrect or ineffective training (workload is too low or too high) or unfavorable training conditions, often lead to dissatisfaction of the fencers.

Particular attention should be paid to capacity overload damage to the locomotor system which, in fencers, is usually based on insufficient preparation and monitoring of specific training, and dysfunction in the area of psychomotor and psycho-vegetative processes due to inadequate regulation of the workload and regeneration cycle. That is why sport-appropriate training planning and control is an indispensable precondition to keeping fencers sound, and for the performance increase projected through training.

The training impulse as it affects the organism as a result of the training load, activates a biological adaptation reaction in the body. It is also referred to as an adaptation phenomenon, whereby a certain stimulus intensity, more specifically an above-threshold stimulus, is prerequisite. The body's stimulus response is dependent on the type of training load (Chapter 2.5). For instance, an endurance workload causes an increase in the amount of sugar stored in the muscles and improves the burning of oxygen. A strength workload on the other hand, leads to an increase in muscle circumference and improves the anaerobic energy supply.

The body's stimulus response takes place as follows: After a certain amount of time a training stimulus of a specific individual performance level is followed by a fatigue phase. Then the regeneration phase follows after the exertion is over.
The training effect is a keloid restoration of the base level towards the end of the regeneration period, which we refer to as **overcompensation**. It is important to know that different types of human tissue have different regeneration time periods. For instance, glycogen can be reproduced within a few hours, while protein resynthesis can take up to eight days.

The exact individual proportioning of load factors is critical to an adequate training effort (load intensity, duration, volume, frequency, density, and quality). Ideally the new training load for physically accentuated training should be set in the overcompensation phase, so that repeated training impulses will lead to a higher performance level. Otherwise, if the intervals between workloads are too long there will be no performance improvement. In training with concentrative-coordinative emphasis, the restoration of the base level for the new workload is indicated.

Training loads that are too frequent, too long, or too intensive prevent complete regeneration after training. The next training stimulus occurs during a non-regenerated function and nutrient changeover. This results in a decrease of the athlete's performance capacity.
Being familiar with the muscular regeneration time periods is the basis for training planning in the area of high-performance. For instance, a regeneration period of 12-24

hours applies for a maximum endurance workload, for strength training 24-36 hours. This data applies to physically fit individuals and can take twice as long for physically unfit individuals. Consuming alcohol within the first four hours after training clearly extends the regeneration period. But in fencing we rarely deal with problems related to overtraining. Deficiencies related to insufficient attention to-, or mastery of such important training principles as orderliness, systematics, and individualization (compare to Chapter 3.4) present a much bigger problem.

Since important energy transmission structures like, for instance, the tendons, are not supplied with blood but are nurtured strictly by diffusion, they have a longer regeneration period and are thus in great danger of being injured by constant training impulses. To prevent this a stabilization phase should be included in every training plan. The supporting apparatus can then compensate with an adaptation reaction.

Flawed training programs do not lead to the intended increase in performance. They can lead to health problems in popular sports as well as professional sports.

After every major workload we can find acidity (acidosis), a shift of electrolytes, water deficit, empty energy reservoirs, and damaged proteins and cell organelles in the muscle. All of these must be regenerated. This can be facilitated and sped up by changing training stimuli, through active processes like cooling down and stretching, but also passively through invigorating baths or massages.

Overtraining

Overtraining (overload) refers to a repeated workload requirement that exceeds the athlete's existing abilities or qualifications. The result is a diminished athletic performance capacity in the training process over a longer time period, combined with subjective and objective symptoms. Overtraining can cause illnesses and is found exclusively in high-performance sports. More frequent injuries are often noticed first, followed by psycho-vegetative disorders. The causes for overtraining are always very complex. The following is a list of possible causes:

- During the training process: disregarding regeneration; demand is increased to quickly; workload volume is too high; workload increase after injury or illness is too great; too many competitions; increased failure experiences; goals are too high.

- Adverse psychological conditions: pressure of expectations is too high; partner conflicts; problems at school or on the job.

- Underlying illnesses: infections in sinus cavities or teeth; viral infections; chronic gastrointestinal disorders with water and mineral deficit due to irregular meals and food allergies.

- Lifestyle-related: chronic sleep deficit due to frequent changes in competition locations; insufficient nourishment during competitions in exotic countries; alcohol and nicotine, as well as other drugs.

Symptoms of overtraining are dependent on the functions of the particular system that is failing. The central nervous system, the vegetative nervous system, the hormonal system, the muscle-energy system and the cardio pulmonary system come into question.

These symptoms are for example:
- Emotional lability, strong mood changes, also aggressive or fatalistic mood.
- Lack of impetus, lack of desire to achieve something.
- Sleep disorders; more often trouble falling asleep, less often sleeping through.
- Lack of concentration, diminished ability to execute motion sequences.
- Shifting of hormonal reactions, increase or decrease of stress hormones, suspension of the menstrual cycle, increase of hormones that catabolize body tissue.
- Muscle weakness accompanied by premature fatigue during minor exertion.
- Tendency to cramp up, and hard muscles.
- Prone to injury, particularly rupture of muscle fibers.
- Overload damage, particularly insertion tendopathy.
- Coordinative disorders with angular motion sequences.
- Weight loss
- Changes in laboratory values like potassium and magnesium deficiency, lactic acid increase even during minor exertion, increase of muscle enzymes and urea.
- Change in resting pulse rate (pulse is definitely higher in the morning before getting up), rarely also a lowering of the pulse rate.
- Increased tendency to feint while changing positions.
- Higher breathing rate.

As previously mentioned, the diagnosis for overtraining is not based on one, but on the sum of many minor symptoms. This very much increases the difficulty of making the correct diagnosis.

Treatment Measures for overtraining
- Taking several weeks off from competition.
- Reduced training or changing the entire training plan (stimulus change, dynamic sampling) but not a total training break.
- Clarification by a specialist of injuries and overload damage.
- Active recuperation with an environment and climate change.

- Change of diet, games and calisthenics.
- Physical therapy, either invigorating or relaxing.
- Treatment of ascertained damage and injuries, substitution of, for instance, minerals, adjustment of misalignment, use of alleviative medications, and also autogenic training.

A special form is the immunosuppression syndrome of the high-performance athlete. In this case the athlete suffers from persistent upper respiratory infections. The cause is a measurable deterioration of immune system activity due to a shift of stress hormones and possibly also endorphins.

The clinical picture should also be treated by a reduction of the workload. Taking immune modulators like Echinacea or zinc, as well as alternating hot and cold water while showering, or taking saunas can also positively impact recovery.

5.7 Typical injuries and capacity overload damage in fencing

Contrary to overtraining with its diffused, gradually beginning symptoms, injuries and capacity overload damage are clearly linked to causes and their consequences. With injuries this link exists between the affecting power and its consequences; with capacity overload damage, which is caused by frequent, uniform force effect, it is between the damage location and the pain reaction of the affected structure, most often the weakest link in the motion chain.

But first here is a summary of a few general aspects of sports medicine.
Fencing has evolved into a true high-performance sport. In the past people started fencing as adults. Over the years it was quickly established that starting basic training during childhood makes sense (compare to Chapter 4). Today, children have to begin fencing at age eight to ten to achieve international success. Result analyses show that most of the fencers who earn medals have already won medals as Cadets or Juniors in comparable competitions. Due to the high performance density, late starters barely have a chance to achieve the same level of success.

Fencing is a technically-tactically determined sport that requires certain basic motor prerequisites, quick reactions, and the ability to concentrate and think and act quickly. The fencers' fitness level and tactical thinking significantly impact the duel. A healthy, trainable cardiopulmonary system and a perfectly functioning metabolism, good psychological and physical regeneration ability, as well as sound sensory organs are also imperative preconditions to being a good fencer. After a certain performance density is

reached, psychological stability is crucial to tournament success. This was elaborated on in Chapter 2.

Due to the increasing commercialization and professionalization in the area of international fencing competition, the classic approach of dividing training into periods is hardly feasible any longer.

The system for international competitions is characterized by an unregulated increase in World Cup tournaments. At the same time dates are individually set by the organizers and entirely ignore considerations of sport methodology. The FIE indirectly forces the fencers or associations respectively, to participate in nearly all World Cup tournaments, since important placement criteria for World Championships and the Olympics are derived from the list of world rankings.

The amount of time spent on the development of the early stages of training with a largely general athletic content like endurance training, strength training, or training of coordinative abilities, has become very limited. A systematic performance buildup is barely feasible any longer.

Then follows the competition phase, which consists of competition blocks of 3-4 competitions in a row, followed by a brief breaks. But the Juniors in particular are often subject to dual demand via their participation in Junior and Actives tournaments. Six competitions in eight weeks are not unusual.
During the subsequent competition-free phase mistakes a corrected, work is done on tactical deficits, injuries are cured, and psychological and physical regeneration takes place.
After this break follows the preparation for the seasonal highpoint, like the World Championships or the Olympics. Here the preparation training serves primarily regeneration, then the buildup of the fitness level, and finally the technical-tactical training.

All of this information shows how enormously important a young fencer's long-term development from student age to Junior age is. Anyone who permits deficiencies here, particularly in the area of fencing as well as the development of general coordinative and fitness-related abilities and skills, jeopardizes the fencer's long-term development through preprogrammed susceptibility to injuries and through performance-limiting deficiencies of the general level of athleticism. Every trainer has guidelines based on training science for the design of long-term performance buildup in junior training (Chapter 4).

Even with constant care from sports physical therapists and physicians sport-related damages can still occur, because the workload capacity of individual structures varies greatly, depending on the period of growth.

The following is a summary of **fencing-specific faulty loading characteristics** that can occur:

- The fencer stands with his side to the opponent to present the smallest possible target area. Initially his weight is equally distributed between both legs, the torso is turned parallel to the pelvis (fig. 2.3.-2). The result is a muscular disbalance and a hyperlordosis of the lumbar spine, which is promoted by a shortening of the hip flexors and knee extensors.
- When doing footwork the center of gravity should always be kept over the center of the pelvis. But that is often not possible when performing a lunge and a flèche attack and can cause overload damage. Also, the simultaneous forward movement of the weapon arm and the forward leg is unphysiological and adversely affects spinal mobility.

The fencer is predestined to have muscular disbalance due to the different demands placed on the movement apparatus. In training it is therefore very important to compensate for these differences with compensatory and supplementary exercises.

Even minor injuries can lead to decreased muscular function via the reflex paths, and thus can also cause faulty loading of joints. That is why the proper treatment and healing of micro trauma is so important.

Fencing injuries

Thanks to improved protective clothing and unbreakable weapons, life-threatening injuries have become much less frequent, but cannot be entirely ruled out.

But occasional injuries are seen on copper strips that are not sufficiently taught or elevated strips that are too high and have sharp edges.

Smaller **lacerations** on the back of the head and the weapon hand, but also on the weapon-bearing arm, are frequent and particularly in foil are the result of a modified fighting style (flick thrust).

As with any sport **contusions, sprains and ligament injuries** cannot be avoided, whereby sprains of the ankle joint are most common.

Muscle fiber injuries have many causes, such as faulty interplay between nerve and muscle, speed versa strength, or previous damage. In case of an acute injury the fight usually has to be discontinued. However, with some muscle fiber injuries the fight can be finished if the injured area has been taped. Painful blisters on the weapon hand or on the soles of the feet can be treated directly by the sports physical therapist. Cushioning of hit-related contusions and ice treatments are often carried out directly at the strip.

Treatment of injuries and damages due to faulty loading

Depending on the diagnostic results, the treating physician takes action or arranges a procedure. Parallel to this is the broad application of physical therapy. Electrotherapy

with low-, mid-, and high-frequency currents is used. The injury can be treated with warmth (fango, infrared light, hot roll) or with cold. Various forms of massages can promote the healing of injured muscles. Functional bandages (taping) quickly allow the return to light training.

In terms of prevention, sports physical therapy can also no longer be dismissed.
A complete regeneration between frequent training and competition workloads can only be achieved by shortening the regeneration time period via physical therapy.

Special physiotherapy – as individual or group therapy, active or passive, water exercises, based on neuro-physiological principles, the sling table to increase strength, endurance, flexibility, coordination, circulation, relaxation, stabilization, and for motion sequences – is effective and necessary.

Manual therapy, as holistic therapy, based on a biomechanical and neurological function analysis for mobilization, stabilization, and sustainment of the functional unit joint-muscle-nerve, continues to gain importance.

Thermo-, hydro-, and electro therapy is used to alleviate pain, improve circulation, regulate tone, and positively impact the metabolic situation.

Various forms of massages being used are the classic massage, connective tissue massage, functional massage, on to myofascial techniques or manual lymphdrainage for pain relieve, fiber orientation, dissolving of agglutination, for decongestion, improved circulation and metabolism, as well as reflex facilitation.

5.8 Long distance travel and immunization

Due to the travel to World Cup tournaments and the exotic locations of World Cup Championships, travel advice and especially immunizations are essential. Since the locations have usually been determined at the beginning of the season, prophylaxis for those fencers being considered should begin early. Vaccinations should start six weeks before departure, since two vaccinations are often required within a four-week period.

Recommended basic vaccinations are: **Diphtheria and Tetanus**. Irrespective of long-distance travel, immunization records should always be checked during any sports examinations. Most often diphtheria-tetanus combo vaccines are used. However, due to the diphtheria component occasionally larger local infections with redness and hardening do sometimes occur. Frequent tetanus vaccinations in surgical outpatient facilities can cause a "Tetanus over-vaccination", whereby the inactive ingredients in the vaccine can

cause allergic reactions. To avoid unnecessary sensitization the ten-year interval between vaccinations should therefore not be shortened. Training can be affected for up to five days. There should definitely be no sports on the day of the vaccination.

Polio: Infantile paralysis – (Poliomyelitis) is an illness that is present all over the world. Occasional booster vaccinations are recommended for everyone, particularly during long-distance travel. The previously administered oral vaccine that could endanger non-vaccinated individuals through contact has been replaced by a new non-live vaccine, which must be administered by injection. Adverse reactions to vaccines are very rare. A triple vaccine against Tetanus, Diphtheria, and Polio is currently used most frequently.

Hepatitis A and B: New vaccination guidelines recommend complete vaccinations for children against Hepatitis B until age16, and it is therefore also covered by health insurance. Hepatitis B causes inflammation of the liver that can lead to severe permanent damage. It is primarily contracted through blood, contact with body fluids of infected individuals, and during medical procedures, as well as unprotected sexual intercourse.

The most serious risk still exists during blood transfusions due to injuries, and during major operations, in spite of careful testing. Protection provided by the immunization can be built up with two vaccinations and can be monitored via serological tests. The vaccinations are usually well tolerated, but can occasionally cause flu-like symptoms.

Since Hepatitis A usually heals without any problems this vaccination is not yet mandatory, but it is recommended for travel to exotic regions. It can be transmitted from water, ice cubes, and from salads to melons, all the way to the swimming pool and a beach with dirty water. Risk of contamination is extremely high in sub-tropic to tropic regions. Although the disease usually takes a mild course, it still causes extended training absences, which is why vaccinations make sense. There are no additional local reactions.

A combination A and B vaccination is available and thus clearly preferable for our top fencers. After three vaccinations in the first year protection will last for ten years.

Vaccinations that should be administered for long-distance travel are:
Yellow fever: In recent times the number of mandatory vaccinations has steadily decreased and yellow fever vaccinations are currently only required by very few countries. They are Central Africa and South America. It is also mandatory when traveling to Asia via one of these countries. The rate of infection from the bite of an infected fly is 100%. Some countries may deny entry without vaccination or quarantine. This vaccination is only

administered at yellow fever vaccination clinics like, for instance, tropical institutes. It is a live vaccine that cannot be given in combination with other vaccines. There should be no intensive training for seven days after immunization, but light workloads should not cause any damage.

Cholera: Immunization offers protection for only six months. One injection is sufficient for a vaccination certificate. There is often redness after an injection. Oral vaccines are still being tested.

Meningococcal meningitis: There are frequent epidemics in Africa and South America. Various strains exist. The vaccine contains material from strain A and C. These types of meningococcus are the most common epidemic-causing pathogens. Protection from the vaccine is very effective and thus makes sense when traveling in high-risk areas and coming in contact with the local population.

Typhoid: Typhoid is an illness caused by salmonellae. It can occur worldwide, but particularly in tropical and sub-tropical regions. Infection occurs via oral ingestion of germs in food that was not properly heated, in dairy products or dairy ice cream, or in raw meat and eggs. Vaccinations are given by injection or orally. Protection from oral vaccine is very effective for approximately six months, and is preferable to the injection because of its tolerability.

Malaria: Malaria is transmitted through mosquito bites. It can occur in many tropical areas on all continents. Due to many years of prophylaxes and therapy many resistant parasite strains have developed, so that reliable protection is often only possible through combinations of multiple agents or through newer, more potent medications.

A vaccination is currently not available.
Since this illness is life threatening, an effective prophylaxis cannot be forgone. Exceptions are extremely brief stays in areas with malaria with strict protection from exposure, or intolerance of malaria prophylactics. But this requires familiarity with malaria symptoms and availability of medical attention within 24 hours. The drug Mefloquine diminishes reaction ability and is therefore not the best choice for fencing tournaments.

Tips for general conduct
Protection from exposure is the central issue. Many medical conditions that affect the course of a competition can be prevented.
(Going to the beach and enjoying exotic fruit can still be done the day after competition).

A word of caution about food: Cook it, peel it, or better not eat it.

Female athletes with travel distinations in other time zones should know that the effectiveness of oral contraceptives might be decreased. Acclimatization can be achieved via daily endurance runs in the morning at an easy pace for a distance of 3 to 5 miles.

5.9 Sports medical care and examination system

The type and intensity of care the fencers receive depends on the age and level of activity of the individual fencer.

Until age 18 every fencer competing in a competition must have a current medical check-up. It is performed by the family pediatrician or physician, whereby special attention is paid to cardiac defects and abnormalities of the locomotor system. Scoliosis and flat feet are often detected in adolescents and should be corrected without fail. These check-ups are required annually. At that time the vacination record should be updated, nutritional information should be provided, and possible training tips or fitness sports should be discussed.

After a mutual agreement it is no longer permitted to obtain health certificates from the physician at the fencing hall the day of competition, since he does not know the fencers well enough and is thus not sufficiently able to assess the risks.

There are different regulations for top fencers. The Deutsche Sport Bund (German Sports Federation) has a comprehensive sports medicine health care system with sports medical check-ups, exercise physiology testing, training control, care and counseling.

Sports medical registration of young fencers begins very early on. The young fencers are examined locally at licensed examination centers according to standardized conditions.

Content should essentially correspond to the preventative and health check-ups of the top fencers. The results must be given to the fencer in written form so a subsequent physician can refer to the information if the fencer should change associations.

Sports medical health check-ups should be carried out once a year as a mandatory basic check-up according to the constantly evolving guidelines of the examination form.

The primary purpose of these check-ups is:
- To ascertain aptitude and to preserve health in terms of general and sport-specific health care in particular.
- To ascertain overall load tolerance via non-specific ergometrics with ECG-monitoring.
- To maintain performance capacity through early recognition and treatment of disorders, acute sports injuries, as well as the onset of sport-related damages.
- Prevention of permanent sport-related damages.

An internist and an orthopedist perform the examinations. If something abnormal is detected during the basic examination, the problem is clarified through additional examinations while treatment is then subject to a free choice of medical practitioners.

Competitive fencing is not advisable for individuals with the following disorders:
- Serious cardiovascular diseases, dysrhythmia, heart defects, hypertension.
- Asthma and cystic fibrosis.
- Uncontrolled type 2 diabetes mellitus.
- Major patellar dysplasia type 3, as per the Wiberg classification.
- Hip dysplasia to hip luxation.
- Spondylolisthesis from second degree on, as per Meyerding.
- Dysfunctions after operations on tendons and muscles.
- Epilepsy with frequent seizures.
- Major vision problems with impaired spatial vision and restricted visual field.

6   Foil fencing

6.1   Particularities of foil fencing

The conventions of foil fencing, particularly the honoring of priority, the predefined target area, and the ban on corps à corps, essentially determine the manner of fighting and thus impact all of the components that determine the performance of the foil fencers.

In foil fencing, the fact that every attack that is carried out in accordance with the rules must first be parried before the attacked fencer has the right to launch his own attack presupposes that the fencer can distinguish a correct attack from an incorrect one, and that he knows how to conduct himself as a matter of principal, with respect to the specific fight situation. The ability to react in accordance with the conventions, with "fencing logic", and to come up with a skillful appropriate technical solution, is a prerequisite to the specific tactical behavior that is adapted to the respective situation.

By preparing the coming about of a fight situation he anticipates, the fencer creates advantages for himself via active maneuvers driven by him, thereby being better able than his opponent to anticipate what will happen next. Since every fencer's thinking – whether he knows it or not – is basically strategy-oriented and he is keen on his final action being as successful as possible, inevitably the maneuvers brought about by both fencers occur in relatively near measure.

In doing so the endured psychological demands largely result from the requirements of having to analyse the situation in near measure and the subjective and/or objective compulsion to act.

Psychologically the demand is defined primarily by the fact that action advantages for all action groups are not created by the actual blade relationship but rather by its respective optimal measure.

The situations created by maneuvering offer the opponent a number of opportunities to take the initiative. This requires an effective, often reflex-like defense. Active preparation ultimately means the necessity of having an effective defense. Only that provides the necessary confidence and opens up the possibility of successfully preparing or utilizing respectively situations for all action groups.

Depending on individual qualifications, one's own strategy and that of the opponent, active preparation is characterized by the parallel situational and resultant requirements.

The dynamic and active progression of movements of a foil fight in which the fight conditions and situations constantly change, places specific demands on technique. The variable execution of one or several consecutive technical elements, that are adapted to the respective situation, is required. A deep flexible fencing stance and a weapon arm that is slightly more bent increase maneuverability. The depth of the lunge varies and requires particular flexibility of the hip joint. The basic positions in modern foil fencing are quarte, sixte, septime, and octave (compare to Chapter 2.3).

The successful foil fencer prefers simple, concise actions that are consciously prepared and whose final phases are characterized by much determination and consistency. The action sequence is brief. The attack is followed by a response or counter-attack respectively, or second intention attacks which are usually followed by no more than two basic strategic elements that end the fighting phase. If in doing so the fight is not interrupted by valid or invalid hits respectively, or by a referee call, the fencers begin to maneuver once again.

It is inconceivable for a fencer with a limited action repertoire to be successful against the multitude of possible foil actions. In a fight he would not be able to develop creative, sudden alternative solutions that are unfamiliar to his opponent, and tactically adapt to the many different opponents.

From a strategic aspect a broader repertoire allows the fencer to successfully react to the developmental directions in terms of fencing style and rule interpretation that take place during the fencer's relatively long developmental process. Unfortunately one can often see attempts at compensating for a lack of versatility with an over-emphasized unilateral performance.

The difference between men's and women's foil fencing, aside from the differently accentuated repertoire due to the different physical prerequisites, is among other things that men's fencing is characterized by a relatively large portion of preplanned actions and deliberately effectuated situations, while the women's fighting style is primarily dominated by their fighting sense and the intuitive exploitation of situations that have developed.

But often the schooling of situational behavior is overemphasized to the detriment of action consequences. Depending on the particular individual qualifications resultant-analytical requirements should also be included in the training of women fencers.

As a result it has been established, that due to a significant improvement in physical qualifications (particularly speed and strength) and the development of new techniques made possible thereby, consistency of actions and the penetrating power of the attack are increased considerably. The balance between attack and defense is thereby severely disturbed. The resulting advantages for the attacker have been reinforced because the warning signal for reaching the "meter warning" has been eliminated. Here the development of the flick thrust with its variations and with or without a "prise de fer" has had a major influence, which has significantly limited the effectiveness of concrete parries, requiring new responses.

An exact interpretation of the conventions makes it difficult to launch a successful attack. The defender can control the attacker's extended weapon arm relatively easily. One successful beat is enough to take priority away from the attacker. Since this is often done with a systematic shortening of the measure, the attacker's failure is predestined.

An initial way out is to continue a forceful attack, which, however, is often combined with the illegal withdrawing of the target area. Another option is a delayed attack without the extended arm. When this is done in combination with major physical effort and an increased attacking speed by strictly running without the conventional footwork, even the referees will have trouble making the right call.

But how can one protect oneself against an attack that is carried out strictly with the body and not the weapon? The only option is to immediately launch one's own attack or better yet, begin to advance. Fencing consistency is an endless series of simultaneous events that are not really simultaneous.

There are only two real possibilities to stop this development. First, it is the referee's job to restore the definition of an attack according to the regulations, and secondly, through better training for foil fencers. Again and again fencers demonstrate how many options one can develop to legally assume priority by retreating.

It is futile to make a prognosis on the direction future development will take. In reality "wanting to win at any price" could always lead to erroneous trends. Such developments can only be successfully counteracted by consistent adherence to the fencing conventions by everyone involved (compare to Chapter 9 and 10).

Imagine a fencer becomes world champion and no one cares. But exactly here lies the lowest common denominator. Only when it is possible to organize foil fencing in such a way that its three main components – the attack, the defense, and the counter-attack – have a nearly equal chance, only then will the fight be worth watching to the interested layperson.

But that is the essential, if not the only chance our sport has at a time when everything is looked at from the angle of media effectiveness.

6.2 Select basic strategic elements

6.2.1 Basic attacks

Basic attacks are attack actions that can be carried out against non-attacking opponents without a direct link to previous attack or defensive actions.

Their application presupposes a certain amount of inactivity on the opponent's part, which can manifest itself in tactical inactivity, insufficient concentration, or too much preoccupation with his own actions. That is why, when choosing the time to launch an attack, next to the opponent's physical situation his psychological situation must be considered as well. Next to the technically faultless execution the success of these attacks depends primarily on the correct choice of measure and moment.

The most advantageous measure for these attacks is also referred to as "critical measure". It is a little closer than "middle measure". Reaching the critical measure through skillful maneuvering is one of the main tasks of the preparatory actions that precede basic attacks.

Beyond that basic attacks are a proven means of fighting opponents who habitually prefer counter attacks. After a deceptive maneuver that convinced the opponent that a feint attack was intended, the basic attack follows in anticipation of a counter-attack, thus leading to an Incontro. A fencer who prefers this type of fighting must be aware of the fact that by doing so he puts himself at the mercy of the referee. The basic attack must therefore be carried out consistently to keep possible wrong calls at a minimum.

6.2.1.1 Direct attacks

Direct attacks are executed with only one movement, meaning in only one fencing tempo without any in between movements by the attacker. Depending on the type of movement they are referred to as "straight thrust" and "angulated thrust".

From a technical point of view the straight thrust is the simplest of all the attacks. Since the point of the blade does not meet with any obstacle (the opponent's arm or weapon) it can quickly reach the opposing target area.

The *straight thrust* can be executed:
*   From an unengaged blade position.

*   From one's own engagement.

*   From blade contact.

Situations in which the straight thrust can be used successfully are described in detail in the following practice examples.

The *angulated thrust* is an individually preferred attack element in foil fencing. Beyond that it is an important element for close quarters and ripostes. In the execution of this attack an angle is created between the blade and the attacker's arm, which is how this action got its name. The angulated thrust can be executed from every direction. Its goal is to render very limited parries or engagements on the same blade plane ineffective or to reach target areas that are not easily accessible (the back).

The angulated thrust can be used:
* If the opponent is in sixte, as a direct attack from below and with the fist turned to the left (the opposing octave parry does not cover up sufficiently.

* If the opponent is engaged in sixte or quarte, starting as a disengagement and ending in the lower opening.

* From the left or the right instead of straight thrusts and from the opposing bind instead of disengagement thrusts.

A special form of angulated thrust is the flick. The idea is to achieve a whip-like effect by utilizing the flexibility of the foil blade. To achieve this effect the blade is "yanked back" just before it reaches the opposing target area, only to be immediately whipped forward.

By stopping any wrist movement at the same time the forward part of the blade continues to move due to the force of inertia and in doing so achieves a slight bending of the blade, which allows it to just make contact with the lower back on the opponent if he is standing erect. This technique is often also referred to as "Bingo", or, erroneously, as a cutover. But the object of this technique is not to disengage a parry, but to penetrate every parry, to essentially achieve a "mal paré".

6.2.1.2 Disengagement attacks

The *disengagement attack* is executed from an opposing engagement or a touch. The objective of a disengagement attack is to reach a target area other than the one covered up by the engagement or the one partially covered by the touch, as well as disengaging opposing defensive actions, engagement attempts, or position changes. Depending on its movement, the disengagement is executed as a disengagement or a cutover.

For a *disengagement* the disengagement is executed with a spiral-like motion of one's blade point around the opponent's guard, hand, and forearm, while simultaneously extending the arm. In doing so the blade point's path should be as minimal as possible and as wide as necessary.

The attack is successful when the opponent is not aware of its beginning until very late. This is achieved by increasing the speed towards the end of the movement and by avoiding any forceful movements and pushing off from the opposing weapon at the beginning of the attack. Both trigger the opponent's defensive reflexes.

With excellent coordination and high speed of movement it is also possible to start the disengagement attack with a brief gliding along the opponent's blade. This leaves the opponent momentarily in the dark as to the real target area, and his defensive action is delayed.

In a cutover the blade moves around the opposing point. In the final phase a straight or an angulated thrust is performed with or without opposition. In certain situations the cutover is more appropriate than the disengagement. Determining factors here are blade position and measure. If the forte of one's blade and the guard are near the opponent's point a disengagement of the same is possible via a movement in time. The path around the guard is longer. In close quarters changing the plane of the line with a cutover is often more advantageous, and occasionally is the only option. Both forms of the disengagement attack are critical components of feint attacks when disengaging an opposing parry, as well as sweep attacks and ripostes when executing indirect thrusts.

It is therefore also necessary to master both forms of the disengagement attack, because here, too, one-sidedness leads to tactical disadvantages. The cutover allows a disengagement of the opposing defensive movement without knowing its exact direction. But its success is largely dependent on the attackers ability to adapt to the rhythm of the defenders parries. The cutover is not recommended against opponents who tend to suddenly close the measure, who make their parries shallow and far away from the body or often prefer counter attacks.

To this purpose it is necessary to comment on the advantages and disadvantages of the cutover as compared to the disengagement. The cutover facilitates a disengagement of the opposing defensive movement without knowing the exact direction of the movement. But this is essential to the successful execution of the disengagement. Thus the cutover is particularly advantageous against fencers who tend to vary their choice of parries. However, it is very vulnerable to opponents who suddenly close the measure while executing an attack since the final thrust in this case often only ends up as a beat.

Methodological recommendations for the schooling of basic attacks
- As individual attack elements direct and disengagement attacks are very difficult to apply successfully. But since they are basic components of nearly all other strategic attack elements, they must play a major role in the basic training of a young fencer. But what young fencer wants to practice a relatively easy to learn motion sequence over and over again without an immediate reward? Just doggedly practicing the motion

sequence without tactical context, violates the original content of fencing as a martial art. The object of our training is not the movement as such, – no matter how exact – but its successful application with respect to the respective engagement situations.

- The basic attacks provide every fencer, coach, and trainer with an unerring indicator for the practical efficacy of their training. Since they are difficult to apply successfully (biomechanical research corroborates this), having success with them is indicative of the fencer's good technical skills.

- This requirement can be met with the following practice examples. Even the successful fencer should not leave these out of his daily training regiment. But before they become an integral part of the training, the fencer must have practiced the previously mentioned basic attacks in their motion sequence as follows:

- The weapon-bearing arm slides into an extended position without lifting or tightening of the shoulder.

- At the moment when the blade point makes contact, the weapon and the arm form a straight line from the blade point to the shoulder.

- Variable start of arm extension during execution with lunge (arm extension simultaneous with the start of leg movement, or leg movement first, then arm movement that overtakes leg movement).

- Variable amplitude and variable progression of the acceleration of leg movements.

Practice examples

The basic idea is to create the most advantageous situation for a basic attack (critical measure, correct time).

1 Middle measure, A and B on guard position
A practices the attack, responds to B's playing with the measure and initially holds the measure.
- B plays with steps forward and backward.
- A follows the step backward with a step forward.
At the same moment that B takes a new step forward, A immediately lunges with a straight thrust.

Since in this exercise A passively waits for the opportune moment to launch an attack, there is the danger that B will use the emerged critical measure for his own attack.
The following exercises actively prepare A for reaching the critical measure.

2 Middle measure, A and B on guard position

A determines the measure and maneuvers with steps forward and backward.

- A carries out his maneuvers with a steady rhythm and tempo (fig. 6.2.-1a).

- B maintains the exact measure.

- After a step forward, A performs only half of the subsequent step backward (even just the indication suffices against nervous fencers), and as soon as B follows he immediately launches his attack (fig. 6.2.-1b).

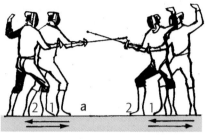

Figure 6.2.-1:
Playing with the measure with steps and attack into the forward movement.

3 Middle measure, A and B on guard position

A maneuvers with a feigned attack (straight thrust) and a half lunge.

- B persistently maintains the measure with a step backward (fig. 6.2.-2a).

- A recovers from a lunge as B moves back and attacks at the moment that B wants to close the wide measure that has developed (fig. 6.2.-2b).

4 Middle measure, A and B on guard position

A takes a double step forward in a short/long rhythm and then immediately moves far back.

- B maintains the measure in the same rhythm.

- Once A has committed B to this rhythm with 1-2 repetitions he suddenly omits the step backward.

- B habitually begins with a step forward.

- A attacks into this forward movement.

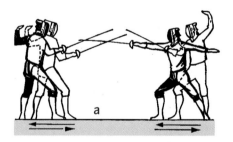

Figure 6.2.-2:
Playing with the measure with a feint attack into the forward movement.

5 Wide measure, A and B on guard position

- A attacks with a forceful feigned attack, but not a full lunge.
- B moves back.
- A begins the maneuver again.
- B stays in place because he previously realized that this feigned attack ends with a measure that does not threaten him.
- At the start of his feigned attack A realizes that B will stop and changes the lunge he started to a step forward-lunge with a straight thrust.

6 Middle measure, A and B on guard position

- A attacks with a feigned attack and a half lunge.
- B evades with a step backward (fig. 6.2.-3a).
- After A has repeated this maneuver several times he stays in the lunge and only returns his blade to the on guard position (fig. 6.2.-3b, phase 1).
- B reacts to the withdrawal of the blade with a step forward.
- A immediately attacks into B's forward movement by dragging the supporting leg behind and going into another lunge (fig. 6.2.-3b, phase 2 and 3).

Figure 6.2.-3: Playing with the measure with a feint attack and attack by dragging behind into the forward movement.

Please note:

- All of the exercises listed here can be further supplemented with variations on so-called footwork elements and also strategic attack elements.

- If these exercises are taught in the form of partner exercises it is essential that B react as the fencer that is being deked. This will enable him to consciously respond to his opponent's intentions in order to achieve combative advantages via appropriate, preplanned counter measures.

- In the following developmental phases the partner's behavior pattern must gradually become competition-like (variable speed, non-rhythmic movements, time changes, disguised changing of measure, immediate egression from critical measure if the opponent has not reacted, etc.).

- In the final developmental phase, measure changes and blade movements must reflect the true behavior of an opponent in combat. But that also means that all of the exercises listed here must be practiced as a whole because, due to his knowledge about the opponent's intentions, the partner can't really be deceived any more with only one exercise.

- It is necessary to point out an important fact in connection with these exercises. From a purely visual point of view the straight thrust in time, for instance, is barely distinguishable from the exercise described under 2. It often happens that identical motion sequences have different tactical intentions. But the designation of strategic elements must reflect the nature of the fencing action. Only then is it possible to specifically orientate the training methodology to the tactical purpose of each movement being learned.

To facilitate the implementation of learned exercises in fencing practice this entire complex should also be practiced in the subsequent from of a conditional assault (practice fight, counter parry).

The exercises always start out at the starting lines. After the starting signal the measure-related work should be structured in such a way that the entire strip is being used. Hits are only counted if leaving the starting zone was accomplished. This form is intended to prevent the fencers from beginning with the actual exercise immediately after taking the first steps.

The ability to maneuver through footwork by means of measure strucutring can only be trained and especially monitored with such mandatory practicing. Dividing the fencing strip into sections is another option for increasing the challenge.

6.2.1.3   Sweep attacks

The difference between these attacks and the direct and disengagement attacks is a preliminary sweeping movement that can be like a thrust or a beat in its execution. They include the *battuta thrust* and the *engagement thrust*.

Variations of these attacks are:
- The glide, a special form of the engagement thrust (characteristic: Contact with the opposing blade is maintained from the start of the engagement until the target is hit).
- The flanconade (glide to the flank) as a variation of the glide.
- The bind (transport) of the opposing blade in a diagonal or circular direction (Riporto).

They are used primarily for:
- Sweeping the opposing blade in line.
- Hampering the opponent's defense.
- Creating a specific opening.

So far the application of the battuta or engagement thrust has been primarily contingent on the lightly or firmly held opposing blade. But this is not a major factor, because every blade can be swept with a beat or a bind. The way the blade is held only determines the force of the beat or the thrust. The crucial factor in applying a battuta or engagement thrust is mainly its intended objective. The opponents generally react differently to the two sweep attacks, regardless of whether they previously held their blade firmly or lightly.

The battuta thrust

The beat on the opposing blade acts as a strong stimulus to which the opponent reacts fiercely. Along with a quick defensive reflex the attacker must occasionally be ready for a touchy testiness. When applied suddenly, this makes the beat an excellent means for interfering with the opponent's attack structure, for camouflaging one's own intentions, and for preparing an attack.

For the same reason an attack with the battuta thrust from a far measure has little chance for success. To hit the target, conditions similar to those for the application of the direct and disengagement attacks must exist with respect to measure and tempo.

The beat makes the opponent's defense against the subsequent thrust more difficult, but it also requires that the attacker have good arm and leg coordination and guide the point accurately.

Against opponents who react to the beat with a reflex action of the appropriate parry, these attacks are executed indirectly, meaning after the battuta with disengagement thrust.

The engagement thrust

Taking the blade, not with pressure on one point but by sliding the blade forward with gradually increasing pressure on the opposing blade, does not cause the opponent to have the same fierce reaction as the battuta. With correct execution and appropriate preparation the opponent recognizes the true intention of the attack very late. During the advance the opponent's blade is engaged.

If the final thrust is made with a disengagement or cutover, emphasizing pressure at the end of the thrusting movement is advisable. This is used particularly with opponents who react with lots of counter pressure.

When using a sweep attack, the attacker has to be much more prepared for counter attacks (displacement counter attacks) than with direct attacks. Consequently he will avoid situations that have a good chance of a successful displacement counter attack (see Chapter 6.2.5.2). The success of a sweep attack depends mostly on the actual engaging or sweeping of the opposing blade via an engagement. This makes a displacement counter-attack impossible.

Methodological recommendations for the schooling of sweep attacks
- Precondition is the mastery of the straight thrust, the disengagement thrust, and the technique for clearing the blade with a beat and an engagement.

- The trainer makes sure that the fencer avoids taking a big swing when clearing the opposing blade. With a disengagement in time he makes him aware of the disadvantage of such a technical error, and by reversing the task (trainer does battuta, fencer the disengagement in time) he proves that a disengagement in time is hardly possible in a critical measure.

- The trainer demands that the (sweep) clearing beat is executed when the opponent's arm is still on its way to blade in line, and he shows the fencer that a beat on the already still blade can easily be disengaged. The practice examples listed in Chapter 6.2.1.1 and 6.2.1.2 can also be used for the preparation of sweep attacks.

The following examples show how the sweep attack can be perfected.

Practice examples
Complex 1
Basic idea: The opponent maneuvers with step forward or with a small lunge. During phrasing the weapon arm is frequently extended. The partner allows the following situation to develop (The fencer is to attack on blade in line. In doing so he has many options.):

1. As the partner advances with blade in line the fencer retreats, engaging the partner's blade with a sixte (he responds without attacking for the moment). When the critical measure has been reached, the attack comes suddenly with a quarte battuta thrust and a lunge in response to the partner's renewed advance.

2. The fencer behaves as in exercise 1, does not engage the sixte, but rather engages the quarte. The attack is made with a sixte glide and a lunge.

3. The fencer again retreats with a sixte engagement, but then immediately attacks with a quarte engagement thrust and forward step – lunge.

4. The fencer behaves as in exercise 3, but engages with a quarte instead of a sixte, and immediately attacks out of the backward movement with a sixte glide and step forward – lunge.

If the partner reacts to the engagement (exercise 3 and 4) with lots of counter-pressure, the fencer must execute the final thrust as a disengagement or cutover thrust. The examples for attack preparation, that are described in these exercises (favorable overall situation) for direct and disengagement attacks, should be added onto.

Complex 2

Basic idea: During exploratory phrasing the opponent proves to be a fencer who reacts to a beat with a reflex defensive counter-beat.

Partner A assumes the role of this fencer; B attacks with a camouflaged beat and disengagement thrust (e.g. camouflaged quarte beat from sixte or octave position, and disengagement thrust against the partner's quarte parry).

Complex 3

Basic idea: During actions against the blade the opponent dodges with disengagements and in doing so he maintains the exact measure. An attack must therefore be made from the far measure and the opposing blade must be seized several times.

1. A tries to engage with an octave, B dodges with a disengagement and retreats. A engages B's blade with step forward in quarte, changes to sixte, and ends the attack with sixte glide and flèche.
2. A again dodges the octave engagement with a disengagement. During the step forward B engages in quarte, then changes to sixte engagement and scores a hit with a cutover thrust.
3. As he advances A engages B's blade in sixte. B retreats and breaks out of the sixte engagement via disengagement. A pursues with step forward-lunge and sixte engagement-disengagement thrust and scores a hit. The exercises in complex 3 can also take on an offensive character if the opponent attacks with a disengagement thrust or improves his position via a change of engagement, instead of just breaking away. All of these options can be varied in complexity for the schooling of decision behavior. For instance, during the step forward A engages B's blade in sixte.

If B then reacts with:
- Change of engagement in quarte, A attacks with disengagement in time against the change of engagement.
- With a disengagement thrust in time and a lunge, A must perform a parry-riposte.
- Step backward and disengagement, A will attack like in exercise 3, with sixte engagement-disengagement, or with a quarte engagement thurst.
- With a step backward and disengagement, A will attempt an attack with sixte or quarte engagement. B dodges the engagement with disengagement in time. A stops his attack and performs a parry-riposte.

The step backward with disengagement can be the conscious preparation for a disengagement attack, particularly if the step backward covered some ground. In doing so B creates a situation that does not contain all of the components of a real sweep attack situation. Recognizing this maneuver should result in the absence of a sweep attack (i.e. not responding to the opponent's intention) or an attack with second intent as the correct solution.

In the following developmental phases the partner varies the different situations and also allows for scenarios for the previously learned attacks to develop. By maneuvering accordingly, he makes it more difficult for the fencer to recognize when a favorable attack situation has developed.

6.2.2   Remise attacks

Remise attacks are attack actions that immediately follow a previous unsuccessful attack, riposte, or counter-attack. The manner in which the attack is continued depends on the measure that developed after the first attack, and on the position and movement of the opposing weapon. We differentiate between direct *remise attacks, disengagement remise attacks, and sweep remise attacks.*

Leg, arm, and trunk movement is contingent on the distance from the opponent and ranges from the upper body bending over and an extended lunge, to repeating the lunge, or to a flèche out of the lunge.

Based on their character, remise attacks can be executed:
• With preplanned intent.
• From a situation with preplanned intent and the finish depending on the opponent's reaction.
• As a spontaneous action to a suddenly arising situation.

6.2.2.1   Direct remise attacks

Direct remise attacks are attack actions that are executed with a straight thrust or an angulated thrust (fig. 6.2.-4) in the same line in which the first attack ended, after a previous unsuccessful attack.

This type is the technically least complicated form of a remise attack. By incorporating a direct remise attack into a simple exercise complex the fencer is most likely to develop the necessary ability to make a correct alternative decision to either perform a counter parry-riposte or a remise attack after the initial attack.

Figure 6.2.-4: Direct remise attack with the upper body bent forward.

Direct remise attacks can be used in the following situations:

- The opponent dodges the attack by moving backward. He does not parry, or only does so briefly or barely respectively, and does not immediately carry out the riposte. Once this peculiarity is recognized the attack is continued in the same line with a straight thrust or an angulated thrust. The leg and trunk movements depend on the specific measure after the initial attack (extended lunge, dragging behind of supporting leg-lunge, flèche, etc.).
- The opponent parries the attacks in the last second, and immediately executes a quick riposte into the high opening without orienting himself. Due to the fencer's forceful and long attack, recovering from the lunge and launching a defense are hardly possible. A direct remise attack with a straight thrust or an angulated thrust and withdrawal of the target area is carried out. In doing so the torso is tilted far forward and to the inside. Due to the speed of the action this form is usually executed without additional footwork.
- The opponent habitually carries out a certain remise attack in a specific rhythm. If this characteristic is identified a remise attack can be executed to block the start of the opposing riposte.

6.2.2.2 Disengagement remise attacks

These are attack actions that are executed after a previous unsuccessful attack, in another opening with a disengagement or a cutover thrust. In terms of technique of movement they are similar to the direct remise attacks, but are usually performed from a slightly farther measure to make the disengagement of the opposing weapon and the thrust into an uncovered opening possible. Footwork preferences are an extended lunge, dragging behind-lunge, and flèche out of a lunge.

- An opponent often responds to an attack with a safe parry without carrying out a riposte. A disengagement remise attack with disengagement or cutover thrust in the unguarded opening is executed (fig. 6.2.-5) to take advantage of this peculiarity

Figure 6.2.05: Disengagement remise attack with extended lunge.

6.2.2.2 Sweep remise attacks

Sweep remise attacks are attack actions that are executed, directly or indirectly, with a sweep attack after a previous unsuccessful attack.

Applicable situations

- The opponent frequently dodges an attack with a measured backward movement and determines the line. A direct remise attack is not possible because priority has passed to the opponent. In this situation the attack can be continued with a battuta thrust in the same line with an extended lunge, or with a flèche (fig. 6.2.-6).

Figure 6.2.-6:
Sweep remise attack with flèche.

- The opponent dodges an attack in on guard position or blade in line. In this situation the attack can be continued with a direct or indirect engagement-thrust (also battuta), dragging behind of the supporting leg with another lunge, step forward-lunge, or other footwork.

Methodological recommendations for the schooling of remise attacks

Preconditions are:

- Mastery of basic attacks and ripostes.
- Tactical skills with respect to remise attacks in connection with the rules of competition.
- Skills for carrying out tactically accurate feigned attacks.
- Ability to perform lunges of varying lengths and at different speeds.

- Before learning the actions it is necessary for the trainer to once again explain and demonstrate the options for application, the various forms of remise attacks and their application in accordance with the rules of competition to the fencer, because a remise attack can only be legally executed if it begins after the opponent's initial unsuccessful attack, in terms of time, prior to an attack or riposte. Exceptions are remise attacks with withdrawal of the target area and with opposition, whereby the attacking fencer cannot be hit by the riposte.

- The various forms of remise attacks are practiced with a variety of footwork under agreed conditions, for the schooling of motion sequences.

- Groups of exercises are designed in which only the initial attack is executed as a planned action. The decision whether and how a remise attack is executed depends on the partner's reaction and behavior pattern.

- A specific form of remise attack is agreed upon to practice primarily the moment of the execution of a remise attack. If all components of the agreed situation are specified after the initial attack (e.g. parries, slight retreat and absence of riposte), the fencer must resolutely continue the attack (e.g. remise attacks with disengagement via extended lunge).

- The execution of remise attacks, as deliberate actions, as actions with previously thought-out intent, require the perfection of feint attacks. The fencer must execute his feint attack according to the opponent's typical actions and reactions. He can influence the measure and the action prerequisites for a remise attack through the type, range, and speed of his feint attacks.

- The trainer (partner) has to simulate the different, some previously mentioned, situations, and in doing so has to take into account the typical behavior of the various opponents.

- At the beginning of the learning process the trainer (partner) offers the fencer the most favorable conditions for executing the actions. Gradually the conditions are changed and made more difficult through varied measure design and blade position, shorter breaks, and faster execution of actions. A faster execution of a planned action at the moment the situation arises and specific preparation of such situations places increasingly higher and competition-like demands on the fencer.

Practice examples
Complex 1
Basic idea: Perfection of motion sequence in remise attacks.

1. • A carries out a quarte engagement with a cautious, short lunge.
   • B parries the attack with a short quarte parry without carrying out a riposte.
   • With an extended lunge A continues the attack with a straight thrust into the not fully protected opening.

2. • A carries out an attack with a sixte engagement-disengagement thrust to the flank and a short lunge.
   • B parries at the last second (apparently surprised) with an octave parry and does not perform a riposte.
   • Subsequently A continues the attack with a disengagement thrust into the high opening via an extended lunge.

3. • A launches an attack with sixte bind-thrust to the flank with step forward-lunge.
   • B dodges the attack with blade-in-line and step backward.
   • A continues the attack with quarte batuta-thrust by dragging behind out of the lunge, and flèche.

4. • A attacks with quarte battuta-thrust and jump forward-lunge.
   • A subsequently continues the attack with quarte engagement-thrust by dragging behind, and step forward-lunge.

Complex 2
Basic idea: After the attack, the measure that has developed and the position of the weapons are different. The remise attack should be executed according to the situation.

1. • A carries out an attack:
   • If B parries the final thrust with quarte parry and immediately executes a direct riposte, A must return to guard from the lunge and parry the riposte (e.g. with a quarte).
   • If B parries the attack with quarte without retreating and does not carry out a riposte, A continues the attack with an angulated thrust and bent over upper body.
   • If B parries by retreating slightly, A continues the attack with a straight thrust by extending the lunge.
   • If B parries with step backward, but then immediately uncovers the opening again without carrying out a riposte, A can continue the attack with a straight thrust via dragging behind-lunge.

2. • A launches an attack:
   • If B maintains the agreed measure, parries the final thrust with quarte, and carries out a riposte, A must use a counter parry-counter riposte.
   • If B parries the final thrust with a short quarte and no riposte follows, A carries out a direct remise attack.
   • If B parries the final thrust with a long quarte (also sixte, etc.) so that the opening is covered, A continues the attack with disengagement or cutover thrust.
   • If B dodges the final thrust and presents blade-in-line, A carries out a sweep remise attack with quarte battuta-thrust (compare to fig. 6.2.-4; 6.2.-5; 6.2.-6). These exercises can be combined in many variations and thereby are very demanding with respect to the partners' concentration and reaction ability. In doing so, every possible change in the measure can be expediently combined with every possible position and movement of the blade. The initial attack action must be arranged.

Complex 3
Basic idea: Schooling of remise attacks in a suddenly arising situation.

1. • A carries out an indirect sixte engagement thrust with jump forward-lunge, returns to guard and counter-parry-riposte.

   • B reacts with step backward and quarte parry, and subsequently carries out a riposte. This attack action is frequently repeated with slight movement, but a fairly constant measure.

   • At a preferably unexpected moment partner B does not carry out a riposte after the parry.

   • Following that, A immediately and quickly reacts with the disengagement remise attack, cutover thrust, dragging behind, and lunge.

2. • A performs a straight thrust with step forward-lunge (very forceful and long). The attack scores a hit and is executed forcefully several times.

   • If B suddenly parries the attack in the last second with quarte and begins a riposte into the high opening, A carries out a direct remise attack with withdrawal of the target area by bending over and slightly to the inside and performing an angulated thrust. A quick recovery from the lunge is no longer possible.

Complex 4
Basic idea: Schooling of remise attacks with previously thought-out intent.

1. • A carries out an attack with octave bind and thrust into the high opening. This attack is executed with a medium, but very soft lunge that does not force the opponent to retreat very far. The execution of the thrust must be such that it forces the opponent (partner) to parry, but does not offer him the safety of riposte.

   • B retreats slightly, takes sixte parry and remains, slightly uncertain, in this position.

   • A continues the attack with disengagement thrust into the uncovered opening by extending the lunge (very quick and forceful!).

2. • A has discovered B's peculiarity of frequently performing an indirect riposte into the high opening at a certain rhythm after the octave parry. He attacks with battuta thrust to the flank with step forward-lunge. In doing so he ends the final thrust very abruptly. At the same moment as B begins his riposte A starts a quick and forceful thrust into the high opening. He thereby blocks the opponent's riposte and is the only one to score a hit.

6.2.3 Parries

Parries are defensive actions that prevent an opposing hit via movements with one's own weapon.

The particular difficulty with defense is that the opposing attack generally occurs when one is in an unfavorable position, and the opponent exploits that moment. Examples of such situations were given in connection with the application of attacks. Contrary to the attack where one has to choose the best possible moment, the parry – if it was not prepared, meaning the opposing attack was provoked and anticipated – must occur during a moment of surprise. It must be a reflex under minimal conscious control. The parry must thus also come confidently and end in a position that provides a favorable starting position for the riposte, even if attention had been focused on something other than the parry.

Training such skills through purely technical exercises is not possible, because they are not just the result of accuracy and speed of movement, but rather depend on other factors (reaction speed, alertness, quick assessment of spatial position, measure, etc.), which are perfected very little or not at all during mere technical training. But to allow these skills to develop strictly through competitions would be an interminable process.

Modern fencing methodology dictates that situations that are characteristic of real fights should be consciously created during training.

To be able to effectively defend one-self, the following questions of detail need to be answered:

• From which line is an attack launched?

• How large is the amplitude of an attack movement?

• What is the execution speed of an attack?

• With what measure did the attack start?

In previous publications parries have been subdivided in a variety of ways. This was mostly done according to the direction of movement. From a tactical aspect we would like to divide the parries into specific parries and general parries.

Specific parries
These only cover the opening threatened by the direction of the opposing thrust. All of the previously learned parries, such as opposition and changes to parries, beat parries, circular parries, etc., belong to this group if they are used to cover an opening that appears to be threatened.

Specific parries also include feint parries that are executed with the goal of forcing the opponent to thrust into a specific opening. The terms "accompanying parry and stop hit" are often seen in this context. The accompanying parries accompany the opponent's feints and the purpose of the stop hit is to parry the actual final thrust. The difference between the two is that the feint parry is consciously used to deceive the opponent. By contrast, the accompanying parry is an after-effect of the opponent's feints.

Since it is an excellent means for an organized defense, the feint parry must have a permanent place in the fencer's training process.

General parries
These are defensive actions that sweep the opposing blade via large circular or semi-circular movements (e.g. the semi-circular prime from sixte). They are used against aggressive opponents and those with stereotypical attacks.

General parries provide a gain in time because they begin before the direction of the thrust is perceived. However, their unpredictable blade relationships and a mostly very narrow measure are a disadvantage, and often make a riposte nearly impossible. They should never be used as emergency parries, rather their use should always be planned. If a general parry is used against an attack that was recognized too late, it is almost always successful. If it is used often and habitually it can also be easily disengaged, which then often leads to a hit.

Methodological recommendations for the schooling of parries
- Learning the parries is not very difficult for the beginner because he is already familiar with the motion sequences from the position changes. But he has to make sure that the final position of the parry conforms to the attack and is occasionally taken higher, lower, closer to the body, or farther away. It is important that the physical lever principle be observed and that one's forte is set against the opponent's foible.

- The successful application of a parry in competition is the result of a complicated process that is influenced by a number of different factors.

- Depending on the character of the attack, the following variations of parries can be used:

- Taking the parry while standing still, with step backward (most frequent form), with step forward, or in a lunge.

- Intercepting the opposing blade at the moment when the attacker begins the lunge (can be used against long, sustained feints; through the parry the attack is practically destroyed at the start).

- Taking the parry at the moment when the attacker's trunk is positioned between his starting position and the final lunge position (most frequently used form of the parry).

- Taking the parry when the opponent's point is already very close to the body and the lunge is nearly completed. The parry is close to the body, the amplitude of the blade movement is broad, the point in quarte and sixte parry points up at a steep angle, in septime and octave parry it points down at a steep angle.

It is important to make sure that the speed of movement corresponds to the respective exercise. Maximum speed is required for the second and fourth options, and for the third variation the speed should correspond to the speed of the attack. As a result this variation is also particularly advantageous in the use of feint parries.

Many textbooks have been written on the execution technique of parries and how to learn it. We will therefore limit ourselves to practice examples that already incorporate tactical tasks and serve the perfecting of the motion sequence.

Practice examples

Situation A
One of the partners provokes a disengagement thrust in time via broad blade movement, subsequent engagement and advance. He prepares the parry with this maneuver. He concentrates on the opposing attack, and in doing so he gains time to take the parry. The other partner occasionally attacks with disengagement thrust and lunge.

Partner A parries with a small step backward and ripostes
- while standing still, if B recovers from the lunge too late.

- with a lunge, if B immediately returns to guard.

- with step backward or with a bent arm, if B continues to advance.

- with disengagement thrust and lunge, if B returns to guard from the lunge and opposes the blade. B can increase the difficulty of the exercise by not reacting (standing still) to A's advance with taking of the blade. This creates a favorable situation for an attack out of the taken engagment, which A is meant to recognize. If B reacts to A's advance without motivation by closing the measure with step forward, A should immediately thrust out of his engagement with bent arm or with step backward.

Additional variations develop the fencer's parry reflexes:
- B attacks with a straight thrust if A returns to the starting position after the engagement.

- B attacks with disengagement thrust feint in time. The parry that A prepared is disengaged by the feint attack. When A realizes that he was not successful with the first parry, he must immediately take the second parry.

The trainer has to make sure that, while preparing the attack, the defending fencer assumes a measure that, on the one hand, lets the opponent think his attack is promising but, on the other hand, also offers the possibility of fending off the provoked attack. The better his parrying ability is the more daring he can be in offering a favorable situation, and the faster the opponent will choose this attack.

Situation B

Bearing in mind the details of a successful defense, the fencer deliberately creates other situations that will provoke the opponent into an attack. Potentially successful situations for a straight thrust, disengagement thrust, cutover thrust, angulated thrust, engagement thrust, or battuta thrust were specified in Chapter 6.2.1.

Fencer B carries out the appropriate attacks to give A opportunity for parry-riposte. Beyond that B can sometimes attack with a feint attack to challenge A to surprise parries, or to respond to the riposte with a counter-parry riposte against which A is meant to defend himself.

Sudden surprise attacks during the preparatory actions or after an attack that just ended are other suitable means for schooling defensive reflexes.

6.2.4 Ripostes

Ripostes are attack actions that follow a successful defensive action. Prerequisite is the parry on whose quality the success of the riposte largely depends.

The motion sequences of the strategic attack elements used for ripostes have already been specified in Chapter 6.2.1. Here we will focus on the particularities of their application. In principle all strategic attack elements and combinations of the same can be used for ripostes.
Ripostes are divided into *direct ripostes, disengagement ripostes* and *sweep ripostes*.

The application possibilities for these three forms depend on measure, blade position, opponent's reaction, and whether or not the preceding defensive action was prepared. In case of the latter, the situation-appropriate use of the riposte would be much more difficult for the fencer to accomplish.

6.2.4.1   Direct ripostes

Direct ripostes are direct basic attacks that immediately follow a successful defensive action. The most frequently used form is the direct riposte carried out with a straight thrust. It is also referred to as *immediate riposte*.

Direct ripostes are carried out in narrow to middle measure. In doing so the measure is determined by the preceding attack action. Ripostes can be successful if the opponent is still physically and mentally occupied with his own attack at the moment they begin.

Angulated thrusts as direct ripostes are mostly carried out with the goal of accessing difficult to reach target areas, or to render the counter-parry of the opponent, who is not retreating after his unsuccessful attack, ineffective.

6.2.4.2   Disengagement ripostes

Disengagement ripostes are disengagements that immediately follow a successful defensive action. In doing so the disengagement has the goal of disengaging a premature or habitually applied defensive movement by the opponent, or to reach a target area other than the one directly opposite.

Disengagement ripostes are also referred to as *indirect ripostes.* It must be pointed out that these are not feints. They are executed at a fencing pace.

Only arrest counter attacks can be used here if one wishes to meet the disengagement riposte with a counter attack. But by no means counter attacks with a gain in time.

The type of disengagement used depends mostly on measure, blade position, and the opponent's reaction. The cutover-riposte is preferred in a very narrow measure.

A peculiarity of disengagement ripostes is that if the opponent does not immediately retreat again, the disengagement must be completely finished in the respective parry position, and only then is the arm extended. The previously described spiral forward movement of the point (Chapter 6.2.1.2) is thus only possible if the opponent retreats again, simultaneously with the execution of the disengagement riposte.

6.2.4.3   Sweep ripostes

Sweep ripostes are sweep attacks that are executed immediately after a successful defensive action. The determining factor is that the attacker retreats with blade in line before the defender has started his riposte. In this case the defender cannot attack directly since he would be lunging against the opposing line. He is therefore forced to disengage it.
Another optional use would be for the defender to make a change after a successful parry to force the uncovering of a particular opening.

The tactical justification for such an action, if it is not an end in itself, is the observation that the opponent is very strong in defending the opening that has been uncovered by the parry, but has revealed weaknesses with respect to the attacks into the opening that has been uncovered by the changeover.

Methodological recommendations for the schooling of ripostes

- Aside from the special features that develop during the execution of ripostes, during schooling of the same the fencer should be made aware from the start of the variety of riposte possibilities from the individual parry positions. Although the immediate riposte is the most commonly used and must occupy an appropriate place in the practice program, here, too, only the fencer, who can behave in accordance with the different situations and has various resolutions for a specific situation, will be successful.

- Often a narrow measure develops during defensive actions. For the riposte to be successful in such a case, the fencer must be made familiar with the particularities of close quarters. In doing so, the direction of the thrust differs strongly from the basic technique. Reaching the opposing target area in the shortest possible way from every blade position in narrow measure requires practice. We consider these exercises to also be a form of schooling of coordinative abilities. In doing so, attention should be paid to the movement restrictions in close quarters specified by the regulations (shoulder axis, over-head hand position).

- In a riposte the thrust direction is usually downward because the valid target area on the lunging opponent is lower.

- Since the opposing advance is utilized, the riposte occurs mostly in narrow measure. To safely score a hit, the point must first be adjusted before the arm is extended. It is also possible to execute the riposte with a bent arm if the opponent continues to advance.

- Attackers who want to avoid the riposte by ducking should be hit on the back (works well with angular thrust from the top).

- Naturally the schooling of defensive elements is always linked with a particular form of ripostes. Naturally, because in fencing only he who scores hits (meaning, he who unhesitatingly uses the psychological advantages that result from a successful defense to score a hit) can be successful. But in the process of perfecting them, the trainer should not let this fact induce him to view these two strategic elements as an inseparable entity. The riposte should not become an automatic appendage to a parry. That would make it truly dangerous.

- The fencer should be made aware that the various forms of riposte application are determined by tactical situations. He must seek out the target and not mechanically execute the parry-riposte (one-two).

- Stereotypical riposting without recognizing or considering the actual tactical situation downright provokes the opponent into remises with evasive maneuvers, or into second intention respectively.

- In contrast, deliberately varying the rhythm in the parry-riposte sequence opens up additional tactical possibilities (false anticipation by the opponent).

Figure 6.2.-8:
Quarte parry-riposte in close quarters with a half volte.

Figure 6.2.-7:
Quarte-riposte in close quarters overhead.

Practice examples

Basic idea: The exercises are based on the assumption that the defense, subject to the opponent's behavior, was deliberately organized.

1 Wide measure, A and B on guard position

- penetrates the critical measure with double step (long-short). With the second step he begins to feint with a straight thrust.

- With a feint parry circular sixte and step backward B forces A into a premature disengagement.
- After the disengagement, A immediately goes into a lunge.
- B parries with quarte while standing still and immediately ripostes.

2 **Same sequence as exercise 1, only**
- B takes a step forward with quarte parry and thereby creates a close quarters situation.
- A remains in a lunge and B first orients himself before starting the riposte.

3 **Middle measure, A and B on guard position**
- A wants to explore with a half lunge and straight thrust.
- B immediately parries with quarte while standing still.
- A realizes the danger and retreats right away, while B immediately starts a direct riposte (straight thrust).
- A retreats further with quarte parry.
- B sees the changed measure and continues the riposte with step forward-flèche and thrust feint-cutover thrust.

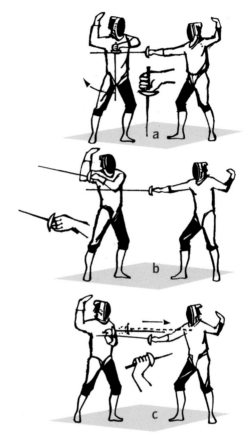

Figure 6.2.-9:
Prime parry-riposte in close quarters as cutover thrust.

4 **Middle measure, A and B on guard position**
Prepared like exercise 3.
- B reacts with quarte parry and step backward without riposting right away.

- A retreats, and while recovering from the lunge assumes a lower blade position.

- Thereupon B executes thrust feint-cutover thrust with double step forward as a preparatory action.

- A merely holds the measure without any further reaction and then begins again with the same preparation. But in doing so he emphasizes the lunge and immediately recovers with blade in line after B's quarte parry.

- B realizes that the situation has changed, maintains contact with the opposing blade and immediately switches over to riposte with quarte engagement thrust and step forward-lunge. At this point it is also possible to switch from quarte bind to sixte, and then attack.

5 Wide measure, A blade in line and B on guard position

- B engages A in sixte, and after engaging the weapon immediately attacks the flank with step forward-lunge and sixte engagement thrust.
- A dodges with step backward and parries with octave.
- B opposes, A now adjusts his behavior based on the timing of the opposition and the measure that developed by B retreating.
- If B opposes right away and in doing so remains in a lunge, A carries out a disengagement riposte while standing still without changing the fist position.
- If B stands up from the lunge and opposes at the same time, A executes a disengagement riposte with lunge.
- If B begins to oppose, then stands up and continues to dodge with quarte parry and step backward, A executes a disengagement thrust feint (due to the changed measure the started disengagement riposte automatically becomes a feint) and disengagement thrust.

6.2.5   Counter attacks

Counter attacks are attack actions that immediately utilize the opponent's actions for preparing an attack or attack actions for one's own attack. They are executed at the same time as the opponent's attack action and exploit inaccuracies (in terms of conventions) or faulty strategic-tactical behavior by the opponent for one's own attack.

Counter attacks are gaining significance in modern fencing, but require a high degree of tactical skill. Through systematic misinformation the opponent must be provoked into behaving in a way that would benefit the execution of the chosen counter-attack. Thus counter attacks require good tactical preparation, but their training again contributes to the effective development of those skills.

6.2.5.1   Counter attacks with gain in time

With regard to their execution, *counter attacks with gain in time* are straight thrusts that take advantage of the convention of priority during their execution.

These counter attacks are carried out in the immediate preparation of basic or compound attacks or during compound attacks by the opponent respectively, and must meet a tempo (fencing time in terms of competition regulations) before the end of the opposing attack.

In their concrete form they are therefore also referred to as *straight thrust in time* and *angulated thrust* in time.

Counter attacks with gain in time are executed in the following situations:

a) When an opponent begins an attack in critical measure with the body without extending the arm. Once this behavior pattern has been recognized and the moment and the type of attack have been detected, the counter attack "straight thrust in time with lunge" is executed into the opponent's first body movement.

b) When the opponent attempts to create a more favorable measure for an attack by maneuvering. He tries to be successful with compound attacks from a longer distance (tactically strong fencers can handle this situation).

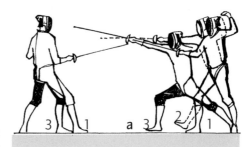

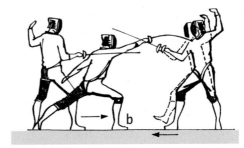

Figure 6.2.-10:
Illustration of a counter attack with gain in time; b) is possible, a) is not possible.

Counter attacks are possible in these compound attacks:
- With a straight thrust in time during a brief break in the compound attack that was provoked by a behavior pattern the opponent was unfamiliar with.

- During the first, second, but at least during the next to last tempo of the opposing compound attack. It is crucial that the hit be placed one tempo sooner, meaning the arm extension for the gain in time has already begun before the opponent begins his final action.

These counter attacks are most often executed before the start of the lunge, in other words, into the opponent's advance. They consist of one action, and their execution is explosive and occurs primarily from a rest position, but never out of one's own backward movement. Deciding if and when

Figure 6.2.-11:
Illustration of a counter-attack with gain in time into the next to last tempo of an attack.

a counter-attack with gain in time can be used depends on the assessment of whether or not the referee will notice the gain in time. The trainer bears lots of responsibility here. Contingencies should be avoided.

Methodological recommendations for the schooling of counter attacks with gain in time
Situation A

Prerequisite is the mastery of a quick, straight thrust with lunge out of a relative rest position and upon reactive demand.

- The trainer or partner creates the above-mentioned situations with the objective of developing perception and recognition of the proper situation for these counter attacks. Initially recognition is facilitated by exaggeration of, for instance, a preparatory movement prior to an attack or swinging for a thrust. The counter-attack is carried out into the agreed but realistic fight situation. It should be noted that the situation is only realistic if all elements of the situation are present, like
- opponent advances into critical measure,
- weapon-bearing arm is adducted,
- attack is started with the body as a recurring action,
- seriousness of the attack.

The moment the situation sets in is initially adumbrated by the aid of a constant rhythm of the preparatory actions.

- The trainer or partner camouflages the setting of the situation by maneuvering. The fencer must execute the counter-attack only when the agreed upon situation has set in.

During this phase training can focus on improving the reaction ability and the ability to make tactical distinctions, and on strengthening technique during explosive, reactive movements.

Situation B

- The developmental steps should be performed similarly, but with more variability of the individual situations. The fencer must learn to recognize the right moment for the start of the counter attack against the various compound attacks, which can occur at varying speeds and rhythms.

Important is that the start of the counter attack occurs at moments during which the opponent is not able fend off or cut short the attack. It is recommended that trainer and fencer work via task reversal. The fencer launches combined attacks, the trainer carries out the counter attack in the right moments. Add to that the step of tactically consciously creating situations for counter attacks. Steadily retreating from the opponent's attacks, if necessary with defensive actions, requires combined attacks from a far measure, if this sequence is apparently unconsciously repeated. After demonstrations by the trainer this step becomes a matter of partner training.

- Based on the beginning of the action, this group of counter attacks also includes *sweep counter attacks*. These are attack actions that begin with a sweep of the opposing line, and that take advantage of the mistakes the opponent makes in his advance.

Figure 6.2.-12:
Illustration of a sweep counter-attack (possible and not possible)

The general situation for this emerges as follows:

- The opponent begins his attack with simultaneous arm extension from a far measure (correct would be: approach with bent arm; extension only begins when the critical measure has been reached). The sweep counter-attack with lunge or flèche takes place during the step or jump forward.

It is important to note that the overall action begins with the sweep movement (quick and forward). The battuta is generally used for a sweep. Fencers with excellent coordination of movement can also use engagements and even transports to sweep.

When using the battuta it is important to emphasize the correct moment of the start of the action (beginning of the attack), unambiguousness in the active taking of the iron, and the correct technical execution, because the referee may interpret the events incorrectly.

Methodological recommendations for the schooling of sweep counter attacks

- The partner must vary his advance from a far measure to the effect, that he begins by irregularly alternating between bending and extending the arm. This will develop the fencer's tactical differentiation ability and helps him to memorize the correct moment for this form of counter attacks more quickly.

- The following variation has been built into schooling to make the fencer aware of the undesirable consequences of a delayed start:

After a calm advance with bent arm, the arm is suddenly extended just before the advance ends, and the attacker immediately goes into a lunge.

If the fencer attempts a sweep counter attack during this phase (this situation requires a parry) it will usually fail, or it will be very difficult for the referee to make a correct interpretation. The sweep is either viewed as an insufficient parry or it is attributed to the opponent as a valid parry.

Practice examples

When schooling counter attacks the blocks of exercises should always be configured in such a way, that the attack on which the counter-attack is based could be executed with equal frequency. A combination with a third exercise, that includes a similar situation but due to the measure or blade position does not permit the execution of a counter attack, simultaneously schools the tactical differentiation ability.

Exercises for the straight thrust in time
1 **Middle measure and quarte touch (no measure play)**
a) A disengages and goes into octave position.
   • A follows with a step forward.

   • A's first forward movement is immediately followed by a counter attack with a straight thrust with lunge or flèche by B.

b) A disengages and goes into octave position.
   After completion of the position change, B immediately begins with straight thrust and lunge or flèche. (Since B starts here, it is obviously not a counter attack).
   • A parries with sixte and immediately ripostes.

c) From the contact in quarte with arm extension and lunge A begins a straight thrust.
   • B parries with quarte and immediately ripostes.

2 **Far measure, A on guard position, B octave invitation (open measure play)**
a) A advances with double step forward (short-long) or jump forward-step forward into the critical measure, and in doing so feints with a slightly bent arm inside – outside – inside – outside, etc.
   • B maintains the exact measure and accompanies with quarte and sixte parry.

   • A continues with thrust feint-disengagement thrust and jump forward-lunge in B's rhythm.

b) A's behavior stays the same.
   • B accompanies only the first step or jump forward with step backward, and after that immediately carries out the counter attack with a straight thrust.

   • A performs a sixte parry and ripostes.

3   Far measure, open blade position, open measure play

a) A begins with quarte engagement and step forward-flèche.
- B avoids the engagement attempt via step backward and by going into octave position.

- A immediately continues aggressively with thrust feint-cutover and step forward-lunge or step forward-flèche.

b) A's behavior stays the same.
- B again avoids the engagement attempt, but accompanies A's thrust feint with only a half step backward and then immediately carries out the counter attack with a straight thrust.

Exercises for the sweep counter-attack

1   Far measure, A and B on guard position

a) A attempts to reach the critical measure via tempo and rhythm changes in the footwork.
- B thwarts this by maintaining the exact measure.
- A attacks from a far measure with an immediate arm extension.
- B immediately begins with quarte battuta in time and hits the target.

b) Same starting position.
- A attacks from a far measure with step-jump forward and picks up speed at the same time. The arm extension begins during the jump. The lunge is completed with lunge or flèche (depending on the measure).

- B tries to maintain the measure, parries the attack with quarte in his final phase and immediately parries.

2   Far measure, A and B on guard position

a) A begins an attack with arm extension and step forward.
- B maintains the measure, thereby forcing A to break off the attack.
- A attempts another attack in the same way.
- B starts the counter attack by engaging the opposing blade in sixte and transporting it to septime during the beginning of the lunge or flèche.

b) Same starting position.
- Following A's first attempt, B stands still and forces A into a disengagement attack via a demonstrative sixte parry (as a feint parry).
- A reacts to the feint parry, disengages it and immediately lunges.
- B dodges with a small step backward, parries with quarte after the feint parry and immediately ripostes.

6.2.5.2 Displacement counter attacks

With respect to their execution, *displacement counter attacks* are disengagement attacks. These counter attacks can be used against all forms of sweep attacks. In their concrete form they are referred to as *disengagement in time* and *cutover in time*.

With both forms it is important that the blades do not make contact, or else the priority will remain with the opponent. In addition the displacement counter-attack should always be combined with a forward movement of the entire body. Displacement counter attacks that are only executed via an arm extension – possibly combined with a bending over of the upper body – are very difficult for the referee to recognize, and thus carry with them the possibility of a faulty judgment (figure 6.2.-13).

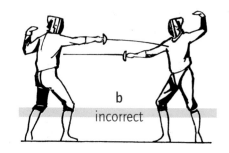

Figure 6.2.-13:
Displacement counter-attack

In addition the forward movement makes it more difficult for the opponent to score a hit at the same time, and makes it easier to correctly judge the action.

Most successful displacement counter attacks usually have to be consciously prepared with maneuvers. This necessity results from the fact that it is impossible to passively await the beginning of a sweep attack against a technically skilled opponent. Contact with the opposing blade is then unavoidable. The only exceptions here are opponents who stereotypically operate with a sweep attack (which are, however, an exception in competition events).

Displacement counter attacks are possible in the following situations:
a) By means of repeated feigned attacks with demonstrative extension of the weapon arm the opponent is presented with a favorable situation for a sweep attack. In doing so the feigned attack can be performed with a step or a quarter to half lunge. It is important to remain in line for only a very brief moment, and then immediately retreat (fig. 6.2.-14a).

With this maneuver the possible moment for a sweep attack is temporally highly restricted. At this moment every forward movement by the opponent becomes a signal for the start of the displacement counter-attack, thus making it successful even if the opponent begins the sweep attack without reaching back at all (fig. 6.2.-14b).

b) The same effect can be achieved via a demonstratively relaxed parry-riposte phrase outside of the critical measure. In doing so the opposing feigned attacks are answered with parry and feint riposte. In the first example the line of the riposte is held only briefly, followed by an immediate retreat.

c) The preparation of a displacement counter-attack against sweep attacks that are executed with a change of engagement differs from the previous examples. A longer period of time is available for the

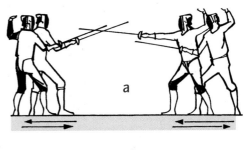

Figure 6.2.-14:
Illustration of a disengagement counter attack situation

beginning of the displacement counter attack. This is due to the fact that with a change of engagement the period of time from the beginning of the movement until the blades make contact is longer than with a direct battuta or engagement respectively.

Once it has been established that the opponent prefers this type of sweep attack, he should be offered the blade for an engagement the way it is shown in the first and also the second example. The retreat comes much later, is calmer, and holds the line. As soon as the opponent begins the change of engagement, the displacement movement immediately follows with simultaneous lunge or with flèche.

Please note:
If the opponent attacks quickly while keeping up the initial bind (there is no change of engagement), a displacement attack is no longer possible.

Methodological recommendations for the schooling of displacement counter attacks
Prerequisite is the mastery of the various forms of disengagement attacks with varying arm and leg coordination.
- The main focus of training must be the ability to tactically differentiate between situations that facilitate displacement counter attacks and those in which their application would be incorrect.

- Preliminary movements to promote identification of the attack moment should be performed not so much during the blade movement, as at the beginning of the forward movement.

- If the fencer is already moving backward the execution of the displacement counter attack should definitely not be required. The taking of the blade should be parried because it will be very difficult for the referee to objectively assess the circumstances.

- Due to the previously listed peculiarities of the cutover, the trompement is the most advantageous form of a displacement counter-attack. But since a successful execution requires particularly good skills, it should not be started prematurely.

Practice examples

1. Derobement (middle measure, A and B on guard position)
A previously noticed that B prefers the quarte engagement attack.
a) A offers B the line with a partially extended arm.
   - immediately takes this opportunity to start a quarte engagement attack.
   - A prevents the engagement attempt with a derobement combined with a half lunge.

b) Same starting position.
   - B manages to make contact with the opposing blade.
   - Subsequently he is no longer able to execute a disengagement attack and immediately reacts to the opposing engagement with a change to quarte parry standing still. Since B cannot break off his engagement attack right away, the parry must be taken very close to the body.

2. Trompement (middle measure, A and B normal fencing position)
A carries out a feigned attack with straight thrust and step forward. Immediately after finishing the step he returns to on guard with the blade and takes an additional step backward (compare to fig. 6.2.-14a).
a) At first B maintains the measure, but plans to immediately attack with quarte battuta thrust upon a redoublement by A.
   - A repeats the preparation and reacts to B's first movement with a cutover thrust in time and lunge (compare fig. 6.2.-14b).

b) With a slight backward movement, B feints keeping the measure and then immediately starts to attack with thrust feint-cutover and step forward-flèche.
   - The moment B's attack begins A has already returned to on guard. He reacts to the thrust feint with quarte and step backward, and tries to answer the final thrust with circular parry-riposte.

6.2.5.3 Stop hits

Stop hits are attack actions that are executed with the goal to block the opposing blade's path to the target area, thereby preventing getting hit at the same time. They can be executed at the start of the opponent's attack action. Their purpose in this case would be to block the opposing disengagement movement.

But the stop hit can also be executed against the final thrust.

In doing so the thrust is executed with simultaneous opposition of one's own blade in order to block the opposing blade. If the fencer who is carrying out the stop hit is also hit he will always be awarded the hit.

With regard to their execution, stop hits are straight thrusts or straight thrusts with opposition.

Blocking the final thrust requires a high degree of certainty in terms of anticipation of the goal and the start of the opposing attack.

An error will turn the intended stop hit into an unjustifiable thrust. The blocking of a final thrust is applicable in the following situation:

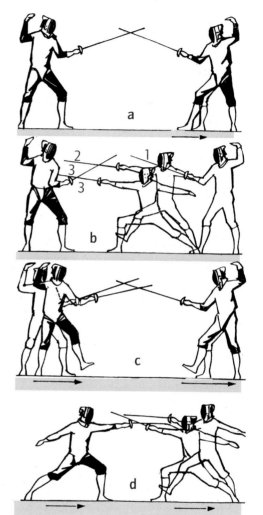

Figure 6.2.-15:
Illustration of a stop hit
(possible and not possible)

It has been determined through observation that the opponent prefers the high outside target area. The fencer deliberately responds to the opponent's attack preparation. In doing so he moves in close proximity to the critical measure.

In addition the preferred target area is presented via appropriate blade movement or blade position. The fencer focuses on the points of reference that will allow him to anticipate the opponent's attack.

Such points of reference are, among others, penetrating the critical measure, changes to the fencing stance, rhythm changes in measure play, or aiming the point. Once the fencer is sure about the start of the opposing attack, he can immediately begin his own stop hit attack (fig. 6.2.-15c, d).

Due to certain particularities we will offer a more detailed description of the execution of the stop hit attack. In our example the point of the blade describes a spiral from front/low/outside to high/inside to high/outside with a simultaneously extended arm. The fist supports the blade movement by gradually going from the starting position to an opposite position high/outside until the hit is delivered (fig. 6.2.-16).

The spiral movement is a necessary requirement for all forms of opposition, because there will always be minor divergences in the straightness of the opponent's final thrust, and the blade movements described here prevent the slipping of the opposing blade.

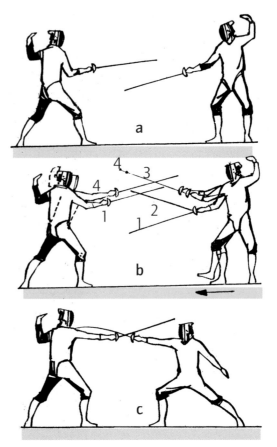

Figure 6.2.-16:
Technical execution of the stop hit attack.

When making contact the blade relationship must be approximately middle of the blade to the opponent's foible, and in landing the hit it must be forte to the middle of the opponent's blade. Hesitating even briefly at the beginning of the stop hit attack leads to blade relationships that make a successful hit impossible.

Stop hit attacks that are executed with the goal to block evasion paths are primarily used against feint attacks. Their execution requires specific knowledge of the type and the beginning of the feint, as well as the intended direction and form of the opponent's evasion, because every possible form has a specific form of stop hit attack assigned to it. In competitions they are therefore used much less often than the stop hit attacks with opposition.

A special form of stop hit attack is the *appuntata*. This stop hit attack is used against indirect ripostes or compound ripostes. With respect to its execution, it is a direct remise. When using the appuntata it is absolutely critical to know the exact form of the anticipated riposte.

An error (e.g. when an indirect riposte was expected after completed quarte parry high/outside, but the opponent thrusts low/inside) will result in the intended stop hit becoming an unjustified riposte. That is why the appuntata is generally the preferred choice only with opponents who habitually carry out indirect or compound ripostes. Otherwise the appuntata must be tactically prepared with maneuvers.

Methodological recommendations for the schooling of stop hits with opposition
- The stop hit motion sequence is initially practiced against a calm extension of the arm while standing still, and subsequently with a lunge.

- Due to the continuously diminishing measure during execution it is particularly important that these changes in the measure are compensated for with the weapon arm.

- A weapon arm that is not totally extended creates more favorable blade relationships. But it is important to note that this spatiotemporal loss must be compensated for with a lunge.

- While learning to recognize the correct situation for the execution of a stop hit they should be combined with the following alternating situations:
    - In the case of a surprise attack or the use of an unexpected form of attack, the stop hit cannot be started in time. The fencer is forced to parry (fig. 6.2.-15a, b).
    - The attack is started in far measure. The fencer must decide if he should wait for the final thrust and then stop hit, or if he should immediately execute another form of counter attack. The decision here depends on the timing of the extending of the weapon arm.
    - If the stop hit is unsuccessful because the opponent attacked into a different opening, contrary to the one anticipated after exploring, additional stop hits during the same fight should initially be avoided.

6.2.5.4   Esquives

Esquives are direct attacks that are combined with a withdrawal of the target area via body movements. The purpose of withdrawing the target area is to avoid also getting hit. They can be executed against the final thrust of all strategic attack elements. Since evasive actions often result in body positions that are disadvantageous to the further fight progression, a successful continuation of the fight after an unsuccessful counter-attack is hardly possible. The esquives can be used at the start of compound attacks as well as against the final thrust. It is important that the fencer carrying out the esquives is not also hit, because the hit will then be given to him.

During his training a foil fencer is oriented to react to counter attacks with a gain in time with a parry only when the counter-attack started one fencing time before his final thrust. Otherwise he will rapidly complete his attack. In its temporal progression the esquives should utilize this proper training dictum by orienting the opponent to unjustified thrusting via a clear succession of

1. extension of weapon arm

2. execution of evasive action,

and not trigger defensive reflexes or a change in the thrusting direction, depending on the opponent's evasive movements.

With respect to their execution esquives are often largely subject to individual peculiarities. Young fencers are strictly prohibited from copying those types of actions they have observed at other fencers. The fencer should be familiarized with the situation for these counter attacks via the subsequently described basic variations. Individual variations can easily be added on to the already acquired skills.

The following are descriptions of three basic variations of the esquives:

Esquives with ducking (passato sotto)
In this form the evasive movement is executed with a reverse lunge with a lowered torso or by getting into a squat position. In both cases it is important that the blade is raised during the thrust (this creates an angle in the wrist between arm and weapon), because the opponent's target area is located on a higher plane. It is important not to start the esquives too soon. Otherwise the opponent will be able to hit the target by changing the direction of his thrust, in spite of the esquives.

Esquives with turning (inquartata)
The majority of all fencers have found a fencing stance in which the line of the shoulders is at an approximately 25° angle to the line of fencing. Of course the direction of attack for the majority of final thrusts corresponds to that. A passing thrust or cross to the opponent against these thrusts (but also against multiple feints inside – outside – inside, that are performed with great amplitude) can be achieved via a quick retracting of the shoulder in the direction of the fencing line simultaneously with the extension of the weapon arm.

Combining the overall movement with a flèche has proven advantageous, since the acceleration achieved thereby makes a reaction by the opponent nearly impossible.

It is important to execute the evasive movement only to the fencing line. Over-rotating will result in having one's back to the opponent, which, if repeated, can lead to a penalty hit. Thus it is not a problem for the opponent to land a valid hit.

The esquive is often combined with a stop hit. In doing so the fist and blade are in a position that corresponds to a direct riposte from septime parry.

Esquives with withdrawing of the target area (arrest)

This form of counter attack is often used against opponents who are physically inferior or those whose attacks are performed stereotypically with a constant depth of attack. The lunging leg is moved back to the supporting leg and the shoulder is brought forward at the same time as the weapon arm is extended.

The hit must be landed on the opponent's shoulder since this is the most forward target area. Some fencers have such excellent command of this form of esquive that they also use them against extended attacks. However, this requires an excellent feel for the measure.

While the last-mentioned form of esquives is only used against a certain type of fencer and does not require specific tactical preparation, the two first-mentioned forms can be used against all opponents. Their tactical preparation is even relatively simple. Through frequent passive retreating against opposing attacks the opponent is provoked into a very aggressive, often uncontrolled "storming forward". The esquive is a very promising means against such an attack.

Methodological recommendations for the schooling of esquives

- In the long term esquives are not a substitute for defense through parries. When repeated frequently their surprise effect is lost. The young fencer should therefore be acquainted with them only after their place in the overall structure of basic strategic elements has been clarified and he has largely mastered all other possibilities of an effective defense.

- The individual forms of evasive movements are practiced separately from the actual thrusting movement. One option for doing this is a practice fight in which the fencer practicing the esquives does not hold a weapon in his hand. He is thus forced to only use body movements to prevent getting hit.

6.2.6   Compound attacks

6.2.6.1 Feint attacks

Feint attacks are combinations of two or more attack elements. The first attack (in case of several feints also the second, third attack, etc.) serves to provoke one or multiple parries and the uncovering of an opening to be able to land a hit with a disengagement attack.

The following elements serve as feints:
- Basic attacks

- Ripostes

- Counter attacks and

- Remises.

Feint attacks get their name from the strategic attack element that is used as a feint, as well as the number and type of displacement parries that end the feint attack.

In fencing multiple, and often different attack elements are often used in one action, and there are many possible combinations.

Feint attacks are very important in modern fencing and are characterized by their versatile tactical application and technical execution:
- Feint attacks can be started from an unengaged blade position (thrust feint), from an opposing engagement (disengagement or cutover thrust feint), from contact or one's own engagement (disengagement or cutover thrust feint).
- All attack elements can be executed as feints.
- Feint attacks can be carried out from varying distances with many different types of footwork and footwork combinations, from a short lunge to several steps and lunge or flèche.
- Accentuated (leading) and sudden feints are used.

Particularly feint attacks against anticipated parries and those taking into account the opponent's reaction during the action are gaining importance in foil fencing (basic counter attacks increase and defense systems are perfected).

Feint attacks to provoke and disengage anticipated parries
This form of feint attack is useful when the fencer has, via maneuvers and feigned attacks, but also through observation and experience, gotten a clear picture regarding the type and timing of the opponent's parry or parry sequence and the measure relationship, before the simple or compound feint attack that is to be executed.

The fencer must therefore learn to recognize or guess the body language, facial expressions, the overall manner of the opponent, etc., as truth or deception.

In the training process the trainer or partner has the important role of simulating these movements by different opponents.

Another important criteria for these feint attacks is the timing of the attack. It helps determine success or failure of these actions and must be actively created during preparation.

Common are

- attacks into the beginning of the forward movement and
- attacks after the forward or backward movement.

The timing of the parry or parry sequence in connection with the measure changes must be grasped at the same time, and has to be taken into account during the execution of one's attack.

Decisiveness, consistency, and speed in the execution of feint attacks are another important characteristic. All exercises must be designed to give the fencer the confidence to execute these attacks. Disruptive factors the fencer cannot react to due to the character of the effected action and the speed of the attack should be incorporated into the exercise in such a way, that, with the appropriate speed and determination, it is possible for the fencer to successfully finish the attack.

Feint attacks are used in the following situations:

- The opponent frequently reacts habitually with a certain parry and a simultaneous step backward to an attack that starts suddenly from a resting position. The feint attack is performed very quickly and forcefully. The arm extension for the thrust feint begins with the jump forward which is executed like a lunge to give the impression of a straight thrust.
- The opponent's reaction to feigned attacks is to temporize and execute late parries in the high line without backward movement. The feint attack is executed with an initially cautious, then forceful lunge. The final phase of the attack is designed with maximum speed and force.

Feint attacks that take into account the opponent's reaction during the action

These attacks are characterized by their taking into account during execution of the attack any changes in the measure and the opponent's different blade movements during the action. The plasticity of the technique of feint attacks must be developed based on the basic technique. This problem must be constantly and continuously addressed in the training process. By perfecting his fencing vision, the kinesthetic sense and the sense of timing, the fencer must be enabled to take the following factors into account:

- Changes in position and movement or of the pressure relationship of the blades.

- Timing of these changes.

- Changes in the measure.

Depending on predisposition and aptitude or also strengths and specialty actions, these skills are used specifically for the perfecting of certain actions and the developing of groups of specialty actions.

Examples of situations for their application are:
- The fight progresses at a high rate of movement. At times the measure is so narrow that the opponent expects a straight thrust. The fencer allows for a quarte parry by the opponent and intents to execute thrust feint-cutover thrust with lunge without being sure about the measure relationship. The opponent retreats with a cautious lunge in response to the start of the attack, in order to then take quarte parry. The fencer is aware of the widening measure and executes the attack with jump forward-lunge.
- Same fight situation as before. But due to the preparation the fencer knows that at a certain threat level the opponent will react with an arbitrary parry in place. The feint attack is started with thrust feint and cautious lunge. At the moment the octave parry begins the fencer realizes the direction of the parry and continues the attack with disengagement thrust and forceful lunge.
- The opponent reacts to feint attacks with quick, small quarte and sixte parries and suggests a backward movement.

The fencer plans a thrust double feint attack with step forward-lunge with the foresight, to pay attention to the opponent's reaction during execution of the action. The opponent comes forward with a prime parry into the start of the feint attack to disrupt the attack.

Since this behavior has frequently been shown in previous fights the fencer can anticipate this reaction. After the initial thrust feint he carries out his attack with just a disengagement thrust to the flank and short lunge.
- In the course of the fight, the opponent parries a sixte glide in the last second with an opposition parry and lands a hit with the riposte.

To take advantage of this reaction the fencer plans a deep glide feint and disengagement thrust in the last second with initially cautious lunge. During the attack the opponent already opposes at the start of the glide feint and takes one step back to be able to safely parry the anticipated disengagement thrust.

The fencer sees the widened measure and the opponent's early opposition, and therefore executes disengagement feint-disengagement thrust with step forward-lunge and lands a hit.

- The opponent's defense system is complicated and opaque. But during feigned attacks with multiple feints he constantly backs up three steps with a few parries, stops suddenly and tries to parry the final thrust or, if the attack is too lengthy and due to the sudden discontinuation of the backward movement goes beyond the goal, he tries to land a hit in close quarters.

- If the defensive rhythm and the type of esquive have been figured out, a multiple feint attack with cutover feint should be executed.

The attack is ended with a lunge at the moment when the opponent is anxious to parry the final thrust and discontinues the backward movement, whereby the weapon is withdrawn. If the opponent now performs an arbitrary final parry, the attack into an uncovered opening is finished with arm extension and lowering of the upper body.

Methodological recommendations for the schooling of feint attacks
Since feint attacks are combinations of already familiar and to a certain degree mastered basic attacks, the following requirements are necessary to perfect them:
- Coordinating several blade movements with a leg movement and arm-leg coordination.

- Executing the action with varying footwork.

- Developing speed and accuracy of blade movements.

- The first methodical step is the breaking down of the feint attack into the components of the feint, the disengagement, and the final thrust, as well as practicing these elements in succession and with breaks. In doing so the partner has the job of helping to determine the breaks via the timing of parries.

- During the training process thrust and disengagement feints are subsequently formed into a fluid overall movement with lunge, via disengagement and final thrust. In the beginning the following principle always applies:

  Arm extension before the start of the lunge! Later, simultaneous arm extension and starting of the lunge, and finally starting the lunge before the arm extension. (Do not allow months of practicing just one of these forms, but rather practice all of them as a group early on!)

- However, during a feint the arm should not be fully extended, so a reserve for the acceleration of the final thrust is available.

- The next step is practicing thrust and disengagement feint attacks with step forward-lunge and jump forward-lunge as a fluid movement with a leading feint, or also with a sudden, aggressive feint and a brief break after the step or jump.

- The degree of the arm extension or the length of the step or jump depends on the measure and the opponent's sensibility. A general rule of thumb is:

- Against nervous fencers who react to any threat with the blade, feints should be carried out with a short aggressive step and with the arm extension executed the same way (one's point just short of the opposing bell guard).

- Against restrained fencers who initially react to threats by holding the measure, feints are carried out with dragging step or steps respectively, and with the arm extension executed the same way, whereby the feint must be brought close to the opposing target area. (To facilitate the subsequent disengagement movement it may be necessary to pull back the weapon arm again by bending the elbow.)

- The coordination of blade and leg movements must be variable in design, and a form of the feint attack should be practiced with varying coordination. (Never tie a blade movement to a specific form or a specific tempo of a leg movement!)

- Very important for the execution of feint attacks is the rhythm in which they are performed. It is possible to force one's rhythm on the opponent. But it is more advantageous to pick up the opponent's defensive rhythm and use it for the execution of one's own attack.

Practice examples

Complex 1
Exercises for the schooling of feint attacks with anticipated parry
1. **Basic idea:** The fencer is supposed to figure out if the opponent's reaction to a feint attack was true or a deception.

- Sudden feint attack with quarte battuta-thrust by A.
- B reacts with jumpy quarte parry and step backward.
- A immediately follows up with an attack of quarte battuta-thrust feint-disengagement thrust with jump forward-lunge.
- At the same time B accompanies A's thrust feint with quarte parry and step backward.

The fencer must decide whether the opponent's reaction was consistent with the character of the feint attack. If that is the case, the serious attack should follow immediately so the opponent won't become aware of his uncontrolled reaction and react differently during the serious attack.

The information the fencer acquired with the feint attack does not always have to be put to use right away, but can also be used again without renewed preparation during the continued fight progression.

2. **Basic idea** as before.
- A carries out a feint attack with sixte engagement-thrust.
- B responds with an obvious, demonstrative sixte parry without backward movement.
- A attacks with sixte engagement-thrust feint-disengagement thrust and lunge.
- B reacts to the thrust feint by A with a counter quarte parry without backward movement.
  (B's reaction was unconvincing. That is why an attack is executed with the foresight that during a serious attack the opponent will take an opposite parry.)

3. **Basic idea:** Determining the moment of the attack.
- B begins with quarte engagement and step forward.
- A responds with a demonstrative step backward.
- B begins again with quarte engagement and step forward.
- A suggests a backward movement, but then changes the time and carries out lunge with disengagement feint-disengagement thrust into the opponent's forward movement.
- B reacts to A's disengagement feint with sixte parry.

4. **Basic idea:** Schooling forcefulness and speed (in this exercise A is fencing left-handed)
- A executes a feint attack with sixte engagement-thrust to the flank with lunge.
- B reacts with octave parry and step backward.
- A expects B to react the same way and carries out a forceful attack with sixte engagement-thrust feint to the flank and disengagement thrust into the high opening with step forward-lunge.
- B reacts to the thrust feint with a straight thrust in time, which A, who is not swayed in the execution of his action, blocks with disengagement thrust into the high opening.

In this exercise it is important that B first reacts to A's thrust feint with a counter attack. If this occurred immediately after A's sixte engagement, it is no longer possible to block the counter attack in this way. Instead of the feint A would have to execute a real attack to the flank.

Complex 2
Exercises for the schooling of attack rhythms
It is possible to force one's attack rhythm on the opponent, but it is more useful to take advantage of the rhythm of the opponent's parries for one's own attack execution. In these exercises we go on the assumption that the opponent has a recognizable parry rhythm.

1. **Basic idea:** The opponent accompanies several feints with small, limited parries with step backward, and resolutely tries to parry the final thrust standing still.
Attack rhythm: short – short – long – short.

- From the opposing quarte engagement A attacks with disengagement double feint and two small steps forward.
- B accompanies with sixte and quarte and holds the measure.
- A emphasizes the disengagement feint, which disengages B's quarte parry, and starts to lunge.
- B tries to parry with circular quarte standing still.
- A disengages this parry with cutover thrust, which is executed during the lunge.

2. Basic idea: The opponent's parry system is complicated and variable, and only the rhythm and backward movement are detectable. The feint attack is executed with cutover feints, irrespective of the type of opposing parries.

- A executes thrust feint-cutover feint with jump forward.
- B reacts to the cutover feint with sixte parry and circular sixte parry and step backward.
- During the lunge A continues with cutover thrust feint-cutover thrust.
- B tries to parry with quarte parry standing still.

Based on this, feint attacks with broken time can also be used. In doing so one or more feints are not suggested (e.g. the second cutover feint). The opponent parries habitually or jumpily, and in doing so uncovers an opening into which the final thrust is executed.

6.2.6.2 Variations of the feint attack

6.2.6.2.1 Feint ripostes

Ripostes are primarily executed as simple feint attacks with varying tactical character, standing still or with a lunge. They are used when the opponent intends to parry the riposte and when, based on the speed and timing of his parries or the measure relationship, there would be a real chance for success.

The feints are executed directly as thrust feints and indirectly as disengagement feints. Kavatation thrust and cutover thrust are used to disengage the opposing parries and to obtain a hit.

Application
After an unsuccessful attack that was repelled with quarte parry, the opponent immediately returns to fencing stance without reacting with an early parry. He intends to repel the riposte with counter sixte parry or direct quarte parry, to then score a hit.

If the opponent's intentions are identified, a feint attack is carried out. After the quarte parry-thrust feint with the start of a lunge follows a disengagement of the opposing parry with cutover, and a thrust into the uncovered opening with the completion of the lunge.

6.2.6.2.2 Feint counter attacks

Counter attacks with thrust feint-disengagement or cutover thrust are used as a special form of counter attack with gain in time. Their application utilizes the convention of priority in that the opponent interrupts his attack (second intention) to parry the anticipated direct counter attack.

Application
In the course of the fight the opponent is hit by a counter attack with gain in time during the execution of a compound attack.
He intends to attack the same way, but plans to repel the counter-attack with quarte parry and to score a hit himself with the riposte.
In this situation the feint attack is carried out in such a way, that a thrust feint with the start of a lunge is executed into the start of the attack. The opponent's quarte parry is anticipated and successfully completed via disengagement thrust into the counter attacks' uncovered opening.

6.2.6.2.3 Remise attacks with feint

Remise attacks are executed with feints when a direct remise attack is not promising due to the measure and another anticipated attack by the opponent.
The attack can be continued from an unengaged blade position with thrust feint or disengagement, in case of opposing parries with disengagement or cutover feint, and also with multiple feints. That mostly happens with dragging behind of the supporting leg or with compound footwork.

Application
The opponent dodges the attack via a backward movement. He parries only briefly with quarte, but does not carry out a riposte, rather takes the blade into on guard position.
The remise attack is executed with dragging behind of the supporting leg, thrust feint with the start of a lunge and cutover thrust with completion of the lunge upon renewed quarte parry by the opponent.

6.2.6.3   Attacks with second intention

Attacks with second intention are executed with the goal of provoking the opponent into an offensive action. This challenges the opponent to a riposte or counter attack that can be answered with a planned defensive action and a riposte, but also with one's own counter attack.

Second intention occupies a dominant place in foil fencing. Its use or non-use is basically an issue of general fighting style. Fencers, who tend to respond to the opponent's intention once it is identified, i.e. letting him proceed, generally prefer the second intention. But there are also fencers who make sure that once the opponent' intention has been identified it does not develop any further. This is not the answer to the question of a promising style. But the trainer must recognize early on which of these basic approaches his fencer is more predisposed to (compare Chapter 2.4). In doing so, he must use the one without leaving out the other.

Individual strengths should in no way lead to one-sidedness in the training process since in the end only the fencer who, aside from having distinctive individual strengths is also able to utilize tactical options in all other areas, will be successful in the long term.

Aside from excellent skills in the handling of strategic defense elements, the fencer must also possess courage, the willingness to take risks, and self-confidence to be able to successfully use the second intention and consciously put himself in critical situations.

The problem with second intention lies primarily in the credibility of the executed attack, which the opponent must regard as first intention. That is why the deception is much more risky than a feint attack. While a feint attack initially triggers a defensive action (which at first is always defensive), the second intention provokes an offensive action. But to provoke the opponent into an offensive action the fencer must first place himself in a measure that is dangerous to him.

To his advantage is the fact that, by preparing the situation well he can greatly limit the opponent's ability to act (type of attack and threatened target area). Schooling the second intention thereby becomes an excellent means for the perfecting of defensive actions. Beyond that it trains observation skills and the anticipation of opposing actions.

The second intention is used primarily
- against habitual ripostes.
- against counter attacks and
- with frequent simultaneous decisions by the referee.

Situations for the possible use of second intention are:
- It has been observed that the opponent habitually executes a certain parry-riposte in a one-two rhythm. Shortly before reaching the critical measure our fencer starts to attack fiercely, namely with the final thrust into the opening that is covered by the opponent's preferred parry. The attack is already begun outside of the critical measure because it is less dangerous to demonstrate sincerity through high speed of movement than to

start the attack in a true measure. In case of the latter, a measure that would be nearly ideal for a habitual parry-riposte would develop after completion of the attack. This could be avoided by simply decreasing the speed of movement, but the result would be that the opponent would recognize this slow attack as a preparatory action.
- By aggressively penetrating the critical measure with a bent weapon arm, an effort is made to deceive the opponent with a mock faulty start of an attack. The counter-attack provoked thereby can then be foiled as follows:
    - via parry-riposte and
    - via a stop hit.

When choosing the parry the respective measure relationships must be taken into account to facilitate a successful riposte. The following applies:
- If the counter-attack is carried out at the beginning of the provocation and usually with a lunge, the sixte parry is most advantageous.
- If the counter-attack is carried out toward the end of the provocation and usually with a lunge, the quarte parry is most advantageous.
- If the counter-attack is carried out with flèche, the prime parry is most advantageous.

- But both of the possible uses of second intention listed here can only be realized if the fencer is able to successfully attack with first intention out of the same type of preparation. In this case the opponent is virtually forced to carry out the actions required for second intention.
- Frequent simultaneity of actions results in simultaneous decisions by the referee. Since a general change of the engagement situation (e.g. switching over to defense) would surely be disadvantageous, this situation must be utilized in the sense of a second intention. The attack is begun a little slower and – as soon as the opponent has also begun his attack – the weapon arm is retracted to parry during the lunge. It is more advantageous to execute the lunge only half way to achieve a favorable measure for one's riposte. A stop hit or a battuta in time are not possible here.

Methodological recommendations for the schooling of second intention
In principle the basic skills for two attack elements and one defensive element are sufficient for the execution of second intention. If these are available the mental preparation of second intention should begin right away. Particularly at this point can a fighting style that does not consist of senselessly lunging at each other best be developed. The fencer soon realizes that it is the mental work during the fight that guarantees the successful application of the skill that he has worked so hard to acquire. He will understand that fencing also means mentally competing against the opponent (training goal and content).

Practice examples

Complex 1
Provoking a riposte
1. **Basic idea:** Answering the riposte with a counter-parry-counter-riposte.
   Middle measure, A and B on guard position
- A begins with a quick step forward and thrust feint.
- B moves back and accompanies the feint with quarte.
- A disengages the quarte and lunges forcefully.
- B parries habitually with sixte and ripostes high.
- A parries the riposte with a high septime while in a lunge, and immediately ripostes indirectly high/inside.

2. **Same basic idea** and same starting position
- A has observed that from the sixte B habitually ripostes low/outside.
- A carries out the same attack as in exercise 1, and after B's sixte parry gets up slightly with a nearly extended arm to pretend to uncover the opening low/outside.
- B ripostes habitually low/outside.
- A parries with octave and immediately ripostes.

3. **Basic idea:** Foiling the riposte with an esquive.
   Middle measure, A and B on guard position
- A carries out the attack as in exercise 1.
- B parries after the accompanying parry quarte with circular quarte and habitually ripostes high/inside.
- A withdraws his target area immediately after the parry by extremely lowering his torso forward/low and at the same time continues his attack.

Complex 2
Provoking a counter-attack
1. **Basic idea:** Provoking a straight thrust in time and its response with parry riposte.
   Far measure, A and B on guard position
- A takes a step forward and at the end of the step provokingly executes quarte battuta. In doing so the arm is not fully extended, but with another step forward the blade changes to the lower line.
- After A's battuta B reacts to the maneuvers with only a step backward.
- A repeats the maneuver.
- B believes there is a chance for a counter attack with a gain in time. After the battuta he only suggests the backward movement and then immediately lunges with a straight thrust high/inside.

- While repeating the maneuver A only pretends to change to the lower line by dropping his point. He parries the counter attack with quarte parry standing still and immediately ripostes.

2. **Basic idea:** Foiling the counter attack with a gain in time via execution of a direct attack.
   Far measure, A and B on guard position
- A maneuvers as in exercise 1.
- B sees a chance for a counter-attack with a gain in time and resolves to immediately attack after battuta if A repeats his maneuvers.
- A expects B's counter attack and immediately performs battuta thrust.
- B executes the planned counter attack, thus causing an incontro.

3. **Basic idea:** Foiling a disengagement feint in time via a stop hit.
   Middle measure, A and B on guard position
- A takes a step forward and makes contact in quarte.
- B holds the measure.
- A changes to sixte engagement with just a suggested step forward and very demonstrative blade movement.
- B holds the measure.
- A abandons the engagement, takes a step backward and starts the maneuver over.
- B could tell by the measure maneuver that A is provoking a displacement counter attack, and intends to only use the disengagement of the change as a feint to be able to disengage A's preferred quarte parry and land a hit high/outside.
- A deliberately designed the maneuver this way and expects the feint attack by B. That is why he does not react to the feint after changing, but blocks B's final thrust himself with a straight thrust with sixte opposition.

Complex 3
1. **Basic idea:** Provoking the final thrust during severely delayed attacks.
- A puts pressure on B with quick, small steps. The weapon arm is briefly extended during the first step, is then withdrawn again with the point high/outside.
- B initially holds the measure, stops after several backward steps and begins to take over the attack (while retreating B must be very careful that a critical measure does not develop and the start of the take-over does not occur stereotypically after a certain number of steps).
- A immediately reacts to the take-over of the attack by thrusting out a delayed attack.
- B does parry–riposte and aids the parry with a step backward.

Please note: A clever variation of this exercise would be for B to simply react to A's final thrust with a displacement parry and after successfully carrying out the same, begin to take over the attack.

2. **Basic idea:** Foiling a feint attack via a stop hit.
- A puts pressure on B with quick, small steps. The weapon arm is briefly extended during the first step, is then withdrawn again with the point high/outside.
- B initially holds the measure, stops after several steps backward and begins to take over the attack (while retreating B must be careful that a critical measure does not develop and the start of the take-over does not occur stereotypically after a certain number of steps).
- A reacts to the take-over of the attack but anticipates second intention by B and wants to successfully use a feint attack against it.
- B reacts to the thrust feint with stop hit followed by an immediate quick retreat.

Please note: For didactic reasons it is necessary to train both exercises in context, and to also incorporate the successful execution of A's feint in exercise 2 into the exercise complex. Only that will guarantee sincerity in the execution and with that the necessary realness of the fight situation. With regard to lesson content, the trainer should make sure that the fencer trains all exercise components (meaning A and B). Here, too, it is certainly possible to incorporate the basic idea 3 from complex 2 into the training material.

7   Epée fencing

7.1   Particulars of épée fencing

The épée is a thrusting weapon. The body of athletic competition rules and regulations made the original dueling weapon into today's sports weapon used in men's and women's fencing. While men's épée has been a part of the Olympic program since the beginning of the modern Olympic games, women's épée fencing only became an Olympic event in 1996, after ten years of international competitions.

It should be mentioned that the épée, with its individual and team competition, is not only represented in the Olympic fencing program, but also as a dueling weapon for modern pentathlon athletes.

The electrical scoring apparatus was developed for épée long before other weapons and was already used in the 1936 Olympics. We are currently very close to the introduction of wireless fencing. The necessity of an electrically objectified scoring apparatus is obvious since in épée fencing, as opposed to other conventional weapons, the fencer who actually lands a hit first always scores the "valid" hit. The time interval for a double hit, which also only exists in épée disciplines, is very brief (1/20 to 1/25 sec.) and during the fight is barely perceptible to the human eye.

In spite of the principal differences between épée fencing and the conventional weapons there are many similarities between foil and épée fencing, particularly with respect to fencing technique. That is probably due to the foil once having been a light practice weapon for the dueling épée.

In today's épée training we generally differentiate between two main directions. Epée fencing that is "foil-like" and épée fencing that is "combat-like". Due to the absence of the conventions of priority and the unrestricted target area (the entire body is a target area), as well as the many different fencing schools and their interpretations, a great variety of individual fencing styles can be observed in épée fencing.

Nevertheless, we can prescind two basic épée fencing styles from the above-mentioned breakdown:
- The épée fencer with "foil-like" training, who reacts "reflex-like" with parries during opposing attacks.
- The fencer with "original épée-like" training, who tends to stop hits during opposing attacks.

The absence of priority in épée presupposes that only the best-prepared attacks can be successful. Defensively there are options for defending with the point or the blade; strategy and tactics are more important than in foil fencing. Special defensive elements are more pronounced in épée fencing. That is why familiar actions from foil fencing, like "second intention" or counter-time (counter-attack against counter-attack) are found more frequently in épée fencing.

Time-wise, épée fencing takes longer. This applies particularly to women's fights, because due to a lower level of athleticism the dynamic for successful attacks is often lacking and an even better choice of time and measure are essential. Patience, experience, strategic-tactical skills, and a good sense of tempo are very important for successfully coping with the many possible variations of an épée fight. The general rule is that in order to have a successful offensive an épée fencer must also have a particularly good defense. On the other hand, a good defense can only be successful if dangerous offensive elements are occasionally incorporated.

Although this characterization applies to tactically top-class fencers, the foundation for this must already be laid early on in youth training. Pursuant to international and national regulations, épée is fought from students to seniors. At the same time the training and competition content must be appropriate for the respective age groups and their performance potential.

The debate over which age is appropriate for children to begin fencing is not based on the choice of weapon. Rather it is the previously mentioned sports theoretical background of the two principal épée fencing styles and the respective fencing school of the trainer that are the deciding factors here. It is possible to start beginners on épée fencing right away but to train initially with the thrusting weapon foil, or to parallel teach foil and épée. Successful épée fencers have been trained with all three versions. The view that foil should be used as the "basic weapon" for training all disciplines over an extended time period to acquire "fencing comprehension" is rarely held any longer.

In learning the technique for the thrust and for partner exercises it must be taken into account that the épée is somewhat heavier and the épée blades are generally much more stiff than the foil. In addition suitable protective wear for typical but "sensitive" épée target areas like the hand or the foot, is often not available during partner exercises.

It is extremely risky to make a recommendation on the "ideal" (calendar) starting age for épée fencing, because fencing, particularly épée fencing, can be a life-long activity. In the interest of the fencing sport, offers should be made to integrate beginners from all age groups into fencing and fencing associations. Epée fencing is particularly well suited for this. The age of beginning épée fencers can also be somewhat higher than in foil.

The better the general athletic-coordinative qualifications are, the better is, of course, the possibility of developing top athletic performances or shortening the initial training steps respectively, to be able to integrate somewhat older beginners into high-performance groups. Although attempts are being made in modern professional sports to achieve maximum efficiency in performance optimization in all stages of training, it is astonishing how individual "career changers" or late starters can always achieve considerable successes in competitive sports such as the complex sport of fencing.

The fencing position for épée fencing

The fencing position for épée fencing has a higher center of gravity. The feet are closer together and the legs therefore bent less (figure 7..-1). In fencing position the weapon arm is straighter than in foil fencing. The forearm forms a straight line parallel to the fencing strip. The point threatens the opposing target area.

The way the weapon is held fulfills a simultaneous covering function via opposition of the bell guard to the opposing point before attacks to the hand and forearm. Due to the size of these target areas, thrusts to the "preceding" target areas of the weapon arm and the lunging leg require a high degree of skill and precision in guiding the blade. Aside from the parries already familiar from foil fencing, the oppositions with the bell guard for defending the weapon arm become very important. One's own point remains in the opponent's line of attack, thereby constantly threatening him.

Withdrawing of the target area and evasive actions as effective defensive actions are used more heavily in épée fencing. The preceding target area of the weapon arm allows for hits to the hand via angulated thrusts and cutovers, whereby thrown thrusts to the hand in the sense of "false cutovers" are often referred to as "bingos" in German-speaking countries (compare to Chapter 8, fig. 8.2.-8 right).

Figure 7.1.-1: Fencing position of an épée fencer; a – front view, b – side view; the valid target area is black.

Holding the weapon in épée fencing

In épée fencing various ways of holding the weapon arm have developed which are in part referred to as individual peculiarities. Loosely extended 2/3 of the way, the weapon arm is held on the sixte-octave line or is moved. The blade is raised slightly in the high line so that the weapon is held similar to sixte position. This relaxed holding of the weapon facilitates excellent guiding of the point and lays a foundation for effective accuracy. The guiding of the weapon in sixte limits the opponent's attack actions since this fencing position is also similar to a defensive position. The point should threaten the opponent as often as possible. A weapon arm with the elbow bent too much limits one's own attack options, and due to the arm's longer extension phase makes it easier for the opponent to launch counter attacks. In contrast, an overly straight arm restricts the variability of actions, there are no quick thrusts, and cutovers directed at the hand are difficult to repel.

Footwork and its coordination with arm movements in épée fencing

The footwork in épée fencing is similar to foil fencing, but there are weapon-specific solutions and differences in the arm and leg coordination. Epée fencers use all three options for the timing of arm and leg movements: first arm – then legs, or first legs – then arm, or arm and legs at the same time. "Arm before leg" is used as the main option.

Epée fencing has a lunging problem, namely that one has a lower body position in the lunge in which the fencer can be hit more easily via counter attacks from above. Due to their flexibility female fencers in particular tend to these, from a tactical standpoint, wrong lunges. A long, deep lunge is only worthwhile with engagements of the blade or an attack in time. Typical are the many options for prolonging the attack that are carried out, for instance, from the lunge with dragging behind and renewed lunge, or via lunge and dragging behind with flèche. The arm is extended during the entire attack action. With a not completely extended arm (slight "loosening" in the elbow joint) the bell guard must remain at the same level. Since the lunging leg as a valid target area must be protected in épée, step-like lunges that make the subsequent maneuvering easier are frequently executed next to "classic" épée lunges.

Depending on the situation and the intent of the further structuring of the fight, the recovery from the lunge can occur in two different ways:

- The elbow is bent at the same time as the lunging leg moves back into fencing position; this permits a variable defense via parries.

- While returning to the fencing position from the lunge the arm remains extended. This makes counter attacks possible and is considered a characteristic peculiarity of épée fencing.

In both versions the holding of the weapon changes, according to the engagement situation, after a complete return to the fencing position.

The flèche is used more often than with the other weapons. It is executed with a high fist position. A frequently used action against attacks to the foot is to retract the lunging leg while simultaneously extending the leg to score with a stop hit.

Epée fencers often don't do "classic" footwork, but rather "hop" similar to a boxer or tennis player. The hops are very small and shallow. In doing so the toes barely leave the ground. The distance between the feet remains constant. This type of "hopping" or "bouncing" is done in place or also during the forward and backward movement. This disrupts the opponent's observation.

In addition there is a preliminary tensing of muscles, which is essential to quick action and reaction. This produces a stronger "internal" sense of rhythm. At the same time these constant movements camouflage the moment of the attack.

Esquives, especially dodging with a very deep squat, are used more frequently in épée fencing than with the other weapons.

The measure in épée fencing

Depending on the target point, the seize of the target area, especially the "preceding" target area of the weapon arm and other peculiarities in épée fencing create varying measure relationships.

During the fight they determine the type of footwork necessary for negotiating the distance to the chosen target point to score a hit.

In épée fencing a narrower measure to the target area closest to the hand and

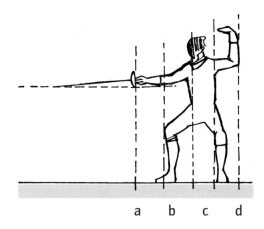

a   b   c   d

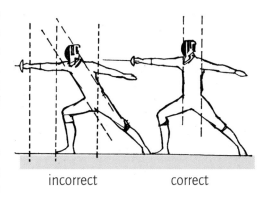

incorrect   correct

Figure 71.1-2:
Different measure depending on the target area

Figure 7.1.-3:
Far measure (to the hand)

253

arm is preferred. The following applies as an orientation for youth training: When the foibles of both fencers make contact these fencers are standing in relation to the target area.

- Wrist in near measure.

- Elbow joint and to the thigh in middle measure, and

- Body and to the foot in far measure (fig. 7.1.-3).

Hits are landed in near measure with just an arm extension, in middle measure with a lunge, and in far measure with step forward-lunge or with flèche.

Advanced fencers orient themselves exclusively on the strategic-tactically determined "critical measure" (compare Chapter 2.4.4).

When choosing the measure the fencer orients himself, on the one hand, on his opponent's bell guard and, on the other hand, on the planned target point. Next to the opposing bell guard the position of the blade (the opponent's holding of the weapon) plays an important role. For instance, if the opponent stands with his weapon pointing to the floor one can hold a narrower measure without risk, because there is little danger of having to react to a surprise action. When a fencer has a longer lunge than his opponent he can hold a measure that allows him to just barely reach the same, which is impossible for the opponent to do because of his shorter lunge. This gives evidence of the subjective character of the "critical measure". Thus it is ideal to be able get close enough to the opponent with one's lunge to hit him, but to be far enough away to be safe from the opposing attack.

The double-hit

An interesting characteristic of épée fencing is the double-hit, which historically originates from the duel, and in the past was most often associated with the disablement of both adversaries. In today's sport of fencing the simultaneous lighting up of both signal lamps within a lag of 1/20 to 1/25 sec. only signifies countable hits for both fencers in épée fencing. With the conventional weapons one fencer is awarded priority when the signal lamps light up simultaneously (incontro), or both hits are not counted (simultaneous action). In foil fencing the time span for triggering the signal lamp is still decidedly longer today than it is in épée fencing. In foil and saber fencing it is therefore possible to train and apply the actions that are protected and authorized by the regulations, while in épée fencing searching for a gain in time is always necessary to be able to land a single hit.

Double-hits contribute to a varying degree to the final result in épée fencing. While there are some fights that are fought almost exclusively with single hits, others will "double" nearly to the final result. This is not always related to the quality of the opponents but is often a matter of similar fencing styles. However, there often is an "inflation" of double-hits in fights with a lower athletic and tactical standard.

In épée fencing double-hits have a special tactical significance, particularly in critical fight situations (4:3, 14:13 and reverse), which, however, should not be overestimated in current, athletic épée fencing. A better choice of tempo and second intention easily prevent an attempt to "systematically" score double-hits during the action. The fencer who is leading in a decisive fight situation should never gamble on a double-hit as an "easy" solution, because he has to be ready for risky, to some extent unpredictable actions (second intent, blade actions) by the opponent. The fencer who is behind should never react by reflex with an accompanying thrust or begin a poorly prepared attack respectively, because with this type of action the risk of a double-hit is too high.

An older peculiarity typical of épée fencing, the double defeat (tie at time lapse), no longer exists in current regulations, which has limited the tactical scope of epée fencing, specifically in team competitions.

7.2 Select basic strategic elements

7.2.1 Basic attacks

Basic attacks are attack actions that are executed against non-attacking opponents without an immediate connection to previous attack or defensive actions. Systematically speaking, basic attacks are divided as follows: *direct attacks, disengagement attacks,* and *sweep attacks.*

The different terms for the attacks are based on the required touching, sweeping, or disengaging movements and the weapon position. The peculiarities of épée fencing require that basic attacks be carried out directly, in opposition, angulated, or thrown. The seize of the target area in épée fencing as well as the preferred portions of the target area (arm, thigh) determine the conditions for the highly differentiated use of basic attacks. One peculiarity results from the fact that counter attacks are launched into every basic attack. A high level of concentration is therefore necessary during every engagement situation.

In addition every direct attack requires diligent, focused, and careful preparation. Receiving a hit via a counter-attack during a direct attack must be avoided. It is therefore important that the amplitude of movement of weapon and weapon arm are kept to a minimum to offer the opponent very little target area for counter attacks. On the other hand, the preceding target areas of the opponent's lunging leg should be hit via precise guiding of the thrust. This presupposes a good technique for landing a hit in the attack, which includes simultaneous defense (particularly of the weapon arm) through opposition of the bell guard to the opponent's blade. In épée fencing basic attacks into the opposing time can be used in the following situations:

- To the arm, thigh, trunk, and foot in (foot tempo) at the moment of critical measure.
- When uncovering openings (hand tempo) during position changes, particularly during schematic changes like raising and lowering the weapon arm.
- At the moment of so called switching points from one direction of movement to another, e.g. when returning to fencing position from a lunge, or after schematic stepping motions (foot tempo).
- At the moment a preparatory action ends and the fencer returns to the starting position (foot tempo).
- When blade movements and footwork take place simultaneously (simultaneous hand and foot tempo).

Much attention should be paid to the training of preparatory actions for creating the situation. The most favorable measure and most appropriate moment (tempo) for the beginning of a basic attack must be created via constant maneuvering.

To orientate to the various measure relationships that develop for the épée fencer due to the larger and preceding target area, orientation to the point and the opponent's bell guard is most advisable. In the fencing position the point is at the same level with the opponent's bell guard and threatens his arm.

Precise thrusting in the different fight situations, excellent coordination between footwork and blade actions, correct tempo, great speed, and the appropriate measure are requirements for the successful use of basic attacks.

7.2.1.1 Direct attacks

Direct attacks are carried out against non-attacking opponents. The opponent is directly targeted with direct attacks, meaning without contact with the opposing weapon and disengagement of the same. For a successful thrust the shortest, most direct path to the target area must be chosen.

Target areas frequently attacked via direct attacks are the hand, the body (especially the upper body), and the leg (foot, knee, and thigh).
Attacks are made with straight thrusts, angular thrusts, opposition thrusts, or flicks.

Direct attacks to the body
These are only successful with the most meticulous preparation. In spite of the constant danger that counter attacks to the arm can already be carried out during the approach of the critical measure necessary for attacks on the body, many épée fencers prefer attacks to the body. The seize of the target area offers favorable conditions for a hit and requires less precision in the guiding of the point. Hits to the body are placed on the front, side, or back area, depending on the fight situation that has developed. The phase of the prepared action usually ends with a feigned attack to the arm, which is

then followed by the direct attack to the body. The moment of surprise is critical to its success. The thrust must be fast and direct and can be angulated, or carried out with opposition or flick.

Swinging motions should be avoided in direct attacks to the body with previous feigned attacks, because such behavior patterns present opportune moments for counter attacks.

Through maneuvering the opponent is forced into positions that cause him to behave incorrectly, preventing counter attacks. Due to the far measure that has to be negotiated, direct attacks to the body mostly end with step forward-lunge or with flèche. Effective measure maneuvers for attack preparation are sudden changes of rhythm and direction of movement, as well as constant phrasing. The larger target area makes it possible to concentrate on measure and tempo. But this is only successful with very good arm-and-leg coordination.

A situation is favorable for attacks to the body when the measure to the body can be bridged with a lunge or flèche and the opposing blade abandons the chosen line of attack because of the deceptive behavior, and therefore does not threaten the attacker's weapon arm. Success is determined by measure and speed, irrespective of the opponent's behavior. The straight thrust is an important element of the basic training, and criteria for the assessment of the training level.

Attacks to the body are used:
• When the amplitude of movement of the opponent's weapon arm is so large that attacks to the arm become difficult, or if the opponent, in response to feint attacks to the weapon arm lowers the same into the low line to withdraw it from the blade maneuvers.
• Against fencers, who react to deceptive attacks to the arm by withdrawing the target area or take the parries close to the body.
• After the referee's "Play!" command, particularly following interruptions. In situations like these, attacks have to be extremely forceful.
• Against fencers, who hold their blade outside of the customary position, thereby not presenting an attackable blade. This is especially typical of fencers with a long-handled French grip. Here a surprise attack to the body can prevent the opponent's timely return from the outside position to a position for a counter-attack.

Methodological recommendations for the perfecting of direct attacks to the body
• Basic requirement for direct attacks to the body is an explosive, well-prepared, sudden final thrust that must be carried out without hesitation. In doing so the time for the speed advantage of the attack action is most important. It is achieved via motion sequences that are executed with maximum speed in one's own time, in the time one has provoked, and as a reaction in the opposing time.

- Careful tactical preparation of attacks is very important. A lot of time should be spent on this during the training process. Ignoring the preparatory actions for attacks creates the risk, particularly in beginner training, of training direct attacks to the body under the wrong conditions. An exception is the thrust to the body during the technical learning process. But here, too, false perceptions may form with respect to the real fight situations. It is therefore advisable to use the weapon with force during attacks to the body to protect oneself from reflex sweeping actions.

- To acquire a reliable thrusting position it is necessary to practice direct attacks against all positions and blade positions. The angle that results in the "bell-right- and point-left-hold" is critical to the adhesion of the point to the target area. Left-handed fencers prefer the shoulder as a target point because it allows them to protect their own shoulder from outside thrusts by holding the fist more to the right.

- Since direct attacks to the body are initiated from far measure with feigned attacks to the weapon arm, and the path to the body can only be negotiated with compound footwork or flèche, practices during the training process should be conducted under these same requirements. Diverging from the direct line of attack should be avoided when directing a thrust.

Figure 7.2.-1: Attack to the body

- Every angulated final thrust initially begins as a straight thrust. The following order applies in the acquirement of movement visualization: form the angle and then do the footwork. To acquire the competitive technique, the coordination between arm and leg movements and the forming of the angle are trained depending on the situation:

Figure 7.2.-2: Direct attack to the arm

(1) Arm extension and forming of the angle standing still, followed by a lunge.

(2) Arm extension and forming of the angle with simultaneous lunge.

(3) Arm extension and forming of the angle in the final phase of the lunge.

In the training process the attacks should always be repeated on different openings and under varying conditions. This ensures the necessary variable and vivid direction of the thrust in a competition. Attacks to the body are essential by virtue of their simple technical function, and should be included early on in the training program for épée fencing.

Practice examples

Basic idea: Creating and utilizing favorable situations for attacks to the body.

1. A carries out feigned thrusts to the hand – B displaces these attacks in far measure.

- At the moment B opens up the measure, A repeats his mock attack to the hand and immediately continues with a direct attack to the body with lunge or flèche.

2. A attacks with deceptive sweep attacks to the arm – B reacts by withdrawing the target area without opening up the measure.

- A's direct attack to the body with flèche, which B wants to foil with a stop hit and subsequent displacement to the rear, comes at the moment the target area is withdrawn. The stop hit remains ineffective (to test the sincerity of counter attacks the opposition position can occasionally be omitted) due to the opposition with which A carries out the attack.

3. A maneuvers with the goal of prompting the opponent to make a forward movement. B responds to the measure play, but holds the far measure and assumes sixte during the forward movement.

- A's direct attack to the body with opposition in quarte (against left-handed fencers opposition in sixte) comes at the moment of B's forward movement.

Practice examples for the four execution options
1. With straight thrust

- A is in octave position.

- B lands a straight thrust with flèche on the shoulder. Arm and leg movement has to start simultaneously. The straight thrust is successful if the opening is large enough or if a hit can be landed before it is covered up again. In this case tempo and very fast action are decisive.

2. With angular thrust

- A is in sixte position.

- B begins a direct attack with step forward-lunge; in the beginning with straight arm extension.

- B attempts to parry with quarte parry.

- Just before the hit, B shifts his fist to the right and forms an angle against the quarte parry. A's body is thereby accessible with an angulated thrust before the final position of the parry has been reached.

3. With opposition thrust

- A is in sixte position.
- B carries out a flèche with opposition thrust in the direction of quarte. A's stop hit is neutralized with increasing opposition until it is blocked entirely. In spite of the opposition the point movement must lead to a hit as fast as possible.

4. With a flick

- A is in octave position.
- From his own octave position B carries out a flèche with flick to A's shoulder or back. An excellent coordination between flèche and flick is necessary to be successful. The advantage of throw-like thrusts is that differences in measure can be compensated for if the blade is bent correctly. If the point moves fast the hit can also land on the shoulder or back. Covered target areas can also be reached with flick, which increases the options for possible hits.

The preparations for direct attacks to the body always begin in far measure.
Additional practice examples are given in Chapter 6 (foil fencing). There much emphasis is placed on creating the critical measure.

Direct attacks to the hand

As "preceding" target areas the arm and the hand are convenient for any kind of attack. This makes it necessary to perfect the precision of the direction of the thrust in – and for these attacks, since the relatively small target area of the weapon arm and the hand requires a high degree of skill and accuracy. The opponent's holding of the weapon, the size of the bell guard, and the constant threat by the opposing blade make the execution of direct attacks to the hand particularly demanding. The attacks must be executed quickly, directly, and precisely, and must catch the opponent off guard.

There is some evidence that suggests that various physical prerequisites with regard to sensory perception are trainable, in particular the ability to optically record fast moving objects (dynamic visual acuity) (compare Chapter 2.2). In épée fencing the eye is focused on the opposing blade or bell guard respectively, because, due to the extremely short distance between the opposing point and one's own hand even very minor movements can be characteristic of dangerous actions. Body and leg movements should be perceived through peripheral vision. The customary distance between the closest target area and the opposing point is between 4 to 40 inches. Time-wise, attacks that are executed within this distance are shorter than the optical-motor reaction capability of a human being.

This problem is especially apparent in the flick to the hand. The well-executed thrust to the hand cannot be parried if the beginning of the movement is not visible, the distance and the tempo are right, and the movement is executed quickly. Due to the above considerations the defender should, as a precaution, direct his point in the anticipated attack direction.

To avoid counter attacks via angulated thrusts to the arm during one's own attacks, direct attacks to the arm are executed with opposition to the opposing point. Direct attacks to the hand are carried out when the opponent during his attack preparations rhythmically changes from low to high blade position, in doing so assumes the sixte position and thereby uncovers the "arm down" opening. The opponent is kept busy with diversionary tactics with the blade and is forced to follow the blade movements. The openings that develop from this are used for direct attacks with angulated thrust to the hand or with direct thrusts to the body. Simultaneously playing with the measure must also create the favorable measure necessary for the attacks.

Opponents, who react to feigned attacks by withdrawing the target area, are directly attacked with flèche. In engagement situations where the opponent executes counter attacks into every attack and opens the measure with "blade in line", direct attacks are carried out only to the arm. With thrusts that miss this target area, the attack must immediately be continued to the next closest target area via opposition of the bell guard to the opposing blade (or via sweep).

Methodological recommendations for the perfecting of direct attacks to the hand

- The training of direct attacks begins with straight thrust high to the arm against the opponent's low fist position. First comes the arm extension with the situation-appropriate forming of the angle or opposition. The hit is landed with step forward. The advantage of this type of exercise is that the sub-elements are easy to control and that there is no changing of the plane, and there are no coordination problems between arm and leg. The next steps are the thrust with lunge,

Figure 7.2.-3:
Angulated thrust to the hand low: a – without rotation with lunge, b – pronated standing still.

261

and finally while standing still. Angulated thrusts to the hand inside are performed from sixte position. With respect to the thrust, it is important that the hand rotation occurs during the initial moment of the thrust and in doing so the point does not leave the line of attack. Raising the point from the low arm position forms the angle for angulated thrusts to the hand low from second or octave position. The moment the measure is right for the attack, the weapon arm is extended in the direction of the point in such a way that the angle between weapon and arm is preserved. The thrust is carried out from octave without rotation, from second with pronation (fig. 7.2.-3).

- With direct and angulated attacks to the hand there are intermediate positions and variations of the fist position during the final thrust. These are mostly individual peculiarities of the fencers that serve the resolution of tactical tasks during a competition.

- With the flick (cutover thrust) to the hand the initial exercises should be performed without footwork, standing still, and with narrow measure. The point is moved from the wrist, as far back as possible. At the same time the arm is brought into the ideal throwing position by moving the elbow backward. The arm's quick forward movement further increases the muscle tension created this way. However, this movement should be slowed down just before the arm is fully extended (like cracking a whip). By virtue of the blade's elasticity the blade, which until now has been bent back, will accelerate forward after the arm has slowed down. This momentum is increased with the wrist until the blade reaches its braking point. After its long acceleration path the blade has reached a very high speed. The blade bends in the direction of the thrust. To achieve valid hits, the point must still be moved forward slightly as it makes contact with the target area. If this technique has been mastered in the fencing position, the cutover thrust must be practiced with step forward and lunge. This technique requires highly developed motor control ability. Due to the versatility of this technique's application possibilities (high, low, outside, inside), it is considered part of the basic repertoire of the modern épée fencer. But particularly in youth training, this technique should not be introduced too soon since the necessary athletic prerequisites, particularly the finger and arm muscles, must first be developed.

- Epée fencing uses a version of the cutover that allows for a hit to be landed behind the bell guard after minimal and very fast point movement. In doing so the impulse comes from the tightened wrist whose initial momentum is gradually transferred "wavelike" to the point via the blade. The point amplitude is no more than 8 inches.

- During training the fencers have to learn that the thrusts must be executed with differentiated strength effort. The amplitude of the point must be kept to a minimum. A successful continuation of the attack or a defensive action, in accordance with the fight situation, must be possible after unsuccessful attacks to the hand. Attacks to the hand are often also used to create favorable conditions for continuing attacks. Particular attention should be paid to this when exploring and camouflaging.

Practice examples

1. • With the changing direction of movement A steadily moves rhythmically forward and backward in far measure. The blade position changes with every backward and forward movement, so that the weapon arm is raised from the lower to the higher line when moving forward, and is lowered to the lower line when moving backward.

   • Partner B is initially passive, mentally determines the moment of the attack accordance with the situation, and begins the appropriate attack in the following situations:

     a. The low thrust to the hand is carried out at the same moment as the stepping forward motion, regardless of the opponent's blade position.

     b. The rhythmic behavior during the forward and backward movement is exploited with the execution of an angulated thrust to the arm low or inside at he same moment as a forward movement with the raising of the weapon arm.

     c. The direct high attack to the arm comes with the lowering of the weapon arm during the backward movement. This complex is trained from the movements of both partners with varying measure, according to the training level. The footwork elements depend on the respective measure during the beginning of the attack as well as the chosen target area.

2. A puts pressure on B with mock attacks, forces him to take steps backward, and pursues the retreating opponent without intending a direct attack. The pressure causes B to dodge moving backward, holding a far measure. When this measure play repeats itself, B suggests a half backward step at the moment A begins his forward movement; A continues his forward movement because he is convinced that B will again dodge backward. At this moment comes a sudden attack to the hand by B.

   Depending on the blade position or the task, the attack execution is direct, angulated, opposing or thrown, low, high, inside, or outside.

Direct attacks to the leg

Direct attacks to the thigh or foot are carried out in engagement situations where the opponent is late moving the lunging leg back from the measure.

Next to the weapon arm, the leg (thigh and foot) is one of the "preceding" target areas in épée fencing. Direct attacks to the thigh are carried out often. They are very successful if they are well prepared. Aside from good preparation, direct attacks to the leg require lots of precision in directing the thrust in order to hit the small target areas thigh, knee, and foot. Direct attacks to the leg must be fast and sudden. Attacks to the thigh are carried out from far measure with extended lunge, and are most often prepared via feigned attacks to the arm. In doing so the entire arm is lowered with the weapon after preparation, so that the arm as a possible target for the anticipated stop hit is removed from the easy to reach plane.

During attacks to the foot the upper body is bent far forward/down to dodge counter attacks with a kind of evasive movement (fig. 7.2.-3 and 7.2.-4). This change in planes makes the defense against thrusts to the foot difficult. At the beginning of training the question often surfaces whether one's gaze can be intently focused on the target "foot", or whether the target is only perceived peripherally.

During the first step the target must be chosen and the point must be guided to the foot with central vision. The fast plane change makes it difficult to guide the thrust and must be practiced often. With a high level of automation a hit to the foot can also be landed without direct vision control, thus making the attack more surprising for the opponent. Attacks to the leg are prepared via feigned actions with the weapon and by constantly changing the measure, with the goal to create favorable situations and moments for this purpose.

Such situations and moments are:
- The opponent delays retracting the lunging leg after recovery from the lunge.

- The opponent responds to mock attacks to the arm with withdrawal of the target area.

- In close quarters situations the thrusts are directed from high sixte or prime parry along the body target area from top to bottom to the thigh or to the foot.

- Through mock attacks to the upper arm the opponent is forced to parry and is distracted. The thrust to the foot with lunge comes at the moment the parry begins.

Figure 7.2.-4: Straight thrust to the knee

- The opponent responds to mock attacks with the withdrawal of the target area by moving the weapon arm or upper body back without footwork. Moments in which the opponent, for his own exploring, moves the lunging leg forward and delays following with the supporting leg, are used to attack.

- The foot is available as an unmovable, attackable target area with every step backward the opponent takes, from the start of the movement until the toe pushes off.

Figure 7.2.-5: Direct attack to the foot

For attacks to the foot special attention must be paid to the choosing of situations and moments. Its incorporation into the youth training program should therefore not be delayed. Top fencers appear to carry out thrusts to the foot while exploiting the opponent's behavior pattern without much preparation. They concentrate on a favorable moment in which the lunging leg is placed far forward and the weapon arm is not extended, and quickly execute the thrust to the foot as a surprise action. For conscious preparation feigned attacks are carried out in the high line.

Methodological recommendations for the perfecting of direct attacks to the leg

- Attacks to the leg are usually preceded by deceptive attacks to the arm or body with the goal to distract the opponent from the true intention. The blade movements are limited; the shoulder and arm muscles must stay relaxed during the thrust. That is how precision and speed are accomplished.

- In the training process limbering-up phases should be included after 3-4 attacks to the thigh or to the foot. During training and competition constant care must be taken to avoid the occurrence of muscle cramps caused by the prolonged holding of the weapon (insufficient precision while thrusting due to local fatigue of the arm and shoulder muscles as well as a reduced range).

- Thrusts to the foot are accelerated from the beginning to the final thrust. In doing so it is very important that the distance to the foot is estimated correctly. The attack should be neither too long nor too short. In unsuccessful attacks the opposing blade is either brought under control or the return back to the fencing position from the lunge is performed with extended weapon arm for the purpose of threatening the opponent's target area and protecting oneself from ripostes.

- Due to the shorter lunge such behavior is not really necessary with attacks to the thigh. Unsuccessful attacks are immediately continued, directly or with opposition, to the body or the hand. In training it is important that attacks to the thigh are carried out from a different measure and from different blade relationships than thrusts to the foot. The point's path to the foot from the high line is longer. Contrary to thrusts to the foot, attacks to the thigh are often carried out direct with opposition or with bind.

Practice examples
Attacks to the thigh
1. A puts pressure on his opponent with forward movements and mock attacks to the arm. B evades the pushing by moving backward and withdraws the threatened target area via heavy bending, lateral displacement and raising up of the weapon arm.
   A uses this moment to launch a feigned attack to B's arm. The thrust is continued to the thigh with the blade shifted downward (exercise should be carried out from different measures (see fig. 7.2.-5).

2. Feigned attacks to the upper arm prompt the partner to carry out sixte parry.
   B's reaction varies (he stands still, moves backward or forward, tries to parry the attacks to the arm with sixte or quarte.)

   The thrust to the thigh is carried out with a lowered blade and half lunge at the moment the parry movements begin (the foot work is chosen according to the specified measure).

3. A attacks with battuta thrusts to the hand.
   B dodges the battuta thrusts by raising and lowering, as well as lateral withdrawal of the arm.

   The immediate thrust to the knee comes at the moment the arm is withdrawn as a target area in one of these directions. Since B anticipates the battuta, it barely needs to be suggested during the real attack.

   B begins the exercise standing still. A can choose the measure as he pleases. B performs one or several steps backward. A adapts to B's measure with the appropriate footwork and executes his final thrust.

Attacks to the foot
1. A evades the attacks to the hand via esquives.
   B's attack preparation is interrupted by a sudden feigned attack to the hand by A. He reacts by reflex with parry or by bending the weapon arm and drawing back the upper body.

   This reaction is used to execute the thrust to the foot at the moment the lunging leg pauses. The feigned attack can only be executed until the opponent's defensive reflex kicks in. From this moment on the attack to the foot must be carried out with constant acceleration.

2. A carries out a direct feigned attack to B's body. At the moment of B's stop hit and the brief pausing of his lunging leg in the middle measure, A executes his final thrust to the foot. This attack can also be carried out with an evasive movement, and its measure as well as technical execution can be varied.

   At the same time conditions have to be created in which counter attacks cannot be taken to the final thrust or remain unsuccessful.

3. A carries out a direct attack to the foot. B pulls his foot back, and with a lunge lands a hit on A's foot while the same is still occupied with recovery from the lunge.

7.2.1.2   Disengagement attacks

Contrary to the direct attack, the final thrust in disengagement attacks is carried out in a different line through disengagement of the opposing weapon and the weapon arm (disengagement), or the opposing point (cutover). Cutover attacks are often used in men's épée fencing, although the bending of the weapon arm at the elbow joint, or an extreme angling of the wrist creates favorable conditions for counter attacks. Because of the risk of a counter-attack the less dynamic cutover action for women is used less often for tactical purposes.
With respect to their technical execution cutover attacks are similar to those in foil fencing.

The disengagement attack is carried out from the opponent's engagement by freeing one's blade from the engaging blade, disengaging the opposing bell guard and thrusting into the next uncovered opening. During the disengagement the point of one's blade describes a forward moving, screw-like motion. The disengagement can take place before blade contact (displacement thrust) and after blade contact (disengagement thrust). In the first case the optical stimulus gives the signal, in the second case the kinesthetic one does. The stimulus response of the proprioceptive reflex is faster than that of the visual reflex. For épée fencing, where the time factor plays a major role, this means that it is better to react via the proprioceptive reflex based on the feel for the blade (kinesthetic control), rather than optical information, the visual stimulus. The path of the blade is like a regular circle. Aside from the consideration of biomechanical principles, this has the advantage that the point can safely free itself from the opposing bell guard and blade, and is thus able to disengage the opposing bell guard without obstruction and hit the arm. The circular disengagement motion is a spiral movement of the point produced by the continuous extension of the elbow.

In épée fencing disengagement attacks are used when it is not possible to reach the target area directly due to the position of the opposing weapon. They are carried out from the opposing engagement, one's own engagement, against contact, as well as at the moment when the opponent makes sweeping attempts.

The disengagement must be as small as possible and executed very quickly. It is important to end the disengagement thrust with opposition to the opposing blade, with a very quick angulated thrust, or with a flick to the arm, if possible.

In épée fencing so called "flicked thrusts " are used in connection with disengagement attacks. The purpose of this type of thrust is to flick the point in such a way that the opponent's parry position (blade position or line) becomes ineffective. By flicking the blade during disengagement with simultaneous thrusting, the thrust lands on the hand or in the crook of the elbow of the weapon-bearing arm.

Disengagement attacks are used against fencers who seek blade contact as part of their basic strategic concept, oppose engagements, and even attack with sweeping actions. The preceding target areas, particularly the arm, are suitable for disengagement thrusts. At the same time it doesn't matter whether the disengagement thrust came from an opposing engagement, from one's own engagement, or is used against a sweep attempt by the opponent (fig. 7.2.6). In every case the time advantage of the hit, which, for instance, permits the use of, remise with disengagement thrust in a parry-riposte, is decisive.

Figure 7.2.-6:
Contact in quarte – disengagement thrust to the arm high/outside

It is not impossible for both fencers to land a hit. That is why actions that carry the risk of double hits should be avoided when one is behind in the score.

Methodological recommendations for the perfecting of disengagement attacks
- The technique for disengagement attacks in épée fencing is different than that in foil fencing. At the same time the blade action is very limited. For good point control it is important not to go past the line of the bell guard during the entire action. To accomplish this, the fist must be raised with a coordinated motion between the point activity and the arm extension. That is how the ideal angle for the hit is achieved. At the same time the bell guard protects one's hand, arm, and shoulder. It is a way to protect oneself from a stop hit from the top.

It is a basic principle of épée fencing to achieve dominance in the high line. The object is to protect oneself on top with the bell guard via the high fist position, while the point prevents counter attacks at the bottom. The disengagement attack is technically executed without rotating the wrist. Even the slightest rotation of the bent blade results in a deflection of the point of an inch or more from the straight line. A good opportunity for self-monitoring is when the unarmed hand holds on to the other forearm at the wrist to prevent possible rotating. Reliability increases when the thrusts are executed in opposition to the line of the probable counter attack.

- In training it should be emphasized that the disengagement thrust is always initiated by the point and continues to accelerate. Disengagement attacks are executed to the arm, body, thigh, and less often to the foot. Next to direct cutovers and opposing thrusts, angular thrusts to the arm are preferred in disengagement thrusts.

- Disengagement attacks should not be executed from the wrist. Due to the difficult to control pivot point that develops between arm, hand, and épée, a loose wrist makes blade control unstable. The ideal épée fencer is very relaxed in the shoulder, loose in the elbow, and firm in the wrist. Against fencers who forego counter attacks, cutover attacks can also be used successfully as surprise attacks. In épée fencing there is a type of disengagement, the so-called "pumping", adopted from foil fencing. In doing so the disengagement is performed primarily by pulling back the arm.

  This solution is risky, but is used as an emergency solution in a fight. In disengagements where the opposing blade, bell guard, or arm is disengaged, the blade is guided with thumb and forefinger of the armed hand. Here the biomechanical conditions are ideal. The movable joint is the point where thumb and forefinger hold the grip. In a disengagement executed from the wrist this point is located in the wrist. The feel for this can be acquired by using an épée with a long French grip, because here blade control is done strictly with the fingers.

Exercises on a fencing dummy that is equipped with a weapon arm and permits disengagement thrusts from one's own engagement are part of a regular training program for épée fencers. Aside from the above exercises, a practice arm can also be used for schooling cutovers and those disengagement cutover attacks typical in épée fencing.

Practice examples

1. Partners A and B are engaging in measure play; when A engages B with sixte in middle measure B attacks:
- With disengagement thrust to the arm inside standing still.
- With disengagement angular thrust to the hand inside and low standing still.
- With cutover thrust high/inside to the hand (disengagement around the blade).
- With disengagement cutover thrust high/inside to the hand (disengagement around the bell guard-flick behind the bell guard).
- With disengagement thrust to the thigh with lunge.
- With disengagement thrust to the body.
  These exercises can be varied against engagement attempts and engagements in all positions and can be trained as displacement thrust before blade contact.

2. A engages B with octave in middle measure and takes a step backward.
- The disengagement attack with lunge to the hand inside, with step forward-lunge to the body high/inside, with opposition to sixte with step forward-lunge or flèche, comes at the moment the stepping motion begins.

3. With a step forward, A takes quarte touch and immediately changes to sixte with step backward.

- B initially remains passive, but at the moment the change begins he carries out a disengagement attack with lunge or flèche to the arm or to the body.

4. A engages B's blade in sixte (quarte, octave) and with stepping motions moves alternately fast and slow, forward and backward, whereby he puts pressure on the blade at different moments.

- B follows the movements while holding the specified measure (middle, near, far). A the moment pressure is put on the blade a disengagement thrust is carried out straight with cutover, opposing or angulated to the arm, body, or thigh.

5. Measure play like exercise 4.

- A attacks with forceful sixte engagement (opposed against the blade). Disengagement thrust to the closest target area (arm high/inside, thigh, or with flèche to the body) is carried out at the moment B gives counter-pressure.

6. Like exercise 5.

- Instead of counter-pressure B carries out a change of engagement.
- Exploiting the moment the blade is released, A executes a disengagement thrust to the arm high/outside with lunge or to the body with flèche.

These exercises demand complete concentration on the measure relationships, the attack moment, and the manner of execution, as well as the objective of the disengagement attacks.

7.2.1.3 Sweep attacks

In épée fencing *sweep attacks* are important attack actions. In doing so the opposing blade has to be swept in such away that a simultaneous thrusting by both fencers (double hit) is prevented. In their technical execution they are similar to sweep attacks in foil fencing (Chapter 6.2.1.3).

But the impact on the opposing weapon is greater, because not only does the conventional right to attack have to be fought for, but the opposing point must also be totally removed from the line of attack. Sweep attacks are carried out with or without opposition, with flick and angulated, to the hand, arm, body, and foot. *Battuta attacks, engagement attacks,* and *coule attacks* are executed as sweep attacks.

- In a **battuta attack** a beat is executed with a forceful motion from the wrist with the middle of one's blade against the foible or middle of the opposing blade. The fencer can rotate his blade during the beat. The alternative with the blade rotation has the advantage of superior épée acceleration.

In doing so the rotation is barely visible because the fist does not move. For a thrust following a beat it is important to use the rebound energy that can be gained from the opposing blade for a quick thrust with arm extension. Carrying out the beat before the arm extension and the footwork in a battuta attack is very important for the learning process. But fencers with good coordinative skills are able to start an attack with lunge or flèche, and due to the proximity of the target area carry out a beat in the course of the movement and score with the immediate thrust.

- **Engagement attacks** have the purpose of dominating the opposing blade. The attacker must establish the necessary blade relationship quickly and forcefully. With one's point in the outside position the opposing blade is engaged on the bell guard and thus dominated. This is done with a quick forward blade action. In doing so it is important for arm extension and footwork to be well coordinated.

- **Coule attacks** are sweep attacks in which the attacker's blade, after making contact with the opposing blade, "grazes" the same briefly or all the way to the point, crosses it, and hits the uncovered opening on the other side with a flick-like movement. The effect of the opponent's reflex counter-pressure with the blade is apparent in that his point moves out of the target zone, so that the attacker is no longer in immediate danger.

A variety of tasks can be accomplished with sweep attacks, such as:
- Removing the opposing blade from the line of attack.
- Uncovering the opening that the final thrust is supposed to go into, with the beat.
- Forcing reactions that provide information about the opponent's behavior during attacks.
- Preventing double hits and counter attacks through engagement of the opposing blade with opposition and bind.
- Making parrying more difficult through beats, and interfering with the accuracy of thrusts in counter attacks (particularly angulated thrusts to the hand), or
- Triggering reflex movements or counter pressure that can be used for follow-up actions via deceptive sweep attacks.

Many situations arise during the fight progression that can be resolved with sweep attacks. Such situations are:
- The opponent disrupts every attack preparation with stop hit or retreats with line. An attack with battuta-angulated thrust to the hand comes at the moment the supporting leg touches down during step backward in far measure, when the opponent holds his weapon loosely.

- Engagement thrust or binds to the thigh or body in middle measure and with a firmly held weapon.

- Fencers, who respond to every attack with stop hit, are aggressively attacked with battuta thrust and opposition to the opposing blade (mostly from far measure with step forward-lunge or flèche).

- Against fencers, who react with counter pressure at the moment of engagement, the attack is begun with engagement, but the final thrust is ended, depending on blade position and measure, with disengagement thrust to the arm, thigh or body.

- Opponents, who move forward with loosely controlled blade, are attacked with battuta angulated thrust to the hand at the moment of a "blade in line".

Methodological recommendations for the perfecting of sweep attacks
- A basic rule for the training of fencers is: Beats are used against fencers who intuitively yield or evade an engagement. It is difficult to bring the opposing blade under control with engagements. With battuta attacks the beat has to be carried out directly before the final thrust, because the opposing point is only briefly cleared from the line of attack. In contrast, the coule attack is ideal against fencers who use opposition against engagement attempts or hold their weapon firmly, because in these the weapon does not have to be dominated. When executing engagement attacks it is important that the opposing blade is completely under control of one's own blade. The forte of one's blade dominates the opposing weapon until one's own hit is executed.

- In youth fencing sweep attacks are a very important part of the training repertoire. But later on these basic guidelines for their application will become increasingly less significant. Epée fencing has become more combative and well thought-out in terms of strategy and tactics. Creating a favorable measure and seizing the right moment are most important. The methodological recommendations on this subject listed in Chapter 6 also apply to épée fencing.

Practice examples
These exercises have been chosen under the aspect of perfecting skills in the application of sweep attacks and the many possible attack forms. They will help with the use of sweep attacks as is appropriate for the situation, in conjunction with choosing the basic versions of measure and tempo as they are described in foil fencing.

1. Partner A moves towards the opponent in fencing position, holding the weapon loosely in middle measure.
- In favorable situations (after rhythm change), B carries out the following attacks against A's high line:
  - Quarte battuta-angulated thrust to the hand inside.
  - Quarte battuta-cutover thrust to the hand high.

- Octave battuta-angulated thrust to the hand high.
- Sixte battuta-angulated thrust to the hand outside.
- Sixte battuta-cutover thrust to the hand outside.

These attacks are executed according to the measure and the target area that is to be attacked (also crook of the arm, leg, or body) with step, lunge, step forward-lunge or flèche.

2. A pressures B with double steps forward from far measure.
- After the second step B suggests a stop hit.
- Against this blade in line follows battuta thrust or a coule attack to the hand, the crook of the arm, the body, the thigh, or the foot.

    As a variation an engagement attack is carried out to the arm in the area of the crook of the arm and to the body, or with engagement attack and bind from quarte in octave to the body low/outside or inside, or with circular bind from sixte to sixte and flicked thrust to the crook of the arm, to the body, or the hand.

3. A attacks from far measure with small step sequences and changes the blade position rhythmically from one position to another.
- B evades the forward movement by opening the measure. At the moment the blade position changes from:
    - high to low, comes an octave engagement thrust to the thigh.
    - low to high, comes an attack during the upward movement, with battuta thrust to the hand, the crook of the arm, or the body,

7.2.2   Remise attacks

Remise attacks are attack actions that directly follow an unsuccessful attack or a mock attack. In épée, due to the absence of conventional rules, they are mostly used as first intention and therefore are strategically assigned to basic attacks. They are a characteristic feature of épée fencing.

We differentiate between *direct remise attacks, disengagement remise attacks,* and *sweep remise attacks.*
- **Direct remise attacks** are attack actions that directly follow an unsuccessful mock attack and are executed into the same target area.
- **Disengagement remise attacks** are executed in an opening that was uncovered by a parry or in another line.
- **Sweep remise attacks** are attack actions that clear the opposing blade from the line of attack at the moment the attack begins or during remise.

Remise attacks require the ability to seize the right moment and to deliver an explosive final thrust. For remise attack all kinds of thrusts may be used and, depending on the engagement situation, these can be directed at all target areas. Preferred are opposition and angulated thrusts. When the opponent retreats with parry after an attack, the remise attack is carried out with remise-lunge or flèche. If the opponent retreats very far in response to the attack, an immediate new attack is required. Since it is very difficult to distinguish a feigned attack from a real attack in épée fencing, every attack attempt by the opponent must be closely watched. Remise attacks are mostly prepared through mock attacks to the arm or initiated via feints.

Remise attacks are promising in the following situations:
- The opponent evades mock attacks by moving backward, and in doing so constantly lowers his weapon arm into octave position. In such situations the attack is continued with flèche to the arm high or to the body (fig. 7.-10).

Figure 7.2.-7:
Flèche attack against withdrawal of target area with simultaneous opening of the measure

- In situations where the defender is delaying the riposte, remise is carried out via angulated thrust to the covered portion – or with disengagement to the uncovered portion of the opening.

- In the case of withdrawal of the target area, the remise attack is carried out to the next closest target area at the moment the threatened target area is withdrawn (e.g. after an attack to the arm a remise attack is carried out to the thigh or with flèche to the body at the moment the arm is bent).

- Opponents, who prematurely suggest defensive actions, are pressured with disengagement – or feint attacks and hit with remise attacks.

- Fencers, who react to attacks with counter attacks (stop hits) are attacked with disengagement remise attacks (engagement or bind). Here remise attacks are often similar to attacks with second intention.

Methodological recommendations for the perfecting of remise attacks
- One of the crucial requirements for a remise attack is seizing the right moment for the start, and the speed of the execution. Resultant is the need to continue the attack without delay if the opponent

- was forced to defend himself and with his blade is in a position, that makes immediate action difficult. Since the speed of the execution plays a critical role in the successful use of remise attacks, this skill must constantly be perfected in training. Remise attacks that are finished with flèche are most successful.

- Raddoppio and flèche are the most commonly used footwork elements in the execution of remise attacks. They should be carried out in varying rhythm. The step-like lunge is used most often as the first element because it opens up favorable conditions for all remise attacks.

- Remise attacks against ripostes that follow a parry without delay, are one peculiarity of épée fencing. When direct ripostes and direct remise attacks are carried out simultaneously it most often results in a double-hit.

Practice examples

1. A carries out a direct attack to the arm high from far measure.
- B takes a step backward with an evasive arm action in a quarte, sixte, octave, or septime-like blade position.
- The direct remise attack with flèche to the body comes at the moment of the evasion before the attack.

2. A carries out a feigned attack to the arm high from far measure.
- B takes a step backward with stop hit to the arm low.
- At the moment of the stop hit A continues his attack with octave engagement thrust and extended lunge.

3. A attacks from far measure with prime battuta thrust to the body high/inside.
- B moves backward with blade in line and dodges the attack.
- Quarte battuta thrust with flèche as a sweep remise attack comes at the moment of the opponent's line.

4. A attacks from far measure with a mock attack to the arm inside with several stepping motions.
- A carries out a remise attack with disengagement thrust and flèche to the body into the backward movements that B combines with quarte parry.

7.2.3 Defensive actions and ripostes

7.2.3.1 Parries

The *parry* is the first effective defensive option against opponents, who operate with basic attacks. The hit is placed with a riposte from the emerging defensive position.

Parries are defensive actions that prevent an opposing hit through movements with one's own weapon. The technical difference between the parry and the counter attack can be seen in the épée's direction of movement. While the épée, during a parry, is moved sidewards or backwards to the opposing blade, the movement during a sweep counter attack is performed during the course of the action, forward, with the point directed at the target area.

As in foil fencing, the parries are identified by their impact on the opposing weapon (beat, press, graze), by the path of the weapon (direct, semi-circular, circular), and by their final position (sixte, quarte, octave, etc.). Due to the large target area in épée fencing the parries' execution becomes very broad and variable. The parry position must be wide enough to offer protection against powerful attacks, and it cannot be too wide so the opening that is created is not uncovered too much.

Parries vary widely in their execution, with a nearly extended arm to a heavily bent weapon arm. At the same time the parry is supported via an opposition position of the bell guard to the opposing blade. Whether the parry is taken with an arm that is heavily bent or nearly straight depends on the depth of the opposing attack. The most favorable blade relationship has been established when the opponent's foible is being dominated by one's own forte with the objective of keeping the opponent away from one's target area.

Contrary to foil fencing, in parries the assumed position cannot be abandoned during riposte to prevent counter attacks or remises via an opposition position. In fights much attention is given to the combination thrust-parry-thrust. An attempt is made to first launch a counter attack to the arm against the opponent's attack, and then directly follow up with a parry. In such cases it is absolutely necessary to combine the parry with stepping motions backward.

The danger of getting hit by a remise attack or not parrying soon enough is considerably greater when the parry is taken in place. The advantage here is a better opportunity for riposte and preventing a long compound attack with a successful ending. Attacks to the thigh or foot are parried with octave, second, or septime parry. To reduce the risk of a disengagement remise attack, the octave parry is initiated with the point. The arm and the bell guard prevent an unauthorized thrust through opposition high to the opposing point (fig. 7.2.-8).

The problems with specific and general parries and the particularities that need to be considered are specified in Chapter 8.2.2.

Application of parries
Parries are carried out with an adducted arm in attacks from far measure forward and attacks from middle measure or near measure, depending on the blade position.

Figure 7.2.-8:
Octave parry against attack to the thigh or foot

Opponents who prefer remises are confronted with parry, and pressure is increased with a shortening of the distance to the opponent. Quarte, sixte, and octave parries in particular are used for this purpose. In situations like these the thrust is carried out with a bent weapon arm.

Methodological recommendations for the perfecting of parries
- In training it is imperative that the épée fencer acquire the ability to vary the execution of parries, meaning he should be able to perform at least two effective parries from the same position. Depending on the situation, he must be able to take these far forward, very close to the body, high and low. He must have mastered the opposition position of the bell guard to the opposing blade, as well as beat-, coule-, and press parry. An épée fencer needs to have the ability and skill of combining the use of parries with the keeping of the correct measures. As strategic defense elements the parries must offer protection in the final position and allow for immediate riposte opportunities.

Practice examples

Once the positions, their changes and engagements have been practiced it is time for their use as parries for the defense against attacks. From the start it is important that the attacks are carried out after serious and proper preparation to create the conditions that are necessary for the perfection of parries.

1. Partner A attacks out of the measure play. B parries these attacks according to the direction of the attack and his own starting position, as follows:

- Thrust to the arm high with direct sixte parry from octave.
- Thrust to the back with sixte coule parry from octave.
- Thrust to the hand low with sixte battuta from octave.
- Thrust to the arm inside with circular sixte parry.

- Thrust to the body low with octave or second parry.

- Flick to the back from octave or second parry.

- Quarte battuta thrust to the arm inside with opposition, with the bell guard to the opposing point.

All of these parries can be effectively mastered through "fight-like exercises" (Chapter 3.1.4).

2. A carries out a direct attack to he arm in the elbow area with step forward-lunge from far measure, and immediately executes a remise attack to the body.
   a) B takes several steps backward and parries the final thrust, or
   b) B suggests a step backward after A's step forward and closes the measure via steps forward with the beginning of a lunge, and parries with quart.

3. A attacks with several steps forward and battuta from far measure, subsequently taking steps backward irrespective of the measure and the partner's behavior. This behavior is repeated several times – B holds far measure and reacts to the battuta thrusts with accompanying parries. He gives pursuit in response to the steps backward. A press parry is carried out at the moment the stepping forward motion begins again.

7.2.3.2 Evasive actions

As strategic defense elements evasive actions (also *displacement parries* or *dodging*) are part of the épée fencer's repertoire. They are defensive actions that prevent an opposing hit via body movements and are identified by retreating, evading to the right or left, ducking, as well as withdrawal of the target area. Esquives are used to support parries. They are particularly effective against opponents who attack vehemently.

A complete overview of the fight must be assured after an esquive action. That is why only evasive actions that can facilitate one's own simultaneous or immediately following attack actions should be used. The most common ones are withdrawal of the target areas weapon arm und lunging leg. Evasive actions by removal are used in every fight via steps or jumps. Esquive by squatting is mentioned for the sake of completeness.

The purpose of esquives is to prevent a hit by opening the measure and at the same time create favorable conditions for ripostes or counter attacks. They are used to defend against opposing attacks in combination with blade movements and without. From a tactical point of view, these behavior patters provoke ripostes. An evasion to the rear with parry tempts the opponent into disengagement ripostes. This creates favorable conditions for the execution of one's own counter attacks.

Evasive actions via withdrawal of the preceding target area are a peculiarity of épée fencing and are used in a variety of ways. As with all evasive actions, the scoring of a hit is prevented via withdrawal of the target area. The target area arm is withdrawn to the rear, to the right, left, top and bottom, depending on the direction of the opponent's attack. In situations where the opponent habitually ripostes to the arm the target area is withdrawn by moving the weapon arm back, which is immediately followed by a riposte.

In the case of foot thrusts with lunge by the opponent, the target area is withdrawn by drawing the lunging leg back to the supporting leg, which is immediately followed by riposte with flèche or lunge.

Methodological recommendations for the perfecting of esquives

- Evasive actions for defending against opposing attacks and for supporting parries in the mentioned forms are all the more effective if they are used suddenly.

- All épée fencers must make it a habit to repel attacks to the thigh or foot not primarily with parries, but with evasive actions, by moving back the lunging leg and immediately launching their own attack. This type of behavior creates a tempo advantage.

- Esquives by removing or moving the weapon arm close to the body most often provoke remise attacks. This is done by drawing the weapon arm back from the line of the blade, via lateral evasion with the weapon arm during angulated thrusts to the arm inside or outside, via increased raising of the weapon arm during angular thrusts from below, as well as the lowering and drawing back of the weapon arm during thrusts from above.

- It must be noted that evasive actions are deliberately used defensive actions, and must be judged as such. They are deceptive in character and are the origin of various types of sudden counter attacks.

Practice examples

Evasive actions via removal
1. A attacks with step forward-lunge.
- B retreats with step backward and blade in on guard position at the moment of the lunge.

2. A attacks with battuta thrust and lunge to the hand.
- B retreats with step backward and adduction of the arm to provide additional protection for the attacked target area at the moment of the lunge.

3. An attack like that in exercise 2, but with subsequent remise to the leg, which was provoked by the moderate evasive action.
- At the moment of the remise comes a withdrawal of the target area via the drawing back of the lunging leg.

In training these exercises can be varied according to the task. Combining esquives with ripostes as well as counter attacks should be emphasized in training.

Evasive actions via withdrawal of the target area
1. A arbitrarily attacks to the hand high, low, inside or outside.
- Depending on the attack, B withdraws the target area by drawing the weapon arm close to the body.

2. A attacks with disengagement and angulated thrust to the hand inside with lunge from far measure.
- B withdraws the target area to the right high in high sixte, and carries out riposte with angulated thrust to the arm inside or high.

Evasive actions are used in a great variety of ways, as these exercises show. It is up to the initiative and the ideas of the trainer and the fencer, to continue to try out better variations.

7.2.3.3   Ripostes

Ripostes are attack actions that directly follow a successful defensive action (parry or esquive). They respond to an opposing attack action. The parry is the basic defense action and forms a technical-tactical unit with the subsequent attack action (riposte, possibly counter riposte).

Prerequisite for a successful riposte is a parry that is taken at the right moment. The parry essentially determines the type and execution of the riposte, and in the reverse, the intended type of riposte determines the choice, type, and execution of the parry. It is the parry that determines the riposte and not the other way around. The riposte is prepared by choosing the parry. The intensity of the pressure or the force of the beat respectively, against the opposing blade determines the type and direction of the riposte, and the direction in which the opposing blade is diverted.

The character of the riposte and the opening one would like to hit determine the position of fist rotation (supination or pronation). The degree of lifting or lowering of the fist is also predetermined via the changeable relationship between parry and riposte. Ripostes can be carried out after any kind of parry: direct, opposed, thrown, with disengagement or with angle. A peculiarity of épée fencing is the riposte with opposition to rule out a simultaneous hit by the opponent. Possible variations are specified under the disengagement attacks (Chapter 7.2.1.3).

7.2.4   Feint attacks

When the defender successfully repels the attacker's basic attacks with parries, the next logical action that presents itself is the *feint attack* to render the opposing defensive actions ineffective.

The feint is a pretend attack with the objective of provoking the defender into a defensive action that will uncover an opening in which the final thrust can land a hit. The feint attack consists of two elements: the feint (as a feigned attack) and the disengagement thrust with disengagement or cutover, with which the opposing parry is disengaged and the hit is scored. All attack elements can be used as feints.

Feint attacks are identified by the strategic attack element that is used as a feint, by the attack number, the type of esquives, and by the attack element that ends the feint attack (e.g. battuta thrust feint-disengagement thrust).

The use of feint attacks requires clarity in terms of how the opponent is likely to react to them. The opponent is forced into his actions through feints. The attacker thereby achieves a tempo advantage. The success of a feint depends on how well the attacker can give the appearance of a real attack. Only in this case will the opponent try to defend the threatened opening.

The feint can be initiated via direct, thrown, angulated, or opposing thrusts. The final thrust is mostly executed as a disengagement thrust, whereby the final thrust can also be executed as a flick or angulated thrust to the hand. Example: The direct battuta thrust to the arm high forces the opponent to defend himself with sixte parry. The provoking parry is disengaged and the final thrust can either be carried out as an angulated thrust to the arm low, or as a disengagement thrust to the arm high. The technical execution of these final thrust movements is identical to that of the disengagement attack. The threat of counter attacks forces the attacker to carry out feint attacks suddenly, quickly, and forcefully, thereby limiting favorable moments for counter attacks and forcing the opponent to defend himself. In addition the thrusts to the arm or body should always be carried out with an opposition to further limit the possibility of counter attacks.

There are different types of beat feints and engagement feints that rule out any realistic chance of carrying out a feint with arm extension after their execution, because the close opposing blade can immediately parry these. In this special case the beat or the engagement has the effect of a feint. The disengagement or cutover thrust follows immediately, instead of the customary arm extension.

Feint attacks require good observation skills, a good feel for the measure, and very precise thrusting. Feint attacks are differentiated by known and unknown outcome.

The type as well as the execution of feint attacks depends on the opponent's behavior, the measure, and the blade position. Feint attacks in épée fencing are similar to those in foil fencing, whereby cutover feints to the hand are used often, but less often to the arm, body, or foot, because in doing so one can easily get hit in a counter attack. The reliability of feint attacks increases when the bell guard, while feinting, is in opposition to the anticipated counter attack. One then only has to pay attention to the parry.

Feint attacks against "known" parries

This refers to feint attacks in which the attacker, due to previous preparatory actions, is sufficiently well informed about the way the opponent will react to a feint. This makes it possible for the attacker to immediately add a final thrust with disengagement after the execution of the required feint, because he has gotten signals regarding the timing and type of the opponent's parry movement and can anticipate them. After the preparation the fencer must have a complete "internal image" of the entire action sequence.

With such a planned action there remains only the question of when (tempo) it can be started. After the start of the action there is no opportunity for corrections; the action program must take place. The required very high speed of action prevents any opportunity for corrections. To regulate the ability to form mental imagines and improve it during training the attacks can be practiced with closed eyes. This can be done in a lesson as well as in partner exercises, or on the fencing dummy. Feint attacks against anticipated parries are necessary, because in competitions against good fencers parries are usually recognized very late and the subsequent reaction with the disengagement takes longer than the amount of time needed to execute the parry.

Feint attacks with "unknown" outcome

In this type of feint attacks (also "feint on sight") the fencer does not have any information at the beginning of the attack about the opponent's behavior. Reliability increases if it can be ascertained early on that the opponent always defends himself with parries, so there is no need to anticipate a counter attack. After the suggestion of a feint the attack is continued in accordance with the opponent's reaction to the feint. Technically this type of feint is executed by slowly starting simultaneous blade and leg movement. The other actions are delayed until the opponent reacts.

At that moment the motion sequence must be accelerated and the hit must be landed in the uncovered opening. The difficulty in doing so is to get close enough to the chosen target area to feign a real threat and still be able to disengage the opposing parry, in spite of the blade relationship. How well the target area can be reached with a major acceleration from the delayed approach is critical in the final phase. This must happen before the opponent uses the next parry. In épée fencing these feint attacks, due to their difficult execution and limited movements and the associated, possibly fast glides by the opponent, are only used by fencers of a very high level. For this special case, the following exercises are used in a lesson: The fencer attacks with delayed straight thrust and lunge. The trainer wards him off with various parries, which the fencer must disengage. The trainer has the option of increasing the intensity by waiting increasingly longer before executing his parry. The task is most difficult when the trainer only parries occasionally. If he doesn't parry at all, the fencer must score a direct hit.

Methodological recommendations for the schooling of feint attacks

- The technical execution of feint attacks is almost identical to those of the individual strategic attack elements. There are differences in the arm extension. In feint attacks the weapon arm extension cannot be too taught in order to still be able to react with parry or stop hits made with opposition to sudden counter attacks by the opponent.

- Opponents, who rarely use parries, are still attacked with feints. In such cases an attack with second intention is recommended.

- Due to the absence of priority in épée fencing, feint attacks are not interrupted when contact is made with the opposing blade. Rather an attempt should be made to foil the opposing action that followed the contact via a stop hit with opposition, and to land one's own hit the quickest way possible. Body feints are used to assist against opponents, who don't react to feints with the weapon.

Practice examples

1. Partner A attacks from sixte position with direct feint thrust to the hand.
- B reacts to the feint with quarte parry.
- A disengages the parry with a disengagement thrust to the crook of the arm.
- B should occasionally respond with quick riposte.

2. B is in quarte position.
- A attacks with a feint to the hand outside and disengages B's sixte parry with a disengagement thrust to the crook of the arm.

3. A executes a feint thrust to the hand from sixte position.
- B parries from octave position with sixte parry.
- A disengages this parry with an angulated thrust low.

4. A attacks from sixte engagement with disengagement thrust feint-disengagement thrust against the quarte parry by B. The final thrust is made to the crook of the arm high/outside.
- B should occasionally carry out stop hit in sixte.

5. A attacks with quarte battuta thrust feint to the arm inside.
- B's reaction with quarte parry is followed by disengagement thrust to the arm outside.

6. A attacks with octave battuta thrust feint to the arm high.
- B's reaction with sixte or quarte parry is followed by disengagement thrust to the arm high in the area of the crook of the arm.

7. A attacks with sixte battuta thrust feint to the arm outside.
- B's reaction with sixte parry is followed by disengagement thrust angulated to the hand inside.

8. A attacks with thrust feint to the arm high.
- B's reaction with sixte parry is followed by disengagement thrust angulated to the arm low or directly to the thigh.
- B's reaction with octave parry is followed by disengagement thrust to the body high/outside or inside. (Additional practice examples can be found in Chapter 6 (foil), and can be used in épée fencing in accordance with their particularities.)

It is recommended that when training feint attacks, particular attention be paid to those that end with disengagement remises. The opponent's behavior in response to attacks is mostly such that the measure is opened very far. Flèche attacks are therefore particularly well suited for continuing attacks.

7.2.5   Counter attacks

The parry is used as a defense against basic attacks. The feint is used as a counteragent against the parry. The simplest defense against feint attacks is the *counter attack*. It is a peculiarity of épée fencing that counter attacks are used very frequently, multifariously, and versatilely in competition.

Counter attacks contain the basic technical attack elements, but strategically they are used against nearly all types of attacks to repel them "offensively". In some fencing schools the counter attack is therefore also referred to as an "active defensive action" during which both attack and defense can be realized simultaneously within one type of action.

Depending on the type of attack, counter attacks are executed against the final thrust or, with feints, they are taken to the first, second, etc., or last tempo. They differ from foil fencing essentially in that they can be carried out in any approach, or in any attack by the opponent without consideration of priority. Counter attacks to the arm, body, or to the leg are preferred. It does not matter whether the approach has direct preparatory or attack character. In every case the hit that was scored 1/20 to 1/25 sec. earlier is decisive.

Counter attacks are essential strategic elements and in many cases determine the outcome of the fight. Combined with subsequent parries and opening of the measure, they considerably hamper the successful execution of other attack elements. Epée fencers, who possess a good defense system and have a well-refined sense of measure and tempo, can execute a counter attack in almost every attack by the opponent. This is done directly, in opposition, thrown, or angulated, depending on the engagement situation, standing still or retreating, with forward movements and with esquives.

Primarily used in épée fencing are: *Displacement counter attacks, stop hit counter attacks, esquive counter attacks,* and *"in between attacks"*.
A peculiarity of épée fencing is the **"in between attack"**, also referred to as stop hit or arrest, or an unauthorized thrust (cut). Contrary to the counter-attack with gain in time in foil and saber, the stop hit or arrest is not about gaining a tempo advantage but merely a time advantage of 1/25 sec., or about the simultaneousness of the hits. An in between attack to the target areas that are not covered by the blade or the bell guard is feasible. The execution of the stop hit (arrest) can be direct, angulated, and thrown. The defender only has the task of landing a hit before the attacker does, and in doing so cannot take the chance of getting shut out by the attacker's blade or bell guard. The appuntata (replacement of the point) is indirect as a stop hit (arrest), or a special kind of arrest as a feint riposte. The in between attack can be executed directly or as a disengagement thrust. The disengagement is not needed to extricate oneself from a sweep attack, but rather to find the quickest way without running the risk of getting shut out.

Example:
- A intends to attack with a feint attack against sixte or circular sixte.
- B is in sixte position and reacts to the feint with disengagement counter attack instead of sixte parry. In the beginning the motion sequence was similar to the sixte parry, but from the start the point is guided forward and down around the opposing bell guard, so that the hit can be placed on the opponent's shoulder.

Displacement counter attacks are used against fencers, who prefer sweep attacks, sweep ripostes, or sweep remises. Following the disengagement an immediate thrust is executed with opposition to the arm, body, leg, or angulated to the hand. In their technical execution they are similar to disengagement attacks. The most common forms of disengagement attacks are direct, thrown, angulated, or opposing disengagement thrusts to the hand and to the arm with simultaneous retreat.

Disengagement counter attacks can disengage from the opposing sweep attack in various ways: with disengagement, displacement, or cutover. A disengagement thrust is executed out of a blade contact; the displacement thrust is executed against the opponent's attempt to establish blade contact. The advantage of the disengagement thrust after contact is that the reaction triggered thereby is proprioceptive, and is faster than a reaction by optical signal. The taking of the blade or the beat only cause a reaction with disengagement, if contact was actually made.

When executing a displacement thrust (with disengagement or cutover) one does not wait until the blades make contact, but rather disengages the opposing blade sooner. The disadvantage is that a sweep attack can be feigned more easily in order to trigger a displacement counter attack. With a counter attack it is possible to begin the cutover movement with or without blade contact. The classic form of displacement counter attacks as a "disengagement in time" with displacement thrust and simultaneous lunge, flèche, or step forward has more significance in modern épée fencing than in foil, because based on the rules of competition blade contact can occur in épée fencing. The conventional priority does not have to be observed. Here the épée fencers with foil-like training are clearly at a disadvantage.

Stop hits (arrests) have the purpose of absolutely preventing the opponent from scoring a hit. The counter attacks block the opponent's attack path with the weapon positions that are characteristic for each situation. This is done by blocking the disengagement during disengagement attacks, disengagement remises, and ripostes, during all feint attacks, or rather by blocking the final thrust in all attacks through opposition. Stop hit counter attacks into the final thrust are always directed at the opposing blade, so that the parry and riposte elements "merge" into one tempo. These are also known as "contractions".

Each stop hit counter attack must be executed with more effort than a free thrust. Prerequisite is, that in doing so the fencer possesses a good feel for the measure and that his handling of the weapon is controlled. They cannot be used in narrow measure.

Esquive counter attacks, which combine counter attacks with simultaneous esquives, are often used in épée fencing. One's target area is withdrawn from the opponent by an esquive and the hit is landed via a counter-attack. Esquives can be backward, sideways, up or down. Very common is the squat, ducking with simultaneous counter-attack in the low openings. Typical are esquive counter attacks that are executed against attacks to the leg. In doing so the attacked lunging leg is pulled back and the thrust is executed to the body, or better yet, to the arm (fig. 7.2.-9 and fig. 7.2.-10).

An acrobatic-looking version would be to jump up at the same time, thereby gaining an even higher position for the arrest (reassemblement).

These esquive counter attacks are best not used against fencers, who reveal the direction of their attack very late and attack suddenly.

Examples:

Figure 7.2.-9: Esquive against attack to the thigh

- Attacks to the leg are part of the peculiarities of épée fencing. As a result the defense of these target areas has also been perfected. For an épée fencer the training of such defensive actions is essential. Evasive actions that result in counter attacks are bound to specific engagement situations and moments. Their possible use, the creating and anticipating of these situations, is a focal point of tactical training that must be greatly emphasized.

Figure 7.2.-10: Esquive against attack to the foot

- Evasive actions in which the upper body leans back, are beneficial in opposing attacks to the foot. These situations and moments usually provoke remise attacks. During a counter attack to the arm low against opponents who often attack with flèche, a fencer should proceed as shown in figure 7.2.-11.
- Several, conspicuously large blade movements during the approach of the opponent, provoke the same into disengagement or feint attacks. Once the behavior and the presumptive attack direction have been explored, a stop hit counter attack is carried out at the moment of the attack.
- In response to the opponent's pushing, the same is tempted with rhythmic deceptive footwork backward and short parries, into executing direct remises. At the moment of remise a stop hit counter attack is carried out to the arm, body, or thigh.
- Displacement counter attacks are carried out against the opponent's sweep attacks the moment they begin, and stop hit counter attacks are executed against the final thrust. During binds a disengagement thrust in time with opposition to the opposing line of attack is carried out at the moment of increased pressure on the blade. If the opponent's attacks begin from far measure, a displacement counter attack is carried out as an angulated thrust to the hand, or with a thrown point to the hand or the crook of the arm. Epée fencers with good abilities and skills in the application of counter attacks can largely forego parries. This type of defense is typical of fencers, who fence with a long-handled French grip.

Figure 7.2.-11:
Counter-attack to the arm
low against flèche attack

Figure 7.2.-12:
Esquive counter-attack
with ducking

Figure 7.2.-13:
Esquive counter-
attack with heavy
ducking against
flèche attack –
"passato sotto"

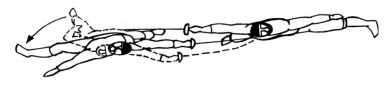

Figure 7.2.-14:
Esquive
counter-attack
with dodging
to the side

Methodological recommendations for the perfecting of counter attacks

- Any thrusts that are used in the execution of strategic attack elements can be used to their full extent as counter attacks. Since the use of counter attacks in épée fencing is steadily increasing, it is recommended to start with the perfecting of basic attacks. At the same time the strategic-tactical differences should be clearly emphasized through situation-appropriate training. This applies to all age and performance levels.

In the training of counter attacks such qualities and skills as courage, a feel for tempo, the willingness to take risks, and reaction speed, are also developed. To improve thrusting skills the target area that is to be attacked is constantly changed for the different thrusts. A distinguishing feature of original épée training is that the beginner learns the counter attack as a first option for successfully confronting opposing attacks. This assures that the counter attack instead of a parry is used as a first reaction.

Practice examples

1. B attacks with a feigned attack to the arm and continues the attack to the thigh.
   * A displaces the attacks to the arm by withdrawing the target area (moving the weapon arm back). At the moment of remise the lunging leg is moved back on the spot and a simultaneous arrest is carried out to the arm high.

2. B attacks with feint (outside/inside) to the arm.
   * A recognized this behavior and already begins the counter attack with a feint to the thigh with opposition to the outside. At the same time A's disengagement to the arm inside is blocked.

3. B carries out feint attacks to the arm and suddenly continues the attack with flèche to the body.
   * In response to the attack to the arm, A opens the measure with step backward. At the moment of the flèche attack comes an esquive forward/low and the thrust to the body from below (passato sotto) (fig. 7.2.-12 and 7.2.-13). Instead of the esquive it is also possible to dodge to the side (fig. 7.2.-14).

4. After several step sequences an attack with battuta thrust and flèche to the body of A is executed from far measure.
   * B holds the measure with several steps backward. A passato sotto with thrust low is carried out at the moment of the battuta attack. Against the same attack a squat forward/low with counter attack is also possible at the moment of the battuta.

5. A attacks with battuta thrust to the thigh from middle measure.
   * B moves the lunging leg back, but only to the supporting leg, and lands an arrest to the arm high, to the body, or on the mask (fig. 7.2.-9).

6. A attacks from far measure (to the bell guard) with battuta thrust and flèche to the body.
   * B withdraws the attacked target area by leaning back, and simultaneously carries out an angulated thrust to the arm low as a counter attack. As a safeguard an immediate parry is added after the counter attack (fig. 7.2.-11).

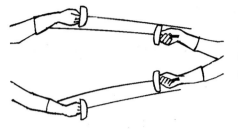

Figure 7.2.-15:
Opposition of the bell guard to the opposing line of attack

Figure 7.2.-16:
Upward withdrawal of the target area against attack to the arm

Figure 7.2.-17:
Esquive with counter-attack to the arm of the attacker

The training of arrests should be incorporated into the training program specifically under the aspect of reaction schooling (moment training). Here success is determined primarily by anticipation and reaction ability, determination, and the powerful, consistent execution of the thrusts.

7.2.6 Attacks with second intention

With the feint attack it is possible to be successful against parries. The counter attack is the strategic solution against feint attacks. And it is best to use the attack "with second intention" against the counter attack.

This strategic element is a type of attack action with a "deliberate and preplanned trap", whereby the goal is to provoke the opponent into a counter attack or a riposte, and to then respond with parry-riposte, disengagement counter attack, or counter riposte. Here the quality of the thought processes is the crucial factor in recognizing whether a string of actions with second intent is being carried out, or whether an improvised, anticipated action is being executed that is controlled by unpracticed, random reflex. As previously mentioned, counter attacks are very dominant in épée fencing.

That is why "second intention" against these counter attacks is more significant here than with other weapons. When carrying out ripostes the counter attack (also one, that leads to a double-hit) must often be prevented. This is done with second intention against the opponent's counter attacks.
It begins with a body movement (body feint), with blade activity, or with forms of sweeps. The counter attack can be executed with forward movements, standing still, and backward. The type of action depends on the opponent's footwork and the distance between the two fencers. Parries are used if the distance is close, binds if the distance is wide. The footwork is the same as that of a parry-riposte.

Methodological recommendations for the perfecting of attacks with second intention
- Second intention is used when the opponent's anticipated reaction is known. This information allows the fencer to predetermine a strategic plan (an action program), whose quality depends on the fencer's strategic abilities (compare Chapter 2.4.3). Without fixed motion sequences with all of the necessary details (spatiality, rhythm, speed, dynamic) these complicated sequences are not feasible.
- Only through available action and movement visualization does the fencer have a chance to succeed. An important criterion is the moment at which the opponent executes the provoked response (counter riposte or counter attack). Actions that take place at an extremely high speed are then no longer consciously controllable. In contrast, the somewhat slower progression makes it possible to recognize the moment of the counter action.
- The ability to accurately guide the blade during fast movements requires perfect technique. For improvement of movement variability and adaptation to the opponent's behavior the second intention must be practiced at varying speeds.

- How realistic the feigned attacks are executed so the opponent is outwitted is important for success. The more surprising the attack situation, the more spontaneous and automatic (reflex) the opponent's reaction.

- It is very difficult to practice second intention in a training situation, since the opponent's reactions are slower than they would be in a competition. Realistic practicing during lessons and partner exercises is very important. During a lesson the trainer is able to imitate different types of opponents to expand the movement adaptation repertoire.

- Well-refined hand-leg-coordination is most important for these types of compound actions with fast execution, such as is necessary for second intention. The necessary skill can be schooled with a variety of exercise forms.

Practice examples

1. The attack with second intention is initiated with the actions that serve the execution of a thrust as a feint attack in the final position.
- A carries out a feint outside/inside with half lunge. – B responds with arrest high to the arm and opens the measure. – A engages with sixte and lands a hit to the shoulder with flèche.
- A as above, – B responds with counter attack straight with lunge. – A returns to the fencing position with sixte coule parry and riposte to the back.
- A as above, – B responds with straight thrust as counter attack, and flèche. – A opens the distance to the back and executes sixte parry-riposte with disengagement low to the hip.
- A as above, – B parries with sixte quarte and ripostes with lunge. – A recovers from the lunge with counter quarte parry and ripostes to the flank with a flick.

2. The attack with second intention is initiated with a sweep attack.
- A attacks with sixte engagement and step forward. – B moves backward with disengagement counter attack. – A pursues him with circular sixte engagement and flèche.
- A as above. – B reacts with disengagement in time with lunge. – A parries with quarte standing still and a riposte with opposition.
- A as above, – B reacts with disengagement thrust and step forward – A lands a hit to the thigh with octave stop hit.
- After the engagement against his blade, B reacts with counter sixte stop hit with lunge. – A parries with ceding counter prime parry standing still and riposte low to the trunk.

3. The attack with second intention that is initiated with an uncovered opening (invitation).

A is in fencing position (on guard) with his blade and uncovers an opening with sixte ("sixte invitation") and step forward. – B reacts with straight thrust as counter attack, with lunge. – A parries this counter attack with quarte parry-riposte standing still.

4. The attack with second intention that is initiated with a body feint.
    A is in octave position and provokes with a body feint. – B reacts with straight counter attack and lunge. – A parries with sixte coule parry and riposte to the back.

The attack with second intention is a very important strategic-tactical means in épée fencing. The attack with second intention remains the only promising action for preventing the undesirable double-hit, during which the opponent lands an arrest to secure his advantage. Its forcefully executed, engagement-like alternative guarantees a high degree of effectiveness, if carried out very aggressively. Good results can be achieved with appropriate combinations, e.g. second intention, parry, and bind.

7.2.7 Feint in time

As a classical action, the *feint in time* is used against opponents, who attack against a counter attack with second intention. In this case the counter attack is merely suggested, and once the parry with second intention triggered by the opponent has been disengaged, the final thrust is executed. The feint in time is an active counter action against an attack with second intention, and thus is a "feint counter-attack".

This action must be consciously prepared, because the attack that is executed with second intention takes advantage of the responding reflex reaction. A very typical situation in a competition fight is for the opponent, if he is far behind, to carry out a vehement attack with second intention just before the end to avoid a double-hit. The appropriate strategic solution against the otherwise rather inconvenient attack is the feint in time. The effect is intensified when the feint is executed simultaneously with lunge or flèche. Here it is an advantage if both the hand and foot tempo can be used for the gain in time.

The necessary prerequisites are developed when a dynamic stereotype is formed with appropriate training exercises that require the feint in time in certain typical situations. This high standard of fencing-cognitive activity requires systematic training, not only in the manual area.

The difficulty in doing so is that the fencer must consciously include the highly automated reflex actions in the action strategy to be able to resolve essential tactical tasks. The desired level of reactions based on reflex and the achieving of maximum reaction ability, should not go so far that responses become uncontrollable. The mental control is prerequisite for this intelligent fencing style.

Methodological recommendations for the schooling of the feint in time
- All types of feint attacks must be thoroughly trained for effective use against all positions. At the same time motor coordination between legs and arms reaches a level of development where conscious control is no longer required.
- Training must include the recognizing of second intention by the following typical characteristics:

  - The attack is slower than a real attack.
  - The sweeps are not as serious
  - The footwork is shorter, slower, and more restrained.
  - The fist position is usually too low.
  - The provocation is too obvious.
  - Individual target areas are left open too demonstratively.

- A skeptical, suspicious behavior pattern must be developed to be able to recognize which parry should be expected.
- It is not the technical execution that is most important, but rather the ability to recognize the opponent's second intention.
- The fencer must be prepared to make quick decisions. While the attacker is the one who decides when the action begins in a feint attack, the opponent gives the "starting signal" for the feint in time. The training goal is to react to the unexpected signal quickly and with the correct feint.

On tactical training in a lesson
- Recognition phase
  The trainer attacks with an attack with second intention. – The fencer reacts with counter attack. – The trainer responds with parry-riposte. – The fencer salvages the situation with counter parry-riposte.
- Implementation phase
- The trainer behaves as above, but after his previous experience the fencer executes a counter attack with feint in time instead of a counter attack.
- After giving notice the trainer executes slow and recognizable attacks with second intention with simple parries; – the fencer reacts with feint in time.
- As above, but the trainer always parries with circular parries.
- The trainer varies his parries, but slowly, until he reaches competition-like speed.

Practice examples

1. A carries out a feint "inside/outside" with lunge as a feint attack with second intention, and intends to parry with quarte; – B reacts with feint in time inside/outside to disengage the quarte parry of the opposing second intention, and lands a hit to the shoulder with flèche.

2. A attacks with sixte engagement in second intention and plans to parry with second parry; – after the opposing bind, B reacts with simple disengagement feint to disengage the second parry, and lands a hit to the hand high with lunge.

3. A attacks with sixte engagement in second intention and wants to parry the opponent's expected counter sixte engagement-riposte with counter change-quarte parry. – B parries with sixte and indicates sixte glide-circular feint-riposte as feint in time against opposing counter change-quarte parry.

4. A beats against the opposing blade with quarte battuta and feints with straight thrust step forward, and wants to land a hit to the back with circular sixte-coule riposte. – B executes feint in time with circular feint and lands a hit to the foot with lunge.

5. A makes a large move with half lunge from on guard to sixte position (invitation) and wants to parry with quarte in second intention. – B reacts with direct feint in time and flèche against quarte parry, and lands a hit to the body.

6. A provokes an attack with high sixte position to be able to react with second intention. In doing so his parry intention is not recognizable. – B reacts with thrust feint-cutover in time to the hand. For this solution (thrust feint-cutover) it does not matter which parry (quarte or sixte) the opponent uses, since the cutover disengages all common parries.

7. A attacks with circular thrust feint against semi circular or circular sixte with lunge in second intention, and allows himself to be parried with the expected counter sixte. – B parries with sixte-second and responds with feint riposte to the counter-sixte parry.

7.2.8 Counter time

A *counter time* is a counter attack against a counter attack that is mostly used against opponents, who execute feint counter attacks (feint in time) against attacks with second intention. In épée fencing counter-time is used often. This composed strategic combination with an otherwise uncomplicated technical execution is the result of good strategic-tactical thinking. The action sequence is initially similar to that of attacks with second intention. But since the opponent responds with feint counter attack, a counter attack is used instead of a parry. For preparation and for deducing actions it must be noted that counter time is always carried out by the attacker.

One generally differentiates between three situations that lead to counter time:

1. Two fencers with good strategic-tactical training, after analyzing the progression of the fight so far, try to take an additional "logical" step in the development of the fight.

So they use a defensive action as a remedy against an offensive action. This role keeps changing back and forth between the two fencers, thus developing action sequences that become increasingly more complicated up to counter time. At this point one employs the so called "reduction' to destroy the logical structure. Familiarizing oneself with this logically composed form is important for being able to correctly predict the opponent's next action or action sequence. This strategic fencing-logical thought and action sequence is generalized and illustrated in figure 7.2.-18.

2. From information about the opponent's habits the fencer learns his typical behavior, e.g. that quarte parry is always followed by a feint riposte, or that he always uses the feint in time against second intention. In this case the opponent is not alerted to one's own plans via long preparation, but is immediately attacked with counter time.

3. The attack in second intention is feigned in such a way that it looks like an action that is not carried out with complete rigor. The opponent very likely expects a renewal. If the opponent is consequently provoked in the same manner, he will react with feint in time. That creates the ideal opportunity for a counter time.

Methodological recommendations for the perfecting of counter time

• During the lesson the specified conditions are such that the trainer, in executing his feint in time, does not know if the fencer will react against the feint with double parry or with counter time. The trainer can thereby prevent any assistance that is not competition-specific.

Didactically it is not necessary to design a counter time exercise in the following way:

• Provocation with step forward, the counter attack is carried out standing still.

• Provocation with step forward, the counter-attack is carried out with opening of the measure backward.

• Provocation with step forward and counter attack with lunge or flèche.

Practice examples

1. A indicates his plan to execute an attack with second intention with sixte-octave (sixte provocation-octave parry) and step forward. – After the analysis B reacts with feint in time and lunge against the feigned parry. – After sixte position A blocks the blade's path high with arrest standing still instead of octave parry.

2. Feigning second intention, A goes from on guard to octave position and suggests a subsequent sixte parry. – B recognizes his intention and reacts with feint in time against sixte parry. – A lands a hit to the shoulder with step backward.

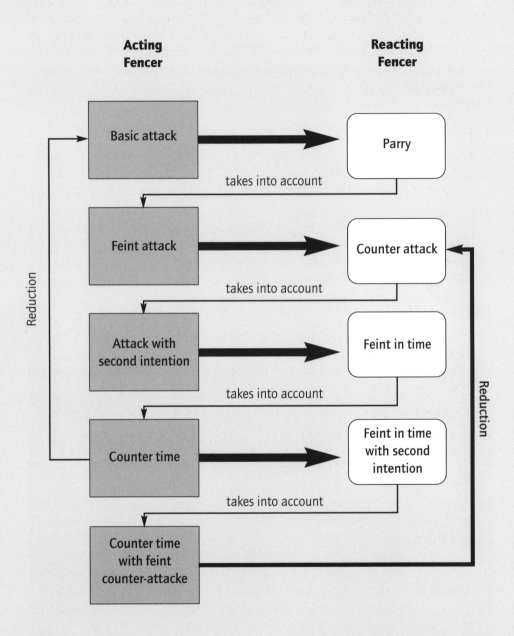

Figure 7.2.-18: Illustration of a fencing-logical strategic though and action sequence.

3. A as above, but from the octave position he does not react with sixte against the planned feint, but rather blocks the blade's path with stop hit in an octave-like position and at the same time takes a step backward.

4. A provokes with an octave position that looks like second intention. – B is uncertain about the subsequent parry because the opponent's intention is not recognizable. He therefore chooses a thrust feint-cutover as feint in time. – A executes an angulated thrust from octave as a counter attack low to the hand against the cutover movement.

5. A as above, but from octave he reacts against the thrust feint-cutover with sixte engagement-thrust and flèche to the arm.

6. Counter time into the feint riposte.
   A feigns an attack with second intention with thrust, but allows himself to be parried with the intention of executing counter parry-riposte. – After the parry B responds with simple feint riposte. – After the opponent's parry A's arm extension remains unchanged. If the opponent abandons the parried blade to carry out a feint riposte, the attacker will arrest the thereby uncovered opening.

8　Saber fencing[1]

8.1　Particularities of saber fencing

Since the late 1980's, saber fencing has undergone some profound changes.
- First of all the manufacturers of fencing equipment made a breakthrough by adapting the saber as the last weapon for use with electrical scoring apparatuses.
  The inherent dynamic of a saber fencer was further increased by independence from subjective decisions by judges because in spite of blade contact, quickly executed cuts were now being recorded and could lead to valid hits.
- Very quickly the fencers began to use the options that had emerged as a consequence to the new requirements, and dispensed with the traditional footwork. The "sprinter" on the fencing strip became the norm.
- In response to this a stipulation was added to the regulations in the mid-90's, limiting footwork to the classical conventional elements. The ban on flèche and cross led to a return of the training of sophisticated tactical and technical finesse, assured an improvement in equal opportunities for the defender, and thus made saber fencing a discipline shaped by dynamics in which attractive action sequences were once again possible.
- Another important advancement in saber fencing is the admission of women's saber in the national and international competition program. Women's saber was successfully performed for the first time as a exhibition competition at the 1998 World Championships. With this the women managed to penetrate the men's final "domain". Starting with the 1998/1999 season, women's saber was included in the official competition calendar of the FIE.

(1) Fencing position, handling of the weapon, and footwork
In saber fencing athletes strive for very elastic footwork. This increases the options for maneuvering and has a positive influence on its effectiveness.

The weapon forms an approximately 100° angle with the forearm and must be held with a minimal amount of tension.

Due to the quick directional changes (forward-backward), the execution of the lunge is not as deep and long as in foil fencing. The dynamic way of fighting requires the saber fencer to have a higher ability and skill level to be able to switch quickly from one element to another. Attack and defensive actions alternate very rapidly. The footwork is characterized by quick changes in the measure as well as an increased frequency in which a switch to a

[1] Use of manuscript by F. Müller, and selective illustrations by H. Hausmann from: Barth et. al.: Fencing, Berlin Sports Publishing 1979

quick lunge is made from the initial lunge to step forward, and from step forward or backward respectively. A saber fencer's footwork is fast, loose, and elastic.

(2) Handling the weapon

The weapon is held and guided in such a way that an angle slightly larger than 100° is formed by the forearm. Characteristic is the minimal tightening of muscles in guiding the saber smoothly and quickly.

The saber is grasped with the second joint of the index finger and the thumb. When landing a hit the point of the weapon is accelerated through finger play.

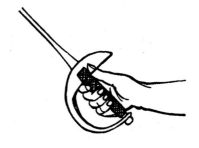

Figure 8.1.-1: Holding the saber

The saber is a cutting and stabbing weapon. This strengthens the offense while it makes the defense more difficult. The stab is used almost exclusively from a defensive position, whereby it opens up a number of tactical options.

Figure 8.1.-2:
Grip and technical execution of a stab

Hand and arm follow the weapon, which is guided by the fingers, while the shoulder joint, if possible, remains in its starting position. Basic cuts are directed at the head, flank, and chest, whereby the cut to the head is by far the most common.

Figure 8.1.-3:
Correct (a) and incorrect (b) execution of a cut. The swinging motion – phase 2 of the illustration – is clearly visible; 1 corresponds to the respective starting position.

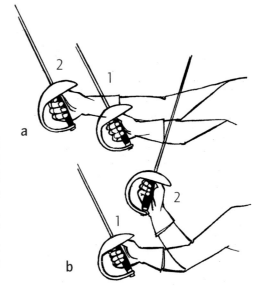

Cuts to the chest are divided into layed down cuts and slicing cuts. The layed down chest cut, like the cut to the head and to the flank, is one of the springy (absorbed) variations of making a hit, while the slicing cut merely "wipes off" the opponent's target area, at chest level on the left side, with a circular motion.

The cut to the arm has recently gained appreciation. Traditionally used defensively as a counter attack with a gain in time, it is now also increasingly used offensively to achieve a gain in time during a potentially simultaneous attack. On principle one should always seek the shortest way to reach the target area.

At the same time the dynamic progression typical in saber fencing, with its constantly changing fight conditions and situations, places high demands on the feel for the measure and working with the measure. The quick changing back and forth between attack and defense, with its different premises with regard to the structuring of the fencing distance (far measure for defense, quickly reaching the critical measure in offense) requires the mental as well as physical ability to comprehend an

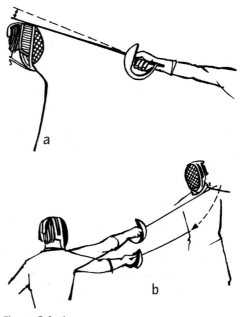

Figure 8.1.-4:
a – Springy (absorbed) head cut, b – slicing chest cut

evolving engagement situation in a split second and use the same to one's own advantage. This requires highly technical and specific training of the weapon handling technique and footwork, and leads to extremely brief actions while trying to achieve objectives. Few quick, successive basic strategic elements rapidly lead to successful scoring of a hit, which, as compared to other weapons, results in a far shorter effective fight time.

(3) The target area

At the bottom it is bounded by the belt line (horizontal line between the two upper ends of the hollow of the groin). Above this line the entire trunk, as well as the head and arms are considered valid target areas.

On the weapon bearing hand the knuckles form the boundary of the valid target area.

Figure 8.1.-5:
Valid target area in saber fencing
(shown in white)

Due to the fact that the arms are also part of the valid target area and cuts are therefore often carried out to the hand or arm, the measure in saber fencing, as a rule, is kept very far. This means that the attacker, in order to be successful, must constantly maneuver to be able to achieve the critical measure necessary for making a valid hit.

Figure 8.1.-6:
Boundary of the hand's valid target area

This constant maneuvering, as well as the fact that a fight situation that will require immediate action can suddenly develop through the opponent's activity, place high demands on the complex of physical and psychological abilities. For a high-performance saber fencer, flexibility, explosive strength, the ability to differentiate, to link, and to concentrate, psychological stress tolerance, feel for rhythm and tempo, are of fundamental importance.

(4) Priority

On principal priority in saber fencing is the same as in foil fencing, meaning the right to attack and the obligation to defend. However, the fencing tempo in saber fencing is significantly lower than in foil, due in no small part to the use of electrical recording

equipment in fencing. The simultaneous attack (attaque simultanée) does not count. Priority is given to the fencer who first initiates an action with the objective of shortening the measure through arm extension.

One peculiarity here is the "blade in line". If the opponent has placed the same in position before the shortening of the measure, it must be cleared first. The hit is awarded to the fencer who first makes contact with the target area with a fluid, accelerated forward movement of his blade in the absolutely final phase. With direct attacks priority changes over to the opponent if the attack ended with a blade parry or was too short.

The defending fencer has further opportunities for gaining priority during blade and compound attacks. If the opposing iron is not encountered during a blade attack (disengagement in time), the right to cut or, – with blade in line, the right to thrust, changes over to the opponent. In a compound attack the opponent has the right to use a counter action (counter attack with a gain in time). But this must be done one fencing time before the attacker's cut, which means that the counter attack must hit before the attacker has begun the final movement of his offensive action.

8.2   Select basic strategic elements

8.2.1 Attacks

In accordance with the modern requirements in saber fencing we differentiate between four basic attacks: *basic attacks*, *long attacks* spanning several stations, *blade attacks* and *compound attacks* or *feint attacks* respectively.

8.2.1.1 Basic attacks

Basic attacks are attacks that can be started without previous offensive or defensive attacks. They can begin out of the fight progression or, more commonly, directly after the referee gives the command "Fence!". Basic attacks are executed against the entire valid target area.

According to assertions from the theory of action, attack preparation and execution can be seen, highly simplified, as three consecutive and interconnected phases:

an orientation phase, a decision-making phase, and an implementation phase. In these phases different psychological and motor processes take place that are necessary for resolving a situational fight task.

(1) Orientation phase

The object of this phase is to perceive and analyze the action situations. This process is the basis for every successful action, but is of critical importance for basic attacks. We will therefore go into more detail here. With the aid of his "perception apparatus" the neuro-physiological definition of which we will forego here, the fencer is able to perceive a large number of optical, muscle motor, tactile, and acoustic impulses that affect the sensory organs, and can thereby clearly and completely assess the fight situation. It is a specific process for gaining information, but it is complicated by the fact that the fight situation must be assessed in very brief time segments, and that the opponent tries to give as little information as possible. It is important that the fencer perceives the most important characteristics of a situation as a whole, i. e., his own movement, the position and movement of the opponent, and whatever preceded a particular situation, all at the same time (compare to Chapter 2.4.4 in particular).

The better the fencer assimilates and processes all of the information in the orientation phase, the greater the possibility that he will make the right decision in each respective situation. As a result such important characteristics as tempo and measure should never be conceived separately or independent of the other characteristics. The result of the orientation phase is the mental recording and understanding of the overall structure of relationships, meaning the specific position of both fencers and their strategic and tactical intentions.

Perception thus becomes an entity of sensation and cerebration, and in its specific and complex form can be referred to as "fighting sense", which continues to develop in its athletic form. Aside from the previously mentioned requirements, the fencer's tactical ability and experience play a decisive role here.

Viewed strictly from the outside, the motor portion of the orientation phase begins with the lifting of the toes. Then follows a small step to initially remain outside of critical measure. The critical measure is necessary for making a valid hit and means that both fencers are obligated to act immediately. Depending on the situation and the length of time, this preparatory phase can be extended arbitrarily. In addition a jump forward-step forward or an arrest is executed first. It is important that the movement is executed smoothly. But in order to be ready to act, the rear leg must quickly be dragged behind.

The execution of the orientation phase is delayed in order to maintain as large a spectrum of actions as possible. At the same time the available alternatives are also determined by the defender's initiative. Possible counter actions against an approach are:

- Blade parry,
- Body parry,
- Counter attacks with a gain in time (counter attack, in between action),
- Sweep counter attacks (pris de fer) and
- Stop hit (blocking the final cut).

(2) Decision-making phase

The decision-making occurs in the second phase. At the same time major thought operations are hardly possible because of a lack of time due to the dynamics of the fight progression. A portion of this mental problem solving is anticipated through strategies. Depending on the strategy, the completed decision is implemented when the best moment has been determined, but most often this or that strategic variation is chosen according to the character of the situation.

Here the thinking largely relates to the preparation of intended (reflex) actions. The beginner must still mentally produce the solution path, but the advanced fencer, due to the frequently repeated, identical or similar specific fight situations and by remembering the successful solution paths, immediately recognizes which method he must use. Such intuitive thought processes are the result of a wealth of experience and the systematic concentration of thoughts during the analysis and solving of tactical problems. They are the product of stabilized technical action elements and good strategic skills that must be acquired after theoretical schooling, through actual practice and in competitions. But in reality the mental process is even more complicated than it can be described here.

Movement is transferred to arm, hand, and fingers, which now take on a leading role and prepare the final or implementation phase.

(3) Implementation phase

The transition from the orientation phase to the final phase during which the decision is implemented, is characterized by the maximum acceleration of the point. The lunging movement begins at the end of this acceleration. The hit lands during the lunge; after this the fencer reaches the final position of the lunge.

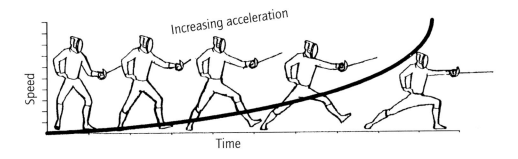

Figure 8.2.-1:
Speed-time progression with suggested action phases of a lunge during a basic attack

While the tactical (operational) thinking prevails in phases 1 and 2, phase 3 is dominated by technical skills. Due to the constantly changing engagement situations the phases alternate, merge, and overlap. Thus the situation must be analyzed constantly. For instance, the actions of the opponent can show that the situation has been assessed incorrectly since the fight developed differently.

Or a decision that was made has to be corrected because one's own plan was given away through a careless move, etc. The ability to make a decision and implement it through constant rapid perceiving and understanding of the situation (based on a good fighting sense), quicker than is possible via all-around deliberation, is called "fight readiness".

The forceful execution of the basic attack is critical to its success. Special preparation of the basic attack is required for the command "Fence!". Since in this case the fencer cannot take advantage of a favorable fight situation, the progression of the orientation phase must already have been run through mentally before the command is given, so the opponent does not get a chance to prepare a counter action, meaning that the decision for a specific action should be made predominantly resultative and not situational. Thus the success of a basic attack with "Fence" essentially depends on the executing fencer's experience, the close observation of the opponent, the processing of information during the fight, and the necessary portion of luck.

Learning and perfecting the execution of a basic attack is done in two steps:

First step
The first step involves the learning of basic technical requirements under standardized conditions. This includes the correct execution of the head cut combined with the respective footwork (arm-leg coordination). This exercise does not yet create fencing-specific conditions since the initial focus is on acquiring movement skills.

Second step
In the second step the training emphasis is placed on the orientation and decision-making phase. Several variations are possible here:
Partner exercise: Far measure

a Fencer A launches an attack to the head; – B allows himself to be hit on the head.

b Fencer A launches an attack to the head; – B varies exercise a and occasionally does a quint parry.

c Fencer A launches an attack to the head; – B varies exercise a and takes anoccasional step backward.

d Fencer A launches an attack to the head; – B varies exercise a and carries out anoccasional counter attack in time.

Fencer A's goal in the orientation phase is to grasp the changed conditions and give a situation-appropriate reaction. At the same time fencer B should apply the variations by alternating them as well as using them in combinations. For the advanced strengthening of skills the exercise can be modified, by having fencer B initially execute a basic attack, which fencer A responds to with a body parry (esquive to the rear) before he starts a counter attack of his own, and B reacts with the described alternatives.

8.2.1.2 Long attack

The *long attack* is an extended version of the basic attack. It is characterized by the fact that it begins in very far measure and is executed with several footwork elements. It consists of preparatory steps, acceleration steps, and the attack step, most often a lunge. The purpose of the preparatory steps is to shorten the fencing distance to the critical measure in a very imposing manner. The long attack is thus equivalent to an orientation phase of the basic attack that has been adapted to the far measure. The movement sequences correspond to those described in the previous paragraph.

Partner exercise: Very far measure

a   Fencer A attacks with preparatory step, moves on to acceleration (step or jump), and lands a hit to the head with lunge. – Fencer B stops (does not extend the measure) and allows himself to be hit.

Variations according to exercise a, b, and d of basic attacks.

b   Fencer A shortens the measure with preparatory steps. – Fencer B "calmly" retreats several steps, but in doing so increases the measure at a different rate than what A is shortening it by. – Just before reaching the critical measure, fencer A begins his acceleration steps and lunge.

Variations according to exercise a, b, and d of basic attacks.

c   Fencer A shortens the measure with preparatory steps. – Fencer B retreats with calm steps, but in doing so he does not increase the measure at the same rate fencer A is shortening it by. – Fencer A begins to accelerate (jump forward-step forward) just before he reaches the critical measure. – Fencer B increases the measure after A's jump. – To bridge this measure fencer A switches back to making preparatory steps and on his second attempt makes a hit with acceleration and attack steps or lunge respectively.

Variations in the second attack according to exercise a, b, and d of basic attacks in Chapter 6.2.1. Here, too, fencer B should apply variations by alternating them as well as in combinations.

Practice suggestions

The acceleration with jump forward-step forward should be minimal, but executed with high speed and frequency. For the lunge as the climax of the attack, the emphasis should be on speed and perfect hand-leg coordination in the final phase.

8.2.1.3 Sweep attacks

In modern saber fencing battuta attacks are clearly preferred for executing *sweep attacks (blade attacks)* because due to the described minimization of the fencing tempo, the electrical scoring apparatus, and the absence of the sensor, engagements have very little chance of success. The most often used beat here is the quarte battuta, followed by the tierce battuta. Due to the perfecting of saber fencing in general and the improved leg and hand speed in particular, the successful execution of a direct basic attack without active counter action by the opponent is made much more difficult.

For unsuccessful attempts with the direct basic attack, battuta attacks are preferred as an alternative over feint attacks, because they cause less of a tempo loss in one's own attack and the beat briefly affects the opponent's concentration and motion sequence. In doing so the beat should be executed directly after the start of the lunging movement, or during the final phase of the attack, for one reason, to safeguard priority, for another, to irritate the opponent in his defensive intention for at least a moment. A swinging motion should definitely be avoided in the execution of the beat. Arm-leg coordination as well as a clean technical execution of the battuta attack is particularly important.

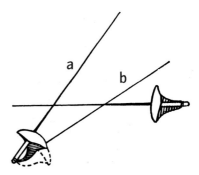

Figure 8.2.-2:
Blade relationships a – correct,
b – incorrect

Battuta attacks consist of two technical movements:
The first movement is in the direction of the opposing blade with the goal of briefly affecting the same. The execution of the movement (blade path) is comparable to a parry movement.

The second movement is in the direction of the target area (hitting movement). Its execution corresponds to that of the final phase of the basic attack.

Partner exercise: Far measure
a. Fencer A shortens the measure with preparatory steps. – Fencer B retreats with "calm" steps, but in doing so does not increase the measure at the same rate fencer A is shortening it by. Fencer B suddenly stops. – Fencer A immediately begins to lunge

when he reaches the critical measure. In doing so he executes quarte battuta with subsequent head cut directly after the start of the lunge. – Fencer B varies with quint parry or counter attack.

b. Simultaneous situation
Both fencer A and B attack with step forward-lunge. – Fencer A carries out a quarte battuta with subsequent head cut along with the lunge. – Fencer B should slightly delay the lunge at the beginning of the exercise so he won't execute it with full intensity, supporting A in his action. Once the fencer has become surer in the execution, this delay can be omitted.

8.2.1.4   Compound attacks

Compound attacks are combinations of two or more attack elements. Paramount are feint attacks which are either executed as expanded basic attacks, or are used selectively as a feint riposte after a parry, or as a counter attack with feint (feint in time). All attack elements prior to the final cut serve as feints with the goal of provoking one or multiple opposing parries to uncover openings, make the defense more difficult, and to deceive the opponent regarding the real attack intentions.

The success of the feint depends on how well the opponent can make his attack that is camouflaged as a feint, look like a real cut or thrust. Only in that case will the opponent actually attempt to defend the threatened opening. If the attack is identified as a feint, the defender won't react to the feint, or he will merely suggest a parry so he can concentrate on the final cut. Due to the very short tempi in modern saber fencing the feint attack that is executed in the critical measure through situational perception, continues to lose its significance. But it is an extremely important and helpful teaching tool in creating understanding for saber fencing, particularly in the younger age groups.

We differentiate between two types of feint attacks:
   The first is the feint attack on anticipated parries.
By closely studying his opponent the attacker has gotten sufficient information on how an executed attack will be parried.

Important information for this is:

- Which parry will be used to repel the attack?

- How will the parry position be taken?

- At what point will the reaction to the parry occur?

Based on this information the attacking fencer will be able to immediately begin with the final cut after executing the feint, since he anticipates the parry movement.

Figure 8.2.-3:
Gripping of the blade in a feint with anticipated parry (a) in contrast to a feint with unknown outcome (b)

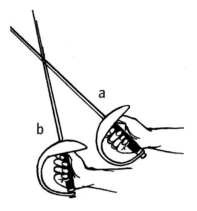

The other form of a feint attack is the feint with unknown outcome
Here the previously mentioned information is not available. After suggesting the feint the attack is continued according to the opponent's behavior. Aside from technical mastery this attack primarily requires the fencer to have good optical perception, quick reactions, and excellent ability to concentrate (see: Orientation phase for basic attacks). In these feint movements the point is held slightly further back, so the fencer is better able to evade the opponent's unknown defensive movements (fig. 8.2.-3b). However, this results in an extension of the tempo, which makes it possible for the opponent to land his own successful hit by executing a quick basic or counter attack. As previously mentioned, the deliberate execution of a feint attack "on sight" is made considerably more difficult by the extremely short tempi in saber fencing.

Based on the nature of the feint attack, – one forces the opponent to parry via a feigned cut to subsequently execute the final cut in the uncovered opening – the following requirements are necessary for the successful execution of a feint:

* The feint movement must be as forceful as possible in order for the opponent to perceive it as a real cut.
* The approach of the critical measure must occur simultaneously with the feint.
* To execute a successful final cut the feint must end before the opponent has assumed the provoked parry.

Partner exercise: Far measure
a Fencer A attacks with head feint-flank cut.
  Fencer B reacts to the head feint with quint parry.

In the beginning the feint movement should be initiated with a step forward. Once the execution of the movement has improved the feint will start with a lunge. The lunge is not started with maximum speed. Particular attention is paid to correct arm-leg coordination

(footwork follows arm movement). Fencer B should parry as late as possible, so fencer A is forced to execute the feint properly.

b Fencer A plays with the measure

Fencer B holds the measure, but does not react to every change, so fencer A, when reaching the critical measure, manages to execute the feint attack.

During these exercises fencer A varies the feint to a chest feint or, with the appropriate invitation from the opponent, to a flank feint.

8.2.2 Parries

Parries are defensive actions in which an opposing hit is prevented via movements with one's weapon, (blade parry), or through withdrawal of the target area (body parry). In the practical application it is important that the parry be posted in the last possible moment.

In doing so the position of the hand should be chosen depending on the measure. Slightly in front of the body for attacks from a large distance, close to the body for attacks from a short distance.

The necessary measure is reached via footwork; however, the fingers determine the final phase of the parry, like the cut.

The body parry (esquive) refers to the withdrawal of the valid target area. This can be done by ducking, dodging, or, the most common way, by retreating. The opponent's attack thereby goes into "space".

The defense against the attack with one's weapon is done via blade parry. In doing so the edge of one's blade must point in the direction of the expected cut. The parry system in saber

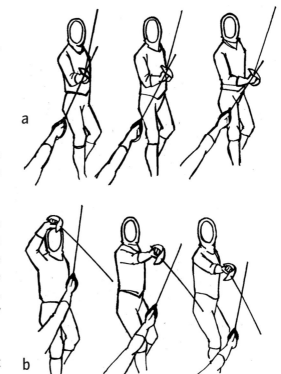

Figure 8.2.-4:
Variable execution of the parry a – according to the depth of the attack. b – according to the direction of the attack

fencing has seven positions of blade parries: the basic positions are tierce, quarte, and quint. They are supplemented by prime, second, sixte, and septime. Sixte and septime are no longer used in today's saber fencing and are listed only for the sake of completeness.

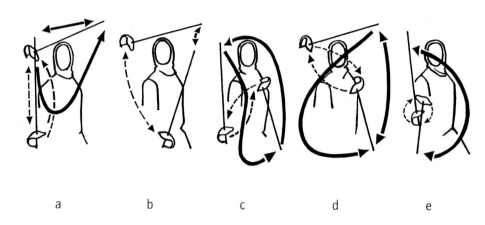

| a | b | c | d | e |

Figure 8.2.-5:
Changes of positions in saber fencing a: tierce-quint, b: quint-quarte,
c: tierce-prime, d: prime-quint, e: tierce-septime

To execute a parry correctly the fencer needs preferably detailed information regarding the type of attack, its length, and the direction of its cut or thrust. The parry is executed at the last moment, so the attacker has no chance to evade the blade movement. This is only possible if the fencer can glean the necessary information from his opponent's movements.

There are various options the defender can choose from to actively bring about the final phase of an opposing attack:

Alternative A
With an accompanying parry executed under tactical considerations, the opponent is tempted into carrying out a cut in a certain opening. The purpose of the accompanying parry is not to repel an attack. It must have the appearance of a reflex parry. The hit is prevented in the very last moment by posting the parry in the "correct" position.

Alternative B
The opponent is put under pressure through active playing with the measure. A quick retreat opens the measure, so a direct cut is no longer possible. The critical measure is created via a suggested counter attack, surprising the opponent, possibly supported

by a feint with the hand. The opponent is thus forced to act and attempts to execute the final cut as quickly as possible without being able to orientate himself with regard to the length and direction of the attack. This uncertainty is used to make one's own hit.

To school a parry it must always be preceded by a cut. For that reason the parry is always practiced in conjunction with an attack.

Partner exercise: Narrow measure
The purpose of these exercises is to practice making a hit or being hit (reducing fear of the cut), particularly with students in younger age groups. In addition the feel for rhythm is also being schooled.

a Fencer A carries out a head cut standing still. – Fencer B reacts with quint parry-riposte to the head (afterwards goes to tierce position). – Fencer A reacts with his own quint parry-riposte to the head.

With beginners it is recommended that the trainer verbally accompany the actions at the beginning of the exercise (e.g., "hit", "defend", etc.).

b Same exercise as a, but the cut is executed with a step forward, the parry with a step backward.

c Same exercise as b, but the chosen openings are determined by the practicing fencers themselves.

The cuts should be executed fluidly but without high intensity to make it easier for the partner to execute a clean parry.

Add-on:
At a more advanced stage elements such as prise de fer or arm stop cut can be incorporated,

Partner exercise: Far measure
a   Fencer A attacks with step forward-lunge and chest cut.
    Fencer B reacts with quarte parry-riposte.

b Fencer A attacks with step forward-lunge and flank cut.
    Fencer B reacts with accompanying parry quarte and tierce parry-riposte.

c Fencer A attacks with step forward-lunge and chest cut.
    Fencer B reacts with accompanying parry quarte and circular parry-riposte.

d Fencer A attacks with step forward-lunge and head cut.
Fencer B reacts with quint parry-riposte.

e Fencer A attacks with step forward-lunge and flank cut.
Fencer B reacts with accompanying parry quint and second parry-riposte.

f Fencer A attacks with step forward-lunge and chest cut.
Fencer B reacts with accompanying parry quint and prime parry-riposte.

g Fencer A attacks with step forward-lunge and head cut.
Fencer B reacts with accompanying parry quint and circular parry-riposte.

Add-on:
- Fencer A's step combination is varied.
- Fencer A and fencer B fence from a simultaneous situation.
- The exercise is fenced from overly large measures.
- Fencer A launches selective attacks on two predetermined openings with step forward-lunge.

Fencer B reacts with the appropriate parry-riposte.

The attack by fencer A should be executed smoothly and without delay.

Add-on:
- Fencer A's step combination is varied.
- The number of possible openings is increased.

Meanwhile a parry-riposte without preparatory action is hardly effective any longer since the parry without preparation can only be fenced theoretically. For this reason the parry-riposte should always be trained with a preparatory action once the technical skills have been mastered.

This inevitably gives the parry-riposte a predominately second intention character. However, the previously described exercises are still described in this chapter.

8.2.3   Counter attacks

Counter attacks are attack actions in which the opponent's immediate attack actions are used for one's own attack. As with other conventional disciplines, the actions preparing the attack are referred to as preparation and thus rule out a classification as an attack. A counter attack can only be effective if the opposing attack is flawed.

Prerequisites for a successful counter attack are:

- Recognition (primarily resultative) of the opponent's incorrect behavior.

- Quick reaction once the situation has been recognized, whereby determination and the willingness to take risks are important in determining the result.

- Precise technique.

- Quick execution of actions.

Counter attacks can be executed as a cut or stab to the entire valid target area, whereby the cut is dominant.

Partner exercise: Overly large measure
Fencer A begins a long attack with preparatory steps. – Fencer B begins his counter attack with step/jump forward-lunge into these preparatory steps. – Fencer A sees the start of the acceleration too late. – Fencer B takes the initiative with a small jump (more suitable than step, because it is one tempo less) and ends the counter attack with a cut.

8.2.3.1   Counter attack with gain in time

Based on their structure, counter attacks with a gain in time are basic attacks with the goal of landing a hit one fencing time sooner than the opponent's attack. They can be executed into any tempo of the opposing attack. This means that a counter attack with a gain in time can also be used against basic attacks if the opponent, once the critical measure has been reached, exhibits incorrect behavior within the spatiotemporal elements of the motion sequence.

Spatial errors by the opponent

- Failure to reach the critical measure, which is necessary for the execution of the attack (beats are too short).

- Errors in the motion sequence (not taking the shortest path).

- Diverging from the shortest path after the start of the attack action (pulling the arm back).

Temporal errors by the opponent

- Insufficient speed during the execution of the action (lack of faith in one's attack priority, thus reaction to the opposing action and loss of time).

In feint attacks the composition of the feint attack (several tempi) can also facilitate a counter attack.

(1) Counter attack with a gain in time offensively

Offensive counter attacks with a gain in time are used primarily in simultaneous situations. They require particularly good arm-leg coordination. The attack is camouflaged by either a delayed preparation or the mock suggestion of a blade – or body parry. But an aggressive attack with lunge is then executed in the last moment. Important is a quick execution of the actions, particularly with the hand.

The cut cannot connect during the flight phase of the lunge, but should lead to a hit directly before or at the beginning of the lunge, because otherwise there will be no obvious gain in time. That is why offensive counter attacks with a gain in time should be executed against the nearest opposing target areas. That is primarily the hand, but the flank and the head are also options. Right-handers have the option of targeting the hand or chest of a left-hander.

Figure 8.2.-6:
Counter attack with a gain in time via head cut (forward movement)

Partner exercise: Far measure
Fencer A parries a simultaneous; in doing so moves too quickly into the critical measure. – Fencer B tries to quickly wrap up the preparation to be able to make a hit with cut-lunge.

Due to the high technical demands, only high-performance fencers should be performing this exercise as a partner exercise. But learning this element in a lesson with a trainer is recommended.

(2) Counter attack with a gain in time defensively

The defensive counter attack with a gain in time is characterized by a backward movement during the execution of the cut. Here retreating serves to assure the gain in time. The arm stop cut is used most often.

Figure 8.2.-7:
Counter attack with a gain in time via arm stop cut (backward movement)

The counter attack to the head is possible when the opponent is already in the critical measure and makes a spatial and/or temporal error in that situation, while the arm stop cut can also be used directly before reaching the critical measure.

The defensive counter attack with a gain in time is not recommended for partner exercises, because the fencer who is to be hit must deliberately make a big error, which could potentially cause a negative training effect, particularly in less experienced fencers. Here, too, one-on-one practice with the trainer is recommended.

8.2.3.2 Stop hits

Stop cut counter attacks are actions that block an opposing final cut or thrust, thereby preventing the attacking fencer from making a hit. They can be executed from two tactical standpoints. The first would be against the final cut of the opposing attack (in doing so an attack action is carried out in the same plane in which the final cut is expected, whereby the bell guard is shifted to the outside to prevent the opposing blade from reaching the target area), the other by blocking the path of the opposing blade.

For instance, the attack head feint-flank via a blade in line can be repelled this way because the blade in line blocks the opposing blade's path to the flank.

In saber the blocking of the opposing final cut or thrust is most common. Priority is determined by virtue of the fact that only the fencer who executes the stop hit counter attack can make a hit. Insufficient blocking of the opposing blade causes the stop cut counter attack to be judged as a temporally unauthorized in between action.

Stop cut counter attacks should only be used when there is certainty regarding which opening the opponent's attack will be executed in.

In simultaneous attacks the stop cut counter attack is carried out in such a way, that with the execution of one's own attack action the fist is shifted in the direction that the opponent's attack is expected to go in. The training of stop cut counter attacks should begin relatively late, because their use presupposes a high level of technical perfection and tactical maturity.

Partner exercise: Far measure
Fencer A executes a flank cut standing still. – In contrast fencer B carries out a cut with lunge, and in doing so turns the edge of the blade to the outside in low tierce position, and with the false edge lands his final cut on the chest.

The action has the drawback of having only one restricted target area available.

- Fencer A executes a head cut standing still.

- In response fencer B carries out a head cut with lunge, and after a successful hit pulls the saber into quarte position, thus putting the opposing blade off its original path.

Add-on:
- Fencer B initially attacks with step forward-lunge.
- In the final phase fencer A attacks with step forward-lunge; in response fencer B attacks with step forward-lunge.

8.2.3.3   Displacement counter attacks/feint in time

Displacement counter attacks are disengagement attacks with disengagements or cutover in time. They are used against opposing blade attacks, whereby the idea is to evade the opponent's intended blade movement. If a displacement attack is carried out in spite of previous contact by the opposing blade, the action is judged as an unauthorized double hit (cut or thrust). Due to the shorter path to the target area (seen in the immediate movement to the opposing target area) the disengagement in time takes priority over the cutover. The success of counter attacks depends on speed of action, technical perfection, the recognizing of the right moment, and reaction speed.

Based on application we differentiate between an active and a passive form. An active form of a displacement attack is characterized by an aggressive forward movement, often executed with a lunge, whereby the hit may be executed as a cut or stab. The passive form is characterized by the execution of a displacement attack with an esquive.

The feint in time must be viewed as a special feature of counter attacks. While it is one of the counter attacks with a gain in time by name, it is not a gain in time in the classical sense, but rather an attack into the opponent's preparation that results in its valuation as a hit. In fact, choosing to use a feint in time depends rather more on the incorrect behavior of the opponent, who interrupts his attack and reacts with a parry to the suggested feint.

The feint in time is used:

- Against opponents who behave inconsistently and, due to a lack of confidence in their attack during counter actions, do not continue the attack but switch to a parry.

- Against opponents who try to be successful using second intention.

- Into the opponent's attack preparation.

The exercises correspond to the exercises for the learning of the feint attack.

8.2.3.4 Esquive counter attacks/"whip-over"

Esquive counter attacks are attack actions that are executed into an opposing attack, whereby the fencer, by withdrawing the target area, tries to avoid getting hit. Since the beginning of the 1990s, a special form of esquive counter attacks, the "whip-over", has taken hold. Related to second intention, it is a thrown cut over the opponent's bell guard to his hand while retreating at the same time. At first glance attributable to arm stop cuts, the use of the esquive with a "whip-over" is particularly common against chest and flank cuts. The development of this action was promoted by the introduction of the e-saber. Like all actively fenced actions in saber fencing, the "whip-over" is mostly used in simultaneous situations.

Partner exercise: Overly large measure

- Fencer A attacks with jump forward-step forward-lunge, preferably to chest or flank, because here the fist is held lower.

- Fencer B responds by executing jump forward-step forward. Into the start of fencer A's arm extension for the final cut, fencer B executes a thrown cut (similar to cutover cut) in the direction of the opposing hand, whereby he takes advantage of the blade's vibration.

Figure 8.2.-8: Illustration of the whip-over

8.2.3.5 Sweep counter attacks/ Prise de Fer

In saber fencing *sweep counter attacks* are also special features of counter attacks. In terms of movement structure they are similar to blade attacks. This special position results from the combination of distinguishing characteristics of counter attacks with a gain in time and stop cut counter attacks. In a prise de fer with a gain in time the referee only allows the impact on the opposing blade if it is timely and is executed in the upper third of the blade.

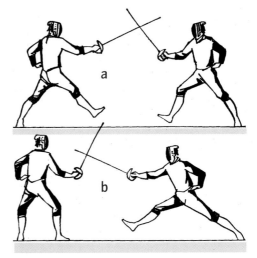

Figure 8.2.-9:
Sweep counter-attack;
a – with correct tempo, b – too late (in this case a parry-riposte must be executed)

The possible use of a sweep counter-attack results from the attacker's incorrect behavior during his approach (strikes too late, approaches too closely with adducted arm, indecisiveness in the execution of the final cut). If the moment of incorrect behavior is missed it is recommended to carry out a parry-riposte, because in this situation, due to the measure and blade relationships that have developed, priority is most often given to the attacker.

From a strategic standpoint, sweep counter attacks are primarily used in the following situations:

- In long attacks with multiple elements.

- After failed attacks, into the immediately following riposte.

- Into the start of the opposing attack, whereby it often assumes the character of an attack-destroying action.

Partner exercise: Overly large measure
a   Fencer A attacks with preparatory steps, whereby he guides the blade, tilted slightly forward, in a calm position.
Fencer B first retreats, then stops and takes over the attack with a quarte battuta and a subsequent direct head cut. If the measure is too far, a coule battuta is also recommended.

b   Fencer A attacks with preparatory steps, whereby he calmly guides his blade in low position. Fencer B first retreats, then stops and takes over the attack with a prime or second battuta and a subsequent direct head cut.

8.2.4   Second intention

Attack with second intention refers to all actions in which the fencer, based on his behavior, provokes a beginning attack action by his opponent, which he foils by using a strategic attack or defensive element.

This element is often used in saber fencing, because due to the great dynamic and the simple but effective basic structure of second intention, a direct basic attack with its tempting prospect of a quick successful hit, can be answered efficiently.

Second intention is used most often with the referee's command "Fence". Due to the "4 m-situation", the fencer has an ever-recurring standard situation at his disposal in which he can arbitrarily combine the various second intention alternatives.

Alternative A:

With a long orientation phase the opponent is induced to execute a counter attack with a gain in time. The opposing attack is repelled with an esquive (body parry) and a big step backward. Depending on the measure, the fencer can now try to score a successful hit with a direct riposte or with a direct attack of his own.

Alternative B:

If the counter attack that is executed after the orientation phase is too long, the fencer must back up the second intention with a blade parry.

Alternative C:

The offensive second intention: Through observation, anticipation, or specific, previous actions it has been established which opening the opponent will strike in. The opposing attack is then repelled with a blade parry without retreating. In doing so the fencer feigns an attack until the flight phase of the lunge, and only in the last moment switches to a quint or quarte parry.

Even if the attacking fencer strikes into another opening, the opposing blade will first touch the parry of the defending fencer since he is not posting the parry, but is actively seeking the opposing iron, thus fencing a type of second attack. The use of a tierce parry is not recommended in this alternative because the risk of a "mal-parry" is too great. This alternative presupposes a high level of fencing-related maturity.

Alternative D:

The second intention with a gain in time: The frequent use of alternative A induces the opponent to a greater depth of attack in the execution of his counter attack. The fencer starts his own counter attack with a gain in time into this long attack.

Partner exercise: Overly large measure

- Fencer A attacks with a jump forward-step forward-lunge.

- Fencer B responds with a jump forward-step forward, interrupts the forward movement, takes a step back with parry-riposte (depending on the final direction of the opponent's final cut).

Add-on:

- Fencer B varies between blade parry, body parry, or continuation of his own attack to a simultaneous.

- Fencer A varies the preparation (step forward-stop element, etc.)

- Fencer A extends his attack, so fencer B has to retreat further to be able to repel the attack.

a Fencer A attacks with jump forward-step forward-lunge and arbitrarily carries out head or chest cut.

Fencer B responds with jump forward-step forward-lunge, with a quint or quarte parry in the last moment. In doing so the parry should be posted far from one's body and actively seek the opponent's blade. The goal of the exercise is for fencer B to parry all of fencer A's attacks.

In preparation to this exercise it is recommended that, for the learning of technical skills and the developing of a sensibility for these actions, fencer A initially execute the head or chest cut standing still, and Fencer B respond with a lunge with quint or quarte riposte.

b Fencer A attacks as in a, but delays slightly, because he is gambling on a body parry by Fencer B.

Fencer B finishes his preparation early and starts a counter attack with a gain in time with head cut-lunge.

8.2.5   Remise attacks

Remise attacks are no longer used in modern saber fencing competitions, and as a strategic element are insignificant. Due to the large valid target area in saber fencing and the added opportunity of scoring with the cut, the riposting fencer nearly always scores a hit.

They are only used for the technical schooling of youth fencers to expand their motor repertoire.

The interested reader can read up on this subject in the respective Chapters 6 (Remise attacks foil) and 7 (Remise attacks épée).

9 International development trends in fencing

Naturally developments in the sport are not seperate from the general development of society. Tendencies toward specialization, toward international integration and thus increased mutual dependence, as well as efforts at increased democratization and thus more equal rights and opportunities, to mention just a few, are of a basic nature and also influence the development of the sport of fencing.

Particularly in the recent past and up to the present, the development trends have been and still are significantly shaped by the efforts to secure fencing's continuing presence in the Olympic program. This essentially defines the core of discussions, petitions, programs, and resolutions up to the present time.

Disregarding certain measures that are shaped by temporary tactical considerations, the following strategic goals are in evidence on a national and international level:

1. Working to broaden the base of the sport.
2. Creating a modern, effective public image of the sport.

Both goals are pursued simultaneously and affect each other. Notable is that all interest groups are largely united with regard to the formulation of the main goals. But some very different methods can to some extent be discerned in the preparation and realization of the respective specific measures. Ccontroversial thoughts will certainly also be presented and discussed here in the future.

9.1 Working to broaden the sport's base

Two lines can be identified in the broadening of the fencing base:
* One is the ambition to preserve or inspire interest in fencing in as many national Olympic committees as possible.
* The other is to strengthen the actual fencing base.

Even after discontinuation of the international confrontation of systems between East and West, the modern competitive sport is, until the very recent past, still an exposed means for the demonstration of national performance ability and thus expression of a country's ability to develop an elite in as many areas as possible. That is why the analysis of the results

Achieved by various countries at prestigious competitions is so important. Based on the amount of effort a country puts into the development of top international results, conclusions can be drawn from the analysis of the results, with regard to the respective sports programs for the particular sport and the respective structural requirements and financial means used.

Much evidence in support of this can be found in the recent past.

For instance, what Germany seeks to accomplish with the "competitive sports structure plan", France is trying to achieve via the "national sports program". Increasingly similar programs are being created in other countries, and taking into account the respective circumstances, they are largely effectively implemented.

Efforts regarding the admission of new sports and disciplines, and thus new chances, into the Olympic program will further this process.

Of course the sport of fencing cannot escape this influence. Countries that, until now, have been under-performing have increased their efforts in changing their performance ranking as compared to previously leading fencing countries. This trend will continue and inevitably leads to constant changes in the ranking order.

Perforce sports-political activities will continue to move beyond the previously, in fencing mostly European core countries. The slogan that summarizes all of these activities is "Magnification of the universality of fencing".

The development of democratic structures as well as trends for the revaluation of confederations from different continents will further promote this, and tends to shift the momentum also to non-European countries. Rational examination suggests that the previous European core countries must not oppose this trend. Results from prestigious competitions like the World Championships and the Olympics show, that previous efforts in this area have not been without success.

Here we can see fencers from many different countries increase their presence in places that promote their respective national image. At the same time it should not be overlooked that this development is essentially accompanied by an objective tendency to increased performance.

Aside from the above-mentioned intentions, this is definitively caused by the heightened transfer of know-how by trainers and athletes from such former top-fencing countries as Hungary, Poland, Rumania, and especially the former Soviet Union after the fall of the "Iron Curtain".

Considerable performance increases have already been achieved in a number of previously under-performing countries through the creation of appropriate structural requirements. The number of trainers with excellent training from the above mentioned countries working outside of their "fatherland" is enormous, and a significant factor in the performance development in those places.

It is expected that this process will result in a tendency to polarized performance. The difference in performance within the individual (also the previously high-performing) organizations and disciplines respectively, such as is already noticeable in individual sub-areas, will continue to increase.

The objectively defined means of most national organizations – and within associations' nations –, in terms of resourcing of personal, financial, and material-technical capacities required for the preparation and realization of top-performances, which continue to grow in volume, have a very limiting effect in the strictly amateur area.

Professional conditions will become increasingly necessary for keeping up in international top-performance fencing. The manner in which the motivational problems – resulting from the polarization – of the fencers who don't belong to the immediate national elite is dealt with, will prove to be an important factor in the stability of the sport.

Long-term stability, particularly in a partner sport, can only be assured by a high degree of real or at least ethical consensus between all parties concerned, regardless of the developmental level of the individuals' achievement orientation.

Aside from these goals, which are mostly shaped by developments motivated by strategic considerations, and in response to this trend, a rising interest in the participation in the sport is expected specifically in areas where goals other than an immediate, existentially significant world class top-performance are aspired to.

To some extent this is already evident now. It can be seen in the development of senior competitive fencing. Here steady progress is also expected due to the creation of new, efficient, structural requirements by the confederations. At the same time the correlation between top performance of the organization and membership development will be very country-specific and largely dependent on the national valency of the sport and appropriate image development.

Many view the **perpetual worldwide expansion of prestigious competitions** along with a simultaneous limiting of the number of eligible fencers as a preferred method for increasing universality.

This is evident in the enormous increase of world-class tournaments in both active and junior fencing and the expansion of the World and European Championship programs in recent years. At the same time this expansion will continue to take place wherever the structural requirements permit. The necessary financial and personal commitment for achieving top performances has increased enormously. There is no end in sight. The resulting compounded polarization is inevitable.

The final stage in this development appears to be a long way off. The competition spectrum in which top performances are achieved, will continue to expand as can also be seen elsewhere, aided by the shifting forward of competitive successes at an increasingly younger age. Representative competitions for pre-cadets are not ruled out.

Even now the issue of training-methodological coping with these new demands from the standpoint of preservation and development of a sophisticated fencing culture, and the balance in implementing selective necessities, particularly with regard to younger fencers, constitutes the real challenge for all parties involved.

These new requirements will force national organizations to adapt their developmental strategies to these trends if they want to live up to their responsibilities regarding the harmonic performance development of young fencers. This must be done with respect to their nominating systems as well as by assuring efficient shares of training and competition in relation to demand and recovery, in view of the respective social conditions. Otherwise it will hardly be possible to prevent a lapse into training-methodological aimlessness and logistical muddle (compare to Chapter 4). Here viewpoints will continue to diverge in the future.

9.2   Creating a modern, popular image of the sport

Based on the growing competition with other sports in the courting of public interest, creating a modern, popular image and heightening the entertainment value of the sport, become increasingly important.

The goal must be to pursue development that is in line with television demand. It is the only way to increase the marketability of the sport and to improve the attention necessary for performance-oriented participation and fundraising. Naturally this development will also have to include intervention in athletic areas. Doing so will require dealing with the participants' increase or loss of motivation respectively, depending on the point of view.

The modification of the competition mode and the competition presentation, the appearance of the fencer, and the exertion of influence on the fighting style are considered areas of primary focus.

(1) Competition mode and competition presentation

Driven by the desire for justness and appeal, the adaptation of the competition mode and competition presentation to the spirit of the times for years has been subject to a constant assimilation and modification process.

Based on the need for a media-compatible presentation commitments can be expected in the following direction:

- Presentation of the event under the pretense of a "show".
- Improved scheduling in competitions (efforts to limit the reasons for interruptions, tightened guidelines for tournament progression, broadening of penalty options, etc.)
- Streamlining of tournaments, and thus more clarity for spectators and journalists.
- More suspenseful competitions due to more equal opportunities for an expanded pool of potential competitors.

The modification of team competitions that has taken place must be pointed out in this context. The current formula seams to find appeal and is spectator-friendly.

This is of particular importance because name recognition of a team or a nation, and thus the spectator's or reader's empathy for the same, is much greater than that of an individual fencer.

Against the background of a constant decrease in the number of accredited individuals and the expansion of Olympic competition, the prospect of team competitions at the Olympics appears to be a particular and as of yet completely unsettled problem.

The elimination of the repechage and the limitation of eligible fencers in individual competition have added suspense, because the chances of a number of nations have thereby improved. This in turn corresponds to the previously described strategy of increasing the suspense during the course of the tournament. Spectacular events anticipated by the spectators are thus much more likely to take place.

However, the debate on how the rules can be made more easily understood for the technically "non-biased" spectator remains a fundamental problem.

Every spectator should be able to at least roughly understand how a particular hit is made. Efforts to make fundamental changes to the regulations for the sake of spectator interest, and therefore challenge the conventions even just partially, would be akin to an invasion of a highly sensitive area of fencing and would affect the basic values of fencing.

But in this area one can always anticipate renewed attempts by the "reformers" and bitter resistance from the "traditionalists" without the certainty of a particular direction in the foreseeable future.

The possible benefits in terms of understandability for the spectator on the one hand, would, on the other hand, limit the versatility and creativity of the sport. With the elimination of the conventions in particular the main argument, that as one of the founding sports fencing also possesses basic values, would be relinquished.

Regardless of how the rules of competition and the tournament mode will evolve, a considerably improved service to the public as well as in the run-up to, and at the tournaments themselves, will have to take place. New communications technologies will be employed to serve potentially interested persons and journalists.

Those interested will be able to follow and comprehend the tournament progression through worldwide current coverage of each phase of the event. The demand in this area for the broader use of technological feasibilies that are already available in the sport today is clearly evident.

The German Fencing Federation's system, which was created and is regularly updated by Heinz Ophardt, has made the organization a leader in this area (compare Chapter 10).

(2) Appearance of the fencer
To improve the fencer's appearance and make it more suitable for television in particular, increasing efforts are under way to move away from the traditional appearance and, in accordance with the spirit of the times, make it possible for the spectators to identify more strongly with the fencer.

Efforts to introduce transparent masks, wireless scoring, the admission of colored fencing suits, and increased advertising opportunities on the fencer, express the desire for show effects and modernity, and promise further development along those lines.

(3) Fight behavior
In this context the development of fight behavior, particularly with regard to its appeal, will remain very important. Precondition to this kind of fight appeal is the for the fencer equally profitable use of as many technical-tactical action groups as possible. It is the only way to counteract lack of action and stereotypical behavior, and to generate some "action".

In awareness of the above-mentioned trends and in appreciation of their responsibility in the continuity of fencing there is a desire, with regard to the devising of rules as well as fencing training, for all participants to feel a stronger obligation toward this goal. It is possible that, against the background of an increased decision-making pressure by the international organization, the appeal of the fighting style of the various disciplines may determine Olympic continuity.

The extent to which it will be possible to create relatively equal chances for attackers and defenders will be a decisive factor here. The expanded technical repertoire, particularly due to the flick thrust in foil and épée, and the elimination of the sensor in saber, parallel with the fencers' physical improvements, have clearly resulted in strategic advantages for the attacker.

Especially young fencers whose defense is not very tight yet, take too little time for proper tactical preparation of their actions and have a tendency to "forward flight". This is one of the main causes for, to some extent, unappealing and low-action fencing with frequent simultaneous actions, particularly in foil fencing with younger age groups.

There are generally several feasible solutions to this problem:
• Consequent adherence to convention regulation by the referee.
• Material-technical changes to the point (mechanical construction of the point), decreased blocking time, definition of a minimum time for landing a hit.
• Deceleration of forward movement through footwork restrictions (similar to rule in saber) and
• Changing the target area to increase risk of attack (sensitive area since this is tangent to conventions).

The continued development of the fighting style's appeal will determine the impact these options will have on improving the image of the sport.

As much as the already mentioned elimination of the repechage has contributed to the streamlining of tournament organization, as lasting can its effect be on the fencers' creativity. It can be expected that the fencer will tend more to the one-sided development of strengths because he may view an important style ameliorating opportunity in a competition as being too risky.

This trend is also reinforced by the fact that the majority of tournaments the fencer is obligated to participate in as per the regulations, do not sufficiently allow him to effectively expand his repertoire.

Depending on the training age of the fencers, training-strategic decisions in particular are indispensable here.

10 Presentation of the sport of fencing

The on-screen duels of D'Artagnan and Zorro, perfectly staged in minute detail, have caused many a spectator to swoon and has enticed many a child into visiting a fencing hall. It is what inspired several of today's top fencers to learn fencing.

And people have always been and still are fascinated by these images. Fencing in the days of d'Artagnan, full of "practical value" for preserving one's life, today is a recreational and competitive sport, children's and senior's sport, and a sport for the disabled. Of course fencing is a sport for women as much as for men.

But not just d'Artagnan, who fought duels larger than life on the silver screen, should spark interest in "non-fencers", rather it is important to make sport fencing itself more popular and present it in an appealing way. But that does not happen on its own. Anyone who is actively involved in fencing in any way should know and utilize measures that have an effect on the public, and do his or her part in continuing to preserve and to spread the fascination with fencing as a dueling sport. Part of this is the proper "selling" of the sport in small and big ways. At the same time it does not matter if it is "just" a youth tournament or the World Championships. Both events must be prepared and presented in a way that is appropriate for the respective audience.

That is why this chapter in a book about "fencing training" focuses on how and what a trainer can and should do "aside", or better yet, along with his "strictly" training activity, to better present the sport and his fencers, be it directly in training or with respect to their media skills. The same applies to the orientation and presentation of fencing tournaments. Most often the trainer is the one who provides the critical information. He is the expert.

Appeal of the sport
The public appeal of a sport depends primarily on how well the sport represents itself. If one asks the question of what a layperson, who knows nothing about fencing, finds so fascinating about this sport when he is confronted for the first time with these weapon duels, the terms "appeal", "drama", and "suspense" come up more than any other. And the trainer has direct influence on these factors.

The appeal and dynamic has two basic components, a coordinative-motor one and a strategic-tactical one:
- The *coordinative-motor component* of the fight consists of very quick and skillful movements and motion sequences. The fencers shine with action sequences the spectators can barely follow. This dynamic is fascinating. To appreciate this the layperson spectator does not have to be able to follow the actions. In figure skating the spectator is not able to see either whether a

triple jump was a Salchow or a Rittberger. He is amazed that a human being can perform such things. That is why fencers are asked to fence "nice action sequences" at fencing exhibitions. It is well received.

- *Strategic-tactically* the allure of a fight lies in the fencers' thought process that the spectators can recognize. One can "predict" from the outside how the fencer will act or react in response to the previous action. Of course this presupposes basic knowledge of the regulations and the strategic-tactical sequences. Such a thought process, that can be explained to the spectator via commentary, is described in Chapter 7, fig. 7.2.-18.

The spectator experiences suspense through continuously landed and received hits. More than 20 in each fight. He just needs to know why which fencer is awarded a hit even though the other landed one, and may be even did so sooner. There usually are few goals in soccer, but the spectator can see them and even make judgments and voice his opinion. That is much more difficult in fencing. More knowledge about rules or simpler rules could be very helpful here. The basic principle to adhere to here would be: "To understand the other's interests and deal with his wishes."

Victory or a successful tournament may sometimes mean a choice between tactics and appeal to the fencer and the trainer, when fencers are standing on the strip without serious action or are "staying limber" in far measure while waiting for time to run out.

A spectator will tolerate temporizing tactical behavior from an athlete who can also fence well and with appeal. When an athlete's tactics are permanently defensive one will already contemplate before the actual fight whether it is even worth watching. Spectators will not be enticed to the fencing strip or in front of the television with "bores". The main event is always the athlete and thus, indirectly, the trainer. It is they who provide "appeal", "drama", and "suspense" through their fencing style. And meanwhile it has surely gotten around that sponsors only appear and organizations only receive the opportunity for television contracts, if fencing has an audience. This vision should transcend the strip and the next victory. Success must be marketable. This should not influence the tactics of an individual fight in an important situation, but rather the overall training of the fencer. Trainer and athlete must remain aware of a sport with appeal, drama, and suspense. The more athletic and dynamic fencers perform their duels, the more suspenseful it is for the spectator (compare also to Chapter 9).

Public relations
"If an event is not reported on, it did not take place." With this quote Emil Beck never misses an opportunity to point out the central point of public relations. Public relations also are fencing's "drum". And something has to be done to really get that drum going.

In German fencing, the success of the women foil fencers at the 1988 Olympics in Soul will be fondly remembered for a long time to come. It was a historic moment when three female German fencers not only became Olympic champions in the team competition, but also won gold, silver, and bronze in the individual competition.

The 2003 foil world champion from Cuba, Peter Joppich, first became aware of fencing back then through these pictures. With such a sensational result the media just jumps on an event like this. Media contacts often develop automatically when a spectacular success materializes. But efforts in making contacts should be made before that.

The following three selective principles offer information for the structuring of public relations from the trainer's point of view:

1. Public relations must be informative
A text, an interview, or a report is informative when the following five questions are being answered: **When? What? Where? How? And Why?**

Public relations work is not limited to newspaper and television reports. Representing the club and training activities in other ways is also part of it. The spectator, listener, or reader wants to, in the figurative sense, "have a look behind the mask". How did an idol become involved in fencing, what does the fencer do outside of training, what is his take on fairness, what does he do in his free time, what does he think about current issues, etc.?

With this analysis the trainer can achieve two things:

- He teaches the fencer to reflect upon his actions and can thus develop basic attitudes about fencing and about him.

- In addition he prepares the fencer to keep others informed about his actions and fencing, namely analytically, regardless of whether the situation is one of joy or anger. That part is particularly difficult in the case of defeat. When someone loses he must also learn how to deal with that.

2. Public relations must be honest
Avoiding exaggeration will pay off. It is just like life itself; too much make-up is bad in the long term. Trainers and athletes don't require special training to act natural in front of the media. The trainer lays the foundation by teaching his fencers to have trust in other people and to be honest to himself and to others. Anyone who has this honesty and this basic trust in himself, his sport, and his surroundings, is also able to outwardly present himself in a way that will reflect an honest and positive image. Now one reader or another

may raise the objection that it is precisely these abilities and qualities that journalists in particular are lacking. That may be true in individual cases. But for the most part the journalism that covers fencing is very satisfactory. This kind of trusting relationship must be cultivated.

3. Public relations must be ongoing

Getting information out continuously is more effective than trying to draw attention to oneself through few actions. The public is almost automatically informed about spectacular outcomes and events.

But what happens for example, when a fencer makes it to the finals of the top eight in a World Cup tournament someplace far away? Who reports on that? If there are no journalists on hand, then the athlete or the trainer become direct sources of information. When someone wants regular media coverage he cannot just contact the editorial department when there is positive news, but must have the courage to also talk about negative results.

The motto here is regularity. The journalists are aware when the fencing events take place. Consequently they also wait for information on the outcome of a tournament. No information at all is worse than a call with information on results, even if sometimes they aren't so great. The journalist waits at the editorial office for information. In this case the reliability of the information source is most important. In the case of the two big sports news agencies in Germany, dpa (German Press Agency) and sid (Sports Information Service), there are also rules about when a report can be given on the "ticker", the information service for all editorial departments.

These two big agencies usually require that a report have national interest. That includes all information on athletes that are active on a national level. It can even be information about junior athletes if they are athletes with good prospects.

Information regarding good work in the youth area of a club or a new trainer, who has started work at the club, etc., belongs in the local (sports) section of the daily newspaper, or in the programming of a local station. The better the information for a journalist is prepared in the run-up, the better the likelihood that something will be printed or broadcast. A proper press release requires concise, simple, and short text, and possibly a good photo.

Having musketeers carry out duels on the tables of guests at a company party, thereby providing entertainment is just one example of a variety of possibilities for keeping the interest in fencing alive.

The personality of the fencer

First it should be pointed out that the object here is not to "change" the personage of a fencer. Here, too, honesty and sincerity is the most important principal. But the idea is to make people aware that every sport depends on how and where it is reported on. This dependence can be influenced. After all the media is interested in "selling" its newspapers or broadcasts. That is why the editor's selection is determined by what the end-consumer wants. In the case of sports this means the appeal of the sport itself.

Journalists keep track of everything and also report on things experienced and things presumed. That includes the fencer's behavior during an interview, on the strip, and in his environment.

The foundation for an appropriately confident manner is laid right from the start at the club and in training. The trainer, who has daily contact with his athletes, must nurture the athlete's strong points on a personal level and give him a healthy amount of self-confidence. Also, or may be even particularly, those trainers active in the area of youth training work precisely within the developmental phase of adolescents that is critical to personality development (see Chapters 2.2 and 4).

It is difficult to say what is required for a successful athlete's personality. Most important is the right achievement at the right time. But what trainer can predict that day? Healthy self-esteem, charisma, reflection on one's actions, analytical ability, exposure to the media, processing of frustration, all of these things can and should enter into training and competitions, as well as early on in the overall education process.

The fencer must understand that he is not simply hunting for a victory but that he also wants to "sell" it. It doesn't matter if the spectators in the hall are friends and family, or if it is in the paper the next day and more of his friends and acquaintances find out about his success. No one demands that the media or the spectators' expectations shape a fight or the fencer's behavior.

But every athlete and every trainer must be aware that the fascination with fencing and the "appeal" of the fencer is not purely determined by victory, by the subsequent interview, or by statements beforehand, but rather by the actual main event, the sport of fencing and the overall conduct of the fencers.

Presentation of tournaments

The public perception of fencing is significantly shaped by the way organizers present their events. Here, too, trainers can be influential in assuring that" their" sport remains interesting.

Nowadays people watch television or attend a sporting event when
- there is lots of money at stake.
- an entire nation is riveted because athletes from that country or club may make a special achievement.
- a likeable person appears on the screen.
- the sport is extremely exciting, or is presented in an appealing way.

The first scenario is still very rare in fencing. But the coverage of so-called super-masters shows, that with more money at stake television is willing to get in on the act. This does not necessarily mean that the number of spectators automatically increases.

The first scenario primarily takes place every four years during the hunt for medals at the Olympics. Based on Germany's fencing history and the amount of medals that have been won, it is certain that the television audience will follow the coverage of Olympic fencing competitions. In Germany the coverage of the women's foil team competition in Atlanta had the second highest viewing rate of the Olympics.

The previous segment mentioned the "likeable personality" of the fencer.
The presentation of the sport is the responsibility of those who organize and hold fencing tournaments.

What happens to a spectator at a fencing event? In many cases he is absolutely lost. A muddle of preliminary rounds with index lists, and climbing as well as relegated athletes, scores of athletes clad in white with their masks all look alike to the outsider. Bright lights and a referee who is gesticulating and assiduously issuing explanations. Suddenly both fencers remove their masks, shake hands, and walk off. One appears to have won, or was it a draw?

It is often said, "a spectator doesn't actually come to watch preliminaries, but only shows up for the finals". He does that because previous experience has led him to do so. But does that mean that we should just let the preliminaries be and only begin to give people an understanding in the final round? Organizers and athletes are asking the question, "Where to begin and where to end, and how much effort is justifiable?

The organizer should put himself in the place of the layperson who enters the hall at any given moment and then needs to comprehend relatively quickly what goes on where. Smaller tournaments should not have electronic screens controlled by computers that automatically display who fences where and why. Even placing nameplates that are handwritten or printed out by computer and enlarged with a copier next to the strip, can be helpful. Programs with the starting numbers and names of the fencers are appropriate when the fencers actually wear the starting numbers so the audience can see them. The comments of an announcer who does not only announce the fights but in addition also explains what certain tournament segments are required for, also serve better comprehension.

Thanks to modern technology it is nowadays also possible for spectators to view the tournament on television monitors. An updated tournament score is shown there at all times. If all of the strips are linked-up, every single hit can be indicated. For a student tournament this amount of effort may seem too much (which does not mean it shouldn't be done), but for an international World Cup tournament it should be the standard. Here the notion that others are not really converting either would be highly inappropriate. It is precisely when "others" are not changing such things, that it is all the more important for at least a few to try. Ultimately every organizer wants to distinguish himself from the rest in a positive way.

It would be ideal if even a layperson entering a fencing hall could interpret everything by himself. That includes things that are self-evident to "fencing insiders", but nevertheless are often overlooked.

Suggestions for more transparency are:
- Visible fight scores at the strip.
- Visible names of fencers at the strip and on the fencers' suits.
- Description of the fencing format.
- Central overview for audience orientation.
- Aids such as leaflets, small brochures, or programs along with the regulations.
- Quick flow of information to the media (results, rankings, position tables, tournament information, press conferences).
- Direct link-up of television networks to the electronic indicator on fencing strips to the direct display of hits (television graphics).

The technical facilities for this have long been created. The German Fencing Federation is one of the leaders in this area (compare to Chapter 9) with a system that was created, and is constantly perfected by Heinz Ophardt.

More than ever, the sport of fencing must see to the setting of a normal standard in the future. All parties involved, athletes, spectators, trainers, physicians, or journalists, should enjoy the sport of fencing. Someone who is interested in it and enjoys it can also convey this joy to others. One has to be on fire to "set light" to others.

The international organization, under pressure from the International Olympic Committees, IOC, is attempting to make fencing more appealing. This modernization refers to the use of transparent masks and wireless fencing.

The visual presentation also plays an important role. At the Olympics in Athens, the spectators for the first time sat on both sides of the fencing strip at the finals. In this case the dark curtain still falls. But correct lighting puts the fencers in the proper perspective and the audience disappears in the dark background: 1,400 to 2, 000 lux of front light in front of the strip as well as a kicker light above the strip make the weapons glitter. The effort is worth it because it creates a "gala" atmosphere. More and more emphasis is also being placed on the optimum presentation of the direct elimination in international competitions. At the World Championships in Leipzig in 2005, these areas will be merged for the first time in an attractive center court. All of this serves to improve the presentation for the spectators inside the hall as well as the television viewers at home.

Pondering whether and how much this increases the appeal of the sport of fencing makes little sense, because it is more of a political than a marketing decision. But, as a matter of principle, the safety of the sport should never be put into question.
The presentation for television viewers in particular, should be made easier in the future. The sport must define itself.

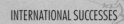

International successes of German fencers at the Olympics and World Championships (after 1945)

Olympics			Gold medals	
1960 Rome	Women's foil	Individual	Heidi Schmid	TSV 1847 Schwaben-Augsb.
1976 Montreal	Men's épée	Individual	Alexander Pusch	FC Tauberbischofsheim
	Men's foil	Team	Thomas Bach	FC Tauberbischofsheim
			Matthias Behr	FC Tauenrbischofsheim
			Harald Hein	FC Tauberbischofsheim
			Klaus Reichert	OFC Bonn
			Erk Sens-Gorius	FC Tauberbischofsheim
1984 Los Angeles	Women's foil	Team	Sabine Bischof	FC Tauberbischofsheim
			Cornelia Hanisch	FC Offenbach
			Zita Funkenhauser	FC Tauberbischofsheim
			Christiane Weber	FC Offenbach
			Ute Wessel	OFC Bonn
	Men's épée	Team	Elmar Borrmann	FC Tauberbischofsheim
			Volker Fischer	FC Tauberbischifsheim
			Gerhard Heer	FC Tauberbischofsheim
			Rafael Nickel	FC Tauberbischofsheim
			Alexander Pusch	FC Tauberbischofsheim
1988 Seoul	Women's foil	Individual	Anja Mauritz-Fichtel	FC Tauberbischofsheim
	Men's foil	Individual	Arnd Schmitt	TSV Bayer 04 Leverkusen
	Women's foil	Team	Anja Mauritz-Fichtel	FC Tauberbischofsheim
			Sabine Bau	FC Tauberbischofsheim
			Zita Funkenhauser	FC Tauberbischofsheim
			Annette Klug	FC Tauberbischofsheim
			Christiane Weber	FC Offenbach
1992 Barcelona	Men's foil	Team	Alexander Koch	OFC Bonn
			Ullrich Schreck	OFC Bonn
			Udo Wagner	FC Tauberbischofsheim
			Thorsten Weidner	FC Tauberbischofsheim
			Ingo Weißenborn	FC Tauberbischofsheim
	Men's épée	Team	Elmar Borrmann	FC Tauberbischofsheim
			Robert Felisiak	FC Tauberbischofsheim
			Uwe Proske	SC Berlin
			V. Resznitschenko	FC Tauberbischofsheim
			Arnd Schmitt	TSV Bayern 04 Leverkusen

Silver medals				
1964 Tokio	Women's foil	Individual	Helga Mees	OFC Castop-Rauxel
1976 Montreal	Men's épée	Individual	Jürgen Hehn	FC Tauberbischofsheim
	Men's épée	Team	Reinhold Behr	FC Tauberbischofsheim
			Volker Fischer	USC München
			Jürgen Hehn	FC Tauberbischofsheim
			Hanns Jana	FC Tauberbischofsheim
			Alexander Pusch	FC Tauberbischofsheim
1984 Los Angeles	Women's foil	Individual	Cornelia Hanisch	FC Offenbach
	Men's foil	Individual	Matthias Behr	FC Tauberbischofsheim
	Men's foil	Team	Frank Beck	FC Tauberbischofsheim
			Matthias Behr	FC Tauberbischofsheim
			Mathias Gey	FC Tauberbischofsheim
			Harald Hein	FC Tauberbischofsheim
			Klaus Reichert	OFC Bonn
1988 Seoul	Women's foil	Individual	Sabine Bau	FC Tauberbischofsheim
	Men's foil	Individual	Udo Wagner	SC Einheit Dresden
	Men's foil	Team	Matthias Behr	FC Tauberbischofsheim
			Thomas Endres	FC Tauberbischofsheim
			Mathias Gey	FC Tauberbischofsheim
			Ullrich Schreck	OFC Bonn
			Torsten Weidner	FC Tauberbischofsheim
	Men's épée	Team	Elmar Borrmann	FC Tauberbischofsheim
			Volker Fischer	FC Tauberbischofsheim
			Thomas Gerull	FC Tauberbischofsheim
			Alexander Pusch	FC Tauberbischofsheim
			Arnd Schmitt	TSV Bayern 04 Leverkusen
1992 Barcelona	Women's foil	Team	Sabine Bau	FC Tauberbischofsheim
			Anette Dobmeier	FC Tauberbischofsheim
			Anja Mauritz-Fichtel	FC Tauberbischofsheim
			Zita Funkenhauser	FC Tauberbischofsheim
			Monika Weber	OFC Bonn
2000 Sydney	Women's foil	Individual	Rita König	FC Tauberbischofsheim
	Men's foil	Individual	Rald Bissdorf	Heidenheimer SB
2004 Athens	Women's épée	Team	Claudia Bokel	FC Tauberbischofsheim
			Imke Duplitzer	
			Britta Heidemann	TSV Bayern 04 Leverkusen
			Marijana Markovic	TSV Bayern 04 Leverkusen

Bronze medals				
1960 Rome	Men's foil	Team	Jürgen Brecht	FC Kurpfalz Edigheim
			Eberhard Mehl	SCR Koblenz
			Tim Gerresheim	FC Rothenbaum Hamburg
			Dieter Schmitt	TV Offenbach
			Toni Stock	FR Nürnberg
			Jürgen Theuerkauff	OFC Bonn
1964 Tokio	Women's foil	Team	Helga Mees	TB Saarbrücken
			Annerose Münch	TSG Weinheim
			Romy Scherberger	TS Freiburg
			Heidi Schmid	TSV 1947 Schwaben-Augsb.
			Gudrun Theuerkauff	OFC Bonn
1988 Seoul	Women's foil	Individual	Zita Funkenhauser	FC Tauberbischofsheim
1996 Atlanta	Women's foil	Team	Sabine Bau	FC Tauberbischofsheim
			Anja Mauritz-Fichtel	FC Tauberbischofsheim
			Monika Weber	OFC Bonn
			Gesine Schiel	FC Tauberbischofsheim
2000 Sydney	Men's saber	Individual	Wiradech Kothny	FG Koblenz
	Women's foil	Team	Rita König	FC Tauberbischofsheim
			Sabine Bau	FC Tauberbischofsheim
			Monika Weber	OFC Bonn
	Men's saber	Team	Wiradech Kothny	FG Koblenz
			Dennis Bauer	FG Koblenz
			Alexander Weber	FC Tauberbischofsheim
	Men's épée	Team	Jörg Fiedler	FC Tauberbischofsheim
			Sven Schmid	FC Tauberbischofsheim
			Daniel Striegel	FC Tauberbischofsheim
			Normann Ackermann	FC Tauberbischofsheim
2004 Athens	Men's épée	Team	Jörg Fiedler	FC Tauberbischofsheim
			Sven Schmid	FC Tauberbischofsheim
			Daniel Strigel	FC Tauberbischofsheim
			Normann Ackermann	FC Tauberbischofsheim

World Championships		Gold medals		
1961 Torino	Women's foil	Individual	Heidi Schmid	TSV 1847 Schwaben-Augsb.
1969 Havana	Men's foil	Individual	Friedrich Wessel	UFC Bonn
1970 Ankara	Men's foil	Individual	Friedrich Wessel	UFC Bonn

1973 Göteborg	Men's épée	Team	Reinhold Behr	FC Tauberbischofsheim
			Harald Hein	FC Tauberbischofsheim
			Jürgen Hehn	FC Tauberbischofsheim
			Joachim Peter	UFC Frankfurt
			Josef Szepesi	SB Heidenheim
1975 Budapest	Man's épée	Individual	Alexander Pusch	FC Tauberbischofsheim
1977 Buenos Aires	Men's foil	Team	Matthias Behr	FC Tauberbischofsheim
			Thomas Bach	FC Tauberbischofsheim
			Harald Hein	FC Tauberbischofsheim
			Klaus Reichert	OFC Bonn
			Albrecht Wessel	OFC Bonn
1978 Hamburg	Men's épée	Individual	Alexander Pusch	FC Tauberbischofsheim
1979 Melbourne	Women's foil	Individual	Cornelia Hanisch	FC Offenbach
1981 Clermont-Ferrand	Women's foil	Individual	Cornelia Hanisch	FC Offenbach
1983 Vienna	Men's épée	Individual	Elmar Borrmann	FC Tauberbischofsheim
	Men's foil	Team	Matthias Behr	FC Tauberbischofsheim
			Frank Beck	FC Tauberbischofsheim
			Mathias Gey	FC Tauberbischofsheim
			Harald Hein	FC Tauberbischofsheim
			Klaus Reichert	OFC Bonn
1985 Barcelona	Women's foil	Individual	Cornelia Hanisch	FC Offenbach
	Women's foil	Team	Cornelia Hanisch	FC Offenbach
			Sabine Bischof	FC Tauberbischofsheim
			Anja Fichtel	FC Tauberbischofsheim
			Susanne Lang	FC Tauberbischofsheim
			Zita Funkenhauser	FC Tauberbischofsheim
	Men's épée	Team	Achim Bellmann	Bayer Leverkusen
			Volker Fischer	FC Tauberbischofsheim
			Thomas Gerull	FC Tauberbischofsheim
			Alexander Pusch	FC Tauberbischofsheim
			Arnd Schmitt	FC Tauberbischofsheim
1986 Sofia	Women's foil	Individual	Anja Fichtel	FC Tauberbischofsheim
	Men's épée	Team	Elmar Borrmann	FC Tauberbischofsheim
			Volker Fischer	FC Tauberbischofsheim
			Thomas Gerull	FC Tauberbischofsheim
			Alexander Pusch	FC Tauberbischofsheim
			Arnd Schmitt	TSV Bayer 04 Leverkusen

Year/Place	Event	Type	Name	Club
1987 Lausanne	Men's foil	Individual	Mathias Gey	FC Tauberbischofsheim
	Men's épée	Individual	Volker Fischer	FC Tauberbischofsheim
	Men's foil	Team	Mathias Gey	FC Tauberbischofsheim
			Matthias Behr	FC Tauberbischofsheim
			Ullrich Schreck	OFC Bonn
			Thorsten Weidner	FC Tauberbischofsheim
			Klaus Reichert	OFC Bonn
1989 Denver	Men's foil	Individual	Alexander Koch	OFC Bonn
	Women's foil	Team	Sabine Bau	FC Tauberbischofsheim
			Annette Dobmeier	FC Tauberbischofsheim
			Anja Mauritz-Fichtel	FC Tauberbischofsheim
			Zita Funkenhauser	FC Tauberbischofsheim
			Susanne Lang	FC Tauberbischofsheim
1990 Lyon	Women's foil	Individual	Anja Mauritz-Fichtel	FC Tauberbischofsheim
	Men's épée	Individual	Thomasa Gerull	FC Tauberbischofsheim
	Women's épée	Team	Eva-Maria Ittner	FC Offenbach
			Ute Schaeper	FC Tauberbischofsheim
			Renate Rieband-Kaspar	OFC Bonn
			Hedwig Funkenhauser	FC Tauberbischofsheim
			Monika Ritz	Heidenheimer SB
1991 Budapest	Men's foil	Individual	Ingo Weißenborn	FC Tauberbischofsheim
1993 Essen	Men's foil	Individual	Alexander Koch	Etuf Essen
	Women's foil	Team	Simone Bauer	FC Tauberbischofsheim
			Sabine Bau	FC Tauberbischofsheim
			Zita Funkenhauser	FC Tauberbischofsheim
			Monika Weber	OFC Bonn
	Men's foil	Team	Alexander Koch	Etuf Essen
			Uwe Römer	FC Tauberbischofsheim
			Thorsten Weidner	FC Tauberbischofsheim
			Udo Wagner	FC Tauberbischofsheim
			Ingo Weißenborn	FC Tauberbischofsheim
1994 Athens	Men's saber	Individual	Felix Becker	TSV Bayer Dormagen
1995 Den Haag	Men's épée	Team	Elmar Borrmann	FC Tauberbischofsheim
			Michael Flegler	FC Tauberbischofsheim
			Arnd Schmitt	Bayer Leverkusen
			Mariusz Strzalka	FC Tauberbischofsheim
1998 La-Chaux-de-Fonds	Women's foil	Individual	Sabine Bau	FC Tauberbischofsheim
1999 Seoul	Men's épée	Individual	Arnd Schmitt	TSV Bayer 04 Leverkusen
	Women's foil	Team	Sabine Bau	FC Tauberbischofsheim

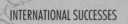

			Gesine Schiel	FC Tauberbischofsheim
			Simone Bauer	FC Tauberbischofsheim
			Monika Weber	OFC Bonn
2001 Nîmes	Women's épée	Individual	Claudia Bokel	OFC Bonn
2002 Lisbon	Men's foil	Team	Ralf Bissdorf	Heidenheimer SB/FA
			Peter Joppich	KSC Koblenz
			Lars Schache	FC Tauberbischofsheim
			André Weßels	FC Tauberbischofsheim
2003 Havana	Men's foil	Individual	Peter Joppich	KSC Koblenz

Silver medals				
1957 Paris	Women's foil	Individual	Heidi Schmid	TSV 1847 Schwaben-Augsb.
	Women's foil	Team	Helmi Hoehle	FC Offenbach
			Ilse Keydel	TK Hannover
			Else Ommerborn	ATSV Saarbrücken
			Helga Stroh	FC Hermannia Frankfurt
			Heidi Schmid	TSV 1847 Schwaben-Augsb.
1958 Philadelphia	Women's foil	Team	Astrid Berndt	TK Hannover
			Helmi Hoehle	FC Offenbach
			Ilse Keydel	TK Hannover
			Helga Mees	TB Saarbrücken
			Heidi Schmid	TSV 1847 Schwaben-Augsb.
1959 Budapest	Men's foil	Team	Jürgen Brecht	FC Kurpfalz –Edigheim
			Tim Gerresheim	FC Rothenbaum Hamburg
			Dieter Schmitt	TV Offenbach
			Jürgen Theuerkauff	OFC Bonn
			Manfred Urschel	TB St. Johann-Saarbrücken
1973 Goteborg	Men's foil	Team	Matthias Behr	FC Tauberbischofsheim
			Thomas Bach	FC Tauberbischofsheim
			Harald Hein	FC Tauberbischofsheim
			Thomas Jäger	OFC Bonn
			Klaus Reichert	OFC Bonn
1974 Grenoble	Men's épée	Team	Elmar Beierstettel	FC Tauberbischofsheim
			Gerd Opgenorth	TUS Clodwig-Zülpich
			Jürgen Hehn	FC Tauberbischofsheim
			Joachim Peter	UFC Frankfurt
			Alexander Pusch	FC Tauberbischofsheim

1975 Budapest	Men's épée	Team	Elmar Beierstettel	FC Tauberbischofsheim
			Reinhold Behr	FC Tauberbischofsheim
			Hanns Jana	FC Tauberbischofsheim
			Jürgen Hehn	FC Tauberbischofsheim
			Alexander Pusch	FC Tauberbischofsheim
1977 Buenos Aires	Men's foil Women's foil	Individual Team	Harald Hein	FC Tauberbischofsheim
			Cornelia Hanisch	FC Offenbach
			Gudrun Lotter	FC Tauberbischofsheim
			Brigitte Oertel	KSC Koblenz
			Ute Kirchels	OFC Bonn
			Karin Rutz	FC Tauberbischofsheim
1979 Melbourne	Men's épée	Team	Christian Adrians	FC Tauberbischofsheim
			Elmar Borrmann	FC Tauberbischofsheim
			Manfred Beckmann	FC Tauberbischofsheim
			Hanns Jana	FC Tauberbischofsheim
			Alexander Pusch	FC Tauberbischofsheim
1981 Rome	Women's foil	Individual	Mandy Niklaus	SC Einheit Dresden
1983 Vienna	Men's foil Women's foil	Individual Team	Mathias Gey	FC Tauberbischofsheim
			Sabine Bischof	FC Tauberbischofsheim
			Cornelia Hanisch	FC Offenbach
			Ingrid Losert	TS Freiburg
			Christiane Weber	FC Offenbach
			Ute Wessel	OFC Bonn
	Men's foil	Team	Hartmut Behrens	SC Dynamo Berlin
			Adrian Germanus	SC Motor Jena
			Klaus Kotzmann	ASK Vorwärts Potsdam
			Jens Howe	ASK Vorwärts Potsdam
			Ingo Weißenborn	ASK Vorwärts Potsdam
	Men's épée	Team	Elmar Borrmann	FC Tauberbischofsheim
			Volker Fischer	FC Tauberbischofsheim
			Rafael Nickel	FC Tauberbischofsheim
			Alexander Pusch	FC Tauberbischofsheim
			Gerhard Heer	FC Tauberbischofsheim
1985 Barcelona	Women's foil Men's foil	Individual Team	Sabine Bischof	FC Tauberbischofsheim
			Matthias Behr	FC Tauberbischofsheim
			Harald Hein	FC Tauberbischofsheim
			Klaus Reichert	OFC Bonn
			Ullrich Schreck	FC Tauberbischofsheim
			Thorsten Weidner	FC Tauberbischofsheim

1986 Sofia	Women's foil	Individual	Sabine Bau	FC Tauberbischofsheim
	Men's foil	Team	Thorsten Weidner	FC Tauberbischofsheim
			Mathias Gey	FC Tauberbischofsheim
			Matthias Behr	FC Tauberbischofsheim
			Ullrich Schreck	FC Tauberbischofsheim
			Thomas Gerull	FC Tauberbischofsheim
1987 Lausanne	Men's foil	Individual	Matthias Behr	FC Tauberbischofsheim
	Women's foil	Individual	Zita Funkenhauser	FC Tauberbischofsheim
	Men's épée	Team	Elmar Bormann	FC Tauberbischofsheim
			Volker Fischer	FC Tauberbischofsheim
			Thomas Gerull	FC Tauberbischofsheim
			Alexander Pusch	FC Tauberbischofsheim
			Arnd Schmitt	TSV Bayer 04 Leverkusen
1989 Denver	Women's foil	Individual	Anja Mauritz-Fichtel	FC Tauberbischofsheim
	Women's épée	Individual	Ute Schaeper	FC Tauberbischofsheim
	Men's foil	Team	Alexander Koch	OFC Bonn
			Thorsten Weidner	FC Tauberbischofsheim
			Mathias Gey	FC Tauberbischofsheim
			Thomas Endres	FC Tauberbischofsheim
			Roman Christen	FC Tauberbischofsheim
	Men's épée	Team	Elmar Borrmann	FC Tauberbischofsheim
			Thomas Gerull	FC Tauberbischofsheim
			Stefan Hörger	FC Tauberbischofsheim
			Günter Jauch	Heidenheimer SB
			Robert Felisiak	FC Tauberbischofsheim
	Men's saber	Team	Felix Becker	OFC Bonn
			Ulrich Efler	OFC Bonn
			Jürgen Nolte	OFC Bonn
			Frank Bleckmann	OFC Bonn
			Jörg Kempenich	OFC Bonn
1991 Budapest	Women's épée	Individual	Eva-Maria Ittner	FC Offenbach
	Men's foil	Individual	Thorsten Weidner	FC Tauberbischofsheim
	Men's épée	Individual	Robert Felisiak	FC Tauberbischofsheim
	Men's foil	Team	Thorsten Weidner	FC Tauberbischofsheim
			Ingo Weißenborn	FC Tauberbischofsheim
			Udo Wagner	FC Tauberbischofsheim
			Ulrich Schreck	OFC Bonn
			Uwe Römer	FC Tauberbischofsheim
1992 Havana	Women's épée	Team	Renate Riebandt-Kaspar	OFC Bonn
			Imke Duplitzer	Heidenheimer SB
			Katja Nass	FC Offenbach
			Dagmar Ophardt	FC Offenbach
			Eva-Maria Ittner	FC Offenbach

1993 Essen	Men's épée	Individual	Arnd Schmitt	Bayer Leverkusen
	Women's épée	Team	Claudia Bokel	OFC Bonn
			Imke Duplitzer	Heidenheimer SB
			Hedwig Funkenhauser	FC Tauberbischofsheim
			Katja Nass	FC Offenbach
1994 Athens	Women's épée	Individual	Katja Nass	FC Offenbach
	Men's foil	Team	Thorsten Weidner	FC Tauberbischofsheim
			Alexander Koch	OFC Bonn
			Uwe Römer	FC Tauberbischofsheim
			Udo Wagner	FC Tauberbischofsheim
	Men's épée	Team	Elmar Borrmann	FC Tauberbischofsheim
			Michael Flegler	FC Tauberbischofsheim
			Arnd Schmitt	Bayer Leverkusen
			Mariusz Strzalka	FC Tauberbischofsheim
1995 Den Haag	Men's saber	Individual	Felix Becker	TSV Bayer Dormagen
1997 Capetown	Women's foil	Individual	Sabine Bau	FC Tauberbischofsheim
	Women's épée	Team	Claudia Bokel	OFC Bonn
			Imke Duplitzer	Heidenheimer SB
			Katja Nass	FC Offenbach
			Eva-Maria Ittner	FC Offenbach
	Men's épée	Team	Elmar Borrmann	FC Tauberbischofsheim
			Michael Flegler	FC Tauberbischofsheim
			Arnd Schmitt	Bayer Leverkusen
			Mark Steifensand	Heidenheimer SB
1998 La-Chaux-de-Fonds	Women's épée	Individual	Dennis Holzkamp	FC Tauberbischofsheim
1999 Seoul	Women's foil	Individual	Sabine Bau	FC Tauberbischofsheim
	Men's épée	Team	Arnd Schmitt	TSV Bayer 04 Leverkusen
			Mark Steifensand	Heidenheimer SB/SF
			Jörg Fiedler	FC Tauberbishofsheim
			Elmar Borrmann	FC Tauberbishofsheim
2001 Nîmes	Women's foil	Individual	Sabine Bau	FC Tauberbishofsheim
2002 Lisbon	Women's épée	Individual	Imke Duplitzer	Heidenheimer SB/FA
	Men's foil	Individual	André Weßels	FC Tauberbishofsheim
2003 Havana	Women's épée	Team	Claudia Bokel	FC Tauberbishofsheim
			Britta Heidemann	TSV Bayer 04 Leverkusen
			Imke Duplitzer	Heidenheimer SB/FA
			Marijana Markovic	TSV Bayer 04 Leverkusen
	Men's épée	Team	Jörg Fiedler	FC Tauberbishofsheim
			Christoph Kneip	TSV Bayer 04 Leverkusen

			Wolfgang Reich	Heidenheimer SB/FA
			Norman Ackermann	FC Tauberbishofsheim
2005 Leipzig	Women's foil	Individual	Anja Müller	FC Tauberbischofsheim
	Men's épée	Team	Daniel Strigel	FC Tauberbischofsheim
			Jörg Fiedler	FC Tauberbischofsheim
			Sven Schmid	FC Tauberbischofsheim
			Martin Schmidt	FC Tauberbischofsheim

Bronze medals

1959 Budapest	Women's foil	Team	Helmi Hoehle	FC Offenbach
			Helga Mees	TB Saarbrücken
			Heidi Schmid	TSV 1847 Schwaben-Augsb.
			Rosemarie Weiss	TS Freiburg
1962 Buenos Aires	Men's foil	Individual	Jürgen Brecht	FC Kurpfalz-Edigheim
1978 Hamburg	Women's foil	Individual	Cornelia Hanisch	FC Offenbach
	Men's foil	Individual	Harald Hein	FC Tauberbischofsheim
1979 Melbourne	Women's foil	Team	Sabine Bischof	FC Tauberbischofsheim
			Cornelia Hanisch	FC Offenbach
			Jutta Höhne	KSC Koblenz
			Ingrid Losert	TS Freiburg
			Ute Wessel	OFC Bonn
	Men's foil	Team	Thomas Bach	FC Tauberbischofsheim
			Matthias Behr	FC Tauberbischofsheim
			Mathias Gey	FC Tauberbischofsheim
			Klaus Reichert	OFC Bonn
1981 Clermont Ferrand	Men's épée	Individual	Elmar Borrmann	FC Tauberbischofsheim
	Men's foil	Team	Matthias Behr	FC Tauberbischofsheim
			Frank Beck	FC Tauberbischofsheim
			Harald Hein	FC Tauberbischofsheim
			Mathias Gey	FC Tauberbischofsheim
			Klaus Reichert	OFC Bonn
1982 Rome	Women's foil	Team	Sabine Bischof	FC Tauberbischofsheim
			Cornelia Hanisch	FC Offenbach
			Ingrid Losert	TS Freiburg
			Gudrun Lotter	FC Tauberbischofsheim
			Christiane Weber	FC Offenbach
1985 Barcelona	Men's foil	Individual	Harald Hein	FC Tauberbischofsheim
1986 Sofia	Men's foil	Team	Adrian Germanus	SC Motor Jena
			Ingo Weißenborn	ASK Vorwärts Potsdam
			Udo Wagner	SC Einheit Dresden
			Aris Enkelmann	SC Dynamo Berlin
			Jens Howe	ASK Vorwärts Potsdam

	Women's foil	Team	Anja Fichtel	FC Tauberbischofsheim
			Sabine Bau	FC Tauberbischofsheim
			Christiane Weber	FC Offenbach
			Sabine Bischof	FC Tauberbischofsheim
			Zita Funkenhauser	FC Tauberbischofsheim
1989 Denver	Women's foil	Individual	Zita Funkenhauser	FC Tauberbischofsheim
	Men's saber	Individual	Felix Becker	OFC Bonn
1990 Lyon	Men's épée	Individual	Arnd Schmitt	TSV Bayer 04 Leverkusen
	Men's saber	Team	Felix Becker	OFC Bonn
			Frank Bleckmann	OFC Bonn
			Uli Eifler	OFC Bonn
			Jörg Kempenich	OFC Bonn
			Jürgen Nolte	OFC Bonn
1991 Budapest	Women's foil	Individual	Sabine Bau	FC Tauberbischofsheim
	Women's foil	Team	Sabine Bau	FC Tauberbischofsheim
			Anette Dobmeier	FC Tauberbischofsheim
			Anja Mauritz-Fichtel	FC Tauberbischofsheim
			Zita Funkenhauser	FC Tauberbischofsheim
			Rosalia Huszti	FC Tauberbischofsheim
	Men's épée	Team	Robert Felisiak	FC Tauberbischofsheim
			Elmar Borrmann	FC Tauberbischofsheim
			Arnd Schmitt	Bayer Leverkusen
			Mariusz Strzalka	FC Tauberbischofsheim
			Uwe Proske	SC Berlin
	Men's saber	Team	Felix Becker	OFC Bonn
			Frank Bleckmann	OFC Bonn
			Jörg Kempenich	OFC Bonn
			Jürgen Nolte	OFC Bonn
			Jacek Huchwajda	FC Tauberbischofsheim
1993 Essen	Women's foil	Individual	Simone Bauer	FC Tauberbischofsheim
			Zita Funkenhauser	FC Tauberbischofsheim
	Men's foil	Individual	Uwe Römer	FC Tauberbischofsheim
	Men's saber	Individual	Steffen Wiesinger	FC Tauberbischofsheim
	Men's épée	Team	Elmar Borrmann	FC Tauberbischofsheim
			Patric Draenert	Heidenheimer SB
			Uwe Proske	SC Berlin
			Mariusz Strzalka	FC Tauberbischofsheim
	Men's saber	Team	Felix Becker	OFC Bonn
			Frank Bleckmann	OFC Bonn
			Uli Eifler	OFC Bonn
			Jacek Huchwajda	FC Tauberbischofsheim
			Steffen Wiesinger	FC Tauberbischofsheim
1994 Athens	Men's épée	Individual	Arnd Schmitt	Bayer Leverkusen
			Thorsten Weidner	FC Tauberbischofsheim

349

1995 Den Haag	Women's foil	Team	Sabine Bau	FC Tauberbischofsheim
			Anja Mauritz-Fichtel	FC Tauberbischofsheim
			Zita Funkenhauser	FC Tauberbischofsheim
			Monika Weber	OFC Bonn
1997 Capetown	Women's foil	Individual	Monika Weber	OFC Bonn
	Women's foil	Team	Sabine Bau	FC Tauberbischofsheim
			Rita König	FC Tauberbischofsheim
			Gesine Schiel	FC Tauberbischofsheim
			Monika Weber	OFC Bonn
1999 Seoul	Men's foil	Individual	Wolfgang Wienand	OFC Bonn
	Women's épée	Team	Imke Duplitzer	Heidenheimer SB/FA
			Claudia Bokel	OFC Bonn
			Kristina Ophardt	FC Offenbach
			Katja Nass	FC Offenbach
2001 Nimes	Men's épée	Individual	Oliver Lücke	OFC Bonn
	Womens' foil	Team	Sabine Bau	FC Tauberbischofsheim
			Monika Weber-Schreck	OFC Bonn
			Gesine Schiel	FC Tauberbischofsheim
			Anja Müller	FC Tauberbischofsheim
	Men's saber	Team	Wiradech Kothny	FC Koblenz
			Christian Kraus	TSG Eislingen
			Michael Herm	TSG Eislingen
			Dennis Bauer	FC Koblenz
	Men's foil	Team	Christian Schlechtweg	SC Berlin
			Ralf Bißdorf	Heidenheimer SB/FA
			Lars Schache	FC Tauberbischofsheim
			Dominik Behr	FC Tauberbischofsheim
2002 Lisbon	Women's épée	Individual	Britta Heidemann	TSV Bayer 04 Leverkusen
	Men's saber	Team	Dennis Bauer	KSC Koblenz
			Harald Stehr	TSG Eislingen
			Michael Herm	TSG Eislingen
			Alexander Weber	FC Tauberbischofsheim
2003 Havana	Men's foil	Team	Peter Joppich	KSC Koblenz
			Ralf Bissdorf	Heidenheimer SB/FA
			Andre Wessels	FC Tauberbischofsheim
			Dominik Behr	FC Tauberbischofsheim
2005 Leipzig	Women's épée	Team	Britta Heidemann	Bayer Leverkusen
			Imke Duplitzer	OFC Bonn
			Monika Soszanska	Heidenheimer SB
			Claudia Bokel	FC Tauberbischofsheim
	Men's foil	Team	Peter Joppich	KSC Koblenz
			Dominik Behr	FC Tauberbischofsheim
			Ralf Bissdorf	Heidenheimer SB
			Benjamin Kleibrink	OFC Bonn

Index

Dr. Heinrich Baer, born 1948, studied medicine in Mainz, and served in the military as a captain in the medical corps and as a doctor in the Air Force. He received his specialist training in internal medicine in Göppingen and in Mainz. Since 1982 he has been in practice as a specialist for general and sports medicine in Heidenheim. Since that time he has been in charge of medical care for the Heidenheim Athletic Association's fencing department as well as tournament medical care. He has been head of the DFB's medicical committee since 1998.

Jochen Färber, born 1967, studied socioeconomics at Augsburg Univeristy. He has been active on a freelance basis at various press-, radio-, and television editorial offices such as Radio 7 Ostalb, dpa, sid, Schwäbische Post, SDR Television, and Eurosport Paris. He was head of the press at F.I.E. and at the Olympic fencing events in Atlanta. He is in charge of public relations at the OSP TBB and DFB.

Dr. Michael Hauptmann, born 1952, has a degree in sports science. He received his doctorate at D. Harre and was an intern at the Institue for General Training Eucation at the German College of Fitnesss Training in Leipzig until 1992. After that he joined the science staff at the Olympic headquarters in Tauberbischofsheim. He has been active for many years in the area of trainer education and continuing education in youth competitive sports.

Claus Janka, born 1943, has a degree in sports science from the German College for Fitness Training in Leipzig, and is a long-time trainer for the German Fencing Association for women's and men's foil. He has guided the national teams to significant successes, is an international category "A" referee and a member of the propaganda committee of the F.I.E., as well as the athletic director of the DFB.

Manfred Kaspar, born 1952, studied at the Trainer Academy in Cologne. He has been a trainer in Bonn since 1979, head trainer at the performance center since 1985, and national trainer for women's épée since 1988. He is a certified fencing master at the DFB and, among others, took Arndt Schmitt to his Olympic victory in 1988, and Rentate Rieband and Claudia Bokel to their World Championship titles in épée.

Peter Proske, born 1940, was educated at a technical school for trainers and studied at the college for sports science at the German College for Fitness Training in Leipzig. He has been a trainer in Leipzig and Dresden since 1963, and has been on the science staff at the fencing club and Olympic headquarters in Tauberbischofsheim since 1992. Among others he trained the Olympic and world champions in men's foil, Udo Wagner and Ingo Weißenborn.

Joachim Rieg, born 1959, has a degree in civil engineering fom the Technical College in Stuttgart as well as a subsequent degree from the Trainer Academy in Cologne. He is the state fencing trainer for the state of Baden-Württemberg and since 1986 has been national trainer for the successful German Junior National Team in men's saber.

Dr. Gabor Salamon, born 1949, is a certified fencing master and has a degree in exercise physiology and conferral of a doctorate in fencing from the sports college in Budapest. He was involved in competitive sports and a trainer for the modern pentathlon in Germany. Since 1991 he has been a fencing trainer in Leverkusen and also was Arndt Schmitt's trainer for many years.

Dr. Arno Schimpf, born 1953, has a doctorate from the university in Frankfurt/Main. He is a sport psychologist at the Olympic headquarters in Tauberbischofsheim, has many years of experience as a psychological advisor and coach in various sports, and for years has been working with professional athletic associations in the area of trainer education.

Andreas Schirmer, born 1958, studied political science and journalism. He has been a journalist with the sports information service since 1979, and editor at the German Press Agency since 1989. He is the author of three books on fencing.

Photo and Illustration Credits

Cover design:	Jens Vogelsang
Cover photos:	dpa picture-alliance, Shrine Production/Robert Beske
Inside photos:	Jochen Färber, Shrine Production/Robert Beske, p. 25, 102, 141, 149, 174, 338
Illustrations (figures):	Hans Hausmann, from "Fencing", Berlin Sports Publishing, 1979